AA004302

DATA ANALYTICS 2016

The Fifth International Conference on Data Analytics

October 9 - 13, 2016

Venice, Italy

DATA ANALYTICS 2016 Editors

Sandjai Bhulai, Vrije Universiteit Amsterdam, the Netherlands

Ivana Semanjski, University of Zagreb, Croatia / Ghent University, Belgium

Printed from e-media with permission by:

Curran Associates, Inc.
57 Morehouse Lane
Red Hook, NY 12571

Some format issues inherent in the e-media version may also appear in this print version.

Printed by Curran Associates, Inc. (2016)

International Academy, Research, and Industry Association (IARIA)
412 Derby Way
Wilmington, DE 19810

Phone: (408) 893-6407
Fax: (408) 527-6351

petre@iaria.org

Additional copies of this publication are available from:

Curran Associates, Inc.
57 Morehouse Lane
Red Hook, NY 12571 USA
Phone: 845-758-0400
Fax: 845-758-2633
Email: curran@proceedings.com
Web: www.proceedings.com

TABLE OF CONTENTS

DATA ANALYTICS 6: BIG DATA

DATA ANALYTICS 2016

Forward

The Fifth International Conference on Data Analytics (DATA ANALYTICS 2016), held between October 9 and 13, 2016 in Venice, Italy, continued a series of events related to data analytics, special mechanisms and features of applying principles of data analytics, application-oriented analytics, and target-area analytics.

Processing of terabytes to petabytes of data, or incorporating non-structural data and multi-structured data sources and types require advanced analytics and data science mechanisms for both raw and partially-processed information. Despite considerable advancements on high performance, large storage, and high computation power, there are challenges in identifying, clustering, classifying, and interpreting of a large spectrum of information.

The event was very competitive in its selection process and very well perceived by the international scientific and industrial communities. As such, it has attracted excellent contributions and active participation from all over the world. We were very pleased to receive a large amount of top quality contributions.

The conference had the following tracks:

- Fundamentals
- Target Analytics
- Sentiment/Opinion Analysis
- Application-oriented Analysis
- Transport and Traffic Analytics in Smart Cities
- Big Data

We take here the opportunity to warmly thank all the members of the DATA ANALYTICS 2016 technical program committee, as well as the numerous reviewers. The creation of such a high quality conference program would not have been possible without their involvement. We also kindly thank all the authors that dedicated much of their time and effort to contribute to DATA ANALYTICS 2016. We truly believe that, thanks to all these efforts, the final conference program consisted of top quality contributions.

Also, this event could not have been a reality without the support of many individuals, organizations and sponsors. We also gratefully thank the members of the DATA ANALYTICS 2016 organizing committee for their help in handling the logistics and for their work that made this professional meeting a success.

We hope DATA ANALYTICS 2016 was a successful international forum for the exchange of ideas and results between academia and industry and to promote further progress in the area of data analytics.

We also hope that Venice, Italy, provided a pleasant environment during the conference and everyone saved some time to enjoy the unique charm of the city.

DATA ANALYTICS Advisory Committee

Fritz Laux, Reutlingen University, Germany
Lina Yao, The University of Adelaide, Australia
Eiko Yoneki, University of Cambridge, UK
Takuya Yoshihiro, Wakayama University, Japan
Felix Heine, University of Applied Sciences & Arts Hannover, Germany
Dominik Slezak, University of Warsaw & Infobright Inc., Poland
Panos M. Pardalos, University of Florida, USA
Michele Melchiori, Università degli Studi di Brescia, Italy
Rudolf Berrendorf, Bonn-Rhein-Sieg University, Germany
Sandjai Bhulai, VU University Amsterdam, The Netherlands
Kerstin Lemke-Rust, Hochschule Bonn-Rhein-Sieg, Germany
Sergio Ilarri, University of Zaragoza, Spain
Les Sztandera, Philadelphia University, USA
Prabhat Mahanti, University of New Brunswick, Canada
Dominique Laurent, University of Cergy Pontoise, France
Ryan G. Benton, University of Louisiana at Lafayette, USA
Erik Buchmann, Karlsruhe Institute of Technology, Germany
Andrew Rau-Chaplin, Dalhousie University, Canada
Takuya Yoshihiro, Wakayama University, Japan

DATA ANALYTICS Industry/Research Liaison Chairs

Qiming Chen, HP Labs - Palo Alto, USA
Alain Crolotte, Teradata Corporation - El Segundo, USA
Tiziana Guzzo, National Research Council/Institute of Research on Population and Social Policies - Rome, Italy
Shlomo Geva, Queensland University of Technology - Brisbane, Australia
Farhana Kabir, Intel, USA
Serge Mankovski, CA Technologies, Spain
Vedran Sabol, Know-Center - Graz, Austria
George Tambouratzis, Institute for Language and Speech Processing - Athena Research Centre, Greece
Yanchang Zhao, RDataMining.com, Australia
Masahiro Terabe, Mitsubishi Research Institute, Inc., Japan
Marina Santini, Santa Anna IT Research Institute AB, Sweden
Mario Zechner, Know-Center, Austria

DATA ANALYTICS Publicity Chairs

Johannes Leveling, Elsevier, Netherlands
Roberto Zicari, Johann Wolfgang Goethe - University of Frankfurt, Germany
Shandian Zhe, Purdue University, USA
Michael Schaidnagel, Reutlingen University, Germany

DATA ANALYTICS Special Area Chairs

Resiliency and Sustainability Through Analytics

Thomas Klemas, Sensemaking-PACOM Fellowship & AIRS, Swansea University/Hawaii Pacific University, UK/USA
Steve Chan, Swansea University & Hawaii Pacific University, USA

DATA ANALYTICS 2016

Committee

DATA ANALYTICS Advisory Committee

Fritz Laux, Reutlingen University, Germany
Lina Yao, The University of Adelaide, Australia
Eiko Yoneki, University of Cambridge, UK
Takuya Yoshihiro, Wakayama University, Japan
Felix Heine, University of Applied Sciences & Arts Hannover, Germany
Dominik Slezak, University of Warsaw & Infobright Inc., Poland
Panos M. Pardalos, University of Florida, USA
Michele Melchiori, Università degli Studi di Brescia, Italy
Rudolf Berrendorf, Bonn-Rhein-Sieg University, Germany
Sandjai Bhulai, VU University Amsterdam, The Netherlands
Kerstin Lemke-Rust, Hochschule Bonn-Rhein-Sieg, Germany
Sergio Ilarri, University of Zaragoza, Spain
Les Sztandera, Philadelphia University, USA
Prabhat Mahanti, University of New Brunswick, Canada
Dominique Laurent, University of Cergy Pontoise, France
Ryan G. Benton, University of Louisiana at Lafayette, USA
Erik Buchmann, Karlsruhe Institute of Technology, Germany
Andrew Rau-Chaplin, Dalhousie University, Canada
Takuya Yoshihiro, Wakayama University, Japan

DATA ANALYTICS Industry/Research Liaison Chairs

Qiming Chen, HP Labs - Palo Alto, USA
Alain Crolotte, Teradata Corporation - El Segundo, USA
Tiziana Guzzo, National Research Council/Institute of Research on Population and Social Policies - Rome, Italy
Shlomo Geva, Queensland University of Technology - Brisbane, Australia
Farhana Kabir, Intel, USA
Serge Mankovski, CA Technologies, Spain
Vedran Sabol, Know-Center - Graz, Austria
George Tambouratzis, Institute for Language and Speech Processing - Athena Research Centre, Greece
Yanchang Zhao, RDataMining.com, Australia
Masahiro Terabe, Mitsubishi Research Institute, Inc., Japan
Marina Santini, Santa Anna IT Research Institute AB, Sweden
Mario Zechner, Know-Center, Austria

DATA ANALYTICS Publicity Chairs

Johannes Leveling, Elsevier, Netherlands
Roberto Zicari, Johann Wolfgang Goethe - University of Frankfurt, Germany
Shandian Zhe, Purdue University, USA
Michael Schaidnagel, Reutlingen University, Germany

DATA ANALYTICS Special Area Chairs

Resiliency and Sustainability Through Analytics

Thomas Klemas, Sensemaking-PACOM Fellowship & AIRS, Swansea University/Hawaii Pacific University, UK/USA
Steve Chan, Swansea University & Hawaii Pacific University, USA

DATA ANALYTICS 2016 Technical Program Committee

Mohd Helmy Abd Wahab, Universiti Tun Hussein Onn Malaysia, Malaysia
Sayed Abdel-Wahab, Sadat Academy for Management Sciences, Egypt
Rajeev Agrawal, North Carolina A&T State University - Greensboro, USA
Fabrizio Angiulli, University of Calabria, Italy
Annalisa Appice, Università degli Studi di Bari Aldo Moro, Italy
Giuliano Armano, University of Cagliari, Italy
Ryan G. Benton, University of Louisiana at Lafayette, USA
Sandjai Bhulai, VU University Amsterdam, The Netherlands
Erik Buchmann, Karlsruhe Institute of Technology, Germany
Luca Cagliero, Politecnico di Torino, Italy
Huiping Cao, New Mexico State University, USA
Omar Andres Carmona Cortes, Federal Institute of Maranhao (IFMA), Brazil
Michelangelo Ceci, University of Bari, Italy
Federica Cena, Università degli Studi di Torino, Italy
Steve Chan, Swansea University, UK
Lijun Chang, University of New South Wales, Australia
Qiming Chen, HP Labs - Palo Alto, USA
You Chen, Vanderbilt University, USA
Qiang (Shawn) Cheng, Southern Illinois University, Carbondale, USA
Been-Chian Chien, National University of Tainan, Taiwan
Silvia Chiusano, Politecnico di Torino, Italy
Liu ChuanRen, Drexel University, USA
Alain Crolotte, Teradata Corporation - El Segundo, USA
Tran Khanh Dang, National University of Ho Chi Minh City, Vietnam
Mrinal Kanti Das, Aalto University, Finland
Ernesto William De Luca, University of Applied Sciences Potsdam, Gernmany
Zhi-Hong Deng, Peking University, China

Shifei Ding, China University of Mining and Technology - Xuzhou City, China
Sourav Dutta, Max-Planck Institute for Informatics, Germany
Sherif Elfayoumy, University of North Florida, USA
Yanjie Fu, Rutgers University, USA
Wai-keung Fung, Robert Gordon University, UK
Cesare Furlanello, Bruno Kessler Foundation, Italy
Matjaz Gams, Jozef Stefan Institute - Ljubljana, Slovenia
Paolo Garza, Dipartimento di Automatica e Informatica Politecnico di Torino, Italy
Shlomo Geva, Queensland University of Technology - Brisbane, Australia
Amer Goneid, American University in Cairo, Egypt
Raju Gottumukkala, University of Louisiana at Lafayette, USA
William Grosky, University of Michigan - Dearborn, USA
Jerzy W. Grzymala-Busse, University of Kansas - Lawrence, USA
Tiziana Guzzo, National Research Council/Institute of Research on Population and Social Policies - Rome, Italy
Michael Hahsler, Southern Methodist University, U.S.A.
Sven Hartmann, TU-Clausthal, Germany
Alois Haselböck, Siemens AG Österreich, Austria
Felix Heine, Hochschule Hannover, Germany
Quang Hoang, Hue University, Vietnam
Tzung-Pei Hong, National University of Kaohsiung, Taiwan
Yi Hu, Northern Kentucky University - Highland Heights, USA
Jun (Luke) Huan, University of Kansas - Lawrence, USA
Joshua Zhexue Huang, Shenzhen University, China
Mao Lin Huang, University of Technology - Sydney, Australia
Sergio Ilarri, University of Zaragoza, Spain
Hajira Jabeen, University of Leipzig, Germany
Olaf Jacob, Neu-Ulm University of Applied Sciences, Germany
Ali Jarvandi, George Washington University, U.S.A.
Wassim Jaziri, Taibah University, Saudi Arabia
Hanmin Jung, Korea Institute of Science and Technology Information, South Korea
Giuseppe Jurman, Bruno Kessler Foundation, Italy
Farhana Kabir, Intel, U.S.A.
Younghoon Kim, Hanyang University at Ansan, South Korea
Daniel Kimmig, Karlsruhe Institute of Technology (KIT), Germany
Thomas Klemas, Sensemaking-PACOM Fellowship & AIRS, Swansea University/Hawaii Pacific University, UK/USA
Boris Kovalerchuk, Central Washington University, U.S.A.
Michal Kratky, VŠB-Technical University of Ostrava, Czech Republic
Srijan Kumar, University of Maryland, College Park, USA
Chao Lan, University of Kansas, USA
Dominique Laurent, University of Cergy Pontoise, France
Aleksandar Lazarevic, Data Science Organization - Aetna, Hartford, USA
Kerstin Lemke-Rust, Hochschule Bonn-Rhein-Sieg, Germany

Johannes Leveling, Elsevier, Netherlands
Cheng Li, University of Michigan, USA
Tao Li, Florida International University, USA
Wenzhe Li, Puhuifinance, China
Yaliang Li, State University of New York at Buffalo, USA
Dan Lin, Missouri University of Science and Technology Rolla, U.S.A.
Wen-Yang Lin, National University of Kaohsiung, Taiwan
Dimitrios Liparas, Information Technologies Institute (ITI) - Centre for Research & Technology Hellas (CERTH), Greece
Shawn (Xiaomo) Liu, Thomson Reuters, USA
Weimo Liu, Fudan University, China
Xumin Liu, Rochester Institute of Technology, USA
Corrado Loglisci, University of Bari, Italy
Fenglong Ma, SUNY at Buffalo, USA
Prabhat Mahanti, University of New Brunswick, Canada
Serge Mankovski, CA Technologies, Spain
Qi Mao, University at Buffalo, The State University of New York, USA
Archil Maysuradze, Lomonosov Moscow State University, Russia
Michele Melchiori, Università degli Studi di Brescia, Italy
Shicong Meng, Georgia Institute of Technology, USA
George Michailidis, University of Michigan, USA
Alessandra Mileo, Insight Centre for Data Analytics - NUI Galway, Ireland
Prasenjit Mitra, Qatar Computing Research Institute - Hamad Bin Khalifa University, Qatar
Victor Muntés Mulero, CA Technologies, Spain
Richi Nayak, Queensland University of Technology, Brisbane, Australia
Feiping Nie, University of Texas at Arlington, USA
Oliver Niggemann, Institut für Industrielle Informationstechnik, Germany
Mikel Niño, University of the Basque Country, Spain
Sadegh Nobari, Singapore Management University, Singapore
Panos M. Pardalos, University of Florida, USA
Dhaval Patel, Indian Institute of Technology-Roorkee, India
Jan Platoš, VSB-Technical University of Ostrava, Czech Republic
Joern Ploennigs, IBM Research, Ireland
Ivan Radev, South Carolina State University, USA
Zbigniew W. Ras, University of North Carolina - Charlotte, USA & Warsaw University of Technology, Poland
Jan Rauch, University of Economics - Prague, Czech Republic
Yenumula B. Reddy, Grambling State University, USA
Manjeet Rege, University of St. Thomas, USA
Vedran Sabol, Know-Center - Graz, Austria
Abdel-Badeeh M. Salem, Ain Shams University Abbasia, Egypt
Marina Santini, SICS East Swedish ICT AB, Sweden
Ivana Šemanjski, University of Zagreb, Croatia / University of Gent, Belgium
Hayri Sever, Hacettepe University, Turkey

Copyright Information

Performance of Spanish Encoding Functions during Record Linkage

María del Pilar Angeles, Noemi Bailón-Miguel
Facultad de Ingeniería
Universidad Nacional Autónoma de México
Ciudad de México, México
e-mail: pilarang@unam.mx, mimibailon@hotmail.com

***Abstract*—Nowadays, many businesses suffer from duplicate records. For instance, information about the same provider, customer or product appears in multiple systems and in multiple formats across the company and simply does not tally from system to system. This situation seriously prevents managers to make well informed decisions. In the case of low data quality written in Spanish language, the identification and correction of problems such as spelling errors with English language based coding techniques is not suitable. In this paper, we have implemented, modified, and utilized three Spanish phonetic coding functions in our prototype called Universal Evaluation System of Data Quality (SEUCAD). A Spanish phonetic coding based on Soundex algorithm, a Spanish Metaphone coding, and a Modified version of the latter were utilized to detect duplicate text strings in the presence of spelling errors in Spanish. The results were satisfactory, athe Spanish phonetic algorithm performed well most of the time, demonstrating opportunities for an improved performance of Spanish encoding during the record linkage process.**

Keywords-— data mining; data matching; de-duplication; record linkage.

I. INTRODUCTION

The existence of duplicate records has strong implications on the use and scope of data. Low data quality affects decision making. For instance, the financial industry has faced several frauds caused by duplicate data. All financial institutions are interested in decreasing the already existing number of duplicates and implementing a more efficiently data handling in order to avoid future duplicate data. In the case of duplicate medical records, when the system is unable to find a reliable patient record the risk of wrong medical treatment, or over-immunization, is present, along with the corresponding cost of unnecessary immunizations, or the risk of adverse effects on patients, etc. Therefore, there has been a significant research in the area of data quality and data matching during the last decade.

We have developed a prototype called Universal Evaluation System of Data Quality (SEUCAD) [1] on the basis of the Freely Available Record Linkage System (FEBRL) [2].

We have previously compared, added and improved a number of data matching methods. Our prototype allows end users to assess density, coverage, completeness [1][3], and performs a complete data matching process in order to identify duplicate records. However, most of the coding algorithms are based on the English language, few approaches are oriented to the Spanish language. Consequently, the encoding algorithms are not efficient enough to detect common errors and misspellings in the process of data matching for the improvement of quality of data. This problem impacts all the industry projects that are related for instance, to data mining, data science, business intelligence, and big data for companies where data are written in the Spanish language.

Our research has been lately focused on the implementation and enhancement of Spanish encoding functions in order to improve the performance of the encoding phase during entity resolution when data have been written in Spanish language.

Within our SEUCAD prototype, the Phonex, Soundex, and Modified Spanish phonetic functions have been previously compared, and our findings published in [3].

The Spanish phonetic coding was proposed in [4], which is an extended Soundex coding, where Spanish characters have been added. Besides, we have modified the Spanish Phonetic Algorithm so the encryption code is resizable, and all white spaces are removed during encoding. The previous comparison showed that the modified version of the Spanish Phonetic Algorithm had a better performance in terms of precision.

The present document shows the implementation of two more Spanish encoding functions: the Spanish Metaphone algorithm [5][6], and a second version of such an algorithm, which applies the same code to similar sounds derived from very common misspellings.

The record linkage outcomes for these three coding functions have been evaluated under a number of different scenarios, where the true match status of record pairs was known. We have obtained precision, recall, and f-measure because they are suitable measures to assess data matching quality.

The present paper is organized as follows: The next section briefly explains the data matching process and how it has been implemented within SEUCAD. Section III explains the phonetic encoding functions proposed from previous research, the enhancements we have implemented on some of them, along with their role within de process of data matching. Section IV presents the experiments carried out, and analyses the results. Finally, the last section concludes the main topics achieved regarding the performance of the encoding functions and the future work to be done.

II. RELATED WORK

The data matching process is mainly concerned to the record comparison among databases in order to determine if a pair of records corresponds to the same entity or not [7]. It is also called record linkage or de-duplication. In general terms, this process consists on the following tasks:

a) A standardization process [7], which refers to the conversion of input data from multiple databases into a format that allows correct and efficient record correspondence between two data sources.

b) Phonetic encoding is a type of algorithm that converts a string into a code that represents the pronunciation of that string. Encoding the phonetic sound of names avoids most problems of misspellings or alternate spellings, a very common problem on low quality of data sources.

c) The indexing process aims to reduce those pairs of records that are unlikely to correspond to the same real world entity and retaining those records that probably would correspond in the same block for comparison; consequently, reducing the number of record comparisons. The record similarity depends on their data types because they can be phonetically, numerically or textually similar. Some of the methods implemented within our prototype SEUCAD are for instance, Soundex [9], Phonex [2], Phonix [2], NYSIIS [10], and Double metaphone [5].

d) Field and record comparison methods provide degrees of similarity and define thresholds depending on their semantics or data types. In the prototype, the algorithms Qgram, Jaro - Winkler Distance [11][12], Longest common substring comparison are already implemented.

e) The classification of pairs of records grouped and compared during previous steps is mainly based on the similarity values that were already obtained, since it is assumed that the more similar two records are, there is more probability that these records belong to the same entity of the real world. The records are classified into matches, not matches or possible matches.

The SEUCAD prototype was aimed to the development of algorithms that reduce the quadratic complexity of the naive process of pair-wise comparing each record from one database with all records in the other database, and how to accurately classify the compared record pairs into matches and non-matches considering attributes dependency.

Nowadays, SEUCAD is able to measure, assess and help during the analysis of data quality process [1] under a number of open and licensed database management system (DBMS), such as Oracle DB, MySQL, IBM DB2, SAP-Sybase Adaptive Server Enterprise, SAP-Sybase IQ, and EnterpriseDB PostgreSQL.

The SEUCAD application extracts the database schema directly from the data dictionary and measures the intrinsic quality of the data through the following indicators: coverage, density, completeness [13]. Since these measures are intrinsically computed through SQL queries, the assessed granularity levels are at database, table and column where applicable as we have done in previous research [14]. Furthermore, the prototype implements a specific framework for the detection, classification and fusion (cleaning) of duplicate records within a number of databases (data matching and de- duplication) with no regard of the type of data source.

During the implementation of some data matching algorithms, we have realized that the coding functions mainly used were on the basis of English language. Such algorithms were not suitable for Spanish written data already stored in our databases. Therefore, we were focused on the implementation and experimentation of Spanish encoding functions in order to improve the performance of the encoding phase during entity resolution.

We have implemented and enhanced two Spanish encoding functions in order to improve the performance of the encoding phase during entity resolution when data has been written in Spanish language, and the corresponding results are shown in the present work.

The aim of the following section is to briefly explain the phonetic encoding functions that we have implemented and enhanced in order to quantify and compare their performance during the record linkage process.

III. PHONETIC ENCODING PROPOSALS TO COMPARE

A. Phonetic coding functions

Phonetic encoding is a type of algorithm that converts a string (generally assumed to correspond to a name) into a code that represents the pronunciation of that string. Encoding the phonetic sound of names avoids most problems of misspellings or alternate spellings, a very common problem on low quality of data sources.

B. Spanish phonetic

The Spanish phonetic coding function compared in the present document is a variation of the Soundex algorithm. Soundex is a phonetic encoding algorithm developed by Robert Russell and Margaret Odell in [9], and patented in 1918 and 1922. It converts a word in a code [15]. The Soundex code is to replace the consonants of a word by a number; if necessary zeros are added to the end of the code to form a 4-digit code. Soundex choose the classification of characters based on the place of articulation of the English language.

The limitations of the Soundex algorithm have been extensively documented and have resulted in several improvements, but none oriented to the Spanish language. Furthermore, the dependence of the initial letter, the grouping articulation point of the English language, and the four characters coding limit are not efficient to detect common misspellings in the Spanish language.

The Spanish phonetic coding was proposed in [4], it is an extended Soundex coding, where Spanish characters have been added. In general terms, the algorithm is as follows:

1. The string is converted to uppercase with no consideration of punctuation signs.
2. The symbols "A, E, I, O, U, H, W" are eliminated from the original word.
3. Assign numbers to the remaining letters according to Table 1.

TABLE I. SPANISH CODING

Characters	Digit
P	0
B, V	1
F, H	2
T, D	3
S, Z, C,X	4
Y, LL, L	5
N, Ñ, M	6
Q, K	7
G, J	8
R, RR	9

We have modified the Spanish Phonetic Algorithm [3] so the encryption code is resizable, and all white spaces are removed during encoding. This model allows us to analyze a larger number of cases where we can have misspellings. The modified Spanish phonetic algorithm is called as soundex_sp in our SEUCAD prototype.

C. The Spanish Metaphone Algorithm

The Metaphone is a phonetic algorithm for indexing words by their English sounds when pronounced, it was proposed by Lawrence Philips in 1990 [5]. The English Double-Metaphone algorithm was implemented by Andrew Collins in 2007 who claims no rights to this work. The Metaphone port adapted to the Spanish Language is authored by Alejandro Mosquera in [6]; we have implemented this function and called as Esp_metaphone in our SEUCAD prototype. Some of the changes applied in order to adjust to the Spanish language are shown in Table II, which considers typical cases of the Spanish language with letters such as á, é, í, ó, ú, ll, ñ, h.

TABLE II. SPANISH METAPHONE

Char	Replacement
á	A
ch	X
C	S
é	E
í	I
ó	O
ú	U
ñ	NY
ü	U
b	V
Z	S
ll	Y

D. Modified Spanish Metaphone coding function

In Spanish language, there are words such as "obscuro", "oscuro" or "combate", "convate" that should share the same code because even they are written different, their sound is similar and the misspelling is common. The second version of Esp_metaphone contains the following enhancements:

The Royal Academy of the Spanish Language reviewed words that originally were written with "ps" as "psicología", and introduced some changes, because "the truth is that in Castilian the initial sound ps is quite violent, so the ordinary, both in Spain and in America, it is simply pronounced as "sicologia". Moreover, our language, differing French or English, is not greatly concerned with preserve the etymological spelling; He prefers the phonetic spelling and therefore tends to write as it is pronounced" [16]. Words that begin with "ps" can be written and pronounced as "s", and are called silent letters; for example, words psicólogo and sicólogo. We have added some cases to the Spanish Metaphone algorithm in order to consider these possible variations in Spanish written words and to assign the same code in both cases. Therefore, in case there is a word that starts with "ps", it will be replaced by "s". A special case with silent letter is presented with words like "oscuro" and "obscuro", where both words have the same meaning so that the use of both is correct. In this case both its meaning and pronunciation is usually the same. Then, in case there is a word that starts with "bs", it shall be replaced by "s". One case of a common misspelling in Spanish language is given with words like "tambien" and "tanbien" were the latter is orthographically wrong, but phonetically is very similar to the former, and in case of typos, the letter "n" is close to letter "m" in a keyboard. Thus, we have decided to replace "mb" by "nb" and assign the same code. We have decided to replace "mp" by "np" and assign the same code in case of words such as "tampoco" and "tanpoco". The words that begin with "s" followed by a consonant are replaced by 'es' such as "scalera" and "escalera". Later all the letters "s" are replaced by "z". Table III shows the additions contained in the Spanish Metaphone version 2.

TABLE III. MODIFIED SPANISH METAPHONE

Char	Replacement
mb	nb
mp	np
bs	s
ps	z

Table IV shows coding from Metaphone and Metaphone_v2, the former is not able to apply the same code to words "psiquiatra", "siquiatra"; "oscuro", "obscuro"; "combate", "convate", "conbate". All these words have the same meaning and in order to identify duplicates they should have the same code.

TABLE IV. SPANISH METAPHONE AND SPANISH METAPHONE V2 CODING

Word	Metaphone	Metaphone_v2
Cerilla	ZRY	ZRY
Empeorar	EMPRR	ENPRR
Embotellar	EMVTYR	ENVTYR
Xochimilco	XXMLK	XXMLK
Psiquiatra	PSKTR	ZKTR
siquiatra	SKTR	ZKTR
Obscuro	OVSKR	OZKR
Oscuro	OSKR	OZKR
Combate	KMBT	KNVT
Convate	KNVT	KNVT
Conbate	KNBT	KNVT
Comportar	KMPRTR	KNPRTR

Conportar	KNPRTR	KNPRTR
Zapato	ZPT	ZPT
Sapato	SPT	ZPT
Escalera	ESKLR	EZKLR
scalera	ESKLR	EZKLR

In the case of code generated by Metaphone_v2 the code is the same, although there are not identical texts because of spelling mistakes but same meaning.

The three coding functions we have explained in this section are meant to increase the similarity between the words written and the sound they represent in Spanish language in order to avoid common Spanish misspelling and errors and enhance the performance of the following steps during the data matching process. For instance, the level of similarity obtained among two words should be increased even in the case of a word was written as "siquiatra" rather than "psiquiatra".

The following section is concerned with the set of experiments we have carried out in order to identify how the coding functions we have implemented within SEUCAD can help to data matching with data written in Spanish language

IV. EXPERIMENTS

We have developed and executed a set of experiments for the record linkage process through four scenarios, each scenario containing a different data-source. In this Section we will explain a) how the quality of the data matching process will be computed ;b) the configuration of all the record linkage process; c) the characteristics of each data-source according to each scenario; and c) the analysis of the outcomes from each scenario.

These experiments are aimed to identify for each data-set which encoding function has the best performance. The performance of the record linkage process is measured in terms of how many of the classified matches correspond to true real-world entities, while matching completeness is concerned with how many of the real-world entities that appear in both databases were correctly matched [7][8]. Each of the record pair corresponds to one of the following categories: True positives (TP). These are the record pairs that have been classified as matches and are true matches. These are the pairs where both records refer to the same entity. False positives (FP). These are the record pairs that have been classified as matches, but they are not true matches. The two records in these pairs refer to two different entities. The classifier has made a wrong decision with these record pairs. These pairs are also known as false matches.

True negative (TN). These are the record pairs that have been classified as non-matches, and they are true non-matches. The two records in pairs in this category do refer to two different real-world entities. False negatives FN). These are the record pairs that have been classified as non-matches, but they are actually true matches. The two records in these pairs refer to the same entity. The classifier has made a wrong decision with these record pairs. These pairs are also known as false non-matches. Precision calculates the proportion of how many of the classified matches (TP + FP) have been correctly classified as true matches (TP). It thus measures how precise a classifier is in classifying true matches [9]. Precision is calculated as TP/(TP+FP). Recall measures how many of the actual true matching record pairs have been correctly classified as matches [9]. It is calculated as: recall= TP/(TP+FN). F-measure is a measure that combines precision and recall is the harmonic mean of precision and recall. Thus, is calculated as 2TP/(2TP+FP+FN).

An ideal outcome of a data matching project is to correctly classify as many of the true matches as true positives, while keeping both the number of false positives and false negatives small. Based on the number of true positives (TP), true negatives (TN), false positives (FP) and false negatives (FN), different quality measures can be calculated. However, most classification techniques require one or several parameters that can be modified and depending upon the values of such parameters, a classifier will have a different performance leading a different numbers of false positives and negatives.

For each data source, the number of total records, the number of duplicated records, the maximum number of duplicated record for an original record, the maximum number of changed fields per item, and the maximum number of record modifications were considered as independent variables. The dependent variables will be the amount of matches, non-matches and possible matches. The quality of the data matching process will be obtained from precision, f-measure, and all the metrics we have already mentioned in this Section. The control variables (also known as constant variables) will correspond to the indexing, comparison and classification steps within the data matching process because the experiments are aimed to identify which coding function will perform the best. All the data sources presented a uniform probability distribution for duplicates. Fig. 1 shows the structure and sample source data utilized for experimentation.

nombre	apellido_pat	apellido_mat	calle
santiago		gonzalez	calle de san gumersindo
david	hernandez	cruz	calle de arnedillo
jessica	perez	martinez	calle de barbara de braganz
martha	sanchez	lopez	calle de jordi sole tura
patricia	garcia	aviles	calle de santa maria reina
alfonso	garcia	hernandez	calle del iridio
adriana	vazquez	gonzalez	calle de jose espelius
tania	mendez	lopez	plaza de arguelles
vicente		reyes	calle de infiesto
angelica	hernandez	brito	calle de los hermanos carpi
maria elena	perez	ramirez	calle de los bascones
isaac	martinez	gutierrez	calle de julia garcia boutan
berenice	ramirez	reyes	calle de elvira barrios
alejandro	alonso	flores	calle de la anunciacion
enrique	cordero	ramirez	calle del gladiolo

Figure 1. Sample of data source

The configuration of indexing, comparison and classification for all scenarios has been the same and repeated for each encoding function (Esp-Metaphone, Esp_metaphone_v2 and Soundex_sp). Such configuration is presented as follows:

1. Indexing: Fields that form the record require to be encoded and indexed in order to avoid a large number of comparisons between records whose fields are not even similar. During the coding phase, we have executed for each experiment one of the coding functions: esp-metaphone, esp_metaphone_v2 or soundex_sp. In order to execute the indexing step, we have chosen "Blocking index" as indexing method based on fields: "nombre", "apellido paterno", "apellido materno", "calle". Fig. 2 shows the configuration utilized for indexing and encoding methods.

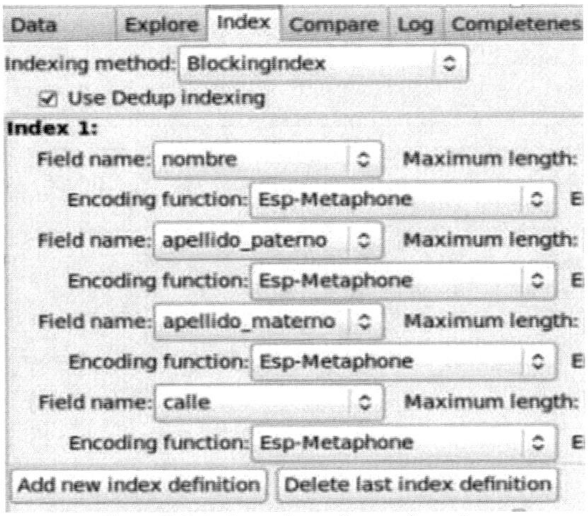

Figure 2. Indexing and encoding configuration

2. Comparison: Once records have been ordered and grouped in terms of the previous fields specified. Each encoded field will be compared. In order to obtain quality measures during the comparison step, we have chosen an exact function "Str-Exact", which requires an exact match on strings compared. This function will be used with the fields named as "nombre", "apellido paterno", "apellido materno", "calle". Fig. 3 shows the comparison specification for the experiments.

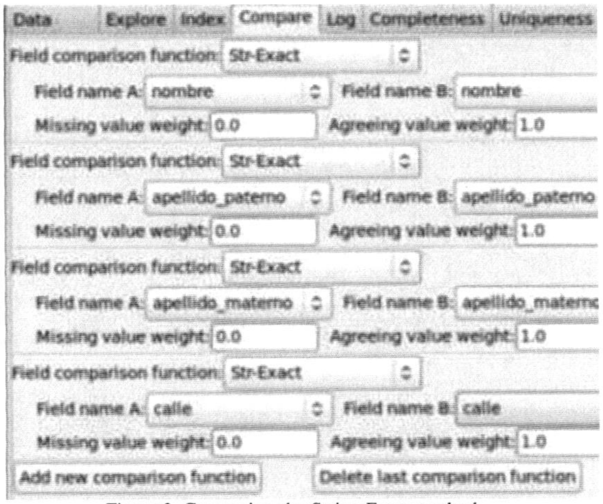

Figure 3. Comparison by String Exact method

3. Classification: In the case of pairs of record classification, we have selected the Optimal Threshold method, with a minimized false method of Positives and negatives, and a bin width of 40 for the range of values to be considered for the output graphic. Fig. 4 shows the classification configuration for the experiments.

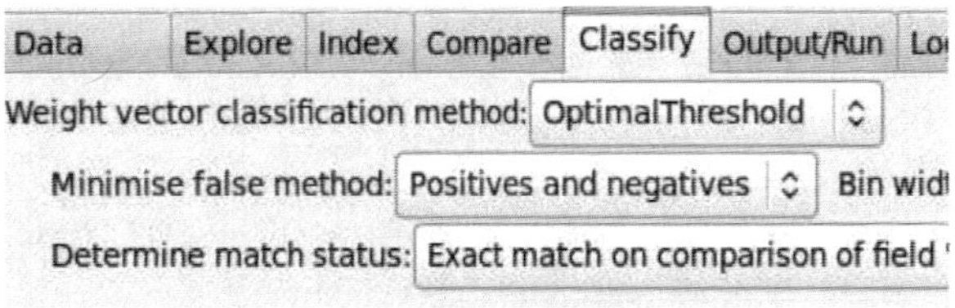

Figure 4. Classification by Optimal Threshold

The following scenarios are presented in order to show the performance of the encoding functions. The corresponding tables show the values of true positives, false positives, precision computed as TP/(TP+FP), and F-measure computed as 2TP/(2TP+FP+FN). The value of false negatives was 0 in all scenarios and encoding functions.

A. Scenario I

The first file was generated with a total length of 1000 records, 100 duplicated records, one duplicated record for an original record as maximum, one change field per item as maximum, one maximum record modification, with a uniform probability distribution for duplicates. The quality metrics obtained for each encoding method are presented in Table V.

TABLE V QUALITY METRICS FOR SCENARIO I

Encode Method	Total Classif.	TP	FP	Precision	F-measure
Metaphone_sp	68	65	3	0.95588	0.977443
Metaphone_v2	69	66	3	0.95652	0.977777
Soundex_sp	76	73	3	0.96052	0.979865

According to the outcomes obtained from the first scenario, we can observe that in the case of the Modified Spanish coding function (soundex_sp), there were 76 record pairs classified, with 73 duplicated record pairs as true positives and 3 record pairs as false positives. Therefore, this method was more precise with 96% than the rest of the functions.

B. Scenario II

The second data source contained a total length of 5000 records, 500 duplicated records, one duplicated record for an original record as maximum, one change field per item as maximum, one maximum registry modification, with a uniform probability distribution for duplicates. The quality metrics obtained for each encoding method are presented in Table VI.

TABLE VI QUALITY METRICS FOR SCENARIO II

Encode Method	Total Classif.	TP	FP	Precision	F-measure
Metaphone_sp	320	319	1	0.9968	0.9984
Metaphone_v2	341	340	1	0.99706	0.99853
soundex_sp	353	352	1	0.99716	0.99581

From Table VI we can observe that the Modified Spanish function classified 353 record pairs, with 352 duplicated record pairs as true positives and 1 record pair mistakenly classified as true match, corresponding then as one false positive. Therefore, this method was 99.7% precise, with more records classified than the Metaphone_sp and Methaphone_v2 with 320 and 341 records classified respectively.

C. Scenario III

The third data source contained a total length of 10000 records, 5000 duplicated records, one duplicated record for an original record as maximum, one change field per item as maximum, one maximum registry modifications, with a uniform probability distribution for duplicates.

The process of record linkage under this scenario showed that the Modified Spanish coding function classified 3622 record pairs out of a total of 5000 potentially to detect, with 3620 duplicated record pairs as true positives and 2 record pairs mistakenly classified as true match. Therefore, this method was 99.94% precise. The Metaphone_sp and Methaphone_v2 phonetic functions obtained less records classified and more false positives than Spanish soundex function. The quality metrics obtained for each encoding method are presented in Table VII.

TABLE VII QUALITY METRICS FOR SCENARIO III

Encode Method	Total Classif.	TP	FP	Precision	F-measure
Metaphone_sp	3333	3324	9	0.997299	0.9986
Metaphone_v2	3489	3480	9	0.99742	0.9987
Soundex_sp	3622	3620	2	0.99944	0.9997

D. Scenario IV

The fourth file has a total length of 1000 records, 100 duplicated records, one duplicated record for an original record as maximum, two changed fields per item as maximum, three maximum registry modifications, with a uniform probability distribution for duplicates.

The Modified Spanish coding function, allowed that 964 record pairs could be classified, the total number of duplicates was actually 2500 records. However, this method did not present any false positive. The rest of the phonetic algorithms were 99% precise with two false positives, but the number of classified records was lower than those with Soundex_sp. The outcomes obtained for each encoding method under scenario IV are presented in Table VIII.

TABLE VIII QUALITY METRICS FOR SCENARIO IV

Encode Method	Total Classif.	TP	FP	Precision	F-measure
Metaphone_sp	812	810	2	0.997536	0.99876
Metaphone_v2	884	882	2	0.99773	0.99886
Soundex_sp	964	964	0	1	1

E. Analysis of Outcomes

According to the outcomes shown in previous section, we can observe that the Modified Spanish Phonetic algorithm was always more precise than the rest of the algorithms. Therefore, the Modified Spanish-Phonetic algorithm allows a higher proportion of how many of the classified matches (TP+FP) have been correctly classified as true matches. The Spanish phonetic algorithm allows a greater number of similarities than the remaining algorithms in all cases, because is more effective codifying Spanish words. The Spanish phonetic algorithm achieved a slightly higher f-measure than the two versions of the Spanish Metaphone algorithm.

The graphics presented in this section, have been generated according to the variation of the coding function in order to observe the behavior of the algorithms. The precision obtained from each encode method for all the scenarios have been compared, graphed and shown in Fig. 5 shows the trend of the contribution of each encoding method to the precision of the classification. As we can observe, the Spanish coding function was above the Metaphone base coding algorithms.

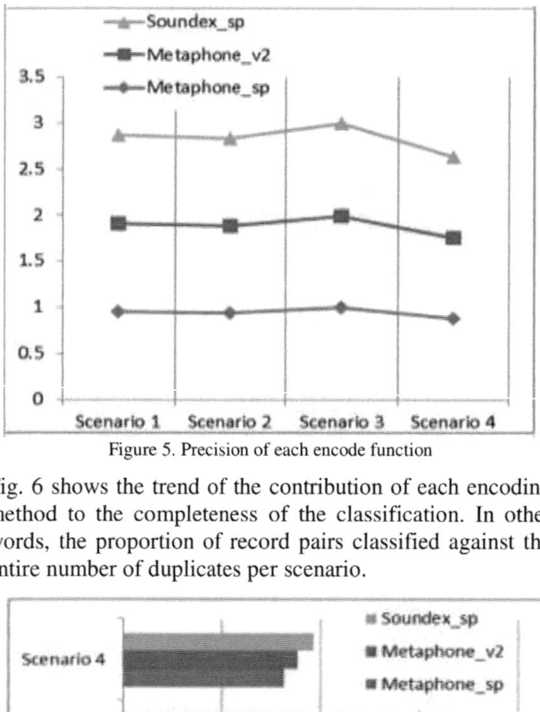

Figure 5. Precision of each encode function

Fig. 6 shows the trend of the contribution of each encoding method to the completeness of the classification. In other words, the proportion of record pairs classified against the entire number of duplicates per scenario.

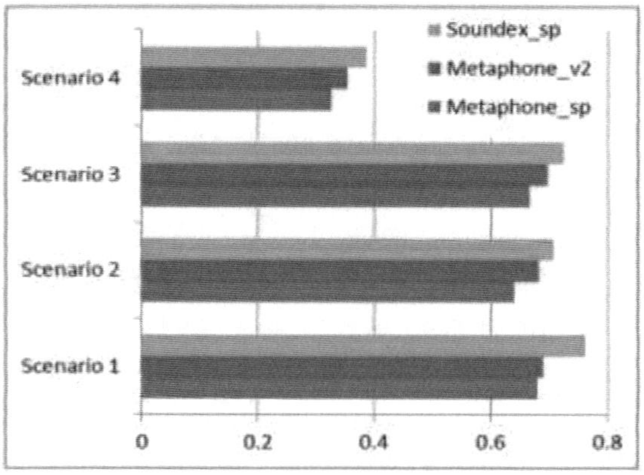

Figure 6. Completeness for each coding function per scenario

According to the outcomes shown in previous section, we can observe that the Modified Spanish Phonetic algorithm was always more precise than the two versions of Metaphone. Therefore, the Modified Spanish-Phonetic algorithm allows a higher proportion of true matches. The Spanish phonetic algorithm allows a total similarity greater than the remaining algorithms in all cases, because is more effective codifying Spanish words.

The Spanish phonetic algorithm achieved a slightly higher f-measure than the rest.

As we can observe from Fig. 6, the Spanish phonetic algorithm obtained a larger number of pairs of records classified than the rest of the phonetic algorithms.

V. CONCLUSION

The problem of detection and classification of duplicate records the integration of disparate data sources affects business competitiveness. A number of encoding, comparison and classification methods have been utilized until now, but there still some work to do in terms of effectiveness and performance.

The present work has evaluated the record linkage outcomes under a number of different scenarios, where the true match status of record pairs was known. We have obtained precision, recall, and f-measure because they are suitable measures to assess data matching quality.

The Modified Spanish Soundex function presented a better performance than the rest of the phonetic functions during most of the experiments. However, it takes the longest execution time with a difference of some milliseconds. It is important to be aware that the performance of a de-duplication system or technique is dependent on the type and the characteristics of the involved data sets, having good domain knowledge is relevant in order to achieve good matching or deduplication results.

We have previously concluded in [3] that the Modified Spanish Phonetic algorithm was always more precise and complete than Soundex y Phonex. Under a new set of experiments we have carried out against a Spanish version of the Metaphone algorithm and an enhanced version of the Spanish Metaphone, the Modified Spanish Phonetic algorithm still having the best performance in terms of precision in the majority of the cases we have experimented during the present research. However, the precision presented for the three Spanish coding functions varies slightly as we have utilized a String exact comparison function, the experimentation with different comparison functions that provide different levels of similarity might give more information regarding encoding effectiveness. We will also focus on performance in terms of massive data processing and its corresponding response time, these elements might give us a better criteria in order to identify the best encoding function.

The proposed framework may also be developed and extended to other languages as part of future work.

ACKNOWLEDGMENT

This work is being supported by a grant from Research Projects and Technology Innovation Support Program (Programa de Apoyo a Proyectos de Investigación e Innovación Tecnológica, PAPIIT, UNAM Project 1N114413 named Universal Evaluation System Data Quality (Sistema Evaluador Universal de Calidad de Datos).

REFERENCES

[1] P. Angeles, et al., "Universal evaluation system data quality," DBKDA 2014 : The Sixth International Conference on Advances in Databases, Knowledge, and Data Applications, vol. 32, pp. 13–19, 2014.

[2] P.Christen, "Febrl a freely available record linkage system with a graphical user interface," Second Australasian Workshop on Health Data and Knowledge Management (HDKM 2008), vol. 80, pp. 17-25, 2008.

[3] P. Angeles, J. García-Ugalde, A. Espino-Gamez, and J. Gil-Moncada, "Comparison of a Modified Spanish Soundex, and Phonex Coding function during data matching process", International Conference on Informatics, Electronic and Vision, ICIEV, Kytakyushu, Fukuoka Japan,ISBN:978-1-4673 6901-5, DOI:10.1109/ICIEV.2015.7334028, IEEE, pp.1-6,2015.

[4] F. M. I. Amon, J. Echeverria, "Algoritmo fonetico para deteccion de cadenas de texto duplicadas en el idioma espanol," Ingenierıas Universidad de Medellın, vol. 11, no. 20, pp. 120– 138, 2012.

[5] L. Philips, "The double metaphone search algorithm," C/C++ Users J, vol. 18, no. 6, pp. 38-43, 2000.

[6] A. Mosquera, E. Lloret, and P. Moreda, "Towards Facilitating the Accessibility of Web 2.0 Texts through Text Normalisation", Proceedings of the LREC workshop: Natural Language Processing for Improving Textual Accessibility, pp. 9-14, 2012.

[7] P. Christen, Data Matching: Concepts and Techniques for Record Linkage, Entity Resolution and Duplicate Detection. Springer Data-Centric Systems and Applications, 2012.

[8] T. Churches, P. Christen, K. Lim, and J. X. Zhu, "Preparation of name and address data for record linkage using hidden markov models." BMC Medical Informatics and Decision Making, vol. 2, no. 1, p. 9, 2000.

[9] M. Odell, R. Russell, "The soundex coding system," American Patent 1 261 167, 1918.

[10] C. L. Borgman, S. L. Siegfried, "Gettys synonametm and its cousins: A survey of applications of personal name-matching algorithms," Journal of the American Society for Information Science, vol. 43, no. 7, pp. 459-476, 1992.

M. A. Jaro, "Advances in record-linkage methodology applied to matching the 1985 census of Tampa, Florida," Journal of the American Statistical Association, vol. 84, pp. 414–420, 1989.

[11] W. Winkler, "String comparator metrics and enhanced decision rules in the Fellegi-Sunter model of record linkage," Proceedings of the Section on Survey Research Methods, American Statistical Association., pp. 354-359,1990.

[12] F. Naumann, J. Freytag, and U. Lesser, "Completeness of Integrated Information Sources", Workshop on Data Quality in Cooperative Information Systems (DQCIS2004), Cambridge, Mass., pp.583-615, 2004.

[13] P. Angeles, F. Garcia-Ugalde, "Assessing data quality of integrated data by quality aggregation of its ancestors", Computación y Sistemas, Centro de Investigación en Computación, Instituto Politécnico Nacional (IPN), vol. 13 No. 3, ISSN 1405-5546, pp. 331-334, 2010.

Leveraging Analytics to Predict Geomagnetic Storms

Impact to Global Telecommunications

Taylor K. Larkin[1] and Denise J. McManus[2]
Information Systems, Statistics, and Management Science
Culverhouse College of Commerce
The University of Alabama
Tuscaloosa, AL 35487-0226
Email: tklarkin@crimson.ua.edu[1], dmcmanus@cba.ua.edu[2]

***Abstract*—Coronal mass ejections are colossal bursts of magnetic field and plasma from the Sun. These eruptions can have disastrous effects on Earth's telecommunication systems and power grid infrastructures costing millions of dollars in damages. Hence, it is imperative to construct intelligent predictive processes to determine whether an incoming coronal mass ejection will produce devastating impacts on Earth. One such process, called "stacked generalization," is an ensemble strategy that incorporates the predictions from a diverse set of models (base-learners) by using them as inputs for another model (a meta-learner). The goal of this meta-learner is to deduce information about the biases from the base-learners and improve generalization to make more accurate predictions. In this work, 30 models are chosen from the R package caret to serve as base-learners in order to predict a geomagnetic storm index value associated for 2,811 coronal mass ejection events that occurred between 1996 and 2014. Two meta-learners are explored: 1) standard linear regression 2) non-negative elastic net regression. Results show that for this dataset, stacked generalization with the latter meta-learner produces the lowest error and performs significantly better than any of the base-learners executed individually. Not only does non-negative elastic net regression have predictive advantages, but it provides sparser solutions and more reliable inferences at the meta-level compared to linear regression. This, in turn, encourages the idea of parsimony and consequently, improves the overall generalization behavior of this technique.**

Keywords–geomagnetic storms; stacked generalization; regularization; predictive modeling.

I. Introduction

Coronal Mass Ejections (CMEs) are massive explosions of magnetic field and plasma components from the Sun (shown in Fig. 1). Typically, a CME travels at speeds between 400 and 1,000 kilometers per second [1] resulting in an arrival time of approximately one to four days [2]; however, they can move as slowly as 100 kilometers per second or as quickly as 3,000 kilometers per second (or around 6.7 million miles per hour) [3]. These phenomena can contain a mass of solar material exceeding 10^{13} kilograms (or approximately 22 trillion pounds) [4] and can explode with the force of a billion hydrogen bombs [5]. Naturally, CME events are often associated with solar activity such as sunspots [3]. During the solar minimum of the 11 year solar cycle (the period of time where the Sun has fewer sunspots and hence, weaker magnetic fields), CME events occur about once a day. During a solar maximum, this daily estimate increases to four or five. One plausible theory for these incidents taking place involves the Sun needing to release energy. As more sunspots develop, more coronal magnetic field structures become entangled; therefore, more energy is required to control the volatility and convulsion. Once the energy surpasses a certain level, it becomes beneficial for the Sun to release these complex magnetic structures [1]. When this force approaches Earth, it

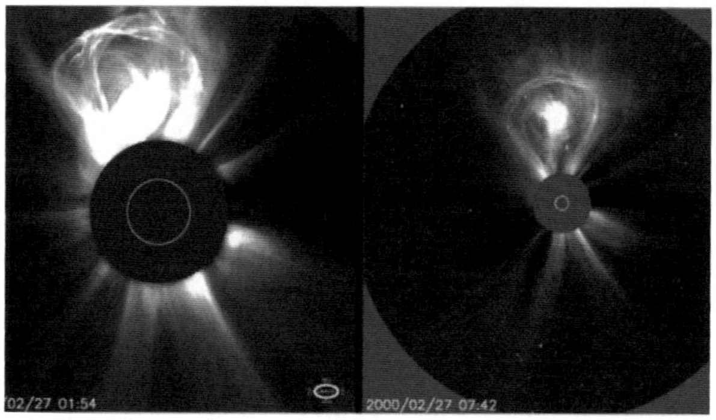

Figure 1. LASCO coronagraph images [3], courtesy of the NASA/ESA SOHO mission.

collides with the magnetosphere. The magnetosphere is the area encompassing Earth's magnetic field and serves as the line of defense against solar winds. The National Oceanic and Atmospheric Administration (NOAA) describes this event as "the appearance of water flowing around a rock in a stream" [6] as shown in Fig. 2. After the solar winds compress Earth's

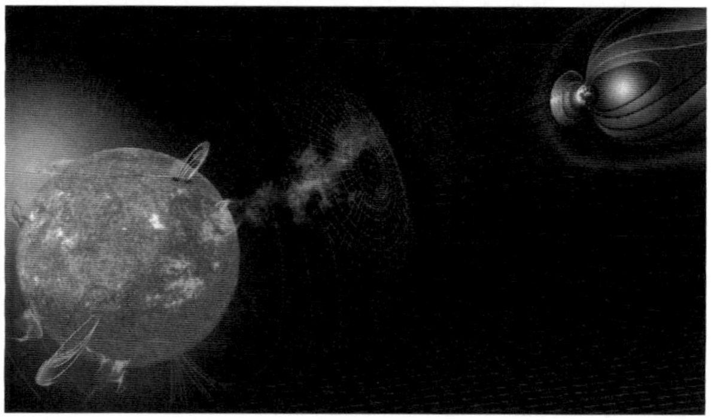

Figure 2. Rendering of Earth's magnetosphere interacting with the solar wind from the Sun [7], courtesy of the NASA's Goddard Space Flight Center.

magnetic field on the day side (the side facing the sun), they travel along the elongated magnetosphere into Earth's dark side (the side opposite of the Sun). The electrons are accelerated and energized in the tails of the magnetosphere. They filter down to the Polar Regions and clash with atmospheric gases causing geomagnetic storms. This energy transfer emits the brilliance known as the *Aurora Borealis*, or Northern Lights, and the *Aurora Australis*, or Southern Lights, which can be seen near the poles.

While mainly responsible for the illustrious Northern Lights, geomagnetic storms have the potential to cause cataclysmic damage to Earth. Normally, the magnetic field is able to deflect most of the incoming plasma particles from the Sun. However, when a CME contains a strong southward-directed magnetic field component (B_z), energy is transferred from the CME's magnetic field to Earth's through a process called magnetic reconnection [8][9][10] (as cited in [11]). Magnetic reconnection leads to an injection of plasma particles in Earth's geomagnetic field and a reduction of the magnetosphere towards the equator [1]. Consequently, more energy is amassed in the upper atmosphere, particularly at the poles. Moreover, this energy is impressed upon power transformers causing an acute over-saturation and inducing black-outs via geomagnetically induced currents (GICs) [12]. Some other residuals of this over-accumulation of energy include the corrosion of pipelines, deteriorations of radio and GPS communications, radiation hazards in higher latitudes, damages to spacecrafts, and deficiencies in solar arrays [13]. These ramifications pose a significant threat to global telecommunications and electrical power infrastructures as CMEs continue to be launched towards Earth [14]. From a business perspective, risk factor mitigation is an absolute necessity within the global business environment [15]. This can be accomplished using advanced analytical techniques on data collected about these phenomena.

The subsequent sections of this work read as follows. Section 2 briefly introduces some previous studies on predicting geomagnetic storms. Section 3 provides introductory detail about the basics of the methodology used, the dataset studied, and the experimental strategy. Section 4 displays and discusses the results. Section 5 concludes with a summary and postulates areas for future work.

II. Background Information

A. Predicting Dangerous CMEs

CMEs present an ever-increasing threat to Earth as society becomes more dependent on technology, such as satellites and telecommunication operations. Nevertheless, because of this increase in technology, more data has been collected about these acts and solar wind in general. This, in turn, has allowed for empirical models to be developed. Burton, McPherron, and Russell [16] presented an algorithm to predict the disturbance storm index (DST) value [17] based on solar wind and interplanetary magnetic field parameters. The DST value is a popular metric to assess geomagnetic activity. Expressed in nanoteslas (nT) and recorded every hour from observatories around the world, it measures the depression of the equatorial geomagnetic field, or horizontal component of the magnetic field; thus, the smaller the value of the DST, the more significant the disturbance of the magnetic field [1]. Many researchers have used this information for building forecasting models to predict geomagnetic storms [18][19].

However, many of these systems only use *in-situ* data, or data that can only be measured close to Earth. To improve prediction, studies have included data from both initial CME observations and the near-Earth solar wind condition [20][21][22], especially considering CMEs remain the source of major geomagnetic disturbances [23][24][25] (as cited in [26]). These have ranged from using logistic regression [21] to neural networks [27][28] to make predictions based on this combination of data. Aside from the work by Dryer et al. [20], which used an ensemble of four physics-based models to predict shock arrival times, the idea of using ensembles of models has not been very prevalent in the literature. Stacked generalization is a type of ensemble that uses the individual predictions from a set of base models as inputs for another model to make a final prediction. This strategy has been the backbone of successful schemes in areas such as predicting financial fraud [29], bankruptcy [30], and user ratings in the famous Netflix Prize competition [31]. Therefore, leveraging more advanced ensemble frameworks for predictive modeling has the opportunity to increase accuracy in this field.

B. Stacked Generalization

The idea of stacked generalization was originally proposed by David Wolpert [32]. It can be simplified in the following way:

- Construct a dataset consisting of predictions from a set of level 0 (or base) learners using a training and a test set. Refer to this as the metadata, *MD*.
- Generate a level 1 (or meta) learner that utilizes the predictions made at the previous level as inputs. That is, train the meta-learner on *MD* as opposed to the original training data.

Often times, the predictions from the base-learners are determined via k-fold cross-validation [33]. Define the dataset $S = \{(y_i, \boldsymbol{x}_i), i = 1, ..., n\}$ where $\boldsymbol{x}_i$ is a vector of predictor variables and y_i is the corresponding response value for the ith observation. Specifically, split the dataset S into k near equal and disjoint sets such that $S_1, S_2, ..., S_k$. Let $S^{-k} = S - S_k$ and S_k be the training and test sets, respectively. Execute the base-learner on the first S^{-k} parts and produce a prediction for the held-out part S_k. Repeat this procedure until each subset of S has been used as a test set. Extract all the hold-out predictions to create *MD*. Because generating the metadata is an independent process across each base-learner, it can be parallelized for faster computation. That is, each base-learner can be trained at the same time. This is key as time plays a pivotal role in geomagnetic storm prediction [22].

The meta-learner's purpose is to gain information about the generalization behavior of each learner trained at the base-level. Popular choices for meta-learners have been linear models [34], especially those with a non-negativity constraint on the estimated coefficients in regression type problems [35][33]. While this ensemble strategy leverages the strengths and weaknesses of the base-learners, it can be prone to overfitting [36]. Therefore, in order to combat this issue, employing regularized linear methods can perform better than their non-regularized counterparts. Reid and Grudic [37] experimented with three regularization penalties: ridge [38], lasso [39]], and elastic net [40]. The authors showed that using stacked generalization with ridge regression as the meta-learner performs well on multi-class datasets. Their findings make sense given the advantages of ridge regression for highly correlated data [38], a natural consequence of well-tuned base-learner predictions. In addition, they commented that using the lasso and elastic net penalties can promote sparse solutions that can reduce the size of the ensemble at the meta-level. Pruning the size of an ensemble model has been explored in other works [41][42][43]. It can lead to better generalization and promote the necessary diversity in the base-learner predictions, or the ensemble members [32].

C. Review of Ridge, Lasso, and Elastic Net

Recall the ordinary least squares (OLS) solution for the coefficients in linear regression [44]:

$$\hat{\beta}^{ols} = (\boldsymbol{X}'\boldsymbol{X})^{-1}\boldsymbol{X}'\boldsymbol{Y} \tag{1}$$

where $\boldsymbol{X}$ is the predictor matrix of dimension $n \times (p+1)$ and $\boldsymbol{Y}$ is the vector of outcomes of dimension $n \times 1$ for n observations and p predictor variables. In particular,

$$\boldsymbol{X} = \begin{pmatrix} 1 & x_{11} & x_{12} & \dots & x_{1p} \\ 1 & x_{21} & x_{22} & \dots & x_{2p} \\ 1 & \vdots & \vdots & \ddots & \vdots \\ 1 & x_{n1} & x_{n2} & \dots & x_{np} \end{pmatrix} \quad \boldsymbol{Y} = \begin{pmatrix} y_1 \\ y_2 \\ \vdots \\ y_n \end{pmatrix}$$

Alternatively, equation (1) can be written as

$$\hat{\beta}^{ols} = \underset{\beta}{\text{argmin}} \sum_{i=1}^{n}(y_i - \beta_0 - \sum_{j=1}^{p} x_{ij}\beta_j)^2 \tag{2}$$

When multicollinearity exists in the predictor matrix $\boldsymbol{X}$, estimates for β can become erratic and demonstrate a large amount of variability. Large positive values of β cancel out with equally large negative values which cause issues for meaningfully interpreting the coefficients [38] [44]. This stems from the predictor matrix $\boldsymbol{X}'\boldsymbol{X}$ being nearly singular. Hoerl and Kennard [38] showed that a smaller mean square error can be achieved through the use of adding a positive constant λ to the diagonal of the predictor matrix

$$\hat{\beta}^{ridge} = (\boldsymbol{X}'\boldsymbol{X} + \lambda I)^{-1}\boldsymbol{X}'\boldsymbol{Y} \tag{3}$$

such that I is a $p \times p$ identity matrix. This makes the solution invertible even if the predictor matrix is not full rank. Hastie, Tibshirani, and Friedman [44] defined ridge regression as a shrinkage method which can be expressed as an optimization problem

$$\begin{aligned} &\underset{\beta}{\text{minimize}} \left\{ \sum_{i=1}^{n}(y_i - \beta_0 - \sum_{j=1}^{p} x_{ij}\beta_j)^2 \right\} \\ &\text{subject to} \quad \sum_{j=1}^{p} \beta_j^2 \leq t, \quad t \geq 0 \end{aligned} \tag{4}$$

such that t controls the amount of shrinkage, or penalty, to introduce.

The ability of ridge regression to effectively penalize the coefficients in a continuous fashion mitigates the unstable behavior of the coefficients in the presence of multicollinearity. However, this penalty only shrinks the coefficients towards zero; hence, no variable selection is taking place. Tibshirani [39] posited lasso which imposes the following formulation:

$$\begin{aligned} &\underset{\beta}{\text{minimize}} \left\{ \sum_{i=1}^{n}(y_i - \beta_0 - \sum_{j=1}^{p} x_{ij}\beta_j)^2 \right\} \\ &\text{subject to} \quad \sum_{j=1}^{p} |\beta_j| \leq t, \quad t \geq 0 \end{aligned} \tag{5}$$

This constraint allows for some of the coefficients to shrink completely to zero for a sufficiently small t. While this has become a wildly popular technique due to its sparse nature, it can have some drawbacks. For instance, it may only select one predictor variable from a highly correlated group. Hence, Zou and Hastie [40] offered the elastic net penalty

$$\begin{aligned} &\underset{\beta}{\text{minimize}} \left\{ \sum_{i=1}^{n}(y_i - \beta_0 - \sum_{j=1}^{p} x_{ij}\beta_j)^2 \right\} \\ &\text{subject to} \quad \sum_{j=1}^{p}((1-\alpha)\beta_j^2 + \alpha|\beta_j|) \leq t, \quad t \geq 0 \end{aligned} \tag{6}$$

which is a convex combination of both ridge and lasso penalties. Note that when $\alpha = 0$ this reduces to the ridge penalty while $\alpha = 1$ is equivalent to lasso. Thus, the elastic net can shrink coefficients to exactly zero while also handling groups of correlated predictor variables.

D. A Suitable Meta-learner

As noted before, it has been shown that a non-negative constrained linear model performs well in stacked generalization for regression tasks. Given the popularity of the penalty functions mentioned in the previous section, a natural extension is to implement a meta-learner that combines these constraints into one model. Recently, Mandal and Ma [45] proposed an efficient multiplicative iterative path algorithm to estimate the entire regularization path for a variety of non-negative generalized linear models with ridge, lasso, and elastic net penalties. Therefore, to capitalize on the results of previous works, this work institutes a regularized linear model with a non-negativity constraint as the meta-learner. That is, with the elastic net Gaussian objective function [46], the following optimization problem is formed:

$$\begin{aligned} \underset{(\beta_0,\beta)\in\mathbb{R}^{p+1}}{\text{minimize}} &\left\{ \frac{1}{2n}\sum_{i=1}^{n}(y_i - \beta_0 - x_i'\beta)^2 \right. \\ &\left. + \lambda\left[\frac{(1-\alpha)}{2}||\beta||_2^2 + \alpha||\beta||_1\right] \right\} \\ \text{subject to} \quad &\beta, \lambda \geq 0, \quad 0 \leq \alpha \leq 1 \end{aligned} \tag{7}$$

In this case, λ has a one-to-one correspondence with t and is considered the shrinkage parameter. By regularizing the coefficients with both a non-negativity constraint and a penalty function, sparse solutions may be realized, even in the presence of high correlation. This meta-learner will be referred to as the non-negative elastic net (NNEN). For comparison, standard linear regression will also be implemented at the meta-level.

III. Methodology

A. Data

Four sources are considered to construct the experimental dataset: near-Earth CME information provided by Richardson and Cane [47] [48], OMNI 2 hourly averaged solar wind data at one AU from the Coordinated Data Analysis (Workshop) Web [49], CME measurements given by the Large Angle and Spectrometric Coronagraph (LASCO) located on the Solar and Heliospheric Observatory (SOHO) satellite [50], and some Sun characteristics recorded by NOAA [51]. These data are combined so that each CME has been assigned interplanetary variable values (such as B_z) prior to the DST minimum during a predicted area of effect on Earth. Establishing these values before the DST minimum gives a lead time prior to the climax of the geomagnetic storms and allows for a more realistic prediction scenario. Also included are the initial measurements about the speed and size of a CME at the time of ejection from the Sun and daily Sun characteristics on the day of ejection. After filtering out missing values and some unnecessary rows, a dataset composed of 2,811 CME events from 1996 to 2014 with 28 predictor variables is ready for analysis.

B. Implementation

1) Experimental Set-up: The analysis is performed in the R environment version 3.2.5 [52], mainly by using the **caret** (Classification And REgression Training) package [53]. This package allows for a streamlined user interface for applying various sets of predictive models from different packages. It has options to perform several resampling techniques to tune model parameters and create visualizations of model performance. The stacked generalization framework is constructed using models from this package. The amount of parameter tuning for all models is assigned at **caret**'s default value with the final parameter combinations determined by those which deliver the lowest root mean square error (RMSE).

The RMSE is calculated from an average of ten repeats of 10-fold (10×10) nested cross-validation to ensure a good estimation of error in the presence of parameter tuning [54]. Furthermore, significance tests between the meta-learner and the individual base-learners are conducted on the population of RMSEs (100 estimates from the 10×10 nested cross-validation) using the corrected repeated k-fold cross-validation test [55]. It is important to test for significant differences to investigate if the extra computation of stacked generalization is worth the effort compared to simply using the best performing model [56]. All base-learners and meta-learners are trained over the same folds with the only difference being that the meta-learners use *MD* as its inputs instead of the CME predictor variables. *MD* is generated using 10-fold cross-validation [34]. Note that this cross-validation is separate from the nested cross-validation used to estimate the error.

2) Learners: Care is taken to make sure a diverse set of base-learners is utilized [41]. The complete list of the 30 models chosen can be found in Table I. As for implementing the NNEN, a custom model is created within the **caret** framework using the *nnlasso* function from the **nnlasso** R package developed by Mandal and Ma [57]. It is important to use a custom model so that this learner is trained on the same folds as the other learners and so that the variable selection takes place within the training folds [44]. As with the popular *glmnet* function in the **glmnet** package [58], two main parameters are tuned in *nnlasso*: the mixing weights of the ridge and lasso penalties α and the amount of shrinkage to be applied λ. For this work, three values of α, $\{0, 0.5, 1\}$, are tested for each iteration in the 10×10 nested cross-validation process. For determining the amount of shrinkage, the values of λ are identified the same way as in **caret**'s implementation of *glmnet*. For the comparison meta-learner, linear regression is executed at the meta-level by calling **caret**'s *lm* method.

TABLE I. LIST OF BASE-LEARNERS

Name	**caret** Method
Bayesian Lasso Regression	*blasso*
Bayesian Regularized Neural Network	*brnn*
Bayesian Ridge Regression	*bridge*
Boosted Linear Model	*BstLm*
Boosted Tree	*bstTree*
Classification and Regression Tree	*rpart*
Conditional Inference Random Forest	*cforest*
Conditional Inference Tree	*ctree*
Cubist	*cubist*
Extreme Gradient Boosting with Linear Booster	*xgbLinear*
Extreme Learning Machine	*elm*
Generalized Additive Model using Splines	*gamSpline*
k-Nearest Neighbors	*kknn*
Lasso and Elastic Net Regression	*glmnet*
Least Angle Regression	*lars*
Linear Regression	*lm*
Linear Regression with Stepwise Selection	*leapSeq*
Multi-Layer Perceptron	*mlp*
Multivariate Adaptive Regression Splines	*earth*
Neural Network with Feature Extraction	*pcaNNet*
Non-Convex Penalized Quantile Regression	*rqnc*
Partial Least Squares	*pls*
Quantile Random Forest	*qrf*
Random Forest	*ranger*
Self-Organizing Map	*bdk*
Spike and Slab Regression	*spikeslab*
Stacked AutoEncoder Deep Neural Network	*dnn*
Stochastic Gradient Boosting	*gbm*
Supervised Principal Component Analysis	*superpc*
Support Vector Machine with Radial Basis Function Kernel	*svmRadialSigma*

IV. Results and Discussion

Table II reflects the results of the analysis. The first column lists both meta-learners and the ten most accurate base-learners ranked in ascending order by the average RMSE displayed in the second column. The third column represents the average RMSE for those CME events which triggered a strong geomagnetic disturbance (DST value ≤ -100 nT) [59]. The asterisk denotes instances where a significant difference between NNEN and the other learners are *not* found at the conventional 0.05 significance level.

Not surprisingly, the top five base-learners are all bagging or boosting ensemble models. However, NNEN yields the lowest RMSE compared to these and all the other learners, even for the strong CME events. In addition, NNEN performs statistically better than all of the base-learners for all CME events and better than the majority for the strong ones. This provides evidence that the implementation of stacked generalization here has more predictive power than using just one model. Ting and Witten [34] indicated in their analysis that stacked generalization delivers substantial improvements in accuracy for larger datasets. This is likely due to a more accurate estimation from the cross-validation process when generating the metadata. Hence, it is probable that with more data, stacked generalization can continue to enhance geomagnetic storm prediction. While the predictive improvements may seem minor at a higher cost in computation, this work, as well as others, show that this ensemble technique can lead to statistically significant improvements even against sophisticated, well-tuned models. Because of the danger that these geomagnetic storms present, even marginal improvements can make a difference.

TABLE II. PREDICTIVE PERFORMANCE

Learner	All CMEs	Strong CMEs
NNEN	**17.64**	**45.35**
Linear Regression	17.75*	45.38*
Random Forest	18.17	49.50
Cubist	18.19	47.61*
Conditional Inference Random Forest	19.06	54.28
Boosted Tree	19.10	51.87
Stochastic Gradient Boosting	19.38	52.33
Extreme Gradient Boosting with Linear Booster	19.46	51.97*
Multivariate Adaptive Regression Splines	19.81	53.29
Generalized Additive Model using Splines	20.06	55.56
Bayesian Regularized Neural Network	20.11	54.24
k-Nearest Neighbors	22.12	67.11

Although it shows its superiority over the base-learners, NNEN does not perform statistically different than simply using linear regression as the meta-learner with only very minor increases in predictive performance. While these techniques may seem equal here, recall that linear regression does not inherently perform variable selection; thus, it utilizes all 30 base-learner predictions. In addition, any attempt at making any inference regarding the coefficients at the meta-level is frivolous due to the high amount of correlation and likely presence of negative coefficients. On the other hand, NNEN selected only 19.39 ensemble members on average during the resampling process. Furthermore, some interpretation regarding the contribution of each ensemble member to the final prediction can be made by analyzing the positive, non-zero coefficients. Hence, NNEN should be preferred over standard linear regression for this dataset since it can produce sparser and more interpretable solutions with statistically similar error. The quality of being able to dynamically select which base-learners are most useful for prediction at the meta-level may help improve on the fixed form bias issues of stacked generalization mentioned by Vilalta and Drissi [60].

Further study of the performance of the base-learners offers interesting directions for future work, specifically with the use of quantile models. The Quantile Random Forest finishes as the 26th least accurate base-learner with a value of 31.60; however, its RMSE on strong CME events has a value of 46.02, which is nearly as accurate as the NNEN. Given that these strong CME events do not occur very often (131 in this dataset) but pose the most risk to society, it makes sense to adapt the meta-learner to focus on a specific quantile as opposed to the conditional mean. In this way, by focusing more on the outliers, better predictions can be made on the more important observations. Naturally, a balance would need to be constructed so that the predictions for weaker storms are not rendered useless.

V. SUMMARY

In this work, stacked generalization is used to predict geomagnetic storms driven by CMEs. Using data from a variety of sources, this technique is executed on a realistic dataset to investigate its predictive performance against using only one statistical model or machine learning algorithm. Based on insights from previous research about regularization and pruning, a NNEN model is implemented. NNEN shows its advantages on this dataset in terms of predictive accuracy while using fewer base-learner predictions. Future work consists of implementing more data for geomagnetic storm prediction to see if further improvements can be made with this methodology. In addition, increasing the number of base-learners can give NNEN more opportunities to find an optimal combination of ensemble members. Moreover, exploring the usage of regularized quantile methods can provide a useful alternative than typical mean predictions. Given the potential cataclysmic damage that CMEs can wreak on telecommunications and power companies, advanced techniques for improving accuracy are an absolute necessity for saving these industries millions of dollars.

ACKNOWLEDGMENT

We would like to thank NASA for their images and the creation of the CME catalog. This CME catalog is generated and maintained at the CDAW Data Center by NASA and The Catholic University of America in cooperation with the Naval Research Laboratory. SOHO is a project of international cooperation between ESA and NASA. In addition, we would like to thank the Goddard Space Flight Center/Space Physics Data Facility (GSFC/SPDF), OMNIWeb, and NOAA for their public use databases.

REFERENCES

[1] T. Howard, Coronal mass ejections: An introduction. Springer Science & Business Media, 2011, vol. 376.

[2] N. Srivastava and P. Venkatakrishnan, "Solar and interplanetary sources of major geomagnetic storms during 1996–2002," Journal of Geophysical Research: Space Physics (1978–2012), vol. 109, no. A10, 2004, pp. 1–13.

[3] N. Oceanic and A. Administration, "Coronal mass ejections," Available: http://www.swpc.noaa.gov/phenomena/coronal-mass-ejections [accessed: 2016-07-27].

[4] R. MacQueen, "Coronal transients: A summary," Philosophical Transactions of the Royal Society of London A: Mathematical, Physical and Engineering Sciences, vol. 297, no. 1433, 1980, pp. 605–620.

[5] N. Aeronautics and S. Administration, "Coronal mass ejections," Available: http://helios.gsfc.nasa.gov/cme.html [accessed: 2016-07-27].

[6] N. Oceanic and A. Administration, "Earth's magnetosphere," Available: http://www.swpc.noaa.gov/phenomena/earths-magnetosphere [accessed: 2016-07-27].

[7] N. Aeronautics and S. A. G. S. F. Center, "Rattling earth's force field," Available: https://svs.gsfc.nasa.gov/10954 [accessed: 2016-07-27].

[8] J. W. Dungey, "Interplanetary magnetic field and the auroral zones," Physical Review Letters, vol. 6, no. 2, 1961, pp. 47–48.

[9] D. H. Fairfield and L. Cahill, "Transition region magnetic field and polar magnetic disturbances," Journal of Geophysical Research, vol. 71, no. 1, 1966, pp. 155–169.

[10] W. D. Gonzalez and B. T. Tsurutani, "Criteria of interplanetary parameters causing intense magnetic storms (dst <- 100 nt)," Planetary and Space Science, vol. 35, no. 9, 1987, pp. 1101–1109.

[11] Y. Wang, P. Ye, S. Wang, G. Zhou, and J. Wang, "A statistical study on the geoeffectiveness of earth-directed coronal mass ejections from march 1997 to december 2000," Journal of Geophysical Research: Space Physics (1978–2012), vol. 107, no. A11, 2002, pp. SSH 2–1–SSH 2–9.

[12] J. Kappenman and V. D. Albertson, "Bracing for the geomagnetic storms," Spectrum, IEEE, vol. 27, no. 3, 1990, pp. 27–33.

[13] S. S. Board et al., Severe Space Weather Events–Understanding Societal and Economic Impacts: A Workshop Report. National Academies Press, 2008.

[14] D. Baker, X. Li, A. Pulkkinen, C. Ngwira, M. Mays, A. Galvin, and K. Simunac, "A major solar eruptive event in july 2012: Defining extreme space weather scenarios," Space Weather, vol. 11, no. 10, 2013, pp. 585–591.

[15] D. McManus, H. Carr, and B. Adams, "Wireless on the precipice: The 14 th century revisited," Communications of the ACM, vol. 54, no. 6, 2011, pp. 138–143.

[16] R. K. Burton, R. McPherron, and C. Russell, "An empirical relationship between interplanetary conditions and dst," Journal of geophysical research, vol. 80, no. 31, 1975, pp. 4204–4214.

[17] M. Sugiura, "Hourly values of equatorial dst for the igy," Ann. int. geophys. Yr., vol. 35, 1964, pp. 1–44.

[18] E.-Y. Ji, Y.-J. Moon, N. Gopalswamy, and D.-H. Lee, "Comparison of dst forecast models for intense geomagnetic storms," Journal of Geophysical Research: Space Physics, vol. 117, no. A3, 2012, pp. 1–9.

[19] T. Andriyas and S. Andriyas, "Relevance vector machines as a tool for forecasting geomagnetic storms during years 1996–2007," Journal of Atmospheric and Solar-Terrestrial Physics, vol. 125, 2015, pp. 10–20.

[20] M. Dryer, Z. Smith, C. Fry, W. Sun, C. Deehr, and S.-I. Akasofu, "Real-time shock arrival predictions during the halloween 2003 epoch," Space Weather, vol. 2, no. 9, 2004, pp. 1–10.

[21] N. Srivastava, "A logistic regression model for predicting the occurrence of intense geomagnetic storms," in Annales Geophysicae, vol. 23, no. 9, 2005, pp. 2969–2974.

[22] R.-S. Kim, Y.-J. Moon, N. Gopalswamy, Y.-D. Park, and Y.-H. Kim, "Two-step forecast of geomagnetic storm using coronal mass ejection and solar wind condition," Space Weather, vol. 12, no. 4, 2014, pp. 246–256.

[23] J. Gosling, S. Bame, D. McComas, and J. Phillips, "Coronal mass ejections and large geomagnetic storms," Geophysical Research Letters, vol. 17, no. 7, 1990, pp. 901–904.

[24] V. Bothmer and R. Schwenn, "The interplanetary and solar causes of major geomagnetic storms." Journal of geomagnetism and geoelectricity, vol. 47, no. 11, 1995, pp. 1127–1132.

[25] B. T. Tsurutani and W. D. Gonzalez, "The interplanetary causes of magnetic storms: A review," Washington DC American Geophysical Union Geophysical Monograph Series, vol. 98, 1997, pp. 77–89.

[26] J. Zhang, K. Dere, R. Howard, and V. Bothmer, "Identification of solar sources of major geomagnetic storms between 1996 and 2000," The Astrophysical Journal, vol. 582, no. 1, 2003, pp. 520–533.

[27] J. Uwamahoro, L. McKinnell, and J. Habarulema, "Estimating the geo-effectiveness of halo cmes from associated solar and ip parameters using neural networks," Annales Geophysicae-Atmospheres Hydrospheresand Space Sciences, vol. 30, no. 6, 2012, pp. 963–972.

[28] A. Singh and P. Mishra, "Prediction of intense geomagnetic storms using artificial neural network," International Journal of Advances in Earth Sciences, vol. 4, no. 1, 2015, pp. 1–7.

[29] A. Abbasi, C. Albrecht, A. Vance, and J. Hansen, "Metafraud: a meta-learning framework for detecting financial fraud," Mis Quarterly, vol. 36, no. 4, 2012, pp. 1293–1327.

[30] C.-F. Tsai and Y.-F. Hsu, "A meta-learning framework for bankruptcy prediction," Journal of Forecasting, vol. 32, no. 2, 2013, pp. 167–179.

[31] J. Sill, G. Takács, L. Mackey, and D. Lin, "Feature-weighted linear stacking," arXiv preprint arXiv:0911.0460, 2009, pp. 1–17.

[32] D. H. Wolpert, "Stacked generalization," Neural networks, vol. 5, no. 2, 1992, pp. 241–259.

[33] L. Breiman, "Stacked regressions," Machine learning, vol. 24, no. 1, 1996, pp. 49–64.

[34] K. M. Ting and I. H. Witten, "Issues in stacked generalization," J. Artif. Intell. Res.(JAIR), vol. 10, 1999, pp. 271–289.

[35] M. LeBlanc and R. Tibshirani, "Combining estimates in regression and classification," Journal of the American Statistical Association, vol. 91, no. 436, 1996, pp. 1641–1650.

[36] R. Caruana, A. Niculescu-Mizil, G. Crew, and A. Ksikes, "Ensemble selection from libraries of models," in Proceedings of the twenty-first international conference on Machine learning. ACM, 2004, pp. 18–25.

[37] S. Reid and G. Grudic, "Regularized linear models in stacked generalization," in Multiple Classifier Systems. Springer, 2009, pp. 112–121.

[38] A. E. Hoerl and R. W. Kennard, "Ridge regression: Biased estimation for nonorthogonal problems," Technometrics, 1970, pp. 55–67.

[39] R. Tibshirani, "Regression shrinkage and selection via the lasso," Journal of the Royal Statistical Society. Series B (Methodological), 1996, pp. 267–288.

[40] H. Zou and T. Hastie, "Regularization and variable selection via the elastic net," Journal of the Royal Statistical Society: Series B (Statistical Methodology), vol. 67, no. 2, 2005, pp. 301–320.

[41] G. Zenobi and P. Cunningham, "Using diversity in preparing ensembles of classifiers based on different feature subsets to minimize generalization error," in Machine Learning: ECML 2001. Springer, 2001, pp. 576–587.

[42] Z.-H. Zhou, J. Wu, and W. Tang, "Ensembling neural networks: many could be better than all," Artificial intelligence, vol. 137, no. 1, 2002, pp. 239–263.

[43] N. Rooney, D. Patterson, and C. Nugent, "Pruning extensions to stacking," Intelligent Data Analysis, vol. 10, no. 1, 2006, pp. 47–66.

[44] T. Hastie, R. Tibshirani, and J. Friedman, The Elements of Statistical Learning. New York: Springer, 2009.

[45] B. Mandal and J. Ma, "l1 regularized multiplicative iterative path algorithm for non-negative generalized linear models," Computational Statistics & Data Analysis, vol. 101, 2016, pp. 289–299.

[46] T. Hastie and J. Qian, "Glmnet vignette," 2014.

[47] H. Cane and I. Richardson, "Interplanetary coronal mass ejections in the near-earth solar wind during 1996–2002," Journal of Geophysical Research: Space Physics (1978–2012), vol. 108, no. A4, 2003, pp. SSH 6–1–SSH 6–13.

[48] I. Richardson and H. Cane, "Near-earth interplanetary coronal mass ejections during solar cycle 23 (1996–2009): Catalog and summary of properties," Solar Physics, vol. 264, no. 1, 2010, pp. 189–237.

[49] J. King and N. Papitashvili, "Solar wind spatial scales in and comparisons of hourly wind and ace plasma and magnetic field data," Journal of Geophysical Research: Space Physics, vol. 110, no. A2, 2005, pp. 1–8.

[50] N. Gopalswamy, S. Yashiro, G. Michalek, G. Stenborg, A. Vourlidas, S. Freeland, and R. Howard, "The soho/lasco cme catalog," Earth, Moon, and Planets, vol. 104, no. 1-4, 2009, pp. 295–313.

[51] N. Oceanic and A. Administration. Index of /pub/warehouse. Available: ftp://ftp.swpc.noaa.gov/pub/warehouse [accessed: 2016-07-27].

[52] R Core Team, R: A Language and Environment for Statistical Computing, R Foundation for Statistical Computing, Vienna, Austria, 2016, Available: https://www.R-project.org/ [accessed: 2016-07-27].

[53] M. K. C. from Jed Wing, S. Weston, A. Williams, C. Keefer, A. Engelhardt, T. Cooper, Z. Mayer, B. Kenkel, the R Core Team, M. Benesty, R. Lescarbeau, A. Ziem, L. Scrucca, Y. Tang, and C. Candan., caret: Classification and Regression Training, 2016, Available: https://CRAN.R-project.org/package=caret [accessed: 2016-07-27].

[54] S. Varma and R. Simon, "Bias in error estimation when using cross-validation for model selection," BMC bioinformatics, vol. 7, no. 1, 2006, p. 91.

[55] R. R. Bouckaert and E. Frank, "Evaluating the replicability of significance tests for comparing learning algorithms," in Advances in knowledge discovery and data mining. Springer, 2004, pp. 3–12.

[56] S. Džeroski and B. Ženko, "Is combining classifiers with stacking better than selecting the best one?" Machine learning, vol. 54, no. 3, 2004, pp. 255–273.

[57] B. N. Mandal and J. Ma, nnlasso: Non-Negative Lasso and Elastic Net Penalized Generalized Linear Models, 2016, Available: https://CRAN.R-project.org/package=nnlasso [accessed: 2016-07-27].

[58] J. Friedman, T. Hastie, and R. Tibshirani, "Regularization paths for generalized linear models via coordinate descent," Journal of statistical software, vol. 33, no. 1, 2010, pp. 1–22.

[59] C. Loewe and G. Prölss, "Classification and mean behavior of magnetic storms," Journal of Geophysical Research: Space Physics, vol. 102, no. A7, 1997, pp. 14 209–14 213.

[60] R. Vilalta and Y. Drissi, "A perspective view and survey of meta-learning," Artificial Intelligence Review, vol. 18, no. 2, 2002, pp. 77–95.

A Framework for Call Center Decongestion Using Sequential Pattern Analysis

Eugene Rex L. Jalao
Department of Industrial Engineering and Operations Research
University of the Philippines Diliman
Quezon City, Philippines
e-mail: eljalao@up.edu.ph

Abstract— **In an effort to improve its customer service, mobile telecommunication companies implemented various customer service channels like call center hotlines, text messaging, email or web self-service where subscribers conduct various after-sales transactions. Nowadays, a hotline call center via a customer service representative is the top choice alternative preferred by subscribers. However, it is noted that the cost of each call when transacting on a hotline is much greater than the cost of the other channels. Furthermore, subscribers get easily irritated when they need to wait for a long time to avail the services. In order to address the problem of reducing hotline calls, as well as to reduce the cost of customer service transactions, subscriber call transactions are analyzed in this paper to predict the next type of call that the subscriber will transact. A sequential pattern analysis methodology is applied and frequent sequences of calls are collected. Given the frequent sequences, the sequences of transaction calls are identified and a corresponding campaign is introduced to intercept the new calls and divert the transaction to less costly customer service channels.**

Keywords: ***call center; decongestion; hotline; sequential pattern analysis;***

I. INTRODUCTION

Delivering good customer service particularly in the telecommunications or telco industry is a must to keep its customers from churning. In this industry, customer service is captured from pre-sales research, to in-life transactions and finally to the renewal of the plan through the procurement of new or upgraded handsets. Basically the entire subscriber life cycle is covered. Hence, to stay with the subscribers every step of the way, these telcos implemented various traditional customer service channels, e.g., physical retail stores, fax numbers, email and contact center hotlines. Subscribers would just transact their needs in one of these channels through the aid of customer service representatives (CSRs).

However, these traditional channels are expensive to maintain and operate. Operating costs include: labor costs of CSRs, rent, and other overhead expenses. In the Philippines, given that the average call and wrap up time metric from the International Finance Corporation is 6 minutes [1], and operating costs of a call center hover from \$8 – \$14 per hour [2], an average call would cost the telco company \$0.8 – \$1.4 per customer transaction. If the hotline receives 100,000 calls per month, this would lead to approximately \$80,000 to \$140,000 operating costs for the telco.

Hence, in an effort to reduce transaction costs, telcos implemented alternative self-service channels to divert subscribers from using the aforementioned traditional costly channels. Some examples of these alternative channels would be: web applications, SMS, and smartphone apps self-service channels. Some companies even utilize social media through official pages to reach their customers. Yet, not all transactions can be deployed in all channels. For example, disputes on billing can only be addressed when talking to a CSR. On the other hand, simple transactions like bill balance inquiry can be done on any channel. The paper by Kumar and Telang [3], presented that the cost of transacting through self-service channels (< 1\$ per transaction) is way cheaper than traditional channels with CSRs (between \$5 and \$10).

On the other hand, a survey by McCarthy and Giles [4] asserts that a phone call with a CSR is the top preferred channel by approximately 75% of the respondents. Additionally, the top most frustrating thing about customer service is the long waiting time to speak to a CSR. Therefore, it is prudent for telcos to keep operating these call centers but on the other hand, having a congested hotline would also lead to negative impacts to their customer service. In essence, telcos would want transactions that can be transacted through self-service channels be diverted from these costly customer service channels.

Given this background, this paper attempts to profile telecommunication subscribers in an effort to decongest call center hotlines and divert possible self-service transactions to other low cost self-service channels. This paper is further divided as follows: Section II provides an overview of current published methodologies, Section III presents the framework of the model while Section VI shows the results and discussion when applied to a local telecommunications company. Section V provides the conclusions and further research.

II. REVIEW OF RELATED LITERATURE

There have been several attempts to decongest a call center hotline through various predictive and prescriptive analytics methodologies.

Forecasting methodologies are considered in [5] - [8]. These models specifically forecast the volume of calls that arrive at a single time interval. These are mainly for operational issues and mainly address the issue of how much work they have to do.

A lot of call centers deal with highly erratic demand that is also time-based. The time-based component is relatively easy to handle by adjusting agent staffing [9]. Some examples would be in [10], where a proposed framework that combines linear programming with simulation to recommend a schedule. Search methods are developed which used queueing theory to produce agent schedules for a multi-skill call center is done in [11]. However, it's the random component that contributes to the complexity of the demand.

Other models tried to reduce the call demand by limiting calls admitted to the hotline. A paper by Omeci et al. [12] proposed a selective form of call admission by selectively admitting calls according to their relative importance to the organization.

Given these solutions, a methodology that could predict the most likely next transaction call type of the subscribers would be beneficial such that low priority transactions can be routed to other low cost channels. A methodology that fits this bill is Sequential Pattern Analysis (SPA). Agrawal and Srikant [13] defined SPA as a methodology to extract frequent sequences within a set of transactions. There have been several applications that used the SPA algorithm: Choi et al. in [14] applied SPA on online-product recommendation systems, Huang et al. in [15] proposed a knowledge-assisted sequential pattern analysis framework to identify the patterns of the uterine contractions as well as labor contractions. Chen et al. [16] in proposed to use SPA to forecast potential customers by identifying attributes with high level of association.

Given the multitude of applications of SPA, this paper hypothesizes that the use of SPA in determining the frequent sequences of calls of subscribers on a hotline can be done to address hotline decongestion.

III. PROPOSED FRAMEWORK

The proposed hotline decongestion framework is composed of three components. These are defined as: (1) the Preprocessing Component, (2) SPA Component and the (3) Campaigns Design Component. This section provides an overview of the different components as follows.

A. *Preprocessing Component*

Call transaction data is extracted from the call database with the following dataset structure as presented in Fig. 1:

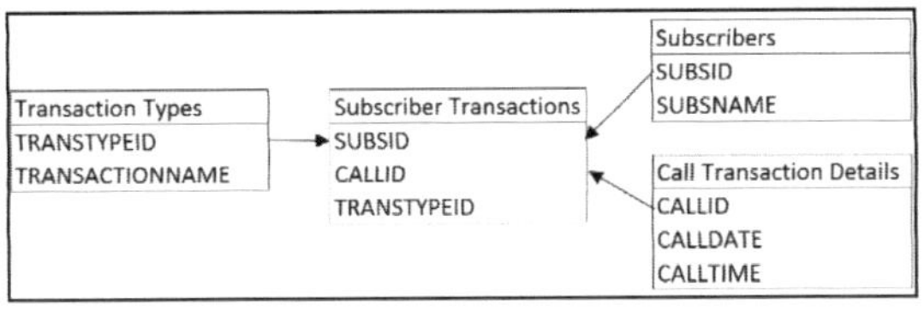

Figure 1. Dimensional Model of required data

The proposed dataset for the SPA component would require to have a granularity of: one row per call with corresponding subscriber and transaction type ID. Hence the following dataset, that joined multiple tables are presented in Fig. 2 as follows:

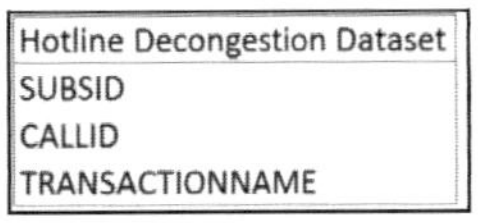

Figure 2. Proposed Dataset Required

Invalid transactions like prank calls, dropped and abandoned calls are likewise eliminated from the dataset leaving only valid transactions. The clean dataset is then sent to the SPA component of the framework.

B. *SPA Component*

In this component, the SPADE (Sequential PAttern Discovery using Equivalence) algorithm proposed by Zaki [17] is utilized on a R Platform. The package "arulesSequences" is utilized as the main library to compute for the frequent subsequences.

The output of this component is a set of frequent sequence of transactions with format as presented in equation (1).

$$<\{\text{transA}\},\{\text{transB}\},\{\text{transC}\},> \ \textit{support} = s \qquad (1)$$

C. *Campaigns Design Component*

Given the result of the SPADE algorithm, corresponding campaigns need to be designed to identify the types of future calls of the subscribers. If the type of call can be done in other low-cost channels, a system is in place to intercept that call and divert that transaction.

To illustrate given the frequent transaction in equation (1), if the subscriber called for {transA} then subsequently called for {transB}, and if {transC} can be done in other channels, a text message from the network can be sent to the subscriber to avail of {transC} in other self-care channels instead of calling the hotline. This would hopefully encourage the subscriber to avail of {transC} in other channels, thus reducing calls in the hotline.

IV. RESULTS AND DISCUSSION

To test the framework, hotline transactions from a leading telecommunications company here in the Philippines are considered and extracted for preprocessing. From the third quarter of 2015, a total of 245,162 calls are extracted from the hotline data warehouse coming from 122,462 unique subscribers. Of the total calls, 23,812 calls are considered invalid since these are invalid transactions and thus are eliminated from the dataset. A snapshot of the final dataset is shown in Fig. 3:

SUBID	TRANSID	TRANS
10454567890	688936812	FOLLOW UP WITHIN SLA
10454567890	688938242	SALES LEAD
10454567890	688939685	SALES LEAD
10454567890	688943163	REFERRED TO OTHER HOTLINE
10454567890	688943751	FOLLOW UP WITHIN SLA
10454567890	688945660	MECHANICS PROCEDURE
10454567890	688945718	SIM RELATED

Figure 3. Dataset Preview of the Data

This dataset is fed into the SPADE algorithm with 1% minimum support setting. Results from the dataset showed that there are 22 sequences of length one transaction and 13 sequences of length two. The 13 sequences are presented in Fig. 4.

```
<{"DEVICE CONFIGURATION"},{"SUCCESSFUL NOT INTERESTED"}> 0.02634287
    <{"DEVICE CONFIGURATION"},{"SUCCESSFUL INTERESTED"}> 0.04060852
     <{"MECHANICS PROCEDURE"},{"SUCCESSFUL INTERESTED"}> 0.01628260
          <{"BILLING INQUIRY"},{"MECHANICS PROCEDURE"}> 0.01084418
      <{"DEVICE CONFIGURATION"},{"MECHANICS PROCEDURE"}> 0.01028891
       <{"MECHANICS PROCEDURE"},{"MECHANICS PROCEDURE"}> 0.01476376
     <{"DEVICE CONFIGURATION"},{"DEVICE CONFIGURATION"}> 0.02413810
    <{"SUCCESSFUL INTERESTED"},{"DEVICE CONFIGURATION"}> 0.01192207
                <{"ACCOUNT DETAILS"},{"BILLING INQUIRY"}> 0.01221603
                <{"BILLING INQUIRY"},{"BILLING INQUIRY"}> 0.02843331
         <{"AFTERSALES REQUEST"},{"AFTERSALES REQUEST"}> 0.01172609
            <{"BILLING INQUIRY"},{"AFTERSALES REQUEST"}> 0.01557218
                <{"BILLING INQUIRY"},{"ACCOUNT DETAILS"}> 0.01315510
```

Figure 4. The 13 frequent sequences of length 2.

Given the results from figure 4, we examine the sequential rule in equation (2) as follows:

$$< \{\text{Account Details}\}, \{\text{Billing Inquiry}\} > \textit{support} = 1.2\% \quad (2)$$

This can be interpreted as: 1.2% of 122,462 or 1470 unique subscribers can be intercepted on the transaction "Billing Inquiry" if they called for "Account Details" beforehand. This could lead to a reduction of at least 1470 calls within a given quarter. The other 12 rules can be designed to maximize the use of the framework to further reduce the number of repeat calls.

V. CONCLUSION AND FUTURE STUDIES

The hotline decongestion framework, composed: (1) preprocessing, (2) sequential pattern analysis, and (3) campaigns design components, is able to profile subscribers in terms of the call type sequences. Frequent call sequences can be extracted and corresponding campaigns can be developed to intercept and divert call transactions to alternative lower cost self-service channels.

Further improvement of the framework is considered in terms of analyzing the inter-arrival time of the calls. The framework currently studies the sequence of calls but not the amount of time in between calls made by the subscriber.

REFERENCES

[1] IFC, "Call Center Pricing," 2016. [Online]. Available: http://www.ifc.org/wps/wcm/connect/75ce96004cf85d4f8752c7f81ee631cc/Tool+9.4.+Measuring+Call+Center+Performance.pdf?MOD=AJPERES. pp. 1 [Accessed: 06-Jul-2016].

[2] World Wide Call Centers, "Call Center Pricing," 2016. [Online]. Available: https://www.worldwidecallcenters.com/call-center-pricing/. pp. 1 [Accessed: 06-Jul-2016].

[3] A. Kumar, and R. Telang, "Does the web reduce customer service cost? Empirical evidence from a call center," *Inf. Syst. Res.*, vol. 23, no. 3 PART 1, pp. 721–737, 2012.

[4] C. Mccarthy, M. Giles, W. W. W. O. Com, and C. Mccarthy, "Customer Service : Where are Telcos Investing ? About the authors," *Ovum Signatue Res.*, no. pp 1-2, November, 2011.

[5] J. Taylor, "Short-term electricity demand forecasting using double seasonal exponential smoothing," *J. Oper. Res. Soc.*, vol. 54, no. 8, pp. 799–805, 2003.

[6] R. Soyer and M. M. Tarimcilar, "Modeling and Analysis of Call Center Arrival Data: A Bayesian Approach," *Manage. Sci.*, vol. 54, no. 2, pp. 266–278, 2007.

[7] J. Weinberg, L. D. Brown, J. R. Stroud, J. W. Einberg, L. D. B. Rown, and J. R. S. Troud, "Bayesian Forecasting of an Inhomogeneous Poisson Process With Applications to Call Center Data," *J. Am. Stat. Assoc.*, vol. 102, no. June, pp. 1187–1199, 2007.

[8] H. Shen, and J. Z. Huang, "Interday Forecasting and Intraday Updating of Call Center Arrivals," *Manuf. Serv. Oper. Manag.*, vol. 10, no. 3, pp. 391–410, 2008.

[9] Z. Aksin, M. Armony, and V. Mehrotra, "Customer Behavior Modeling in Revenue Management and Auctions: A Review and New Research Opportunities," *Prod. Oper. Manag.*, vol. 16, no. 6, pp. 665– 688, 2007.

[10] M. T. Cezik, and P. L'Ecuyer, "Staffing Multiskill Call Centers via Linear Programming and Simulation," *Manage. Sci.*, vol. 54, no. 2, pp. 310–323, 2008.

[11] A. N. Avramidis, A. Deslauriers, and P. L'Ecuyer, "Modeling Daily Arrivals to a Telephone Call Center," *Manage. Sci.*, vol. 50, no. 7, pp. 896–908, 2004.

[12] H. E. Ormeci, E. L., and A. N. Burnetas, "Admission policies for a two class loss system with random rewards," *IIE Trans.* \, vol. 34, no. 9, pp. 813–822., 2002.

[13] S. Agrawal, and Rakesh; Ramakrishnan, "Mining sequential patterns," *Proc. Elev. Int. Conf. Data Eng.*, pp. 3–14, 1995.

[14] K. Choi, D. Yoo, G. Kim, and Y. Suh, "A hybrid online-product recommendation system: Combining implicit rating-based collaborative filtering and sequential pattern analysis," *Electron. Commer. Res.*

Appl., vol. 11, no. 4, pp. 309–317, 2012.

[15] Z. Huang, M. L. Shyu, J. M. Tien, M. M. Vigoda, and D. J. Birnbach, "Prediction of uterine contractions using knowledge-assisted sequential pattern analysis," *IEEE Trans. Biomed. Eng.*, vol. 60, no. 5, pp. 1290–1297, 2013.

[16] W. C. Chen, C. C. Hsu, and J. N. Hsu, "Optimal selection of potential customer range through the union sequential pattern by using a response model," *Expert Syst. Appl.*, vol. 38, no. 6, pp. 7451–7461, 2011.

[17] M. J. Zaki, "SPADE: An efficient algorithm for mining frequent sequences," *Mach. Learn.*, vol. 42, no. 1–2, pp. 31–60, 2001.

Tracking Cyclists and Walkers: Will it Change Planning and Policy Processes?

João Bernardino, Mafalda Lopes
TIS - Consultants in Transport, Innovation and Systems S.A.
Lisbon, Portugal
e-mail: joao.bernardino@tis.pt, mafalda.lopes@tis.pt

Predrag Živanović, Slaven Tica, Branko Milovanović, Stanko Bajčetić
University of Belgrade – Faculty of Transport and Traffic Engineering
Belgrade, Serbia
e-mail: p.zivanovic@sf.bg.ac.rs, slaven.tica@sf.bg.ac.rs, b.milovanovic@sf.bg.ac.rs, s.bajcetic@sf.bg.ac.rs

Giacomo Lozzi
POLIS - Promotion of operational links with integrated services, Association internationale
Bruxelles 1050, Belgium
e-mail: glozzi@polisnetwork.eu

Abstract—**Tracking cyclists and walkers may open a new window of opportunities for urban planning and policy. Data analytics about where, when, how, why, how far, how fast and from and to where people walk or cycle, will be available cheaply and quickly. It is our hypothesis that this will cause a change in transport planning and decision making processes. How, and to what extent, will this happen? Through what actors? With what kind of information? For what types of action? Who will want it and why? Will it generate a positive outcome? We approach some of these questions by elaborating on the technical potential of tracking data towards cycling and walking planning and policy analysis, interpreting the results of a stakeholder consultation and observing the approaches and outcomes of some cases of application. We conclude that tracking data analysis is likely to become a relevant part of cycling and walking planning and policy processes in the near future, not only for the efficiency gains in technical analysis, but also crucially in the communication between actors.**

Keywords-tracking; walking; cycling; GPS; mobility tracking; transport planning, transport policy.

I. INTRODUCTION

The ubiquitous presence of smart mobile phones accompanying individuals, and its technological development, is facilitating the tracking of those individuals, with multiple applications. An opportunity is created by the fact that tracking data allows to characterize the movements of individuals in ways that may be used in mobility planning and policy processes. In the scope of motorized traffic, tracking data is already being applied in citizen information [34] and traffic model calibration [35][36]. When it comes to cycling and walking, applications in the scope of infrastructure and communication planning and policy are yet less mature, although there are already a few cases to record, either analysing data through common geographic information system (GIS) tools or even already with dedicated user interfaces (BikePrint tool [37]). These experiences are mostly part of research projects, and even though several cities have already applied tracking data, there has been no time to mature them into systematized local planning processes. It is thus not yet clear what the actual influence of tracking data might become in the future.

To contribute to such assessment, we provide a review about the positioning of tracking information in relation to current cycling and walking planning and policy practices, identifying what it adds to existing information, interpreting the results of a stakeholder consultation and reviewing some already existing applications. We finally elaborate on how tracking data could influence and change cycling and walking planning and policy processes in the future, considering also the issue of the quality of data obtained.

The stakeholder consultation included two surveys and a workshop. The first survey targeted mobility planners and approached 92 respondents from 25 European countries. The second survey was targeted at user representatives and collected 63 responses from 15 countries. The workshop targeted planners, researchers and user representatives and involved 27 participants from 12 European countries (details are provided in [27]). The samples were based partly on calls within the network of European cities POLIS [38] and partly based on calls by the entities taking part in the TRACE project [39], under which these activities were executed. The samples in question may be characterized by a higher than average interest of the participants in innovative urban mobility initiatives and a specific focus on cycling and/or walking issues. The samples were fairly representative in terms of countries, except for the user representatives survey, which has an overbalance of two countries (Portugal – 33% of respondents; Italy – 15%).

Section II of this document starts by reviewing what is the role data and planning support systems play in urban mobility processes. Section III describes the traditional methods on data collection for monitoring travel behaviour. Section IV digs into what tracking data could add to these processes, both from the perspective of the comparison with the data provided by traditional methods and from the perspective of stakeholders. Section V introduces some cases of application. Finally, based on the observations of the previous sections, section VI elaborates about the ways how tracking data might influence cycling and walking planning and policy processes, including the identification of its limitations and challenges.

II. Data and Planning Support Systems in Urban Mobility Planning Processes

Reference [1] notes the influence of data in planning and policy processes in the following way: "data can help establish baselines, identify trends, predict problems, assess options, set performance targets, and evaluate a particular jurisdiction or organization. Which indicators are selected can significantly influence analysis results. A particular policy may rank high when evaluated using one set of indicators, but low when ranked by another."

In this scope, it is firstly interesting to obtain a measure of the extent to which data is being applied in the field of active mobility. The planners' survey asked which types of information were being used for cycling and walking planning in the respondents' sites. About 26% of the said that no type of network related quantitative data is considered locally for cycling. The number increases to 76% in the case of walking, showing that the use of data is much higher for cycling than walking. Qualitative information has a significantly wider use across cities than quantitative information (Fig. 1). On the other hand, asked about which types of barriers they found to be the most relevant to achieve existing priorities, respectively 51% and 62% identified the lack of data as one of the issues.

For our aim, the relevant question is why data is being (or not) used. And building on it, how could the new tracking data add to planning and policy processes. In this section we provide a review on the application of data in urban mobility and specifically cycling and walking policy.

Data is used in distinct ways depending on the context and inherent needs of the relevant actors. The work [2] points that "transport data needs may be assessed on the project basis, the business basis or the system basis. The purpose, content and extent of data needs are different for these three bases".

In Europe, best practices have been synthesized and are widely disseminated by the European Commission's Sustainable Urban Mobility Planning guidelines [32]. This guide advocates four main stages of the planning process. Data plays an important role in all of them:

A. Preparation: data is used to analyse the current mobility situation and develop alternative scenarios that might result from different policies and measures.

B. Setting of the objectives: to set targets, the level of accuracy of the previously collected data should be assessed

C. Elaboration of the plan: monitoring and evaluation process should be defined, and the impact of a particular measure will be assessed on the basis of data.

D. Implementation: data is collected to measure target user behaviour and target achievement, allowing for a better understanding of the system and correction actions.

Structured guidance in the specific scope of cycling has been given by European projects like PRESTO [40], BYPAD [41] and CHAMP [42], which include a role of data in the scope of their normative planning frameworks. They put a particular emphasis on planning related linear aspects like the diagnosis of the current situation and on the monitoring and evaluation of actions carried out. A structured approach towards the collection of data for cycling policy is given by [33], which attempts to provide guidance to cities. Depending on the aims of data collection, several questions are presented as to how to communicate the data, such as:

- Who is the primary target group?
- Who are secondary target groups?
- How should data be presented?
- Should other media also be involved?
- Who is to draw up the final cycling account?
- Is the cycling account to be politically approved or are they simply informative?
- How can it be ensured that politicians, municipal staff and citizens are aware of the cycling account?

As assumed by several of these guidance initiatives, the advocated planning stages and their intermediate steps are actually a dynamic, non-linear process. In the real world, not strictly shaped by the desirable approaches of guidelines, the processes are often chaotic and strongly framed by political and organizational short-term issues. In that scope, it is an interesting and rather under-studied issue what is the actual role of data in real world urban mobility planning and policy.

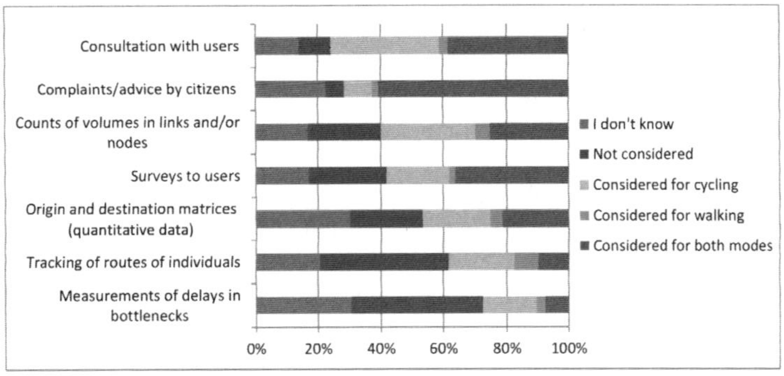

Figure 1. Type of information considered for cycling and walking (planners survey)

While we did not find such analyses in the strict scope of data collection, they are embedded in a wider field within the scope of mobility, which is the use of planning support systems (PSS). PSS refer to information and analysis tools which provide support by identifying problems and testing solutions, by translating data into relevant information applicable for planning purposes. In other words, PSS may be defined as "an information framework that integrates the full range of current (and future) information technologies useful for planning" [3], with the purpose of either projection to some point in the future or estimation of impacts from some form of development [4].

The accumulated experience, including the evaluation of its (lack of) success, is interesting to interpret the ability of data in ultimately influencing planning and policy processes.

Reference [5] describes the advantages of PSS as providing analytical and communicative support. From an analytical perspective, the PSS can provide valuable feedback on the necessary iterations that are part of a negotiation task. From a communication perspective, the PSS may spark an active and content-based dialogue among the involved participants and improve the collaboration and communication among different disciplines. However, the authors warn that the support capabilities of a PSS can also have a negative effect on conducting a task, an idea also supported by [6], who argue they can become performative, thereby steering rather than supporting the process.

Reference [8] assesses the history of PSS use, claiming that there has been a significant evolution, powered by new technologies for disseminating information. This, coupled with the development of intrinsically visual tools such as GoogleMaps [43], has led to the common media of communication becoming predominantly visual. As such, PSS have evolved to graphic and related media in contrast to its origins in numerical data processing. The interactivity of these systems has also developed considerably. An assessment of spatial planning practice at the end of the 20th century however suggested that the adoption and use of geo-information tools are far from widespread and far from being effectively integrated into the planning process.

Reference [4] claims that the largely successful history of urban transportation modelling systems in the United States suggests that three factors are required for computer-based tools to be widely used in practice: a shared commitment to a well-defined methodology, extensive government support, and the ability of available tools to provide needed outputs for a substantial user community.

Some authors [9] attempted to identify the main factors blocking the widespread usage of PSS by launching a web survey directed to people involved in planning practices from all around the world. The participants were asked to classify the importance of potential bottlenecks. The main obstacles were identified as:

- Little awareness among planners of the existence of PSS and for the purposes for which PSS can be used;
- Lack of experience with PSS;
- Low intention to start using a PSS among users.

The authors suggest that marketing actions accompanying the launch of the PSS are essential in order to give PSS a good chance to prove itself as a means for improving spatial planning practice. Other researchers [10] consider that the PSS are stuck in a vicious cycle: although there are many PSS in existence, generally speaking PSS have not yet become widely applied in planning practice. As a result, few lessons are actually being learned about the effective integration of PSS in planning practice, and this lack of experience hampers the further improvement of PSS technology and its application.

Reference [11] considers that there are several barriers that explain this lack of integration, which can be divided in institutional/procedural discrepancies (*i.e.,* separate planning institutions, formal processes, financial arrangements, *etc.*) and substantive differences (*i.e.,* different planning objects, information *etc.*). In a web survey, the author identified additional barriers to the widespread usage of PSS, noting that these relate mostly to "softer issues":

- PSS are implemented too late rather than too early in the planning process;
- PSS are implemented too far removed from the political process;
- They do not fit the land use and transport planning process,
- PSS do not sufficiently support the generation of new strategies, although they do support the evaluation of strategies;
- Lack of transparency;
- Low communication value (*i.e.,* PSS which are not understandable for planners, stakeholders and politicians);
- Conflicting interests between land use and transport actors are the main barrier to successful integration, with 'lack of a common language' in second place and 'lack of political commitment' as third.

Other authors [12] consider that there is an implementation gap between the PSS and the actual planning decisions. In order to overcome this gap, it is advisable for the development of the PSS to be intertwined with the planning process itself. The authors consider that the transparency of the output and the assumptions of the models that are part of the PSS are improved through discussions and continuous explanations by the modellers.

A relevant conclusion for our analysis is that the application and influence of data in planning and policy processes is more complex than the picture provided by linear urban mobility guidance, being framed by diverse and contextual political, organizational and individual elements.

Another dimension to this review of PSS use processes is that the influence of data in this context also depends on how it is presented. As pointed by [1], an "activity or option may seem desirable and successful when measured one way, but undesirable and ineffective when measured in another. It is therefore important to understand the assumptions and implications of different types of measurements". For example, bicycle counting and surveys may provide different conclusions regarding the bicycle use trends [13]. This calls for data collection methods and an appropriate choice of accurate indicators.

In further sections of this paper, we try to understand how tracking data can influence planning and policy, not in view of desirable normative planning frameworks, but rather actual planning and policy processes.

III. DATA COLLECTION METHODS FOR MONITORING TRAVEL BEHAVIOUR

Travel behaviour may be monitored either by observing what users do or by asking them about what they do. In the scope of cycling and walking, the traditional methods used are counting and surveys.

Counting allow to quantify the number of users passing in a given place. They are a physical measure associated with a point, a section or an area. The most relevant indicator collected from counting is the volume of users or vehicles in the given element of infrastructure. The most common motivation of local authorities to apply counting is related to the measurement of the achievement of some type of target with regard to bicycle traffic, while prioritising certain measures among others, or to monitor specific measures on individual routes are also found to be related to counting [13]. With the later scope, it is also possible for example to measure speeds or delay times through more sophisticated technology.

Counting does not allow knowing who the user is, from where to where he goes or why. To obtain more detailed data about the users and their trips, surveys are used. Different survey methods can be used and survey data can be quantitative or qualitative. Three broad types of surveys may be identified: general/population-based surveys, intercept surveys and travel diaries [14].

General surveys are of static nature, in the sense that they do not relate to specific trips or sites, but they tend to capture routine travel behaviour of the users, focusing on general behaviour, like for example usual mode of transport to work, usual distance, or usual number of trips. General surveys also provide a good opportunity to know the personal characteristics of the user. Their application is frequently made in the scope of the elaboration or monitoring of general mobility plans [13]. They may also be used to predict what users would do in the face of some transport supply change, in the form of a stated preference survey.

The intercept survey refers to directly interviewing cyclists or pedestrians, *i.e.,* capturing them while they are cycling or walking. This allows both to approach directly the user target in question but also to target by the place where users are passing.

Travel diaries provide the transport planner specific information about each trip realized during a period. This data collection method has a number of drawbacks, however: large burden placed on respondents, high costs, decrease in the quality of the recorded data and missing trips, especially if the diary is made over several consecutive days. Reference [15] highlights 'non-response' as the most pressing problem in all surveys (response rates around 20-30 percent from a mail-back survey, 40-60 percent from a telephone survey, and 60-75 percent from a face-to-face interview).

A problem faced in many travel surveys, and in particular in the scope of cycling and walking, is that they assume trips are taken by only one mode, while many trips involve more than one mode. "Last-mile" connections to and from public transport trips are the best-known example of missing multimodal information, such as walking to a bus stop, or carpooling to a park-and-ride station [16].

TABLE I. IDENTIFICATION OF GAPS IN DATA RELEVANT FOR TRANSPORT PLANNING AND POTENTIAL OF TRACKING DATA TO FULFIL THOSE GAPS

Input data for transport planning	**Traditional methods**		**Tracking based methods**			
	Surveying	**Counting**	**GPS**	**GPS + GIS**	**GPS + SMS/app**	**GPS + GIS + SMS/app**
User data - socioeconomic						
Gender, age, occupation, address, *etc.*	yes	no	no	no	yes	yes
Travel data - individual						
Origin	yes	no	yes	yes	yes	yes
Destination	yes	no	yes	yes	yes	yes
Journey start time	yes	no	yes	yes	yes	yes
Journey end time	yes	no	yes	yes	yes	yes
Exact routes	no	no	yes	yes	yes	yes
Transport mode(s)	yes	yes	no	yes	yes	yes
Travel purpose	yes	no	no	yes	yes	yes
Transfer nodes	yes	no	no	yes	yes	yes
Transfer time	yes	no	no	yes	yes	yes
Network data						
Road data (type and condition)	yes	no	no	yes	no	yes
Nodes data (bottlenecks, delays, *etc.*)	no	yes	no	no	no	yes
Links data (link speeds, bottlenecks, delays)	no	yes	no	yes	no	yes
Absolute volumes	no	yes	no	no	no	no
Public transport data (stops, lines, routes, *etc.*)	yes	yes	no	yes	no	yes
Parking data (location, quantity)	yes	yes	no	no	no	yes
Zones data	yes	no	no	no	no	yes

Note: The classification given in the table to each item is subjective. In some cases with classification "no", the data in question may potentially be extracted by the concerned method but it would imply high costs and is not common (*e.g.*, surveys could incorporate GIS tools allowing the user to provide exact routes). In other cases with classification "yes", the capability may not yet be fully developed (or fully accurate) with current tools, but such may be expected in the near future (*e.g.*, transport mode identification from tracking tools).

IV. What Does Tracking Data Add?

A. *Tracking and traditional data collection methods*

The growing importance of promoting and improving conditions for cycling and walking is evident in today's urban planning practice. One of the major issues for not putting cycling and walking on an equal footing with motorised transport modes is arguably the lack of data. Good quality and reliable input data are crucial for efficient transport planning processes.

Table I indicatively reviews gaps in data relevant for transport planning from traditional data collection methods. Surveying lacks or implies high costs in obtaining network and travel data. Additionally, for some relevant types of data, it does not provide necessarily accurate data, but only the perceptions of users (concerning, for example, travel time), which may be both an advantage and a disadvantage. On the other hand, counting only gives partial network data, while socioeconomic and travel information is absent.

Tracking allows to characterize network data with a level of detail and capability to obtain indicators that is not possible by other methods. This is achieved if combined with GIS tools, through which a map matching operation allows to allocate GPS trajectories to the existing network. When movement trajectory is obtained via an application from mobile phones, the same application is an opportunity to establish a channel of communication with the user, allowing to obtain the type of socio-economic information normally extracted by common surveys. Tracking data combined with GIS tools and an application interface with users thus seems to at least potentially cover all data needs, with one exception and one significant difficulty:

- Tracking data does not allow to infer absolute volumes, only relative volumes, since it does not capture all users. To obtain absolute flow volumes, counting are still essential;
- Tracking combined with an application allows asking specific question to users; however, it is questionable that this is possible to do within reasonable representativeness of the sample.

Overall, the comparison of these methods suggests that tracking provides network data that was previously not possible or difficult to obtain. At the same time, traditional methods will still fill some gaps, as also suggested by [31].

B. *New indicators and visualizations*

The location and time data provided by tracking allows for a variety of analysis fields and approaches. Table II outlines the most relevant and potentially feasible indicators identified in the stakeholder consultation [27]. These indicators can be grouped into origins/destinations, flows and volumes, level of service and surface quality. Additionally, relevant derived visualizations like isochrones or parking spot attraction (based on local arrivals) were particularly highlighted as useful. Another element referred was the ability to visualize and compare the tracking based indicators with other indicators like slopes, pollution or accident data.

TABLE II. TRACKING DATA INDICATORS

Indicators	Space dimension	Unit
Volume of users	Link, node, area	users/time
Number trips originated and ended per zone (origin/destination)	Area	users/time
Volume per origin-destination	Area-Area	users/time
Speed average	Link, area	kilometre per hour
Speed standard deviation	Link, area	kilometre per hour
Level of service and/or congestion	Link, path, node, area	percentage
Distance average	Area-Area	meters
Trip time average	Area-Area	minutes
Waiting time	Link, path, node, area, area-area	time
Waiting time per user	Link, path, node, area, area-area	time /user
Quality of surface	Link	rugosity index

An additional interesting outcome of the planners' consultation is that the importance given to different types of indicators varies with local context (Fig. 2). If divided into two groups according to the local modal cycling share – into *champions* and *starters* – it becomes clear that in *champion* cities, respondents give more importance to indicators related to the performance of the existing network (like speeds and delays), while in *starter* cities they tend to be more interested in indicators that help to define a network (like number of trips per origin and destination).

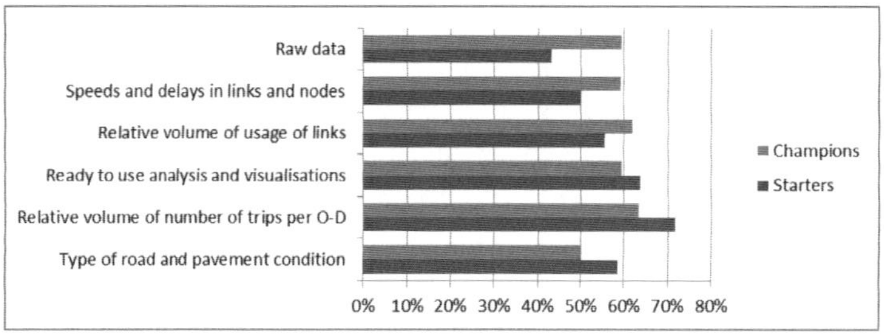

Figure 2. Indicators planners would like to obtain from tracking data, according to the city profile in terms of level of cycling adoption

C. *Contributions to a mobility vision (Workshop)*

The "Tracking data for planning and policy" workshop explored how tracking data could influence planning and policy, from mobility vision to operations [27].

A starting point of the workshop conclusions was that changing the mobility paradigm away from car use is a difficult task, which requires a strong dialogue between actors that promotes the sharing of information and ideas. In this process, tracking will help redefining the policy vision by providing evidence and helping quantifying goals: vision is not a technical matter, but it needs technical support.

More particularly, it was a wide belief that tracking data could give visibility to ideas and groups of users commonly disregarded by traditional planning and data collection methods, helping to increase the community engagement and participation. Tracking will help reinforce the idea that users are persons, not numbers, thus enabling setting goals and approaches more suited to the target groups: if you want to build a city for people, you have to have data on people. The underlying vision is to drive change based on the evidence of user demand, i.e., on what people actually want.

Another dimension of reflection referred to the trends in collection of tracking data. According to the recent trends, tracking data will be pervasive and standard within few years. Coupled with the widespread use of other big data, it might have significant impacts on the planning process. Tracking data provides continuous and current information, richer detail, user segmentation, and can complement other types of data. This contributes to making better diagnoses, test ideas, monitor and evaluate actions, develop multimodal policies and improve the network design.

Another relevant aspect raised is that by accessing data continuously, tracking will shorten the temporal horizon of activities and programs: with tracking there is no need to wait for the "elephant paths" (i.e., the destruction of grass by people walking along he shortest path across a field).

However, stakeholders also stressed that, when using tracking for planning, it is important to keep in mind that it should not be seen as a goal in itself or as the only basis for establishing goals and visions. Like motor traffic models, tracking may reinforce the idea that mobility is solely an engineering question, while personal choices, equity, lifestyle and citizens' well-being should not be forgotten.

V. Cases of Application

The stakeholder consultation allowed to identify some cases of influence of tracking based information in planning and policy processes. Five representative cases are presented, which refer to different aspects of those processes. None of those cases is part of a systematic use of tracking data in local planning procedures; they rather refer to applications of research projects or ad-hoc uses of the available data. All the collected cases refer to cycling, which is coherent with the fact revealed by the stakeholder survey that planners show a higher interest to apply tracking in the scope of cycling.

A. *Case 1: Identifying user preferences through Strava to select the ideal path for a cyclepath (Lisbon)*

In Lisbon, there was an internal discussion in the municipality about the ideal path for a new cycle path, considering a balance between distance and slopes. The question was put which path would the users prefer. The observation of the Strava Heat Map (Fig. 3) available in the web allowed to conclude that most users preferred to follow the path with the shortest distance, even if it had a higher slope and more intense traffic. This led to the decision to build the cycle path in this link instead of the alternatives.

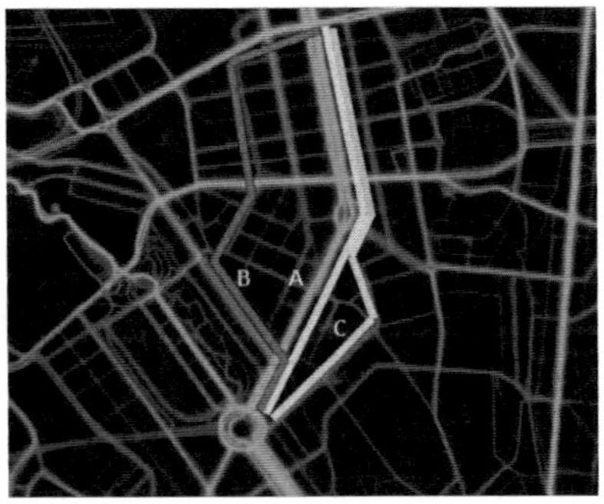

Figure 3. Path development choices in Lisbon (Source: author's elaboration based on Lisbon municipality staff's description and Strava Heat Map)

B. *Case 2: "Cycling is faster" area definition and communication to citizens (Leuven)*

In Leuven, the cycling and car tracking data allowed to map the areas of the city from which each of the modes of transport is faster in trips towards the train station (Fig. 4). This information was then used to communicate to citizens with the objective to promote more cycling in relation to car use. The campaign was based on outdoor posters spread in the frontier within which cycling was faster than car [28].

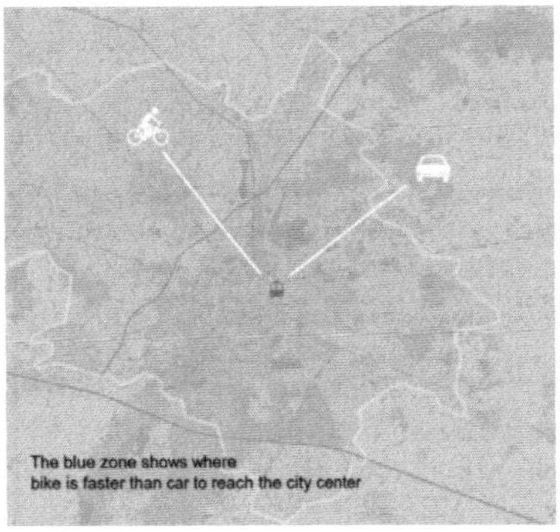

Figure 4. Areas where each mode (cycling vs car) is faster towards train station in Leuven (Source: [28])

C. Case 3: Defining position for bike parking (Bologna)

In 2015, the Municipality of Bologna decided to install 1.000 new bike racks in the city centre of Bologna. The issue was to determine the places and the number of racks per place in order to maximize their efficacy. The Local Mobility Agency and the Municipality decided to study the origins/destinations coming from GPS data collected during the European Cycling Challenge 2015 [44] (Fig. 5). The result was a set of locations and a number of racks per location based on real needs of cyclists, an "evidence-based" approach that gave strength and concreteness to the decision.

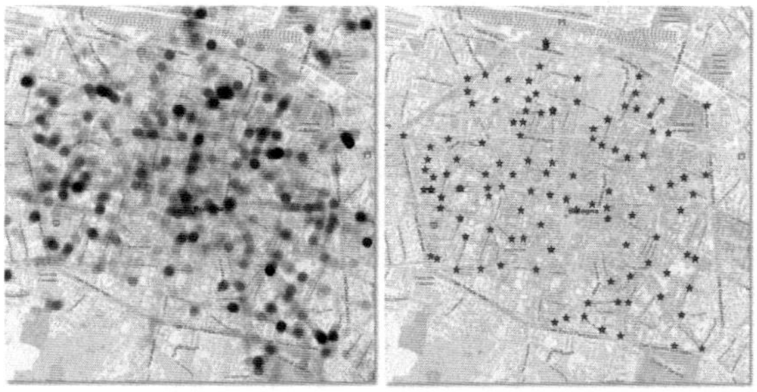

Figure 5. Bicycle parking location selection (right) based on tracked trip destinations (left) in Bologna (Source: SRM – Reti e Mobilità Srl,)

D. Case 4: How would a new cycle highway improve travel times? (Eindhoven)

In Eindhoven (Fig. 6), an analysis of the cycle tracking data through the BikePrint tool allowed to closely calibrate the speeds practised in each link, as well as the travel times from each zone to the city centre. Based on that information, a test was made to check what would be the time benefits per zone of building a cycle highway [18].

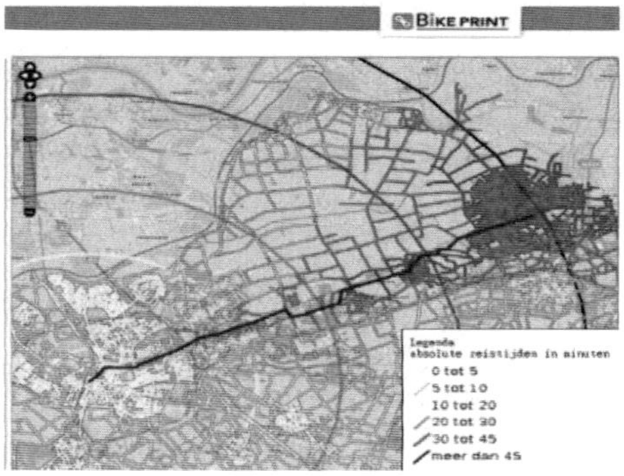

Figure 6. Analysis of travel time reduction by implementation of a high speed cycling lane in Eindhoven (Source: [18])

E. Case 5: Identification of user sub-optimal choices and improve information to users (Leuven)

A new high speed cycling route was developed at the north side of the rail line in Leuven (Fig. 7).

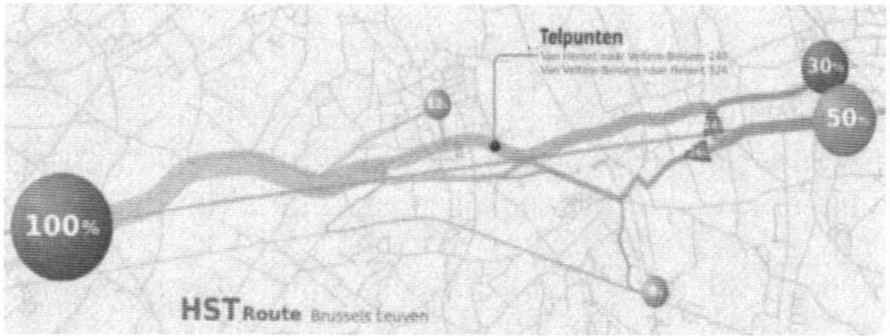

Figure 7. Bicycle user route choices between a high speed route and an old route in Leuven (Source: [28])

However, the tracking data revealed about half of the users coming from the south side of the line were still using an old route when they would be able to ride faster if they followed a certain link towards the north route. From this information, the municipality put better information at the relevant intersection to inform the users that they could proceed to the high speed cycle route [28].

VI. How could tracking data influence planning and policy processes? Some speculative hypotheses

When asked whether they believed that tracking data would be useful to their municipality or region, most respondents of the planners' survey replied that it would – 85% and 68% respectively in the scope of cycling and walking. When asked if tracking based information could be useful for a set of elements, the respondents replied positively to all of them. But it is noteworthy that despite they valued technical aspects like effectiveness of the actions and defining priorities, the one which was rated the highest is "communication to policy makers" (Fig. 8).

A different perspective is the perspective of the users (cyclists and walkers). In the user representatives' survey, 74% agreed that the use of tracking data would have the potential to "radically" improve planning practises. About the uses of tracking data, user representatives saw the highest potential in using it for their own purposes as a communication tool for lobbying policy interventions, followed by understanding priorities for intervention and providing information to users (Fig. 9).

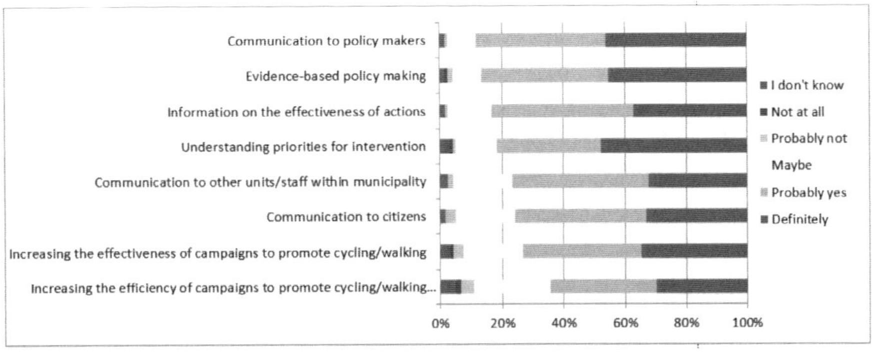

Figure 8. Planners survey responses: "Do you believe tracking based information could be useful for…?"

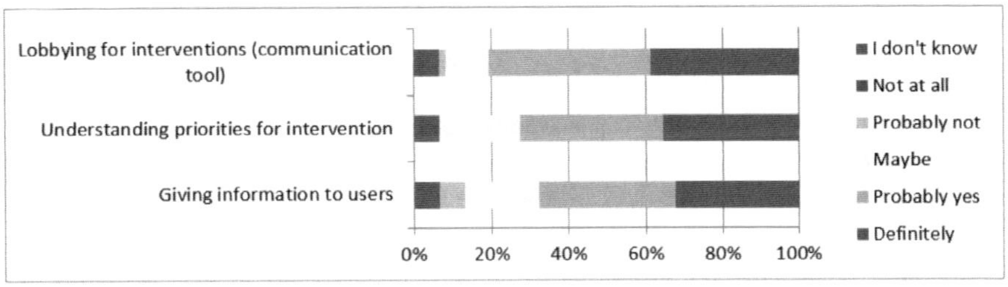

Figure 9. User representatives survey responses: "In your opinion, would tracking based information be useful to your organization for …?

Considering the collection of stakeholder views and the observations described in the previous sections, we elaborate on plausible *hypotheses* about the future role of tracking in cycling and walking planning and policy.

A. Functions of tracking data

Tracking data may have multiple functions interfering in policy and planning process:

A simple tool for Communication. A potential of tracking data is its apparently powerful communication ability. Because it makes cyclists or walkers visible to the decision maker, to the general public or to planners themselves, tracking visualizations seem to have the ability to influence opinions and decisions, at least in the short term.

Demand and infrastructure performance analysis. The location and time data provided by tracking allows for a variety of analysis fields and approaches, whether they be about the level of service of the infrastructure or knowledge about the demand and its preferences, at a micro or macro level, per type of user, schedule, weather or location.

Monitoring of measures. Tracking data allows to see in much detail how demand changed whenever a measure is introduced in the local mobility system.

Like other policy and planning tools, it may be that tracking data and related tools will become intrinsically connected within the process of planning and decision making. We could say that it will have become a building block of the process. At that point, its influence would be structural and part of the paradigm of urban mobility. It is desirable that such influence of a tool is a positive one and not biased towards certain objectives opposed to others, or that it is not only illusionary contributing to some objective. This was the case in the past of transport models, which ignored other modes of transport and failed to show planners and decision makers that addressing congestion through more space for cars was feeding a never ending feedback loop. In its own ways, cycling and walking tracking information use has a risk of creating biases.

B. Stakeholders under influence of tracking

Stakeholders may use or be influenced by tracking information in several ways. We will describe a scenario where tracking influences a system of interrelations between different actors in the planning and decision making process. The system is constituted by planners in the field of cycling and walking, planners from other fields, decision makers and the citizens, which may include the general public but also user activists (Fig. 10).

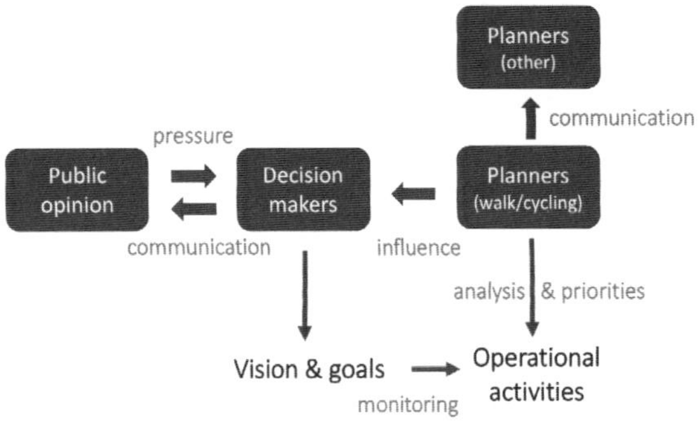

Figure 10. Roles of tracking data in the planning process (Source: author)

First of all, cycling and walking planners may use tracking information to develop better analyses and properly define priorities for action. But they can also use tracking information to communicate and sometimes influence other actors. That could be the case with other technicians within the organization who might have different views or distinct languages –the visual and quantitative power of tracking data helps to show that cyclists and walkers have needs and face movement constraints. 55% of the planners' survey respondents said that conflicting views were one of the main barriers in relation to achieving the existing priorities in the scope of cycling (30% for walking).

The same goes for the planners' relation with decision makers. Here, the influence might happen not only on operational decisions but also at a higher level of vision definition. Showing the evidence on the entropy of walking, or the choices of cyclists towards safer or quicker paths, may trigger the decision maker's appetite for giving priority to improving the conditions for walkers or cyclists.

Tracking information will also give decision makers the additional assurance that will be able to communicate with the public in an effective way. Through the network information provided by tracking data, they will be able to use numbers to describe the problem and show the positive effects of solutions. This ability to argue based on empirical evidence will provide decision makers more confidence to take politically risky decisions.

The communication between decision makers and public will also occur in the opposite direction. Activism towards cycling or walking can in the same way find in tracking data a powerful tool to argue for the improvement of their conditions, showing that there are users and describing their problems through data, makes it more inevitable for the interlocutor politician to act.

VII. QUALITY OF DATA

The quality of input data in transport planning analyses may have significant influence on the accuracy of the conclusions. [19] claim no study has systematically examined the implications of using low-quality big data for traditional analyses. Nevertheless, there are two main elements related to quality of data for the purpose of realizing analysis meaningful for mobility planning.

The first one is the accuracy of the location data, which depends on the instruments and methods of measurement used by the application. Several issues affect the accuracy of GPS data: trees and buildings obscuring GPS signals, the geometric arrangement of the GPS constellation of satellites, and the quality of the GPS unit [20]. Because of this, GPS routes can appear to bounce around to either side of an actual route when accuracy is decreased. But for tracking routes longer than only the shortest walking trips, modern GPS devices represent a relatively accurate and inexpensive way to record natural travel data [21]. A recent study that tested algorithms for calibrating GPS-observed walking trips to actual trips had the best results when trips were more than 3 minutes long and more than 30 meters in distance [22]. This deficiency of GPS can be mitigated by implementing a primary data processing phase prior data usage for planning and/or other purposes. Some authors [23] have described a series of procedures that have been developed to manipulate data collected from GPS devices carried by people or placed in personal vehicles, and used to produce records of the trips made over a period of days or weeks. In their paper they give insight on different steps within data processing, from converting continuous GPS logs into trip-based records and trip identification, to overcoming of various deficiencies. These include cold start problems, particularly the case for movements of a vehicle over a distance of one or two kilometres and for short walks with a wearable GPS, where a ''cold start'' receiver may not record position, or when the trip is long enough for position to be acquired, but the resulting trip will be shown to be shorter in length and duration than the real trip). Another issue addressed is the correction for signal loss in ''urban canyons'', tunnels, and under other circumstances. The authors claim to have reached a 95% correct rating in identifying real trips, while at the same time reducing the time and effort required to process data up to 75-80% of the amounts of time required for a manually assisted procedure.

The other issue is the representativeness of the sample. Since different user groups have distinct preferences and behaviour profiles [30], it tends to be important that the sample has a realistic representation of those user groups. To guarantee that this happens, it is not enough to obtain a sufficiently large sample, but also that specific groups are not being excluded from the sample for some reason [25].

[24] gave a comprehensive review on a state-of-the-art of the travel behaviour studies categorized by trajectory data types. All selected empirical studies have drawn conclusions about the population based on the sampling dataset. According to [19], there have been three large-scale travel surveys that have relied entirely on GPS technology, two of these in the USA. The first exclusively GPS household travel survey conducted was by the Ohio Department of Transportation, in the Cincinnati metropolitan area with a sample of 2608 households [15]. Sampling for the pilot and the main surveys used an address-based sampling procedure [15]. GPS data was complete in 80% cases and the data was used to derive travel parameters, *i.e.*, average daily No of trips (mobility rate), trip distance, travel time, travel purpose, *etc.* Data was presented for all days and weekdays, and on the personal and household level. Reference [15] has reported that a high level of representativeness for the sample was achieved. Their primary conclusion was that it is feasible to undertake a GPS-only household travel survey. They also recommend a longer period of measurement to be used in future surveys.

According to the results of the stakeholder consultation, there are three typical problems of sample representativeness:

- *Leisure vs. utilitarian cyclists:* the most developed segment of tracking applications is related to the promotion of sports or physical activity in general. For example, the STRAVA [45] heat map is available for any user and site. In starter countries with a low level of cycling, even applications primarily targeted at utilitarian trips, like the

European Cycling Challenge, do attract individuals who cycle for leisure. Leisure minded cyclists have different preferences in terms of destinations and path choice to utilitarian cyclists and are generally not suitable as a sample for the purpose mobility planning. In European Cycling Challenge application in Bologna, currently the tool attempts to distinguish utilitarian from sports users by filtering the trips by some areas of the city or schedule.

- *Experienced cyclists vs. starters:* this distinction is particularly relevant in the context of starter or climber cities, where the cycling network is not fully developed and there are very significant differences between users in terms of their ability and willingness to use the car network for cycling. Initiatives that collect data about existing cyclists tend to attract experienced cyclists, who are the more willing to participate in these kind of initiatives. However, the stronger is their identity as a cyclist, the more likely are they to be far away from the average in terms of choice preferences. When the target of the planner is to take into account the preferences of users who are not very experienced or have a strong cyclist identity, this effect should be considered. A possible way to isolate the differences among different groups is to ask the application users how they identify themselves in terms of their experience and cycling identity.
- *Info excluded users:* walkers with specific needs like elder people and children are also the ones who tend to be excluded from the use of smart mobile phones, which are the devices that make it viable to track the movements of users. This biasing factor is difficult to overcome and the planner may have to assume that the data is not representative for these types of users. If data from these users is particularly important, the planner may require different data collection methods and a specific campaign targeted at these users.

Overall, it seems to be important that the analyst is critical about the type of sample represented by the data and the implications that may have for the validity of the analysis that is realized. The application of samples from different sources may minimize the problem or, at least, provide an opportunity to compare data. Obtaining specific information about user characteristics also provides the chance to compare results for different user groups.

VIII. Conclusions

With the aim of assessing the potential of tracking data to change cycling and walking planning and policy processes, this paper reviewed (i) the analytical capabilities resulting from tracking data, considered (ii) the views of relevant actors in a stakeholder consultation and collected some (iii) initial experiences on the application of tracking data.

Tracking data obtained though users' mobile devices opens up an opportunity to obtain new cycling and walking activity information. Such data can be treated through GIS tools to produce quantified information about the state and performance of the cycling or walking network. Indicators like speeds, delays, relative volumes, trip origins and destinations and their paths, collected for every part of the network, become possible. This information allows to better assess bottlenecks, user information, monitoring the effects of measures or studying user preferences in ways

Mobile applications doing tracking (and possibly interacting with the user) could thus complement and significantly replace traditional data collection methods. Two main limitations to this were identified: firstly, tracking data does not provide absolute volumes in the network, for which countings data will still be needed; secondly, the sample of tracked users may have biases.

Considering the new technical analyses that are made possible, such new tool theoretically promises to enable better diagnoses and decision making towards cycling and walking provision. This is also the belief of the planners and user representatives consulted under this work.

However, such capability does not guarantee by itself that the use of tracking data will be embraced within planning and policy processes. The review of past applications of planning support systems shows that not always they are successful in penetrating the planning and policy practices. Or, in cases where they are, there is a risk that these planning support systems end up steering decisions based on partial information rather than supporting a conscious decision making – as motor traffic models which ignored costs on cycling and walking.

A different, perhaps even more crucial dimension of the influence of cycling and walking tracking data, is its communication ability. "Communication to policy makers" was evaluated as the most relevant application of tracking information by planners. According to these actors, tracking data makes cyclists and pedestrians more "visible", and thus more prone to be considered as a priority in decision making processes. Communication between staff of the local authorities and communication to citizens have also been cited in the survey as important functions of tracking data. Some of the practical cases presented in this paper show actual examples of how the tracking data has been applied both in internal dialogue between planners and decision makers and in citizen information. Tracking data does therefore not only provide potential analytical ability, but could also be a powerful instrument for communication.

Acknowledgment

This paper is based on results of the project 'Opening the cycling and walking tracking potential – TRACE', under grant agreement No 635266 – European Union's Horizon 2020 research and innovation programme.

We thank all the participants in the surveys and workshop.

References

[1] T. Litman, "Developing indicators for comprehensive and sustainable transport planning", Transportation Research Record: Journal of the Transportation Research Board, (2017), pp. 10-15, 2007.

[2] Z. Huang, "Data integration for urban transport planning", PhD thesis, Febodruk BV, Enschede, The Netherlands, 2003.

[3] R.E. Klosterman, and E. Richard, "Planning Support Systems: A New Perspective on Computer-Aided Planning, Journal of Planning Education and Research", vol. 17, pp. 45-54, 1997.

[4] R. K. Brail, "Planning Support Systems Evolving: When the Rubber Hits the Road," in Complex Artificial Environments: Simulation, Cognition and VR in the Study and Planning of Cities, J. Portugali, Ed. Berlin, Heidelberg: Springer Berlin Heidelberg, pp. 307–317, 2006.

[5] P. Pelzer, G. Arciniegas, S. Geertman, and S. Lenferink, "Planning Support Systems and Task-Technology Fit: a Comparative Case Study", Applied Spatial Analysis and Policy, pp. 1-21, 2015

[6] H. Smith, G. Wall, and K. Blackstock, "The role of map-based environmental information in supporting integration between river basin planning and spatial planning", Environmental Science & Policy, 30, pp. 81–89, 2013.

[7] Brail, R. K., "Planning support systems for cities and regions", Lincoln Institute of Land Policy, Cambridge, Massachusets, 2008.

[8] J.S. Stillwell, S. Geertman, and S. Openshaw, eds., Geographical information and planning: Advances in spatial science, Berlin: Springer Verlag, 1999.

[9] G. Vonk, S. Geertman, and P. Schot, "Bottlenecks blocking widespread usage of Planning Support Systems", Environment and Planning A, vol. 37. Pp. 909-924, 2005.

[10] G. Vonk and S. Geertman, "Improving the Adoption and Use of Planning Support Systems in Practice", Applied Spatial Analysis, vol. 1, pp. 153-173, 2008.

[11] M. te Brömmelstroet, "Making planning support systems matter: improving the use of planning support systems for integrated land use and transport strategy-making", PhD thesis, University of Amsterdam, 2010.

[12] M. te Brömmelstroet and P. Schrijnen, "From planning support systems to mediated planning support: a structured dialogue to overcome the implementation gap", Environment and Planning B:Planning and Design, vol. 37, pp. 3-20, 2010.

[13] A. Niska, A. Nilsson, M. Wiklund, P. Ahlström, U. Björketun, L. Söderström, and K. Robertson, "Methods for Estimating Pedestrian and Cycle Traffic", Survey and Quality Assessment, VTI Report 686, 2010.

[14] A. J. Richardson, E. S. Ampt, and A. H. Meyburg, "Survey methods for transport planning", Melbourne: Eucalyptus Press., 314 p., 1995.

[15] P. Stopher, L. Wargelin, J. Minser, K. Tierney, M. Rhindress and S. O'Connor, "GPS-Based Household Interview Survey for the Cincinnati, Ohio Region", Abt SRBI, Incorporated, Cincinnati, OH, 2012.

[16] "Transportation Research Circular E-C183: Monitoring Bicyclist and Pedestrian Travel and Behavior", 2014.

[17] R. Greene-Roesel, M. C. Diogenes, D. Ragland, and L.A. Lindau, "Effectiveness of a Commercially Available Automated Pedestrian Counting Device in Urban Environments", TRB Annual meeting CD-ROM, 2008.

[18] D. Bussche and P. V. de Coevering, "BikePRINT–In Depth Analysis of Cyclist Behaviour and Cycle Network Performance Using GPS-Tracking Technology." European Transport Conference 2015. 2015.

[19] A. Vij and K. Shankari, "When is big data big enough? Implications of using GPS-based surveys for travel demand analysis", Transportation Research Part C, vol. 56, 446–462, 2015.

[20] J. Wolf, S. Hallmark, M. Oliveira, R. Guensler and W. Sarasua, "Accuracy Issues with Route Choice Data Collection by Using Global Positioning System", In Transportation Research Record: Journal of the Transportation Research Board, No. 1660, pp. 66–74, 1999.

[21] S. Bricka, J. P. Zmud, J. L. Wolf, and J. Freedman, "Household Travel Surveys with GPS: An Experiment", In Transportation Research Record: Journal of the Transportation Research Board, No. 2105, pp. 51–56, 2009.

[22] G.-H. Cho, D. A. Rodríguez, and K. R. Evenson, "Identifying Walking Trips Using GPS Data", Medicine and Science in Sports and Exercise, Vol. 43, No. 2, pp. 365–72, 2011.

[23] P. Stopher, C. FitzGerald, and J. Zhang, "Search for a global positioning system device to measure person travel", Transport. Res. Part C: Emerg. Technol., vol. 16 (3), pp. 350–369, 2008.

[24] Y. Yue, T. Lan, A.G.O. Yeh, and Q. Li, "Zooming into individuals to understand the collective: A review of trajectory-based travel behaviour studies", Travel Behaviour and Society, vol. 1, pp. 69–78, 2014.

[25] N. Facchiano, A. Kingman, A. Olore, and D. Zuniga, "Sampling Strategies for Error Rate Estimation and Quality Control (Project Number: JPA0703)". Worcester Polytechnic Institute. Available from: https://www.wpi.edu/Pubs/E-project/Available/E-project-042308-150804/unrestricted/JPA-0703_JHMQP_FINAL.pdf. April, 2008.

[26] E. Bossuyt, J. Christiaens, N. Deham, E. Franchois, and I. Vleugels, "Assessment of the potential and conditions for use in behaviour change initiatives", Report, Project TRACE – Walking and Cycling Tracking Services, 2016.

[27] J. Bernardino et al., "Walking and Cycling Tracking for Planning Information and guidelines on using tracking data for mobility planning", Report from project TRACE, 2016.

[28] I. Semanjski, "Move platform, i-Know consortium presentation", 1st TRACE Take-Up Group meeting. Brussels, January 21, 2016.

[29] www.fietstelweek.nl, Retrieved 16 February 2016.

[30] I. Semanjski, A.J. Lopez Aguirre, J. De Mol, and S. Gautama "Policy 2.0 Platform for Mobile Sensing and Incentivized Targeted Shifts in Mobility Behavior." Sensors 16.7 (2016): 1035. 2016.

[31] G. Romanillos, M. Zaltz Austwick, D. Ettema, and J De Kruijf, "Big data and cycling." Transport Reviews 36.1 (2016): pp. 114-133.

[32] European Union, "Guidelines. Developing and Implementing a Sustainable Urban Mobility Plan", Brussels, 2013.

[33] Nordyske cykelbyer, Process plan for preparation of a cycling account, Published online at http://www.nordiskecykelbyer.dk/upload/NonPublic/Proces_plan_cycling_account.pdf , 2013.

[34] Wikipedia contributors, "Google Traffic," Wikipedia, The Free Encyclopedia, https://en.wikipedia.org/w/index.php?title=Google_Traffic&oldid=718736727 [retrieved: August, 2016].

[35] A. Kesting and M. Treiber, "Calibrating car-following models by using trajectory data: Methodological study." Transportation Research Record: Journal of the Transportation Research Board 2088 (2008): pp. 148-156, 2008.

[36] E. Brockfeld, R. Kühne, and P. Wagner, "Calibration and validation of microscopic traffic flow models." Transportation Research Record: Journal of the Transportation Research Board 1876 (2004): pp. 62-70, 2004.

[37] www.bikeprint.nl/ [retrieved: August, 2016].

[38] http://polisnetwork.eu/ [retrieved: August, 2016].

[39] TRACE – Walking and cycling tracking services, Horizon 2020 under grant agreement No 635266. http://h2020-trace.eu/

[40] http://www.rupprecht-consult.eu/nc/projects/projects-details/project/presto.html [retrieved: August, 2016].

[41] www.bypad.org/ [retrieved: August, 2016].

[42] http://www.champ-cycling.eu/ [retrieved: August, 2016].

[43] https://www.google.rs/maps/ [retrieved: August, 2016].

[44] http://www.cyclingchallenge.eu/ [retrieved: August, 2016].

[45] https://www.strava.com/ [retrieved: August, 2016].

The 100-fold Cross Validation for Small Sample Method

Shuichi Shinmura
Faculty of Economics, Seikei Univ.
Tokyo, Japan
e-mail: shinmura@econ.seikei.ac.jp

***Abstract*—We establish a new theory of discriminant analysis by mathematical programming (MP) and develop three MP-based optimal linear discriminant functions (Optimal LDFs). Those are Revised IP-OLDF based on a minimum number of misclassification (minimum NM, MNM) criterion by integer programming (IP), Revised LP-OLDF by linear programming (LP) and Revised IPLP-OLDF that is a mixture model of Revised LP-OLDF and Revised IP-OLDF. We evaluate these LDFs with two support vector machines (SVMs), Fisher's LDF and logistic regression. Although we could compare these LDFs by six different small samples, we could not validate these LDFs by the validation samples. Therefore, we developed "100-fold cross validation for small sample" method that is a combination of k-fold cross validation and re-sampling sample (The Method). By this break-through, we can validate seven LDFs with the 95% confidence interval (CI) of error rates and the discriminant coefficients in the training and validation samples. Especially, we can select the best model with minimum mean error rates in the validation sample (M2) instead of the leave-one-out (LOO) procedure. We compared seven LDFs using six different datasets and showed that the best models of Revised IP-OLDF are better than the other six best models by the Method.**

Keywords- ***Fisher's LDF; logistic regression; two SVMs; three Optimal LDFs (OLDFs); Best Model; LOO.***

I. INTRODUCTION

We establish a new theory of discriminant analysis by MP-based OLDFs [28]. In statistics, the discrimination means the method to classify class/object categories by independent variables. On the other hand, classification of cases by independent variables is cluster analysis. Three OLDFs, namely Revised IP-OLDF, Revised LP-OLDF, and Revised IPLP-OLDF [22] are validated with hard-margin SVM (H-SVM), soft-margin SVM (S-SVM) [29], Fisher's LDF [3] and logistic regression [1] by the "100-fold cross validation for small sample" method (The Method). It is a combination of k-fold cross validation and re-sampling sample. If we fix k=100, we can obtain the 95% confidence intervals (CIs) of error rates and the discriminant coefficients in the training and validation samples [17] [18] [20] [23]-[25]. When we fixed k=10 at first, we noticed we were not able to get 95% CIs. LOO procedure [6] cannot offer 95% CIs. There are four serious problems with discriminant analysis [21] [26]. Only Revised IP-OLDF [12] - [16] can discriminate the cases on the discriminant hyperplane exactly. Other LDFs cannot discriminate these cases correctly (Problem1). All LDFs except for H-SVM and Revised IP-OLDF cannot discriminate linear separable data (LSD) theoretically (Problem2). Problem3 is the defect of the generalized inverse matrix and effects the quadratic discriminant function (QDF) and regularized discriminant analysis (RDA) [5]. Although statisticians developed discriminant functions based on the variance-covariance matrices, we found many defects. Most statisticians misunderstand that the discriminant analysis is the inferential statistics as same as the regression analysis. Although Fisher proposed Fisher's LDF and established the theory of discriminant analysis, he never proposed the standard error (SE) of error rate and discriminant coefficients (Problem4), nevertheless Fisher's LDF assume Fisher's assumption. In this paper, we discuss on Problem4 and propose the Method using iris data [2] because it is relevant evaluation data of discriminant analysis. Because the iris data is not LSD, we cannot discuss H-SVM for this data.

In Section 2, we explain five MP-based LDFs. In our research, we compare two statistical LDFs and five MP-based LDFs by the Method. We code the Method of Fisher's LDF and logistic regression by JMP script [7] and do not discuss in this paper. We discuss five MP-based LDFs coded by LINGO [8].

In Section 3, we explain the Method. By this break-through, we can validate seven LDFs by the 95% CIs and best models. Genuine statisticians established the inferential statistics by their creative brain and theoretical distribution. Because the Method is a computer-intensive approach by computer power and software of MP and statistics, we had better consider the Method is not traditional inferential statistics that is more straightforward than LOO procedure.

In Section 4, we explain the results of iris data by the Theory because Fisher's LDF is most suitable for iris data. Fisher proposed Fisher's LDF under Fisher's assumption that two classes have the same normal distributions and two different means. Because statisticians have difficulty to develop good test statistics for Fisher's assumption, we usually obtain MP-based LDFs and logistic regression better results than Fisher's LDF for many real data, most of whom may not satisfy Fisher's assumption.

In Section 5, we summarize the results by the Theory using CPD data [9], Swiss banknote data [4], student data [11], six pass/fail determination using exam scores [19] and Japanese automobile data [28].

II. MP-BASED LDFS BY LINGO

A. The Iris Data in Excel

We explain the Method using iris data that is critical evaluation data in the discriminant analysis. It consists of three species as follows: setosa, versicolor, and virginica. Each species has 50 cases. There are four variables, such as: X1 (petal width), X2 (petal length), X3 (sepal width) and X4 (sepal length). Because we can separate the setosa from other two species by the scatter plot quickly, we usually omit the setosa and focus on the two-class discrimination of versicolor (y_i =1) and virginica (y_i = -1) in Table 1. All values of class2 are changed negative values. We define Excel range name 'IS' that is "B2:F101." LINGO can retrieve 'IS' array values by "IS = @OLE( );" function and use it as LINGO array name 'IS.' Next, we define the Excel range name 'CHOICE' that is "I2:M16" in Table 2. Fifteen rows correspond the models from the full model (X1, X2, X3, X4) to the 1-variable model (X1). If the model includes the variable, the value is '1,' otherwise it is '0.'

TABLE I. THE IRIS DATA IN EXCEL

	A	B	C	D	E	F
1	species	X1	X2	X3	X4	y
2	versicolor	7	3.2	4.7	1.4	1
...	versicolor	...	...	...	...	1
51	versicolor	5.7	2.8	4.1	1.2	1
52	virginica	-6.3	-3.3	-6	-2.5	-1
...	virginica	...	...	...	...	-1
101	virginica	-5.2	-3	-5.1	-1.8	-1

TABLE II. RANGE NAME SUCH AS CHOICE

SN	p	X1	X2	X3	X4	c
1	4	1	1	1	1	1
2	3	0	1	1	1	1
3	3	1	0	1	1	1
4	3	1	1	0	1	1
5	3	1	1	1	0	1
6	2	0	0	1	1	1
...	...	...	...	...	...	...
8	2	1	0	0	1	1
12	1	0	0	0	1	1
13	1	0	0	1	0	1
14	1	0	1	0	0	1
15	1	1	0	0	0	1

After optimization, we output three arrays, such as the "NM, ZERO and VARK100" to the Excel range name by "@OLE( ) = NM, ZERO, VARK100;" function. "NM: (N2: N16)" stores 15 NMs. "ZERO:(O2:O16)" stores the number of cases on discriminant hyperplane of 15 models. "VARK100: (P2:T16)" stores the coefficients of 15 models.

B. Five LDFs to Solve Original Data by LINGO

In this paper, we explain the model by LINGO, which is the solver developed by LINDO Systems Inc. [8]. We develop six LDFs; those are Revised IP-OLDF (RIP), Revised IPLP-OLDF (IPLP), Revised LP-OLDF (LP), H-SVM and two S-SVM (SVM4 for penalty c=10^4 and SVM1 for penalty c=1). In this paper, we consider two S-SVMs are different LDFs. The Revised IP-OLDF in (1) can find the right MNM by "MIN=Σe_i;" because it can directly find the interior point of an optimal convex polyhedron (OCP) [10]. If case $\mathbf{x_i}$ is classified, e_i=0. If case $\mathbf{x_i}$ is misclassified, e_i=1. Because the discriminant score becomes negative for the misclassified case, Revised IP-OLDF selects alternative support vector, such as "y_i* (${}^t\mathbf{x_i}$ **b**+ b_0) = 1 - M*e_i=-9999" instead of "y_i*(${}^t\mathbf{x_i}\mathbf{b}$+$b_0$) =1" for misclassified cases.

MIN=Σe_i; (1)
y_i* (${}^t\mathbf{x_i}$ **b**+ b_0) >= 1 - M* e_i ;
b: p independent variables, b_0: the intercept,
$\mathbf{x_i}$: (1*p) case vector if data is (n*p),
(${}^t\mathbf{x_i}$ **b**+ b_0): the discriminant score,
M: big M constant, such as 10000,
y_i: y_i= 1 for class 1 and y_i = -1 for class2,
e_i: 0/1 integer variable corresponding $\mathbf{x_i}$.

We can define this model in 'SUBMODEL' section of LINGO. 'RIP' is the sub-model name of Revised IP-OLDF. We can solve and control this IP model by this name. "@SUM and @FOR" are two essential LINGO loop functions. "@SUM (N(i): E(i))" means "$\Sigma_{i=1}^n$ E(i)". "@FOR(N(i):" defines n constraints, such as "@SUM(P1(j): IS(i, j) * VARK(j) * CHOICE(k, j)) >= 1-BIGM*E(i)); for i=1,...,n". "@FOR(P1(j): @FREE (VARK(j))); for j=1,...,p" defines the discriminant coefficient **b** as the free decision variable." "@FOR(N(i): @BIN(E(i))); for i=1,...,n" defines that 'e_i' are 0/1 integer variables. By these function, we can define a compact model. If we insert '!' before "@FOR(N(i): @BIN(E(i)));", it changes the only comment, and 'e_i' becomes non-negative real decision variable by the default. This model is Revised LP-OLDF. Therefore, we define the model of Revised LP-OLDF named 'LP' that is the second SUBMODEL.

```
SUBMODEL RIP (or LP):
 MIN=ER; ER=@SUM(N(i):E(i));
 @FOR(N(i):
 @SUM(P1(j):IS(i,j)*VARK(j)*CHOICE(k,j))
      >= 1-BIGM*E(i));
 @FOR(P1(j): @FREE(VARK(j)));
 (or !) @FOR(N(i): @BIN(E(i)));
ENDSUBMODEL
```

Third, we define Revised IPLP-OLDF. In the first stage, we discriminate the data by Revised LP-OLDF. In the second phase, we discriminate the restricted cases misclassified by Revised LP-OLDF. Therefore, we must distinguish two alternatives stored in the array 'CONSTANT' and Revised IP-OLDF discriminate only the misclassified cases by the "SUBMODEL IPLP" that is restricted Revised IP-OLDF.

```
SUBMODEL IPLP:
  MIN=ER; ER=@SUM(N(i):E(i));
  @FOR(N(i):@SUM(P1(j):IS(i,j)*VARK(j)*CHOICE(k,j))
        >= 1-BIGM*E(i));
  @FOR(P1(j): @FREE(VARK(j)));
  @FOR(N(I)| CONSTANT(i)#GT#0:@BIN(E(I)));
  @FOR(N(I)| CONSTANT(i)#EQ#0:E(I)=0);
ENDSUBMODEL
```

In the 'CALC' section, we insert the below statements for Revised IPLP-OLDF that is a mixture model of Revised LP-OLDF and restricted Revised IP-OLDF.

```
@SOLVE(LP);
@FOR(N(i):@IFC(E(I)#EQ#0:CONSTANT(i)=0; @ELSE
   CONSTANT(i)=1;));
MNM=0; ER1=0; MNM2=0; ER2=0;
@FOR(P1(J):VARK(J) =0; @RELEASE( VARK( J)));
@SOLVE(IPLP);
```

S-SVM has two objects in (2). These two objects are combined by defining some "penalty c." We must define the value of penalty in the CALC section. In this research, two S-SVMs, such as SVM4 and SVM1, are examined. We know the mean error rates of SVM4 are almost better than SVM1. If we delete the second object "c* Σe_i" and "-M*e," it becomes H-SVM that is not used in this paper.

$$\text{MIN} = \|\mathbf{b}\|^2/2 + c^* \Sigma e_i ; \quad (2)$$
$$y_i^* ({}^t\mathbf{x}_i\, \mathbf{b} + b_0) >= 1 - M^* e_i ;$$
$\mathbf{b}$, $\mathbf{x}_i$, $({}^t\mathbf{x}_i\, \mathbf{b}+ b_0)$, y_i,: same in (1)
c : penalty c, e_i: non-negative decision variable.

```
SUBMODEL SSVM:
MIN=ER;ER=@SUM(P(J1):
VARK(j1)^2)/2+Penalty*@SUM(N(i):E(i));
 @FOR (N(i): @SUM(P1(j):IS(i,j)*VARK(j)*
   CHOICE(k,j)) >= 1-E(i));
 @FOR (P1(j): @FREE(VARK(j)));
ENDSUBMODEL
```

If we insert five LDFs before the 'CALC' section, we can easily discriminate the original data by five LDFs.

C. Discrimination of the Iris Data by LINGO

We can discriminate the iris data by MP-based LDFs using "SETS, DATA, five SUBMODELs, CALC, and second DATA" sections. In the 'SETS' section, "P, P1, N and ERR(MS)" are one-dimensional sets, element numbers of those are 4, 5, 100 and 15 defined in 'DATA' section. Set 'P1' has one-dimensional array 'VARK' that stores the discriminant coefficient of one discriminant model. Set 'N' has two one-dimensional arrays. 'E' stores the 100 binary integer values of 'e_i' and 'CONSTANT' stores 100 discriminant scores. "MS" has the two one-dimensional arrays. 'NM' and 'ZERO' store the number of misclassifications (NM) and the number of cases on the discriminant hyperplane. If we discriminate the data by RIP, 'NM' column shows MNMs of 15 models. From 'ZERO' column, we can confirm Revised IP-OLDF is free from the Problem1. Because other LDFs cannot avoid the Problem1, all LDFs must check these numbers. Now, we cannot trust the output of NMs by statistical LDFs. 'VARK100' stores 15 coefficients of Revised IP-OLDF.

```
MODEL:
SETS:
 P; P1: VARK; P2; N: E, CONSTANT; MS: NM, ZERO;
 D(N, P1):IS; MB(MS, P1):CHOICE;
 VP(MS, P1):VARK100;
ENDSETS
DATA:
 P=1..4; P1=1..5; N=1..100; MS=1..15;
 CHOICE, IS = @OLE( );
ENDDATA
! Here, insert six SUBMODELs (LDFs).
CALC:
@SET('DEFAULT'); @SET('TERSEO',2);
 K=1; G=1; LEND=@SIZE(MS);
@WHILE(K#LE#LEND:
@FOR( P1( J): VARK( J) = 0;
@RELEASE( VARK( J)));NM=0; Z=0; Penalty=10000;
@SOLVE(RIP); !Change the submodel name.;
 @FOR(P1(J1): VARK100(@SIZE(MS)*(G-1) +K, J1)
      =VARK(J1)*CHOICE(k,J1));
 @FOR(n(I): CONSTANT(i)= @SUM(P1(J1): IS(i,J1)
               *VARK(J1)*CHOICE(k,J1)));
 @FOR(n(I): @IFC(CONSTANT(i) #EQ#0: Z=Z+1));
 @FOR(n(I): @IFC(CONSTANT(i) #LT#0: NM=NM+1));
   NM(K)=NM; ZERO(K)=Z; K=K+1);
ENDCALC
DATA:
      @OLE( )=NM, ZERO, VARK100;
ENDDATA
END
```

III. THE THEORY

A. The Method Outlook

In this paper, we proposed the Method, as follows [17].

*1) Let n be the number of cases and p be the number of variables including the intercept y_i (y_i = 1 for class1; y_i = -1 for class2). We copy the original data (n-cases by p-variables) 100 times and generate pseudo-population sample (100*n cases by p-variables).*

*2) We add the random number to this sample (100*n cases by (p+1)-variables) and sort it in ascending order by the random number. We divide this sample by 100 sub-samples and add the sub-sample number from 1 to 100.*

*3) We use 100 sub-samples as the training samples (n cases by (p+1)-variables) and the pseudo-sample as the validation sample (100*n cases by (p+1)-variables). This operation implies us that we re-sample 100 sub-samples from the pseudo-population. If we consider one sub-sample is the training sample, and other 99 sub-samples is the validation sample, we cannot estimate results uniformly because 100 validation samples are different. Moreover, if we fix the validation sample uniquely, we can control the training samples and validation sample very easy. For example, we can validate the validation sample generated by the original data because both samples are the same distribution. Moreover, we can get 95% CIs of the discriminant coefficients and propose the best model as model selection procedure instead of LOO procedure.*

B. How to generate the re-sampling sample and prepare the data in Excel file

We generate re-sampling sample from the original iris data and evaluate seven LDFs by the Method. Each species compose of 50 cases with 4-variables and classifier y_i. We copy each species 100 times. We add the random number (R column) as the seventh variable and sort it in ascending order in Table 3. Variable names "A1:X1 and R" are located in cells "A1 and G1." We consider this dataset is a pseudo-population and the validation sample that has the same statistics values, such as the average and range as the original data. We can control many research datasets and reduce mistakes.

TABLE III. RESAMPLING SAMPLE: ES

A1:X1	B1:X2	C1:X3	D1X4	y_i	SS	R
x(1,1)	x(2,1)	x(3,1)	x(4,1)	1	1	
				1	....	
				1	1	
				1	....	
				1	100	
				1	...	
x(1,5000)	x(2,5000)	x(3,5000)	x(4,5000)	1	100	
-x(1,5001)	-x(2,5001)	-x(3,5001)	-x(4,5001)	-1	1	
				-1	....	
				-1	1	
				-1	....	
				-1	100	
				-1	...	
-x(1,10000)	-x(2,10000)	-x(3,10000)	-x(4,10000)	-1	100	

Next, we divide this sample into 100 sub-samples and add the sub-sample number (SS column) from 1 to 100 as the sixth variable. Each sub-sample consists 100 cases and seven variables in Table 3. Six variables excluding 'R' are input by "ES= @OLE ();" in the 'DATA' section of next 'D.' The '@OLE ( )' function input the data ES on Excel range name, such as "A2: F10001" if the cell of 'X1' is located in `A1', and define the LINGO array ES. The 100 sub-samples play the training samples, and a total re-sampling sample is used as the validation sample. We consider the validation sample is a suede-population, and the training samples are the samples from the suede-population. We should fix the validation sample uniquely and evaluate the training samples by suede-population.

C. Set Notation Model by LINGO

Fisher never formulated the equation of SE for error rate and discriminant coefficient. If we discriminate the data by the Method, we can easily calculate the 95% CIs of error rates and discriminant coefficients. We obtain the Philosopher's Stone to validate seven LDFs by six small datasets. 'SET' section defines six one-dimensional sets, such as P, P1, P2, N, MS, and G100. "P, P1, and P2" are the number of independent variables, the number of (independent variables + intercept) and the number of (independent variables + intercept + sub-sample No.), respectively. These dimensions of elements in 'DATA' section are 4, 5 and 6, respectively. Only 'P1' defines one-dimensional array named 'VARK' with 5-elements that store the discriminant coefficients of the training sample.

Five sets "N, N2, MS, MS100 and G100" are one-dimensional sets, the elements of those are 100, 10000, 15, 1500 and 100 elements, respectively. Two-dimensional set 'D(N, P1):' with 100*5 has the same size array 'IS' that stores the 100 sub-sample with p-variables as the training samples. "D2(N2, P2):" with 10000*6 has the same size array 'ES' that stores the resampling-sample as the validation sample. The set ERR(MS, G100) with 15*100 has four arrays. The IC and IC_2 store MNM or NM in the training and validation samples. The EC and EC_2 store the number of cases on the discriminant hyperplanes in both samples. The set SS(N2, MS) with 10000*15 has the array SCORE2 that stores the discriminant scores of 15 models. The set VVV(MS100, P2) with 1500*6 has the array VARK100 that stores 1500 coefficients of the 100 training samples.

In the DATA section, we define nine parameters values and input two arrays, such as CHOICE and ES. The 'CHOICE' stores the pattern of 15 models showed in Table 2. The 'ES' stores the validation sample in Table 3. In CALC section, the training sample IS with 100*5 chooses 100 rows of ES by the sub-sample number (SS column).

D. Total Model with CALC Section by LINGO

After we define the "SETS and DATA" section, we insert six LDFs described in 'B' of Section 2. We divide two parts of the 'CALC' section. The first part is the default setting of output, global search, QP, multi-thread, etc.

```
MODEL: The Method for the Iris data;
SETS:
  P; P2; P1: VARK;
```

```
N:; N2: ; MS : ; MS100 : ; G100 :;
D (N, P1):IS;
D2 (N2, P2):ES;
MB (MS, P1): CHOICE;
ERR(MS, G100):IC, IC_2, EC, EC_2;
SS(N2, MS):SCORE2;
VVV(MS100, P2):VARK100;
ENDSETS
DATA:
P=1..4; P1=1..5; P2=1..6;
N=1..100; N2=1..10000;
MS=1..15; G100=1..100; MS100=1..1500 ;
BIGM=10000; ! for SVM4;
CHOICE, ES=@OLE();
ENDDATA
! Here, insert five LDFs described in 'B' of Section 2.
```

```
CALC:
! Reset all options to default; @SET('DEFAULT');
! @SET('TERSEO',1);!Allow for minimal output;
@SET('TERSEO',2);
!Global solver (1:yes, 0:no); @SET('GLOBAL',1);
!Quadratic recognition (1:yes, 0:no);@SET('USEQPR',1);
!Multisarts (1:Off, >1 number of starts);
@SET('MULTIS',1);
!Number of threads; !@SET('THRDS',4);
!Print output immediately (1:yes, 0:no);
@SET('OROUTE',1);
!No need to compute dual values; @SET('DUALCO',0);

K=1; Lend=@SIZE(MS);
@WHILE (K#LE#Lend: f=1;
@WHILE (f#LE#100:
  @FOR(D(i, j): IS(i, j)=ES( @SIZE(N)*(f-1)+i, j));
    MNM=0; ER1=0;MNM2=0;ER2=0;
  @FOR( P1( J): VARK( J) = 0;@RELEASE( VARK( J)));

  @SOLVE ( RIP );! Set the submodel name here;

  @FOR(P1(j): VARK100(100*(k-1)+f,j)=VARK(j));
    VARK100 (100*(k-1)+f, @SIZE(P2))=K;
@FOR(n(l):SCORE(l)=@SUM(P1(j):IS(l,j)*VARK(j)*
    CHOICE (k, j)));
@FOR(n2(nn):SCORE2(nn,K)=@SUM(P1(j):ES(NN, j)*
    VARK(j)*CHOICE(k, j)));
@FOR(n(l): @IFC(SCORE(l)#LT#0: MNM=MNM+1));
@FOR(n2(nn):
  @IFC(SCORE2(nn,k)#LT#0:ER1=ER1+1 ));
@FOR(n(l):@IFC(SCORE(l)#EQ#0: MNM2=MNM2+1));
@FOR(n2(nn):@IFC(SCORE2(nn,k)#EQ#0:ER2=ER2+1 );
IC(K,f)=MNM;EC(k,f)=ER1;
IC_2(K,f)=MNM2;
EC_2(K,f)=ER2;
f=f+1);
ENDCALC
```

```
DATA:
 @OLE( )=IC, EC, IC_2, EC_2, VARK100, SCORE2;
ENDDATA
END
```

The second part of CALC section controls the optimization models that consist two loops. The big loop is repeated 15 iterations by "K=1,…,15." The small loop is repeated 100 iterations by "f=1,…,100." If we set "@SOLVE (RIP);," we can discriminate the iris re-sampling sample by Revised IP-OLDF. If we replace this command by "`SOLVE(SSVM);," S-SVM discriminate the datasets. We can choose SVM4 or SVM1 by setting "Penalty=10000 or 1" in Calc section. In the second DATA section, we output six results on Excel arrays. "IC and EC" are the 100 MNMs in the training samples and 100 NMs in the validation samples. "IC_2 and EC_2" are the 100 numbers of cases on the discriminant hyperplane in the both samples. From these figures, we calculate the mean error rates, such as "M1 and M2" in the both samples. 'VARK100' are the 1500 discriminant coefficients of 15 models. We can calculate the 95% CI of discriminant coefficients. "SCORE2" are the 10000 discriminant scores.

IV. Results of Iris Data

A. *Results of Original Data*

We investigate all combinations of discriminant models ($15 = 2^4 - 1$). Table 4 shows the 15 models from 4-variables model to four 1-variable models. The column 'SN' is the sequential number of models. The column 'Var.' denotes the suffix of variable name. The column 'RIP' is the MNMs of Revised IP-OLDF. We can confirm "MNM monotonously decreases ($MNM_k \geq MNM_{(k+1)}$)." For example, the forward stepwise technique of the regression analysis chooses the variable as follows: X4, X2, X3, and X1 in this order. The MNM of four models decreases as follows: 6, 3, 2, 1. We can confirm the monotonous decrease of MNM by other model sequences, such as X1, X2, X3, X4 in this order. The MNM of four models decreases as follows: 37, 25, 2, 1. Therefore, we cannot choose the model having minimum MNM as the best model because we always choose the full model. Six discriminant functions represent the following abbreviations in the table. SVMs are SVM4/SVM1. Revised LP-OLDF is LP. Revised IPLP-OLDF is IPLP. The logistic regression is 'Logi.' Fisher's LDF is LDF. Six columns after 'RIP' are the difference (Diff2) between (NMs of seven discriminant functions – MNM). We omitted Revised IPLP-OLDF from the table because NMs are the same as MNMs. All NMs of each model should be greater than equal to MNM because MNM is the minimum NM in the training samples. The last row shows the number of models with a minus value of 'Diff2'. Revised LP-OLDF has two minus values. This fact means that Revised LP-OLDF is not free from the Problem1. We cannot judge the Problem1 by models having "Diff2 >= 0," because we must check 'ZERO.' Although this data is expected to give the right results for Fisher's LDF, QDF and RDA, these functions based on variance-covariance matrices are not superior to MP-based LDFs. Bold numbers of 'Diff2s' among each seven discriminant functions are maximum values. There are 23 maximum values among Fisher's LDF, QDF and RDA. On the other hand, there are 15 maximum values among SVM4, SVM1, and Logi. Roughly speaking, we judge Fisher's LDF, QDF and RDA are inferior to other LDFs, although this judgment is not clear.

TABLE IV. MNM AND EIGHT DIFF2

SN	Var.	RIP	SVMs	LP	Logi.	LDF	QDF	RDA
1	1,2,3,4	1	1/0	1	1	**2**	**2**	**2**
2	2,3,4	2	0/**2**	0	0	**2**	**2**	1
3	1,3,4	2	0/0	0	0	1	1	**2**
4	1,2,4	4	**3**/1	**3**	0	1	2	1
5	1,2,3	2	2/4	2	2	5	**6**	4
6	2,4	3	1/1	**3**	0	0	2	2
7	3,4	5	**3**/2	1	1	**3**	0	2
8	1,3	4	1/**3**	1	0	2	2	2
9	1,4	6	**1/1**	0	0	**1**	0	0
10	2,3	5	0/0	**1**	0	**1**	**1**	**1**
11	1,2	25	2/2	2	0	0	**4**	**4**
12	4	6	**0/0**	**0**	**0**	**0**	**0**	**0**
13	3	7	0/0	0	0	**1**	0	0
3	1	37	0/0	-3	0	0	**3**	**3**
15	2	27	**5/5**	-2	0	**5**	**5**	**5**
		-	0	**2**	0	0	0	0

1) *Diff2 of Revised IPLP-OLDF is omitted from the table because all values are zero.*
2) *Column 'SVMs' denotes both values of SVM4/SVM1.*

We cannot select the best model by MNM or error rate in the training samples. Until now, we have two options to choose a good model from the original data or training sample. The first option is the LOO procedure. The second option is to evaluate models by the model selection statistics of regression analysis. Table 5 is the result of all possible combination of models. The column 'Model' shows 15 models from 4-variables model to 1-variable model. The column 'p' indicates the number of variables. Within the same 'p,' models are descending order of "R-square (R2)". The column 'Rank' is the ranking within the same number of 'p.' This procedure is very powerful because we can overlook all models and simulate the forward and backward stepwise techniques. Both techniques choose the same models, such as: (X4) -> (X4, X2) -> (X4, X2, X3) -> (X4, X2, X3, X1). Therefore, we can easily choose a good model among these four models. Model selection statistics, such as AIC, BIC, and Cp statistics, choose the full model as a good model. However, these statistics usually select different models by other data. Therefore, we cannot usually decide a good model by these statistics uniquely.

TABLE V. THE RESULT OF ALL POSSIBLE COMBINATION

Model	p	Rank	R2	AIC	BIC	Cp
1,2,3,4	4	1	0.78	143.49	158.22	5.00
2,3,4	3	1	0.77	148.70	161.09	10.37
1,3,4	3	2	0.76	151.80	164.18	13.59
1,2,4	3	3	0.73	163.89	176.27	27.16
1,2,3	3	4	0.70	174.19	186.58	40.09
2,4	2	1	0.72	163.52	173.52	27.39
3,4	2	2	0.72	165.00	175.00	29.19
1,3	2	3	0.70	172.71	182.71	39.07
1,4	2	4	0.69	176.43	186.43	44.12
2,3	2	5	0.63	192.14	202.14	67.61
1,2	2	6	0.25	263.97	273.97	237.44
4	1	1	0.69	174.27	181.83	42.12
3	1	2	0.62	193.68	201.25	71.72
1	1	3	0.24	262.02	269.59	236.18
2	1	4	0.09	280.07	287.63	301.87

B. *Results by the Method*

Table 6 shows the results of 15 models by the Method. The first 15 models of RIP show all possible combination of models from a 4-variables model to a 1-variable model shown in column 'Model'. "M1 and M2" columns are the mean of error rates in the both samples. 'M1' decreases monotonously the same as MNM, because M1 is the average of 100 MNMs. Therefore, M1 of the full model is always minimum value theoretically. We can confirm this fact by the values of M1 in the table. Although M2 of the full model happen to be the minimum value, and it is 2.72, this may be caused by the reason this data has only four variables. We consider the model with minimum M2 is the best model. We claim the best model has good generalization ability. The column 'Diff' is the difference between (M2 - M1). Because a 1-variable model (X4) has a minimum value of 'Diff,' these statistics is not useful to choose the best model. We confirmed this fact by many types of research.

We summarize 15 models of other LDFs in two rows. The first row corresponds to the full model. All LDFs choose the full model as their best models. Those M2s are 3.03, 3.00, 2.98, 2.70, 3.07, and 3.18 %, respectively. The second row corresponds to the model with minimum 'Diff.' Last two columns, such as "M1Diff & M2Diff" are the differences between (M1/M2 of other LDFs – those of RIP). If we focus on 'M2Diff' of the full model, those are 0.31, 0.28, 0.26, -0.02, 0.35 and 0.46 % higher than Revised IP-OLDF, respectively. Therefore, six LDFs are not so bad than Revised IP-OLDF. The values of 'M2Diff' are almost less than those of 'M1Diff.' This fact may imply that Revised IP-

OLDF over-fit the training sample. We observed this defect only in this data. The column 'Diff' is the difference between (M2-M1). We misunderstand the model with a minimum value of 'Diff' has good generalization ability. If we check the 'Diff,' we can understand this claim is not right. Especially, although 'Diff' of Fisher's LDF is -0.42%, this result is caused by the high value of M1, such as 40.72%. We claim the full model of Revised IPLP-OLDF has good generalization ability among seven LDFs. CPU times showed in full model rows tell us Fisher's LDF and logistic regression are slower than MP-based LDFs.

TABLE VI. THE COEFFICIENTS OF SEVEN LDFS

RIP	M1	M2	Diff.	Model	
1 12m11s	0.56	**2.72**	2.16	X1, X2, X3, X4	
2	0.96	3.03	2.07	X2, X3, X4	
3	1.37	3.42	2.05	X1, X3, X4	
4	2.68	5.07	2.39	X1, X2, X4	
5	1.55	3.70	2.15	X1, X2, X3	
6	3.61	5.79	2.18	X2, X4	
7	2.44	4.39	1.95	X3, X4	
8	2.91	4.82	1.91	X1, X3	
9	4.23	5.69	1.46	X1, X4	
10	4.29	7.03	2.74	X2, X3	
11	22.74	27.27	4.53	X1, X2	
12	5.40	6.08	**0.68**	X4	
13	5.88	7.25	1.37	X3	
14	25.75	28.24	2.49	X1	
15	35.67	38.93	3.26	X2	
SVM4	M1	M2	Diff.	M1Diff.	M2Diff.
1 8m43s	1.21	**3.03**	1.82	0.65	0.31
12	6.00	6.06	**0.06**	0.60	-0.02
SVM1	M1	M2	Diff.	M1Diff.	M2Diff.
1 8m42s	2.23	**3.00**	0.77	1.67	0.28
12	6.16	6.28	**0.12**	0.76	0.20
LP	M1	M2	Diff.	M1Diff.	M2Diff.
1 4m20s	1.15	**2.98**	1.83	0.59	0.26
12	5.74	5.83	**0.09**	0.34	-0.25
IPLP	M1	M2	Diff.	M1Diff.	M2Diff.
1 16m39s	0.56	**2.70**	2.14	0.00	-0.02
12	5.44	6.08	**0.64**	0.04	0.00
Logistic	M1	M2	Diff.	M1Diff.	M2Diff.
1 18m	1.36	**3.07**	1.71	1.50	0.35
15	40.68	40.30	**-0.38**	5.01	1.37
LDF	M1	M2	Diff.	M1Diff.	M2Diff.
1 16m	2.76	**3.18**	0.42	2.20	0.46
15	40.72	40.30	**-0.42**	5.05	1.37

Table 7 shows the three percentiles of the discriminant coefficients and the intercept. To fix the "intercept=1," we divide the original five coefficients by the value of (original intercept + 0.00001) to avoid the zero divide if original "intercept=0." By fixing the intercept, we can understand the meaning of the 95% CI of coefficients clearly [26]. Before adjusting the intercept, we struggle many 95% CI of coefficients include 0 because the signs of intercept almost have both plus and minus values [24]. Although Shinmura [17] proposed this idea, we could not obtain good results because we did not fix the intercept. Four 95% CI of the full model of Revised IP-OLDF includes zero, and we cannot reject the null hypothesis at 5% level. On the other hand, we can reject three coefficients of a 3-variables model (X2, X3, X4) at 5% level.

TABLE VII. THE 95% CI OF LDFS

	%	X1	X2	X3	X4	C
RIP	97.5	4.55	5.35	9.94	12.31	1
	50	0.06	0.11	-0.23	-0.41	1
	2.5	-5.59	-11.94	-6.93	-6.34	1
	97.5		**1.25**	**-0.06**	**-0.14**	1
	50		**0.18**	**-0.15**	**-0.54**	1
	2.5		**0**	**-0.53**	**-1.36**	1

If we choose the medians as the coefficient, we get the LDF in (3). Although we judge the full model of Revised IP-OLDF is the best model, the 95% CI of Revised IP-OLDF tells us this model may be redundant and suggest a 3-variables model as a useful model. There is a mismatch between our judgment of the model selection using M2 and the 95% CI of discriminant coefficients in the best model. We usually experienced this uncertainty in inferential statistics, also.

$$RIP = 0.18*X2-0.15*X3-0.54*X4+1. \quad (3)$$

We cannot reject four coefficients of Revised LP-OLDF in (4), three coefficients of Revised IPLP-OLDF in (5), and two coefficients of SVM4 in (6). We can reject only four coefficients of SVM1 in (7). If we check a 3-variables model, we can reject three coefficients of four LDFs the same as Revised IP-OLDF. Before we did not fix the intercept, we lost many research time and had no knowledge about the discriminant coefficients. To summarize these results, we cannot obtain clear results of the 95% CI of the coefficient.

$$LP = 0.06*X1+0.13*X2-0.21*X3-0.46*X4+1 \quad (4)$$
$$IPLP = 0.52*X1+0.11*X2-0.21*X3-0.39*X4+1 \quad (5)$$
$$SVM4= 0.06*X1+0.13*X2-0.22*X3-0.43*X4+1 \quad (6)$$
$$SVM1=0.08*X1+0.11*X2-0.28*X3-0.28*X4+1 \quad (7)$$

V. CONCLUSION

In this research, we specified how to discriminate the original data and re-sampling data by the Method. We can compare five MP-based LDFs and two statistical LDFs. We obtain remarkable results.

1) We propose the new model selection procedure as the best model of each LDFs. We can easily compare and evaluate seven LDFs by the best models because we can evaluate seven LDFs by the minimum mean values of M2. In many evaluations, Revised IP-OLDF and Revised IPLP-OLDF is the best. Next, logistic regression is superior to SVM4 in many trials. M2 of SVM1 is almost greater than M2 of SVM4. Fisher's LDF are almost the worst except for the iris data.

2) Next, IP-OLDF found the Swiss banknote data is LSD, and 16 models including (X4, X6) are linear separable models. Other 47 models are not linear separable models. We can conclude H-SVM and Revised IP-OLDF can recognize LSD theoretically. Other LDFs are not free from the Problem 2. It is hard for us to find LSD occasionally. We locate the pass/fail determination of exam scores give us good research data for linearly separable models [19]. By these examinations, the error rates of Fisher's LDF are 20% worse than Revised IP-OLDF with MNM=0. Therefore, we claim the discriminant functions based on the variance-covariance matrices are fragile for the discrimination of data that has many cases nearby the discriminant hyperplane. We had better re-evaluated the old principal researchers discriminated by these functions.

3) Many statisticians struggle to select feature of microarray datasets because it has many variables (genes) (Problem5). Only Revised IP-OLDF can select feature naturally and shows that high dimensional gene space consists several small disjoint unions of gene sub-spaces those are linearly separable. Therefore, we can analyze these small gene sub-spaces by the common statistical methods [27].

4) The Method solves Problem4 for six MP-based LDFs instead of LOO [6]. Revised IP-OLDF solves Probleml, 2 and 5. H-SVM solves Problem2. Other LDFs can not solve Problem1and Problem2 theoretically.

5) We should not use the iris data for evaluation of discriminant analysis because it cannot tell us the differences of discriminant functions.

REFERENCES

[1] D. R. Cox, "The regression analysis of binary sequences (with discussion)," J Roy Stat Soc, B20, pp.215-242, 1958.

[2] A. Edgar, "The irises of the Gaspe Peninsula," Bulletin of the American Iris Society, Vol. 59, pp. 2-5, 1945.

[3] R. A. Fisher, "The Use of Multiple Measurements in Taxonomic Problems," Annals of Eugenics, Vol. 7, pp. 179–188, 1936.

[4] B. Flury and H. Rieduyl, " Multivariate Statistics: A Practical Approach," Cambridge University Press, 1988.

[5] J. H. Friedman, "Regularized Discriminant Analysis," Journal of the American Statistical Association, Vol. 84/405, pp. 165-175, 1989.

[6] P. A. Lachenbruch, and M. R. Mickey, "Estimation of error rates in discriminant analysis," Technometrics, Vol. 10, pp.1-11, 1968.

[7] J. P. Sall, L. Creighton, and A. Lehman, JMP Start Statistics, third ed, SAS Institute Inc. 2004.

[8] L. Schrage, Optimization Modeling with LINGO, LINDO Systems Inc. 2006.

[9] S. Shinmura, "Optimal Linearly Discriminant Functions using Mathematical Programming," Journal of the Japanese Society of Computer Statistics, Vol. 11/2, pp. 89-101, 1998.

[10] S. Shinmura, "A new algorithm of the linear discriminant function using integer programming," New Trends in Probability and Statistics, Vol. 5, pp.133-142, 2000.

[11] S. Shinmura, Optimal Linear Discriminant Function using Mathematical Programming, Dissertation, March 200, pp. 1-101, Okayama Univ., 2000.

[12] S. Shinmura, "Enhanced Algorithm of IP-OLDF," ISI2003 CD-ROM, pp.428-429, 2003.

[13] S. Shinmura, "New Algorithm of Discriminant Analysis using Integer Programming," IPSI 2004 Pescara VIP Conference CD-ROM, pp.1-18, 2004.

[14] S. Shinmura, "New Age of Discriminant Analysis by IP-OLDF –Beyond Fisher's Linear Discriminant Function-," ISI2005, pp.1-2, 2004.

[15] S. Shinmura, "Comparison of Revised IP-OLDF and SVM," ISI2009, pp.1-4, 2007.

[16] S. Shinmura, "Overviews of Discriminant Function by Mathematical Programming," Journal of the Japanese Society of Computer Statistics, Vol. 20/1-2, pp. 59-94. 2007.

[17] S. Shinmura, "The optimal linearly discriminant function," Union of Japanese Scientist and Engineer Publishing. 2010.

[18] S. Shinmura, "Beyond Fisher's Linear Discriminant Analysis –New World of the discriminant analysis-," 2011 ISI CD-ROM, pp.1-6. 2011.

[19] S. Shinmura, "Problems of Discriminant Analysis by Mark Sense Test Data," Japanese Society of Applied Statistics, Vol. 40/3, pp.157-172, 2011.

[20] S. Shinmura, "Evaluation of Optimal Linearly Discriminant Function by 100-fold cross-validation," 2013 ISI CD-ROM, pp.1-6, 2013.

[21] S. Shinmura, "End of Discriminant Functions based on Variance-Covariance Matrices," ICORE201, pp.5-16. 2014.

[22] S. Shinmura, "Improvement of CPU time of Linear Discriminant Functions based on MNM criterion by IP," Statistics, Optimization and Information Computing, Vol. 2, pp. 114-129. 2014.

[23] S. Shinmura, "Comparison of Linearly Discriminant Functions by K-fold Cross-validation," Data Analytic 2014, pp.1-6, 2014.

[24] S. Shinmura, "The 95% confidence intervals of error rates and discriminant coefficients" Statistics, Optimization and Information Computing, Vol. 3, pp.66-78, 2015.

[25] S. Shinmura, "A Trivial Linear Discriminant Function. Statistics," Optimization, and Information Computing, Vol.3, pp. 322-335, 2015. DOI: 10.19139/soic.20151202.

[26] S. Shinmura, "Four Serious Problems and New Facts of the Discriminant Analysis," In E. Pinson, F. Valente, B. Vitoriano (Eds.), Operations Research and Enterprise Systems, pp.15-30, Springer (ISSN: 1865-0929, ISBN: 978-3-319-17508-9, DOI: 10.1007/978-3-319-17509-6), 2015.

[27] S. Shinmura, "Matroska Feature Selection Methods for Microarray," Biotechno 2016, pp.1-8, 2016.

[28] S. Shinmura, "New Theory of Discriminant Analysis after R. Fisher," Springer, 2016. ISBN 978-981-10-2163-3

[29] V.Vapnik, The Nature of Statistical Learning Theory. Springer-Verlag, 1995.

Improving Process Mining Prediction Results in Processes that Change over Time

Alessandro Berti

SIAV
35030 Rubano PD (Italy)
Email: alessandro.berti89@gmail.com

Abstract—**In this paper, we propose a method in order to improve the accuracy of predictions, related to incomplete traces, in event logs that record changes in the underlying process. These "second-order dynamics" hamper the functioning of Process Mining discovery algorithms, but also hamper prediction results. The method is simple to implement as it is based exclusively on the Control Flow perspective and is computationally efficient. The approach has been validated on the Business Process Intelligence Challenge 2015's Municipality 5 event log, that contains an interesting shift in the process due to the union of the municipality with another municipality.**

Keywords–Concept Drift; Process Mining; Prediction.

I. Introduction

Business processes are constantly evolving to adapt to new opportunities, and continuous improvement is needed for a company in order to remain at the top. In some cases, the quality of a process can be measured in time: for example, in Service Desk tickets, avoiding to break service level agreements is important. Knowing in advance which instances are most critical, assigning more resources to them, may be vital for some organizations.

Here arises the need of a good prediction algorithm for process instances. Process Mining provides some techniques to predict the completion time of instances, however they assume the underlying process to be static, obtaining in many cases poor results. In this paper, we provide an approach to improve existing prediction results by considering the fact that the process changes over time. This is the first approach in the field. An assessment done on Business Process Intelligence Challenge 2015's Municipality 5 event log shows that the approach actually improved the prediction results in a process that changed over time.

The rest of the paper is structured as follows. In Section 2, we present Process Mining techniques and a classication of concept drifts in processes. In Section 3, the method to consider concept drifts in the predictions Is introduced. In Section 4, we show some results on the BPI Challenge 2015 log. We conclude in Section 5.The rest of the paper is structured as follows. In Section 2, we present Process Mining techniques and a classication of concept drifts in processes. In Section 3, the method to consider concept drifts in the predictions Is introduced. In Section 4, we show some results on the BPI Challenge 2015 log. We conclude in Section 5.

II. Background

Process Mining [1] is a relatively new discipline that aims to automatically discover and measure things about processes. It mainly uses automatic recordings of events which are event logs. Sub-disciplines of Process Mining are process discovery [2], that aims to automatically discover the process schema starting from an event log, process conformance [3] that is useful to see differences between a de-jure process model and the current executions of the process (recorded in the event log), process performance [2] that wants to identify bottlenecks inside business processes starting from event logs, and process-related predictions which will be analyzed later. Event logs are organised in traces that are collections of events serving to a particular purpose. For example, a trace might regard a single case served by an Help Desk process. Meanwhile, events can be described by several attributes, including:

- The activity that has been performed.
- The originator of the event (the organizational resource that has done the event).
- The timestamp (the time in which the event has been executed).
- The transition of the event that refers to the state of execution (a "complete" transition means that the activity actually ended, a "start" transition means that the activity started).

The trace itself can be characterised by several attributes (for example, in an Help Desk system, the severity of the case might be an attribute). The minimum timestamp of its events can be considered as start timestamp of the trace, and the maximum timestamp of its events as end timestamp. Many times, there is only a transition ("complete"), so the trace might be described (in the Control Flow perspective) by the succession/list of its activities. This is a condition required by some Process Discovery algorithms, like the Heuristics Miner [4] that aims to discover the process schema by calculating the dependency between activities. This means that if in all occurrences of an event log an activity (1) is followed by another activity (2), then Heuristics Miner can discover a process schema in which activity 1 is always followed by activity 2. So, Heuristics Miner analyzes (among the others) the paths in a trace: a path is a direct succession of activities in a trace. For example, if a trace contains (analyzing only the Control Flow perspective) the activities ABCDE then all the paths contained in the trace are: AB BC CD DE. A path belongs to a trace if it is contained in the trace. An important definition provided for later use is about the belonging of a trace to a time interval. A trace, with *start* as the start timestamp and *end* as the end timestamp, belongs to a time interval $[t_1, t_2]$, if one of the following three conditions is satisfied:

1) $start \leq t_1 \leq t_2 \leq end$
2) $t_1 \leq start < t_2$

DiffInt(log,I_1,I_2)
Require: An event log log, time sub-intervals I_1 and I_2.
$Tr_1 = \{tr \in log, tr \in I_1\}$
$Tr_2 = \{tr \in log, tr \in I_2\}$
$RelImp_1 = \left\{ \left(path, \frac{\#occ.\ path.}{\#Tr_1}\right) | \exists tr \in Tr_1, path \in tr \right\}$
$RelImp_2 = \left\{ \left(path, \frac{\#occ.\ path.}{\#Tr_2}\right) | \exists tr \in Tr_2, path \in tr \right\}$
$AllPaths = \pi_0(RelImp_1) \cup \pi_0(RelImp_2)$
$D = \{\}$
for $P \in AllPaths$ **do**
if $P \in \pi_0(RelImp_1)$ *and* $P \in \pi_0(RelImp_2)$ **then**
$D[P] = \frac{Abs(RelImp_1[P] - RelImp_2[P])}{Max(RelImp_1[P], RelImp_2[P])}$
else
$D[P] = 1$
end if
end for
return D

Figure 1. The algorithm to calculate the difference between the paths' importance in two different sub-intervals.

Importance(tr,D)
Require: A complete trace tr, difference of importance of paths between intervals D.
return $avg_{(A_1,A_2) \in Paths(tr)}\{1 - D[(A_1, A_2)]\}$

Figure 2. The algorithm to calculate the importance of a trace tr in the difference of temporal contexts described by the dictionary D.

Similarity(log,tr_1,tr_2,$intervals$)
Require: An event log log, an incomplete trace tr_1, a complete trace tr_2 (used for prediction purposes), collection of time sub-intervals $intervals$.
if $\exists I \in intervals | tr_1 \in I, tr_2 \in I$ **then**
return 1
end if
return $\max_{I_1, I_2 \in intervals | tr_1 \in I_1, tr_2 \in I_2} Importance(tr = tr_2, D = DiffInt(log, I_1, I_2))$

Figure 3. The algorithm to calculate the similarity between the temporal context of two traces, one of them is incomplete and the other is complete and used for prediction.

3) $t_1 < end \leq t_2$

It might be important also to consider the difference between complete and incomplete traces. The last ones are being reported in the log, although their execution is not finished. The distinction is somewhat difficult to make, [5] can be referred for further discussion. A possible way to detect incomplete traces is applying heuristics to the end activities: if the end activity of a trace can be found as an end activity in many other traces, then it is considered to be a complete trace, otherwise incomplete. The succession of the activities of an incomplete trace might be shared with a complete trace, being a "prefix". An interesting task about incomplete traces might be the prediction of their attributes. For previous work on prediction tasks, [6] that mainly describes a method for the prediction of the remaining time of incomplete traces. Basically, the idea is to build an annotated "transition system" (the explanation of this concept is skipped, as it is not firmly connected with the explanation of the method. For further discussion, see [6]), that is learned from previous executions, i.e., complete traces, using an abstraction mechanism. In [7] is proposed a method to predict the remaining time based on sequential pattern mining.

A further step is the one explained in [8]. The prediction of the remaining time is calculated using these two factors:

- The likelihood of following activities, given the data collected so far.
- The remaining time estimation given by a regression model built upon the data.

Basically, this method is an improvement over [6] because it considers not only the Control Flow perspective, but also other events' attributes, identifying the ones that are relevant to the prediction of the remaining time. A process specialist could insert artificial attributes to events (for example, the workload of the resources, or the work in process), in order to improve the prediction. However, an aspect somewhat ignored in predictions is the fact that the underlying process might change during time. As [9] reports, changes might induce one of the following drifts:

- Recurring drifts: these ones refer to changes that happen in some moments of the year (seasonal influence) or some other recurring changes (for example, a financial process might change near the financial closure of the year).

- Sudden drifts: these refer to big changes in the process: the "old" process cease to exist, while a "new" process starts to be applied.
- Gradual drifts: these refer to a gradual shift from an "old" process to a "new" process. This might be done to let the organizational resources learn the new process.

A method to identify and to cope with changes in the process is described always in [9]: at a first time you have to identify change points in the process (i.e., the times when the process is different), after that you have to identify the region of the change and the type of the change (recurring, sudden, gradual drifts). The last step exploits this knowledge to "unravel" the evolution of the process, describing the change process. Basically, an application of the classical Process Discovery algorithms (for example Heuristics Miner [4], Inductive Miner [10]) can be reliable only in time intervals that contains a consistent, without-drifts process. The same is valid for the prediction algorithms, as a prediction based on the entire process (that might be changed meanwhile) is not-so-accurate. However, also a prediction based only on the last iteration of the process might be incomplete and not-so-accurate.

III. Method

The proposed method wants to overcome the limitations of both a prediction based on the entire process, and a prediction based only on the last iteration of the process (it might be a restricted time interval). A method to detect change points and analyze them is not proposed, for this scope, [9], [11] can be referred; the proposed method starts from the assumption to know where change points are (this could also be done with an interview to organizational resources). Starting from the overall time interval of events contained in an event log, it is supposed that there is a collection of time sub-intervals covering the entire time interval and in which the underlying process is constant.

The method is based on the knowledge of a distance measure between two time sub-intervals. This way, you have a method to say how much reliable a complete trace (that might be following a slightly different process) is in the prediction of an incomplete trace that is based on the last iteration of the process. The proposed algorithm in Figure 1 measures the distance path by path, as some paths might be equally present in both intervals. Algorithm in Figure 1 basically works calculating the relative importance of each path in each of the subintervals (that is the ratio of the number of path's occurrences and the number of traces), and then comparing this quantity between the intervals. The reliability of the trace in the context of a prediction can be then calculated using the algorithm in Figure 2. It is proposed to use the average (done on all the paths of a trace) of the distance calculated using algorithm in Figure 1. Other statistics (like the maximum of the distance) proved to be less reliable.

Algorithm in Figure 3 uses the previous two algorithms, starting from a couple of traces (the first of them is the one to predict), the event log and the subdivision in sub-intervals. It tries to find two sub-intervals, containing respectively the two traces (with the meaning explained in Background) that are at a minimum distance, so maximising the similarity. This has been done in order to avoid giving unnecessary low weights of similarity to traces whose duration has been longer than the sub-intervals in which the underlying process is constant.

Then, to obtain the prediction, one could use van der Aalst's [6] algorithm, weighting the traces used for the prediction through algorithm in Figure 3.

IV. Results

The proposed algorithms have been tested on the BPI Challenge 2015's Municipality 5 event log (DOI 10.4121/uuid:b32c6fe5-f212-4286-9774-58dd53511cf8). The log describes a very complex process, with many activities, and is particularly interesting because this municipality (Municipality 5) got merged with another municipality (Municipality 2, DOI 10.4121/uuid:63a8435a-077d-4ece-97cd-2c76d394d99c) at a certain point of time, and the process became different. Some different time intervals can be identified:

1) The first one, going from the start of the log to June 2013, in which Municipality 5 was substantially departed from Municipality 2.
2) The shift one, going from June 2013 to June 2014, in which Municipality 5 get merged with Municipality 2.
3) The second one, going from June 2014 to the end of the log, in which Municipality 5 is already united with Municipality 2.

These sub-intervals were identified with a resource analysis, seeing that the resources working in the process got more numerous, and the point of the shift is comprised between June 2013 and June 2014. Being these sub-intervals roughly identified, the shift interval will be ignored for prediction purposes, and the focus will be on the first and the second interval, in which the underlying process is different.

The algorithm proposed by van der Aalsts [6] is used as prediction (of the remaining time) algorithm, weighting the traces used for the prediction using Algorithm 3. All the traces in the log have been considered as completed ones, so for the prediction purposes a prefix of each one has been taken, the completion time has been predicted and compared to the effective completion time. The effectiveness of the prediction was measured using two standard measures (Mean Absolute Percentage Error (MAPE) and Root of Mean Squared Percentage Error (RMSPE)), briefly explained below. Here, A_i is relative to the actual value (the effective completion time) and F_i is relative to the predicted completion time.

$$MAPE = \frac{1}{n}\sum_{i=1}^{n}\left|\frac{A_i - F_i}{A_i}\right|$$

$$RMSPE = \frac{\sqrt{\sum_{i=1}^{n}(A_i - F_i)^2}}{n}$$

In Table I, there are some results of the application of the algorithm in Figure 1 to Municipality 5 event log. The first column describes the path, the second and the fourth report the count of the paths in the respective time intervals, the third and the fifth report the relative importance (the average of the occurrences of paths inside traces). The sixth column is then calculated as the ratio of the absolute difference of the relative importances and the maximum of the two relative importances. You can see that for some paths there is a big difference in importance between intervals. This reflects the big change in the underlying process.

TABLE I. DIFFERENCE IN IMPORTANCE OF SEVERAL PATHS IN THE DIFFERENT INTERVALS. THIS REFLECTS THE CHANGE IN THE UNDERLYING PROCESS.

Succ. of act.	Count(1)	Rel.Imp.(1)	Count(2)	Rel.Imp.(2)	Diff.Imp.
01_HOOFD_011,01_HOOFD_012	362	0.4707	155	0.6078	0.2256
01_HOOFD_490_1,01_HOOFD_490_2	295	0.3836	1	0.0039	0.9898
01_HOOFD_480,01_HOOFD_490_1	275	0.3576	1	0.0039	0.9890
01_HOOFD_030_1,08_AWB45_020_2	194	0.2523	1	0.0039	0.9845
01_HOOFD_370,01_HOOFD_375	185	0.2406	1	0.0039	0.9837
01_HOOFD_030_2,01_HOOFD_015	182	0.2367	3	0.0118	0.9503
01_HOOFD_330,09_AH_I_010	178	0.2315	119	0.4667	0.5040
01_HOOFD_380,01_HOOFD_430	170	0.2211	1	0.0039	0.9823
01_HOOFD_195,01_HOOFD_250_1	163	0.2120	8	0.0314	0.8520
01_HOOFD_050,04_BPT_005	139	0.1808	51	0.2000	0.0962
08_AWB45_005,08_AWB45_010	137	0.1782	5	0.0196	0.8899
04_BPT_005,01_HOOFD_065_1	137	0.1782	1	0.0039	0.9780
01_HOOFD_250_2,01_HOOFD_330	134	0.1743	1	0.0039	0.9775
01_HOOFD_101,01_HOOFD_180	124	0.1612	1	0.0039	0.9757
02_DRZ_010,01_HOOFD_050	122	0.1586	1	0.0039	0.9753
01_HOOFD_196,01_HOOFD_200	117	0.1521	12	0.0471	0.6907
04_BPT_005,01_HOOFD_061	116	0.1508	1	0.0039	0.9740
01_HOOFD_065_0,01_HOOFD_061	107	0.1391	2	0.0078	0.9436
13_CRD_010,01_HOOFD_480	98	0.1274	141	0.5529	0.7695
08_AWB45_005,01_HOOFD_196	95	0.1235	28	0.1098	0.1112
01_BB_540,01_BB_775	92	0.1196	14	0.0549	0.5411
01_HOOFD_510_0,01_BB_540	92	0.1196	1	0.0039	0.9672
01_HOOFD_010,01_HOOFD_030_2	88	0.1144	2	0.0078	0.9315
08_AWB45_010,08_AWB45_020_0	88	0.1144	59	0.2314	0.5054
01_HOOFD_490_4,01_HOOFD_500	82	0.1066	2	0.0078	0.9264

TABLE II. RESULTS RELATED TO THE PREDICTION OF REMAINING TIME OF TRACES WHEN THE ACTIVITIES AND THE TIMESTAMPS OF THE FIRST TWO EVENTS OF A TRACE ARE KNOWN.

Start of trace	N. of trac.(1+2)	MAPE(1+2)	RMSPE(1+2)	MAPE(1)	RMSPE(1)	MAPE(2)	RMSPE(2)
01_HOOFD_010,01_HOOFD_011	512	92.8544	7596039.2797	**72.1547**	**5758334.0360**	**29.4204**	**3684134.2904**
01_HOOFD_010,01_HOOFD_030_2	178	3.5637	9587638.9410	3.5637	9587638.9410	**1.0269**	**497670.2839**
01_HOOFD_010,01_HOOFD_015	89	0.7490	7087620.4087	0.7490	7087620.4087	0.9472	**537482.9933**
01_HOOFD_010,01_HOOFD_065_2	51	0.3856	4639109.3841	0.3856	4639109.3841	0.9343	**733715.3557**
01_HOOFD_010,01_HOOFD_020	45	6466.2098	5150725.7065	**5897.2386**	**4897063.7661**	**1157.3147**	**1237980.3061**
01_HOOFD_010,02_DRZ_010	13	21.1334	6483207.2943	**5.0226**	**2740205.8570**	**20.1936**	**5823588.8817**
01_HOOFD_030_2,01_HOOFD_010	11	1.4041	30442608.9241	**1.3705**	**28448527.4061**	**0.8268**	**6779677.5687**
01_HOOFD_011,01_HOOFD_020	8	0.8641	3540610.0560	**0.5266**	**2475832.0442**	**0.6885**	**2767641.7088**
01_HOOFD_010,01_HOOFD_100	7	116.1590	49573665.1192	**53.6666**	**45699111.1204**	**4.6097**	**9047583.6599**
01_HOOFD_010,08_AWB45_020_2	6	0.4237	2882146.0787	0.4237	2882146.0787	0.8300	**2054337.2500**
01_HOOFD_065_2,01_HOOFD_010	4	1.0459	8758215.5171	1.0459	8758215.5171	**0.9356**	**3509933.2780**
01_HOOFD_010,04_BPT_005	3	48.0765	6306318.0537	**7.8786**	**2877381.7631**	48.0765	6306318.0537
01_HOOFD_010,01_HOOFD_180	2	0.3875	3894038.0000	0.7555	5147446.2190	0.3875	3894038.0000
01_HOOFD_010,01_HOOFD_190_2	2	3.7315	114725504.0000	3.7315	114725504.0000	**0.9044**	**47393188.8894**
01_HOOFD_460,01_HOOFD_010	2	0.0496	1410228.0000	0.0496	1410228.0000	0.9016	14055460.3380
01_HOOFD_065_2,01_HOOFD_100	2	0.8069	1443136.0000	0.8069	1443136.0000	0.9809	**1114929.5283**

In Table II, we present some results related to predictions. Three different conditions have been compared:

- The prediction (of the remaining time) relative to a prefix of a trace (belonging to the first or second time interval), using for the prediction all the traces in the log.
- The prediction relative to a prefix of a trace belonging to the first interval, using for the prediction all the traces weighted accordingly to the algorithm in Figure 3.
- The prediction relative to a prefix of a trace belonging to the second interval, using for the prediction all the traces weighted accordingly to the algorithm in Figure 3.

The prefix is formed by the first two activities. The results are then grouped based on their prefix.

In Table III the same techniques are applied to a prefix containing the first three activities of the trace. In many occurrences prediction results obtained by weighting the traces using algorithm in Figure 3 are improved in comparison to the classical technique.

V. CONCLUSION AND FUTURE WORK

In this paper is proposed a method to consider process drifts in the prediction of traces' attributes. At best of the author's knowledge, this is the first approach in the field (so there are not comparisons with other methods). The method assumes that the times in which the process changes are already

TABLE III. RESULTS RELATED TO THE PREDICTION OF REMAINING TIME OF TRACES WHEN THE ACTIVITIES AND THE TIMESTAMPS OF THE FIRST THREE EVENTS OF A TRACE ARE KNOWN.

Start of trace	N. of trac.(1+2)	MAPE(1+2)	RMSPE(1+2)	MAPE(1)	RMSPE(1)	MAPE(2)	RMSPE(2)
01_HOOFD_010,01_HOOFD_011,01_HOOFD_020	482	97.8206	7609140.4442	**74.4032**	**5684585.8721**	**32.2999**	**3779530.8508**
01_HOOFD_010,01_HOOFD_030_2,01_HOOFD_015	122	14930.5165	10071033.0171	14930.5165	10071033.0171	**424.3935**	**411018.8551**
01_HOOFD_010,01_HOOFD_015,01_HOOFD_020	88	0.7528	7113510.0065	0.7528	7113510.0065	0.9469	**544560.6131**
01_HOOFD_010,01_HOOFD_030_2,01_HOOFD_065_2	35	0.5755	6048120.8883	0.5755	6048120.8883	0.9416	**742048.0423**
01_HOOFD_010,01_HOOFD_020,03_GBH_005	32	0.5460	5410643.3730	0.5460	5410643.3730	0.8779	**907541.9461**
01_HOOFD_010,01_HOOFD_011,01_HOOFD_015	25	2.1717	8279672.0234	2.1717	8279672.0234	**0.8312**	**1897717.0886**
01_HOOFD_010,01_HOOFD_065_2,01_HOOFD_030_2	24	0.3386	3596116.9073	0.3386	3596116.9073	0.9599	**758544.5811**
01_HOOFD_010,01_HOOFD_065_2,01_HOOFD_011	10	0.2136	1730206.6639	0.2136	1730206.6639	0.8376	**1539281.7300**
01_HOOFD_030_2,01_HOOFD_010,01_HOOFD_015	9	1.5834	34502687.4489	1.5834	34502687.4489	**0.8614**	**5178829.1068**
01_HOOFD_010,02_DRZ_010,04_BPT_005	9	36.2173	7428347.0140	**6.8727**	**2504995.6683**	36.2173	7428347.0140
01_HOOFD_010,01_HOOFD_020,01_HOOFD_015	9	28662.2724	3743629.8187	28662.2724	3743629.8187	**1827.3567**	**1201595.5150**
01_HOOFD_010,01_HOOFD_030_2,01_HOOFD_100	8	0.6689	7220627.9116	0.6689	7220627.9116	0.9488	**2202998.4987**
01_HOOFD_010,01_HOOFD_030_2,01_HOOFD_020	6	0.5900	6852557.9972	0.5900	6852557.9972	0.8914	**3524148.5139**
01_HOOFD_010,01_HOOFD_011,01_HOOFD_012	5	4.4923	6541984.7061	**4.3511**	**4989471.1460**	**1.0229**	**5111010.0414**
01_HOOFD_010,01_HOOFD_065_2,01_HOOFD_020	5	0.1980	1989049.6259	0.1980	1989049.6259	0.9366	2165896.7836
01_HOOFD_010,08_AWB45_020_2,01_HOOFD_011	5	1.9712	4342968.0844	1.9712	4342968.0844	**0.6074**	**1762686.1021**
01_HOOFD_010,01_HOOFD_030_2,08_AWB45_020_2	5	1.4118	18454190.2346	1.4118	18454190.2346	**0.8784**	**7320269.2102**
01_HOOFD_011,01_HOOFD_020,02_DRZ_010	4	0.9579	5093072.7121	**0.7281**	**2374478.6397**	0.9579	5093072.7121
01_HOOFD_010,01_HOOFD_065_2,01_HOOFD_015	4	0.1935	1518991.7059	0.1935	1518991.7059	0.9385	1783136.1910
01_HOOFD_010,01_HOOFD_065_2,01_HOOFD_100	3	2.0393	25282013.7310	2.0393	25282013.7310	**0.9485**	**8849956.0681**
01_HOOFD_010,02_DRZ_010,01_HOOFD_011	3	1.9991	3157732.3759	**1.9245**	**2524545.0040**	**0.3542**	**2102105.9026**
01_HOOFD_011,01_HOOFD_020,03_GBH_005	3	1.1284	4899912.1248	1.1284	4899912.1248	**0.6089**	**3021026.5790**
01_HOOFD_010,04_BPT_005,01_HOOFD_065_0	2	0.8638	7474836.0000	**0.7944**	**5532054.4569**	0.8638	7474836.0000
01_HOOFD_065_2,01_HOOFD_010,01_HOOFD_030_2	2	2.6098	25116980.0000	2.6098	25116980.0000	**0.9108**	**11058921.0330**
01_HOOFD_010,01_HOOFD_100,01_HOOFD_065_2	2	0.3275	13389370.0000	0.3275	13389370.0000	0.9616	21201323.5022
01_HOOFD_010,01_HOOFD_100,08_AWB45_020_2	2	1.9679	44208424.0000	1.9679	44208424.0000	**0.9351**	**21257607.3203**
01_HOOFD_010,01_HOOFD_065_2,01_HOOFD_190_2	2	0.0147	144842.0000	0.0147	144842.0000	0.9882	4932713.5820
01_HOOFD_010,01_HOOFD_180,08_AWB45_005	2	0.3875	3894038.0000	0.7555	5147446.2190	0.3875	3894038.0000
01_HOOFD_010,01_HOOFD_020,01_HOOFD_011	2	1.2573	12031792.0000	1.3985	**11188363.6467**	**0.6438**	**8663993.7255**

known. All these changes, might they be seasonal, gradual or sudden, split the overall time interval into subintervals in which is assumed that the process is constant. The discovery of these times could be done in an automated way, for example using the algorithm described in [9], or manually through an interview. For each time sub-interval, you can observe how many times two activities are in direct succession; after that, you could compare the distributions measured in the different sub-intervals. This is useful to understand how much the process is different between different sub-intervals, and to give a different weight to the different (complete) traces one could use to predict the outcome of an incomplete trace. This is useful in each type of prediction, as the prediction of the remaining time in a trace.

The described algorithms are pretty easy to implement, and are not computationally expensive (the implementation has been realised in a plain Python script). However, the approach considers only the control flow perspective, and ignores other perspectives (like the data perspective and the resource perspective) in which the process could change over time. Indeed, changing roles inside an organizational process might change the throughput times, because of different skills, changed workloads and difficulties in collaboration between different work groups. Some literature can be cited related to social and work psychology [12], [13], [14] that give insights on how much inter-group relationships are important for organizational performance. Generally, one could identify inter-group distances in a process by measuring times elapsed between activities performed by different roles. This can be related to the Lean Manufacturing concept of Flow Rate [15], [16], [17]. Another aspect is related to the group's Transactive Memory [18], [19], [20]. Transactive Memory is a psychological concept that could be explained as "group memory" and is related to the specialization and the coordination of the group [21], [22]. Indeed, a change in the work group's structure that could be motivated by a change in the process, can hamper a lot the group's performance, because of the newcomers' need to know the rest and the roles of the group, or some people exiting the group. It is a pity that Transactive Memory in groups is generally difficult to measure [23], because it's a powerful tool to measure group performance.

There is also scope to research related to non-instantaneous events that could include several transitions (start, complete, stop, resume) [24], as the framework described here works only for instantaneous events (each trace could be described by a succession of conclusive activities). Overall, the proposed method seems to be good performing on the BPI Challenge's Municipality 5 log. In that log, the process changes after the union with another municipality (Municipality 2). Not in every event log, however, a change in the underlying process can be registered. In that case, the method is useless.

Moreover, current results related to prediction of attributes (e.g., remaining time) are not that good, even with the proposed improvement. There is something more to come in order to get good and reliable predictions.

REFERENCES

[1] W. e. a. Van Der Aalst, "Process mining manifesto," in Business process management workshops. Springer, pp. 169–194, 2012.

[2] W. Van Der Aalst, Process mining: discovery, conformance and enhancement of business processes. Springer Science & Business Media, 2011.

[3] W. M. Van der Aalst and A. K. A. de Medeiros, "Process mining and security: Detecting anomalous process executions and checking process conformance," Electronic Notes in Theoretical Computer Science, vol. 121, pp. 3–21, 2005.

[4] A. Weijters, W. M. van Der Aalst, and A. A. De Medeiros, "Process mining with the heuristics miner-algorithm," Technische Universiteit Eindhoven, Tech. Rep. WP, vol. 166, pp. 1–34, 2006.

[5] W. e. a. Van Der Aalst, "Workflow mining: a survey of issues and approaches," Data & knowledge engineering, vol. 47, no. 2, pp. 237–267, 2003.

[6] W. M. Van der Aalst, M. H. Schonenberg, and M. Song, "Time prediction based on process mining," Information Systems, vol. 36, no. 2, pp. 450–475, 2011.

[7] M. Ceci, P. F. Lanotte, F. Fumarola, D. P. Cavallo, and D. Malerba, "Completion time and next activity prediction of processes using sequential pattern mining," in Discovery Science - 17th International Conference, DS 2014, Bled, Slovenia, October 8-10, 2014. Proceedings, pp. 49–61, 2014.

[8] M. Polato, A. Sperduti, A. Burattin, and M. de Leoni, "Data-aware remaining time prediction of business process instances," in Neural Networks (IJCNN), 2014 International Joint Conference on. IEEE, pp. 816–823, 2014.

[9] R. J. C. Bose, W. M. van der Aalst, I. Žliobaitė, and M. Pechenizkiy, "Handling concept drift in process mining," in Advanced Information Systems Engineering. Springer, pp. 391–405, 2011.

[10] S. J. Leemans, D. Fahland, and W. M. van der Aalst, "Discovering block-structured process models from event logs containing infrequent behaviour," in Business Process Management Workshops. Springer, pp. 66–78, 2014.

[11] J. Martjushev, R. J. C. Bose, and W. M. van der Aalst, "Change point detection and dealing with gradual and multi-order dynamics in process mining," in Perspectives in Business Informatics Research. Springer, pp. 161–178, 2015.

[12] H. Tajfel, "Social psychology of intergroup relations," Annual review of psychology, vol. 33, no. 1, pp. 1–39, 1982.

[13] ——, Social identity and intergroup relations. Cambridge University Press, 2010.

[14] B. E. Ashforth and F. Mael, "Social identity theory and the organization," Academy of management review, vol. 14, no. 1, pp. 20–39, 1989.

[15] R. Shah and P. T. Ward, "Lean manufacturing: context, practice bundles, and performance," Journal of operations management, vol. 21, no. 2, pp. 129–149, 2003.

[16] T. Melton, "The benefits of lean manufacturing: what lean thinking has to offer the process industries," Chemical Engineering Research and Design, vol. 83, no. 6, pp. 662–673, 2005.

[17] C. Cassell, J. Worley, and T. Doolen, "The role of communication and management support in a lean manufacturing implementation," Management Decision, vol. 44, no. 2, pp. 228–245, 2006.

[18] D. M. Wegner, "Transactive memory: A contemporary analysis of the group mind," in Theories of group behavior. Springer, pp. 185–208, 1987.

[19] R. L. Moreland and L. Myaskovsky, "Exploring the performance benefits of group training: Transactive memory or improved communication?" Organizational behavior and human decision processes, vol. 82, no. 1, pp. 117–133, 2000.

[20] J. R. Austin, "Transactive memory in organizational groups: the effects of content, consensus, specialization, and accuracy on group performance." Journal of Applied Psychology, vol. 88, no. 5, p. 866, 2003.

[21] L. Argote, "An opportunity for mutual learning between organizational learning and global strategy researchers: transactive memory systems," Global Strategy Journal, vol. 5, no. 2, pp. 198–203, 2015.

[22] C. Heavey and Z. Simsek, "Transactive memory systems and firm performance: An upper echelons perspective," Organization Science, 2015.

[23] K. Lewis, "Measuring transactive memory systems in the field: scale development and validation." Journal of Applied Psychology, vol. 88, no. 4, p. 587, 2003.

[24] A. Burattin, "Heuristics miner for time interval," in Process Mining Techniques in Business Environments. Springer, pp. 85–95, 2015.

Real-Time Knowledge Map Services on National R&D Data

Kang-Ryul Shon
Korea Institute of Science and Technology
Daejeon, Korea
krshon@kisti.re.kr

Han-Jo Jeong
Korea Institute of Science and Technology
Daejeon, Korea
hanjo.jeong@kisti.re.kr

Cheol-Joo Chae
Korea Institute of Science and Technology
Daejeon, Korea
cjchae@kisti.re.kr

Chul-Su Lim
Korea Institute of Science and Technology
Daejeon, Korea
cslim@kisti.re.kr

***Abstract*—The National Science & Technology Information Service (NTIS) provides knowledge map services with an integrated information of national R&D information and science & technology information. In order to solve the request of the users in real time, this paper presents a real-time knowledge map service that retrieves and aggregates the needed data and creates the map services on the fly. To select and aggregate the needed information on the fly, we used the slice and dice method, which is one of the most widely used methods in data warehousing and on-line analytical processing (OLAP) approach. In addition, we show some examples of knowledge map services, which analyze and visualize the status and the topic-trend of the national R&D information based on the real-time data selection and aggregation.**

Knowledge Map; Map Service; NDSL-NTIS; Real-Time Analysis ; Slice and Dice

I. INTRODUCTION

Knowledge maps can be divided into two types: one is a knowledge map used in the area of knowledge management to store, manage and process the organizations' data as knowledge, the other is a knowledge map for analyzing and representing knowledge extracted from the science & technology documents. The knowledge map in the knowledge management area is focused on designing and structuring the organizations' internal knowledge and processes to enhance the knowledge management and business processes [1]. On the other hand, the main purpose of the knowledge map in the science & technology area is to represent the science & technology knowledge by allowing users to navigate the knowledge [2] the same way a general map allows users to browse and navigate a region and an area in the map. In this research, we focus on the knowledge map of representing the science & technology knowledge as our goal is to integrate the R&D data and to assist users to browse and navigate the R&D data in terms of such knowledge-based approach.

National Science & Technology Information Service (NTIS) [3] provides such knowledge map services with an integrated information of national R&D information and science & technology information obtained from NTIS and National Digital Science Library (NDSL) [4]. In this research, a real-time knowledge map service, which selects and aggregates a part of knowledge map data and creates the knowledge map services on the fly, is introduced.

II. KNOWLEDGE BASED KNOWLEDGE MAP SERVICE

In this section, the knowledge-map service system in NTIS is introduced. As shown in Figure 1, the NDSL-NTIS Knowledge base is created based on a national R&D ontology for integrating the national R&D data, such as research projects, research papers, patent, and project reports. The system has as goals 1) to integrate the national R&D data obtained from NDSL and NTIS, which are two major repositories and service of national R&D data servicing in Korea, 2) to provide a topic-based information search on the integrated data, and 3) to provide knowledge map services based on the analysis and knowledge processing.

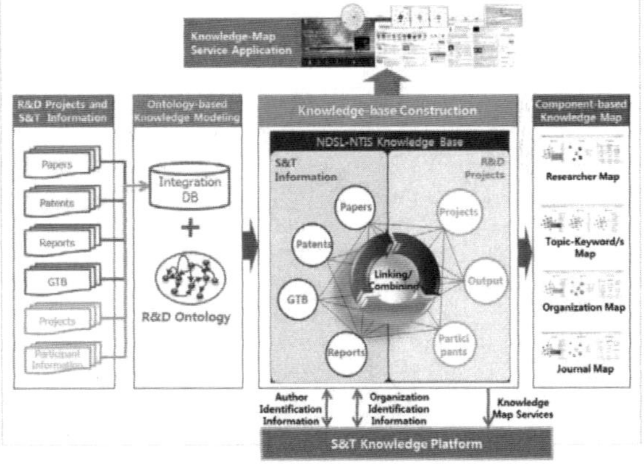

Figure 1. Overall System Architecture

III. REAL-TIME KNOWLEDGE MAP SERVICES

As described in Figure 2, users can select (Slice) a part of knowledge map data using a filtering-based search. Then, the part of the data are selected (Dice) and aggregated into a knowledge map on the fly applying the slice and dice method, which is one of the widely used methods in on-line analytical processing (OLAP) approach [5]. Lastly, the knowledge map services, such as R&D output analysis and trend analysis map services could be created based on the aggregated data in real time using 'd3' Java script Library for visualized graph.

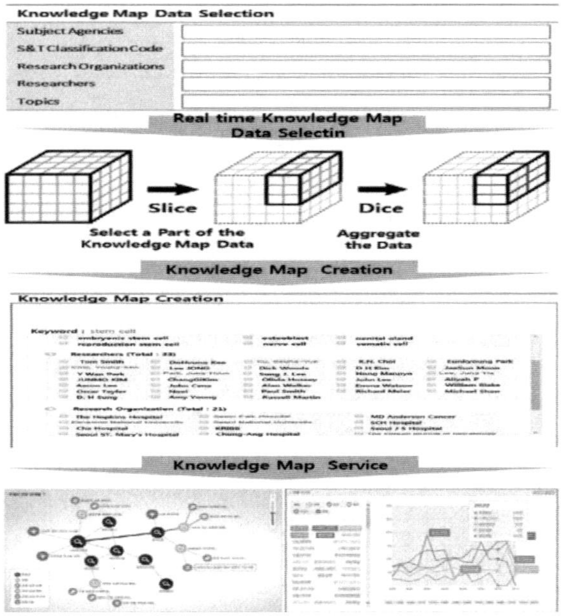

Figure 2. Real-Time Knowledge Map Creation

A. *Real-Time R&D Output Analysis Map Service*

Figure 3 shows a real-time R&D output analysis map service. Basically, the national R&D project data is filtered and retrieved from the filtering-based search. Then, the project data is firstly clustered based on the topics, and the clustered data is aggregated with the number of the related R&D projects and the total amount invested for the R&D projects. Lastly, top N topics are selected based on the number and the amount of the related R&D projects. Based on the selection and aggregation, the R&D output analysis map service is created with the selected topics and their related R&D output data.

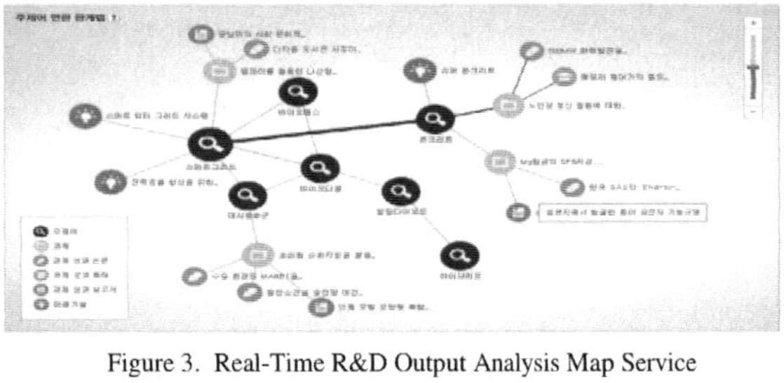

Figure 3. Real-Time R&D Output Analysis Map Service

B. *Real-Time R&D Trend Analysis Map Service*

Figure 4 shows a real-time R&D trend analysis map service. As similar with the R&D output analysis map service, the R&D project data is selected and filtered by users and the data is aggregated based on the topics. The aggregation can be done in two ways: the first is aggregating by the number of R&D output data, and the second is aggregating by the total amount of R&D investment. In addition, the aggregation can be performed by the number of each R&D output data at the user's request. After the aggregation is done, the R&D trend graph is created with the aggregation by year.

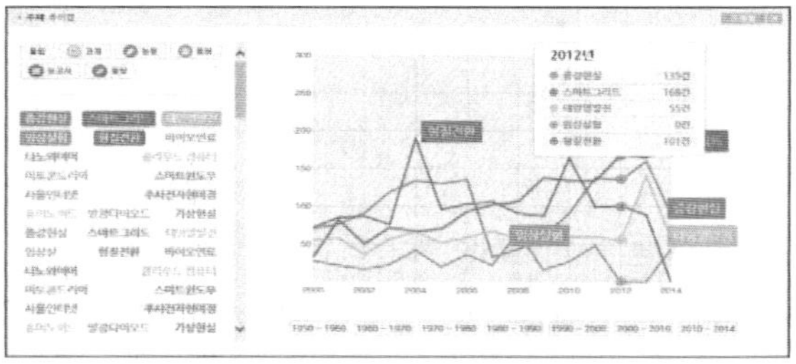

Figure 4. Real-Time R&D Trend Analysis Map Service

IV. CONCLUSIONS

In this paper, we introduced the real-time knowledge map services, which select and aggregate the knowledge map data and create the knowledge map service upon the user request. To select and aggregate the knowledge map data, the slice and dice method is used. We also introduced the examples of the knowledge map services, which represent and visualize the knowledge map data in the form of network and graph. In future research, we will elaborate on the keyword focused processing methods to minimize user interaction for the knowledge map construction.

ACKNOWLEDGMENT

This research was supported by Maximize the Value of National Science and Technology by Strengthen Sharing/Collaboration of National R&D Information funded by the Korea Institute of Science and Technology Information (KISTI).

REFERENCES

[1] L. Businska, I. Supulniece, and M. Kirikova, "On data, information, and knowledge representation in business process models," In Information Systems Development, Springer New York, pp 613-627, 2013.

[2] R. Klavans and K. W. Boyack, "Toward a consensus map of science," Journal of the American Society for information science and technology, vol. 60, no. 3, pp 455-476, 2009.

[3] "National Science & Technology Information Service (NTIS)," URL http://www.ntis.go.kr/

[4] "National Digital Science Library (NDSL)," URL http://www.ndsl.kr/

[5] R. Kimball and R. Margy, "The data warehouse toolkit: the complete guide to dimensional modeling," John Wiley & Sons, 2011.

Multilingual Sentiment Analysis on Data of the Refugee Crisis in Europe

Gayane Shalunts

SAIL LABS Technology GmbH
Vienna, Austria
Email: gayane.shalunts@sail-labs.com

Gerhard Backfried

SAIL LABS Technology GmbH
Vienna, Austria
Email: gerhard.backfried@sail-labs.com

Abstract—**The refugee crisis in Europe was one of the biggest challenges in summer-autumn 2015. The problem drew the highest attention in media and was the discussion topic of politicians and responsible organizations. The current article presents multilingual sentiment analysis of the traditional media content covering the topic. Sentiment analysis forms an integral part of multifaceted media analysis. The dataset comprises relevant articles from eighty of the most circulated traditional media sources in English, German, Russian and Spanish, compiled in the course of three months. The temporal sentiment classification per language demonstrates how the attitude towards the crisis differs across the languages and geographical areas. The further sentiment analysis and visualizations of various aspects illustrate in details the distribution of positivity/negativity among media sources and their target languages.**

Keywords*–*Multilingual sentiment analysis; refugee crisis.

I. Introduction

Sentiment analysis refers to a classification task in Natural Language Processing (NLP) community, the goal of which is commonly to determine the objectivity (objective/subjective) or polarity (positive/negative) of the input data. The main parameters defining the scope of a sentiment analysis approach are the target language, domain and media type (traditional or social media). The most common application is the monitoring of public opinions in marketing (product reviews) and politics (election campaigns). Whereas the research field is active, most publications are limited to the domains of movie and product reviews in English only. Sentiment analysis methods can be divided into two broad categories: machine-learning- and lexicon-based methods [1]. Machine learning methods are implemented as supervised binary (positive/negative) classification approaches, in which classifiers are trained on labeled data [1] [2]. However, the dependence on a labeled dataset is considered a major drawback, since labeling is usually costly, time-intensive and even impossible in some cases. In contrast, lexicon-based methods use a predefined set of patterns (referred to as a sentiment dictionary or lexicon) associating each entry with a specific sentiment score and do not require any labeled training data. Here, the challenge lies in designing an appropriate sentiment lexicon. Lexicon-based methods are tuned towards specific target domains, media types and the respective language style, e.g., formal language on traditional media and colloquial language on social media. A comparison of eight state-of-the-art sentiment analysis methods is performed in [1]. All experiments are carried out using two English datasets of Online Social Networks messages. The methods compared are SentiWordNet [3], SASA [4], PANAS-t [5], Emoticons, SentiStrength [6], LIWC [7], SenticNet [8] and Happiness Index [9]. They report that the examined sentiment analysis methods have different levels of applicability on real-world events and vary widely in their agreement on the predicted polarity. Sentiment analysis of the textual data relevant to disasters/crises aims to provide additional structured information to the responsible organizations for situation analysis in various phases of disaster/crisis management [10].

The current article makes the following contributions: 1) Compiles automatically a corpus of news articles covering the refugee crisis in Europe in a period of a quarter in summer-autumn 2015 (36702 articles in total). The articles originate from 80 of the most circulated traditional media sources in English, German, Russian and Spanish, 2) investigates the temporal development of the data volume per language, 3) performs sentiment analysis per language, 4) detects the sentiment polarity across media sources and their languages and generates visualizations of different aspects. The authors choose to employ the SentiSAIL software tool [11] among numerous existing state-of-the-art sentiment analysis methods to carry out the above remarked experimental setup. SentiSAIL performs multidimensional sentiment analysis in terms of languages, domains and media types. It is integrated into the SAIL LABS Media Mining System (MMS) for Open Source Intelligence [12]. MMS is a state-of-the-art Open-Source-Intelligence system, incorporating speech and text-processing technologies [11]. SentiSAIL performs an important part of MMS automatic multifaceted processing of unstructured textual data. It addresses the content of both traditional and social media in English, German, Russian and Spanish, supports the domains of general news and particularly the coverage of disasters/crises. The performance evaluation of SentiSAIL on a trilingual traditional media corpus, as well as on an English social media dataset for comparison with other state-of-the-art methods, is reported in [11]. The experiments in [11] showed that the performance of SentiSAIL and human annotators are equivalent. SentiSAIL was also used to analyze the social media data in German, concerning the European floods 2013 [13]. The choice of SentiSAIL is motivated by the following advantages of applicability in the current scenario: 1) SentiSAIL supports all the languages mentioned, unlike other sentiment analysis approaches, which handle only a single language content. E.g., SentimentWS [14] and [15] target only German, [16] [17] - Russian, Sentitext [18] and [19] - Spanish. The authors in [20] adapted the English semantic orientation system [21] to Spanish, comparing several alternative approaches. 2) SentiSAIL is adapted to the domain of news articles and especially the coverage of disasters/crises in the traditional media. The authors in [22] also target the domain of news, limited only to English though.

The paper is organized as follows: Section II clarifies the methodology of the SentiSAIL tool. Section III gives detailed information about the experimental corpora. Section IV presents the experimental setup, performance evaluation and results. And finally, Section V draws conclusions from the work presented.

II. SentiSAIL Methodology

SentiSAIL is a multilingual sentiment analysis tool addressing the domain of general news and particularly the coverage of disasters/crises in general news [11]. It employs the algorithm of one of the state-of-the-art sentiment analysis methods SentiStrength [6]. SentiStrength, like [21], is a lexicon-based approach, using lexicons of words associated with scores of positive or negative orientation. SentiSAIL also supports stemming of the lexicon patterns, which is particularly important for the processing of inflective languages, such as Russian or German. The intensification/boosting and negation of the lexicon words, as well as the polarity scoring of phrases and idioms, intend to model the structure and semantics of the language observed. The innovative contribution of SentiSAIL [11] lied in expanding the SentiStrength algorithm into new domains (general and disasters/crises related news), multiple languages (English, German, Russian and Spanish) and to the granularity level of full articles. In the scope of the crises domain were considered both natural and humanitarian crises, like the refugee crises in Europe. The adaptation of SentiSAIL to the crises domain was achieved by means of manual compilation of sentiment terms from relevant texts. Examples of such terms are "donation", "volunteer" (positive terms), "underfeeding","xenophobic" (negative terms).

Whereas SentiStrength is optimized for and evaluated on social media content, SentiSAIL targets both social and traditional media data. The social media features are parameterized and may be disabled during traditional media processing. The SentiStrength and SentiSAIL features are compared in [11] on a self-compiled traditional media corpus, reporting the SentiSAIL performance improvement in English to be slight and considerable in German and Russian. SentiSAIL, like [23], solves a dual classification task by classifying a text into one of the following 4classes: positive, negative, mixed (both positive and negative) or neutral (neither positive, nor negative). The dual classification scheme is motivated, as humans exhibit the ability to experience positive and negative emotions simultaneously [24]. The class of the input text is obtained by taking the following steps: 1) the sentiment on the granularity level of line is determined by obtaining a pair of positive/negative scores by averaging the respective positive/negative scores of the sentiment patterns present in the line. Algorithms other than averaging were also employed in this step without a significant impact on the final classification rate [11]. 2) The sentiment on the granularity level of document is calculated likewise as a pair of positive/negative scores by averaging the pairs of the positive/negative scores of all lines respectively. 3) The final sentiment class of a text is produced by double thresholding of the pair of the positive/negative scores on the granularity level document: classification of the positive and negative classes is straightforward. Documents passing both thresholds are classified into the mixed class, those failing both thresholds are classified as neutral.

III. Data Collection

The multilingual corpus covering the humanitarian crisis of refugees in Europe was collected automatically using the SAIL LABS Feeder for web content a web-crawler aimed at the collection of textual content from feeds and web-pages [12]. The tool can be scheduled to collect traditional media sources on a regular basis. A multilingual corpus (English, German, Russian and Spanish) was compiled to reflect a variety of views in particular geographical regions and formed by cultural differences and political influences. Twenty out of the most circulated traditional media sources per language were chosen in order to obtain equal distribution among languages. The period observed is a quarter from July to September 2015

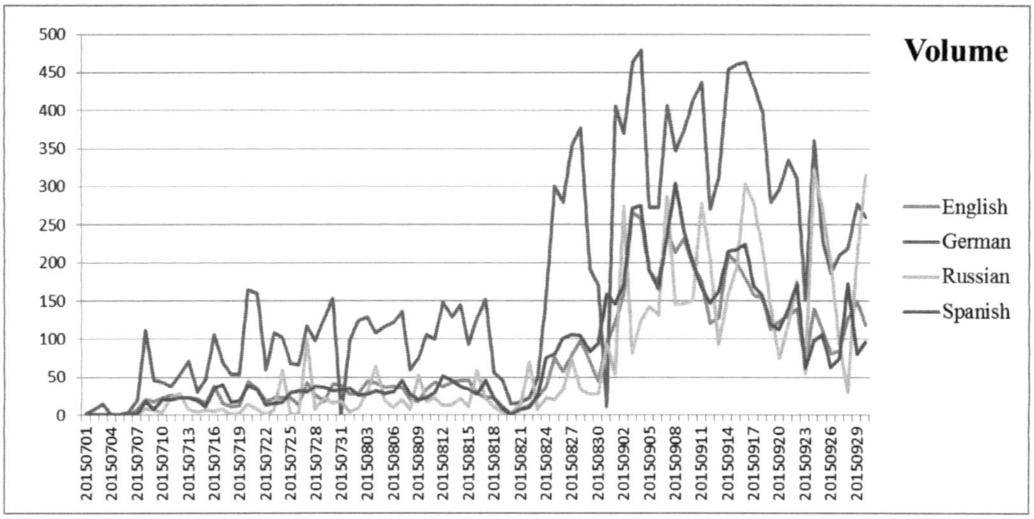

Figure 1. Temporal chart of the data volume per language (horizontal axis - date, vertical axis - article count).

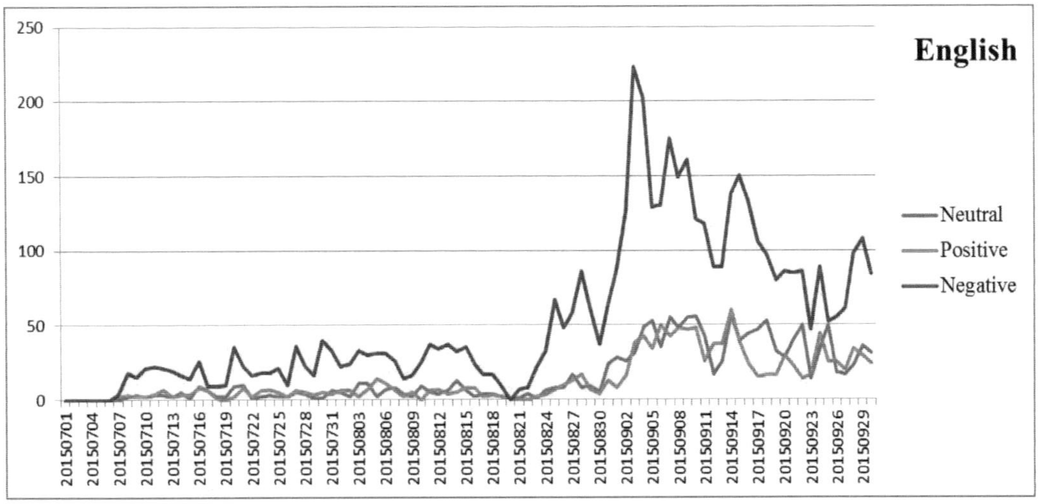

Figure 2. Temporal sentiment analysis of the English data (horizontal axis - date, vertical axis - article count).

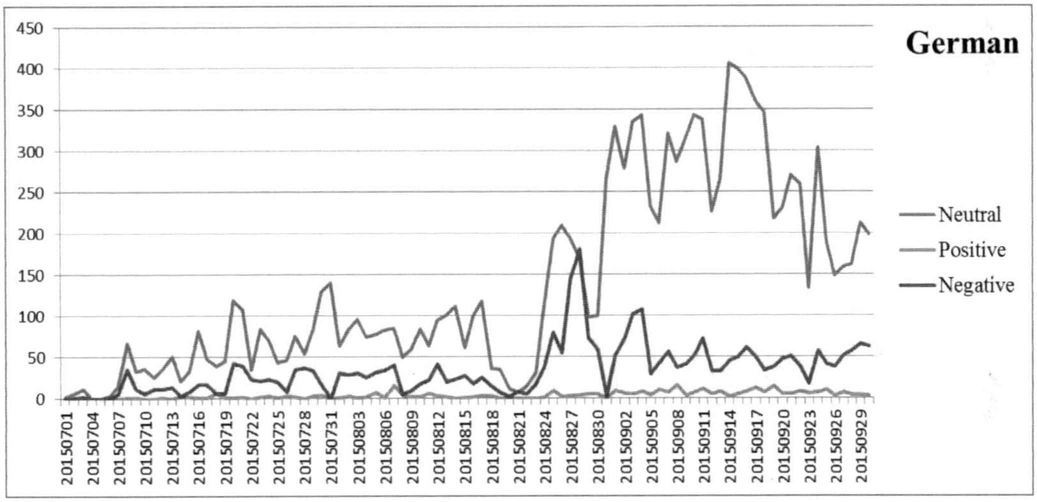

Figure 3. Temporal sentiment analysis of the German data (horizontal axis - date, vertical axis - article count).

on a daily basis. The number of the collected articles in the mentioned period in English is equal to 6580, in German 16669, in Russian 6459 and in Spanish 6994. A total of 36702 articles relevant to the refugee crisis were analyzed.

IV. The Experimental Setup and Results

In order to have a picture about the development of the refugee crisis and how actively the selected multilingual traditional media sources covered those, firstly the temporal distribution of the data volume among languages is examined. Fig. 1 depicts the daily volume of the compiled data per language in the period from July the 1st to September 30th. The data volume growth is noticeable for all languages starting from August 25th, coinciding with the dates of the deepening of the refugee crisis. It is also visible from the chart that the traditional media sources in German paid more attention to the problem, generating the highest volume of content among the four languages monitored. This tendency may be explained by the fact that the German speaking countries Austria and Germany were confronted with the crisis immediately by a vast stream of refugees.

The temporal sentiment analysis of the selected traditional media sources in English, among those CNN and BBC, is displayed in Fig. 2. The vertical axis represents the number of articles per sentiment class, the horizontal axis the issue dates of the articles. The articles, classified in the mixed class, are assigned both to the positive and negative classes. As observed in Fig. 2, the negative sentiment is generally dominating during the whole period. The term refugee(s), associated with a slightly negative score, is excluded from the sentiment patterns in all languages, in order not to bias the classification of the whole corpus towards negative sentiment. Fig. 3, Fig. 4 and

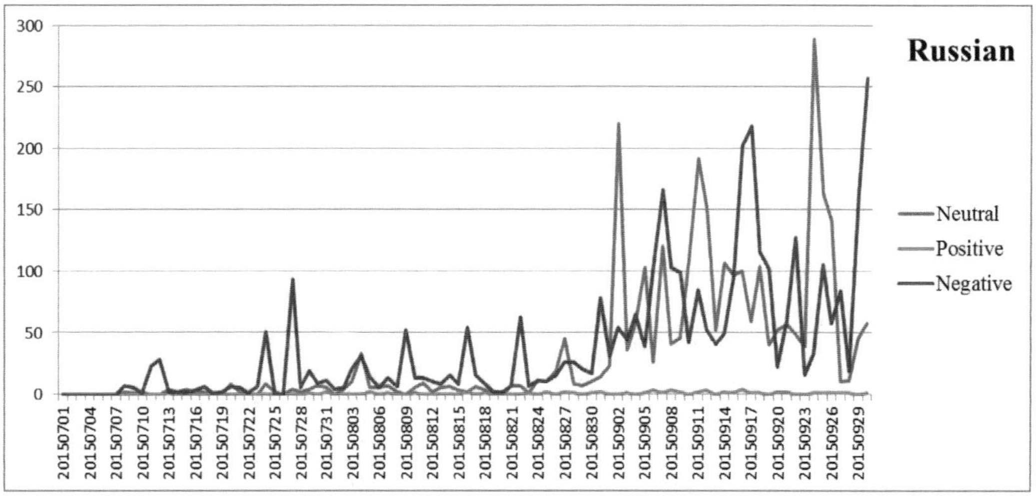

Figure 4. Temporal sentiment analysis of the Russian data (horizontal axis - date, vertical axis - article count).

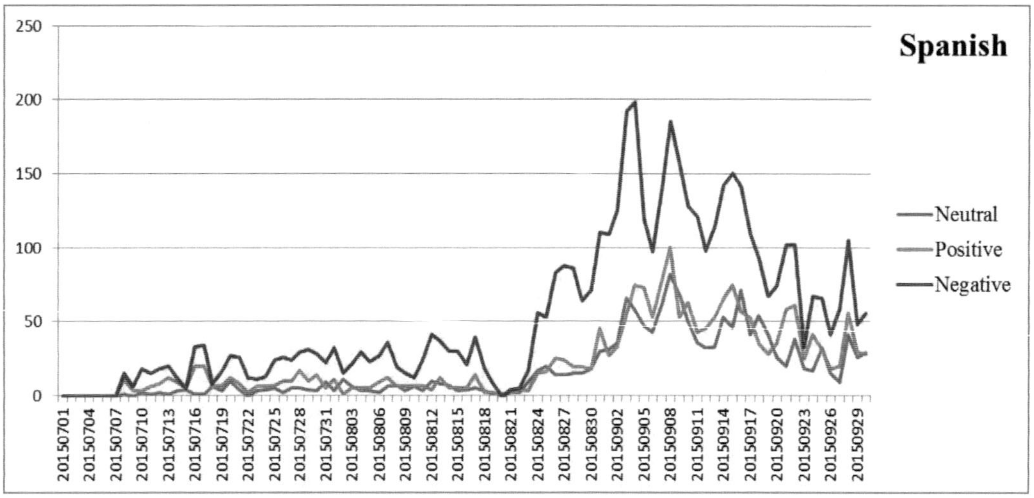

Figure 5. Temporal sentiment analysis of the Spanish data (horizontal axis - date, vertical axis - article count).

Fig. 5 portray the equivalent temporal charts of the distribution of the sentiment classes on German, Russian and Spanish share of the corpus respectively. Comparing the four multilingual charts, one may conclude that whereas the negative sentiment is highly prevailing on English and Spanish media sources, the German media stands out by dominating neutrality. The Russian corpus analysis reveals high rates of both negative and neutral sentiment (Fig. 4). One can also find correlations with the crisis events examining the sentiment distribution diagrams. For example, the global maximum of the negative sentiment on the English data is observed on September 3rd (Fig. 2), coinciding with the date, when a three-year-old boy drowned in his Syrian familys attempt to reach Greece from Turkey. On the other hand, the global negative maximum on the German media is located on August 28th (Fig. 3), when 71 refugees were found dead in the back of a freezer truck in Austria. A closer look at German articles, carrying positive sentiment, revealed phrases, such as Ich bin stolz Deutscher zu sein (I am proud to be German); Eine der größten Spendenaktionen der vergangenen Jahre ist gelungen (One of the biggest donation activities of the past years succeeded); Hilfsbereitschaft (willingness to help), etc.

Table I demonstrates how positivity, negativity and neutrality are distributed among the four languages, covering the sensitive topic of the refugee crisis. The most positive media language is Spanish with 27.61% positive content, the least positive is the Russian one with only 2.35% positive articles. Note for comparison that the average positivity rate of the whole multilingual corpus is 13.13% (Table I). The highest negativity rate is observed on the English media coverage with 72.3% negative rate, whereas the German media spreads the lowest negativity with 23.6% negative rate. The average negativity rate on the whole multilingual corpus yields 52.9%.

TABLE I. THE POSITIVITY, NEGATIVITY AND NEUTRALITY RATES IN PERCENT PER LANGUAGE.

	English	German	Russian	Spanish	Average
Positivity rate %	19.61%	2.96%	2.35%	27.61%	13.13%
Negativity rate %	72.3%	23.6%	45.6%	70.2%	52.9%
Neutrality rate %	19.7%	74.3%	53.2%	21.7%	42.2%

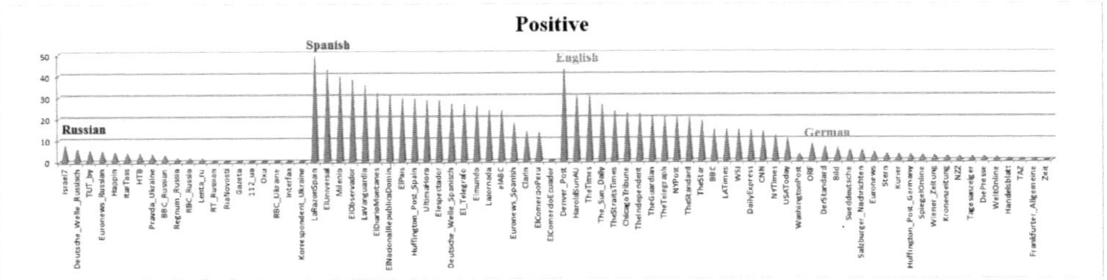

Figure 6. The rate of all positive articles in % per media source.

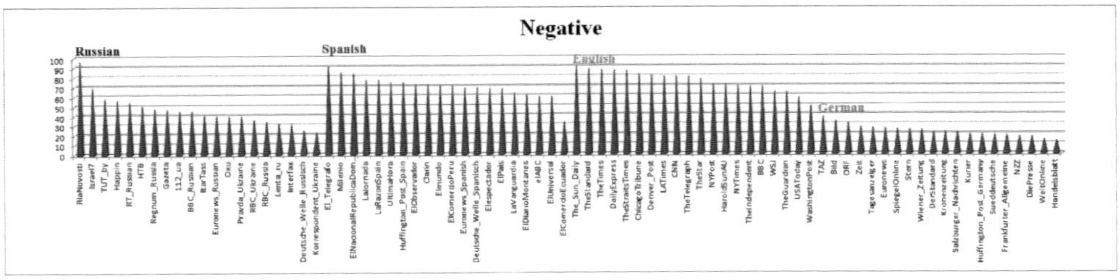

Figure 7. The rate of all negative articles in % per media source.

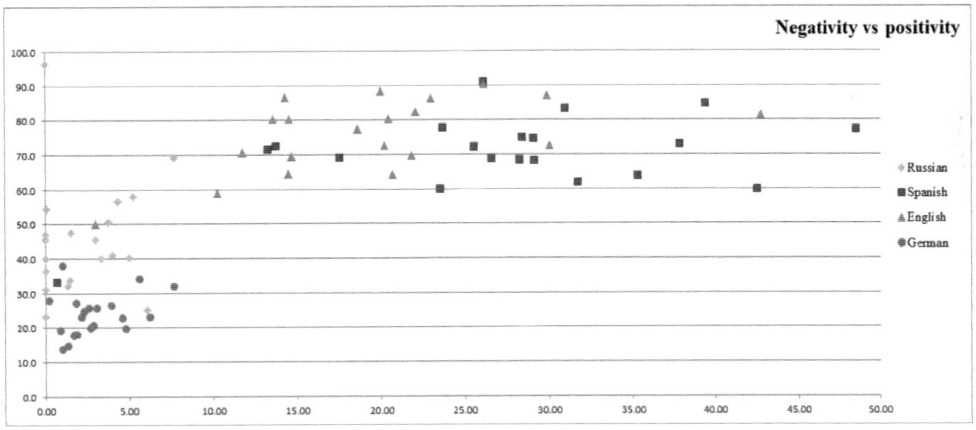

Figure 8. The rate of negativity (vertical axis) vs positivity (horizontal axis) in % per media source and language.

The German corpus also stands out with the highest neutrality rate (74.3%), which is considerably higher than the average neutrality rate of the complete dataset (42.2%) (Table I).

The next facet of our multilingual sentiment analysis portrays the distribution of the positive and negative sentiment per media source to reveal the most positive/negative sources. Fig. 6 depicts the positive rate in percent for the 80 media sources, labeled by their language. Fig. 7 is the corresponding chart for the negative sentiment. The most positive media source is the Spanish La Razon Spain with 48.55% positive content, the least positive ones are the Russian Ria Novosti, Gazeta, 112 Ukraine, Oxu, RBC Ukraine, Interfax and Korrespondent Ukraine, lacking positive content completely (Fig. 6). The most negative media source is the Russian Ria Novosti with 96.3% negative articles, the least negative one - the German Handelsblatt with 13.6% negativity rate (Fig. 7). Fig. 8 shows a visualization of the positivity vs negativity rates in percent per media source and language. Here, an interesting tendency of clustering per language is noticeable: 1) The German media sources shape a well-defined cluster of low negativity and low positivity. 2) The Russian media sources form a cluster of low positivity and moderate negativity. Here, the clear outlier is Ria Novosti with 96.3% negative and 0% positive content. The clustering is not so clearly notable in cases of the English and Spanish corpora. Here, one may conclude, that whereas both media languages spread highly negative content (exceeding 59%), the range of the distribution of the positivity is very broad. The outliers from the tendency are the English Washington Post (3% positivity vs 50% negativity) and the Spanish El Comercio Ecuador (0.74% positivity vs 33.1% negativity).

V. CONCLUSION

The paper presented sentiment analysis of traditional media data on the 2015 refugee crisis in Europe, originating from a vast number of multilingual, highly circulated sources of traditional media. The languages, covering the humanitarian tragedy, were English, German, Russian and Spanish. The observed time span was a quarter year in summer-autumn 2015. The initial experiment compared the data volume per language of the automatically compiled corpora. The German data volume was considerably higher than those of the other languages, explained by the fact that German speaking countries faced the crisis immediately. The second experiment employed SentiSAIL software tool to perform sentiment analysis per language. The outcome of the experiment was that the dominating sentiment on the English and Spanish corpora was the negative one, whereas on the German and Russian data the neutral one. The final experiment visualized and illustrated the distribution of the positivity and negativity rates among all multilingual sources, revealing a tendency towards clustering per language. In a larger context, these results form part of our contrastive analysis of media coverage of disasters across multiple languages and media.

REFERENCES

[1] P. Gonçalves, M. Araújo, F. Benevenuto, and M. Cha, "Comparing and combining sentiment analysis methods," in Proc. of the 1st ACM Conference on Online Social Networks (COSN). Boston, USA: ACM, 2013, pp. 27–38.

[2] B. Pang, L. Lee, and S. Vaithyanathan, "Thumbs up?: sentiment classification using machine learning techniques." in Proc. of the ACL conference on Empirical methods in natural language processing (EMNLP), Philadelphia, PA, USA, 2002, pp. 79–86.

[3] A. Esuli and F. Sebastiani, "Sentiwordnet: A publicly available lexical resource for opinion mining," in Proc. of the 5th Conference on Language Resources and Evaluation (LREC06, 2006, pp. 417–422.

[4] H. Wang, D. Can, A. Kazemzadeh, F. Bar, and S. Narayanan, "A system for real-time twitter sentiment analysis of 2012 u.s. presidential election cycle," in ACL (System Demonstrations), 2012, pp. 115–120.

[5] P. Gonçalves, F. Benevenuto, and M. Cha, "Panas-t: A pychometric scale for measuring sentiments on twitter," CoRR, vol. abs/1308.1857, 2013.

[6] M. Thelwall, K. Buckley, G. Paltoglou, D. Cai, and A. Kappas, "Sentiment Strength Detection in Short Informal Text," J. American Society for Information Science and Technology, vol. 61, no. 12, Dec. 2010, pp. 2544–2558.

[7] Y. R. Tausczik and J. W. Pennebaker, "The psychological meaning of words: Liwc and computerized text analysis methods," Journal of Language and Social Psychology, vol. 29, no. 1, 2010, pp. 25–54.

[8] E. Cambria, R. Speer, C. Havasi, and A. Hussain, "SenticNet: A Publicly Available Semantic Resource for Opinion Mining," in AAAI Fall Symposium: Commonsense Knowledge, 2010, pp. 14–18.

[9] P. S. Dodds and C. M. Danforth, "Measuring the happiness of large-scale written expression: songs, blogs, and presidents," Journal of Happiness Studies, vol. 11, no. 4, 2009, pp. 441–456.

[10] G. Backfried et al., "Integration of Media Sources for Situation Analysis in the Different Phases of Disaster Management: The QuOIMA Project," in Proc. of European Intelligence and Security Informatics Conference (EISIC), Uppsala, Sweden, 2013, pp. 143–146.

[11] G. Shalunts and G. Backfried, "SentiSAIL: Sentiment Analysis in English, German and Russian," in Proc. of the 11th International Conference on Machine Learning and Data Mining, ser. MLDM '15, Hamburg, Germany, 2015, pp. 87–97.

[12] G. Backfried et al., "Open Source Intelligence in Disaster Management," in Proc. of the European Intelligence and Security Informatics Conference (EISIC). Odense, Denmark: IEEE Computer Society, 2012, pp. 254–258.

[13] G. Shalunts, G. Backfried, and K. Prinz, "Sentiment analysis of German social media data for natural disasters," in Proc. of the 11th International Conference on Information Systems for Crisis Response and Management (ISCRAM), University Park, Pennsylvania, USA, 2014, pp. 752–756.

[14] R. Remus, U. Quasthoff, and G. Heyer, "Sentiws - a german-language resource for sentiment analysis," in Proc. of the 7th conference on International Language Resources and Evaluation (LREC), Valletta, Malta, 2010, pp. 1168–1171.

[15] S. Momtazi, "Fine-grained german sentiment analysis on social media," in Proc. of the 8th International Conference on Language Resources and Evaluation (LREC). Istanbul, Turkey: European Language Resources Association (ELRA), 2012, pp. 1215–1220.

[16] I. Chetviorkin and N. Loukachevitch, "Extraction of Russian Sentiment Lexicon for Product Meta-Domain," in Proc. of the 24th International Conference on Computational Linguistics (COLING), Bombay, India, 2012, pp. 593–610.

[17] I. Chetviorkin and N. Loukachevitch, "Evaluating Sentiment Analysis Systems in Russian," in Proc. of the 4th Biennial International Workshop on Balto-Slavic Natural Language Processing, Sofia, Bulgaria, 2013, pp. 12–17.

[18] A. Moreno-Ortiz, C. Perez-Hernandez, and M. A. Del-Olmo, "Managing multiword expressions in a lexicon-based sentiment analysis system for spanish," in Proc. of the 9th Workshop on Multi-word Expressions, Atlanta, Georgia, USA, 2013, pp. 1–10.

[19] V. P. Rosas, C. Banea, and R. Mihalcea, "Learning Sentiment Lexicons in Spanish," in Proc. of the 8th International Conference on Language Resources and Evaluation (LREC). Istanbul, Turkey: European Language Resources Association (ELRA), 2012, pp. 3077–3081.

[20] J. Brooke, M. Tofiloski, and M. Taboada, "Cross-Linguistic Sentiment Analysis: From English to Spanish," in Proc. of Recent Advances in Natural Language Processing (RANLP). Borovets, Bulgaria: RANLP 2009 Organising Committee / ACL, 2009, pp. 50–54.

[21] M. Taboada, J. Brooke, M. Tofiloski, K. Voll, and M. Stede, "Lexicon-based methods for sentiment analysis," Computational Linguistics, vol. 37, no. 2, 2011, pp. 267–307.

[22] A. Balahur et al., "Sentiment analysis in the news," in Proc. of the 7th International Conference on Language Resources and Evaluation (LREC). Valletta, Malta: European Language Resources Association (ELRA), 2010.

[23] T. Wilson, J. Wiebe, and P. Hoffmann, "Recognizing Contextual Polarity: An Exploration of Features for Phrase-Level Sentiment Analysis," Computational Linguistics, 2009, pp. 399–433.

[24] G. J. Norman et al., "Current Emotion Research in Psychophysiology: The Neurobiology of Evaluative Bivalence," Emotion Review, vol. 3, no. 3, 2011, pp. 349–359.

The Impact of Machine Translation on Sentiment Analysis

Gayane Shalunts*, Gerhard Backfried*, Nicolas Commeignes*

*SAIL LABS Technology GmbH
Vienna, Austria
Email: {gayane.shalunts, gerhard.backfried, nicolas.commeignes}@sail-labs.com

***Abstract*—The article explores the impact of Machine Translation on sentiment analysis, employing the combination of two state-of-the-art tools - the multilingual sentiment analysis tool SentiSAIL and the Machine Translation tool SDL Language Weaver. The original corpora are in German, Russian and Spanish in the domain of general news. The output language of translation is English. Firstly, the work presents the development and evaluation of SentiSAIL features in a newly supported language - Spanish. Further experimental setup reveals that the performance rates of sentiment analysis on the original and translated corpora are comparable. Thus a given tool, performing high quality Machine Translation from a target language to English, can eliminate the necessity to develop specific sentiment analysis resources for that language.**

Keywords–Sentiment analysis; machine translation.

I. INTRODUCTION

Sentiment analysis refers to a classification task in the Natural Language Processing (NLP) community, the goal of which is commonly to determine the polarity (positive/negative) of the input text. Whereas subjectivity analysis deals with the detection of private states (opinions, emotions, sentiments, beliefs, speculations) [1], classifying the textual input as objective/subjective. The main parameters defining the scope of a sentiment analysis approach are the target language, domain and media type (traditional or social media). Due to automation and the ability to process big amounts of data, sentiment analysis has found a broad range of applications in marketing, e.g., monitoring of public opinions of product reviews [2] [3] [4], political science, e.g., observation of public opinions during election campaigns, social science, economics, etc. Generally, sentiment analysis approaches may be divided into lexicon-based and machine-learning-based groups [5]. In machine learning approaches labeled data is employed to train classifiers [5] [6]. The demand of costly labeled data and the narrow context of applicability are the major drawbacks of these methods. Lexicon-based methods use a predefined list of words as features, also referred to as *sentiment dictionary* or *lexicon*, where each word is associated with a specific sentiment [5]. Here, the challenging task is to obtain a sentiment dictionary applicable in various contexts. Thus lexicon-based methods are tuned to cover specific target domains and media types, as traditional media exhibits formal language and social media - colloquial language, slang.

Whereas the research field is very active, the majority of publications are limited to the domains of movie and product reviews in English only. Here a straightforward question arises, if the performance of the state-of-the-art Machine Translation (MT) systems allows to translate an input text in an original language into English and to apply sentiment analysis in English afterwards. The objective of the current work is to evaluate the effect of MT on sentiment analysis. The goal of the evaluation is to compare the performance of the SentiSAIL tool on original German, Russian and Spanish corpora and on the corresponding corpora in English, translated employing the MT tool SDL Language Weaver [7]. The performance of SentiSAIL on the original self-compiled corpora in German and Russian is reported in [8]. The current paper also contributes an equivalent annotated traditional media corpus in Spanish and evaluates the classification of SentiSAIL on it. The comparison examines the impact of two factors on sentiment analysis - the translation noise and the difference of sentiment lexicons in English and original languages. Note that the English sentiment lexicon is well-tested and more extensive than those in other languages, which is likely to lead to better performance in English. The comparison reveals equivalent performance rates of sentiment analysis on original and translated data, leading to a conclusion that the state-of-the-art MT systems can provide an alternative to the costly development of language features to realize sentiment analysis in multiple languages.

SentiSAIL is a multilingual sentiment analysis system [8]. It employed the methodology of the lexicon-based system SentiStrength [9] and expanded it into the domains of general and disaster related news multilingually. The SentiStrength and SentiSAIL features in English, German and Russian are compared in [8] on a self-compiled traditional media corpus, reporting SentiSAIL performance improvement to be slight in English and considerable in German and Russian. SentiSAIL is integrated into the SAIL LABS Media Mining System (MMS) [10], which is a state-of-the-art Open-Source-Intelligence system, incorporating speech and text-processing technologies. Sentiment analysis forms a part of MMS automatic multifaceted processing of multilingual unstructured textual and speech data.

The paper is organized as follows: Section II reviews the literature on the impact of MT on sentiment analysis, as well as sentiment analysis in German, Russian and Spanish. Section III clarifies SentiSAIL methodology and the development of Spanish resources. Section IV presents the experimental setup, performance evaluation and results. And finally, Section V draws conclusions from the work presented.

II. LITERATURE REVIEW

The authors of [11] explore the impact of MT on sentiment analysis in French, German and Spanish. They employ three MT systems for comparison - Bing Translator [12], Google Translate [13] and Moses [14]. An original dataset in English was divided into training and testing sets. Afterwards corresponding training and testing datasets were generated by translating the original English data into French, German and Spanish by the three MT systems mentioned above. Classification models were trained and tested per language in two different experimental scenarios, using unigrams and bigrams as features. Firstly, training and testing datasets were created per language by each translator separately. The performances of the sentiment analysis on original English and translated corpora were comparable. The performance difference reached 8% in the worst case. Secondly, the corresponding training datasets generated by the three translators were combined together, resulting in increase of the noise level and performance drop. The paper concludes that the state-of-the-art MT systems are reliable enough for creating training data for languages other than English.

The approach in [2] experiments with polarity-annotated datasets in English and Turkish from the domain of movie and products reviews. The authors report that the polarity detection task is not affected considerably by the amount of the artificial noise introduced by MT. [15] proposes two approaches for mapping existing subjectivity resources in English to Romanian. The first approach builds the Romanian lexicon by translating the Opinion Finder lexicon [16] using a bilingual dictionary. The second approach generates a subjectivity-annotated corpus in Romanian by projecting annotations from an automatically annotated English corpus. The authors find out that the corpus projections preserve subjectivity more reliably than the lexicon translations. This observation was also made in their previous work, stating that subjectivity is a property associated not with words, but with word meanings [17].

Three further approaches for generating subjectivity resources in a target language from English are presented by [18]. The approaches on Romanian and Spanish show promising results, being comparable to those obtained using manually translated corpora. In the first approach the annotations of the Multi-Perspective Question Answering (MPQA) corpus are automatically translated, yielding subjectivity annotated sentences in Romanian. In the second one, they use the automatically translated entries in the Opinion Finder lexicon to annotate a set of sentences in Romanian. In the third experiment, the direction of translation is reversed to verify the assumption that subjective language can be translated and thus new subjectivity lexicons can be acquired for languages lacking such resources.

Another method to build lexicons for languages with scarce resources is presented by [19]. In this research, the authors apply bootstrapping to generate a subjectivity lexicon for Romanian, starting with a set of seed subjective entries, using electronic bilingual dictionaries and a training set of words.

The authors of [20] translate the MPQA corpus from English into 5 languages - Arabic, French, German, Romanian and Spanish. Their empirical results indicate that including multilingual information while modeling subjectivity is able not only to transfer English resources into other languages, but can also improve subjectivity classification in the source language itself. They showed that an English classifier was improved by using out-of-language features, achieving a 4.9% error reduction in accuracy with respect to using English alone. The work proposed by [3] constructs a polarity co-training system, using the multi-lingual views obtained through the automatic translation of English product-reviews into Chinese.

Further articles address sentiment analysis in languages, examined in the current work - German, Russian and Spanish. A German language sentiment analysis method, called SentimentWortschatz or SentiWS, is presented in [21]. The approach targets the domain of financial newspaper articles and respective blog posts on a German stock index [21]. The sentiment lexicon is developed from the General Inquirer (GI) lexicon [22] by semiautomatic translation into German using Google Translate and is manually revised afterwards. The lexicon post-translation revision included the removal of inappropriate words and addition of words from the finance domain [21]. The usage of the GI lexicon as a base is justified by the fact that it is widely accepted in the sentiment analysis community and has a broad coverage. Another method in German, introduced by [23], targets the domain concerning German celebrities. The approach utilizes the SentiStrength tool [9] and permits the classification of mixed sentiments. Here also the English opinion dictionary was automatically translated into German and manually improved afterwards by two German native speakers.

The publications [4] [24] illustrate the sentiment analysis research in Russian. Authors in [24] propose an approach for domain specific sentiment lexicon extraction in the meta-domain of products and services. [4] describes and evaluates the state-of-the-art sentiment analysis systems in Russian.

The authors of [25] present a lexicon-based sentiment analysis system in Spanish, called Sentitext, which employs three major feature sets - the dictionary of individual words, the dictionary of multiword expressions and the set of context rules. They conclude that the proper management and extensive coverage of multiword expressions is critical for successful textual sentiment analysis. Sentitext is also used in [26] to detect sentiments on Twitter messages in Spanish. [27] describes machine learning technique for opinion mining in blogs. The experimental Spanish corpus was created by their Emotiblog system. The authors of [28] adapt an existing English semantic orientation system [29] to Spanish, comparing several alternative approaches. Their experiments prove that although language-independent methods show decent baseline performance, automation cost is considerable and the development of language-specific knowledge and resources provides the best long-term improvement. [30] introduces a framework, where the Spanish lexicons derived from manually and automatically annotated English lexicons yield an accuracy of 90% and 74% respectively.

III. SENTISAIL METHODOLOGY AND SUPPORT OF SPANISH

The SentiSAIL sentiment analysis tool, introduced in [8], performs processing of both traditional and social media data. The target domains in traditional media are the general news and particularly the coverage of disasters/crises in general news. In addition to English, German and Russian the current version of SentiSAIL supports also Spanish, French and Arabic. In this work we introduce SentiSAIL in Spanish - the development of Spanish resources and the performance evaluation on a self-compiled traditional media corpus (Section IV).

SentiSAIL employs the algorithm of SentiStrength [9]. SentiStrength, like [29], is a lexicon-based approach, using as the main feature list a lexicon of sentiment patterns associated with scores of positive or negative orientation. The positive patterns are weighed in the range [1; 5], the negative ones - [-5; -1] in a step 1, e.g., "charming" 4, "cruel" -4. To account for the formation of diverse words from the same stem (inflection and declension), stemming of the lexicon words is implemented. E.g., "sympath*" will match all the words starting with "sympath", e.g., "sympathize", "sympathizes", "sympathized", "sympathy", "sympathetic", etc. The text to be processed is treated as a Bag of Words, and each word is compared to the predefined stemmed lexicon patterns for matching. Employing unigram sentiment terms as the main feature introduces less noise during translation compared to higher level n-grams. In order to model the structure and semantics of the language observed the following additional feature lists are employed:

Boosters. Sentiment words may be intensified or weakened by words referred to as *boosters*. E.g., "less charming" will weigh 3 and "very cruel" -5.

Negations. It is assumed that negating a positive word inverts the sentiment to negative and weakens it twice, whereas negating a negative word neutralizes the sentiment. E.g., "not charming" scores -2, whereas "isn't cruel" equals 0. The boosters and negations affect up to 2 following words.

Phrases and idioms. We define a *phrase* as a combination of words, expressing sentiment only in the given sequence, e.g., "high quality" 3. An *idiom* is also a combination of words, but unlike a phrase it expresses a figurative, not literal meaning, e.g., "crocodile tears" -2. Idioms and phrases score as a whole, overriding the scores of their component words. The sentiment lexicon comprises the polarity of individual words (*prior polarity*) [31]. The polarity of a word in a sentence (*contextual polarity*) may be different from its prior polarity [31] and is determined in the context of negations, boosters, phrases and idioms.

SentiSAIL, like [32], solves a dual classification task by classifying a text into one of the following 4 classes: positive, negative, mixed (both positive and negative) or neutral (neither positive, nor negative). The dual classification scheme is motivated by the human ability to experience positive and negative emotions simultaneously [33].

The class of the input text is determined as a result of taking the following steps:

1) The sentiment on the granularity level of line is determined by computing a pair of positive/negative scores using a combining algorithm. Three combining algorithms were applied with no significant difference on the final classification accuracy [8]. The algorithms are listed below:

a) *Maximization*. The scores of the most positive and the most negative terms of the line are assigned to its positive and negative scores respectively.

b) *Averaging*. Positive and negative scores of each line are calculated respectively as the average of its all positive and negative word scores.

c) *Aggregation*. Positive and negative scores of each line are obtained from respective aggregation of the scores of all positive and negative words of the line, bounded by the maximum positive and negative values.

2) The sentiment on the granularity level of document is calculated likewise as a pair of positive/negative scores by averaging the pairs of the positive/negative scores of all lines respectively.

3) The final sentiment class of a text is produced by double thresholding of the pair of the positive/negative scores on the granularity level document. The classification of the positive and negative classes is straightforward. Documents passing both thresholds are classified into the mixed class, those failing both thresholds are classified as neutral.

Though SentiStrength comprises the mentioned feature lists in 14 languages, the lexicons in languages other than English are short and lack stemming. The development of the SentiSAIL lexicon in Spanish comprised four stages.

At the first stage the initial SentiStrength short lexicon in Spanish (286 words) is taken as a base and improved. We prefer to revise and expand the lexicon manually, since automation introduces also false hits [28]. A Spanish native speaker went through the SentiStrength lexicon, performing stemming and removing incorrect terms.

At the second stage the patterns from the parallel SentiStrength lexicon in English were translated into Spanish, stemmed and scored manually. At this step automation is not realizable, as the stemmed patterns may not be meaningful words (e.g., sympath*). Though the automatic translation of meaningful words may also be ambiguous due to multiple meanings. In addition weights of equivalent words in different languages may also vary due to cultural factors.

At the third stage additional sentiment words were manually selected and added from the sentiment dictionary generated by [30].

The fourth stage of the lexicon extension aims to cover the domains of general news and natural disasters. A database of 100 articles in Spanish from the target domains was collected from the web with that purpose. Half of the articles were chosen randomly as the training dataset, from which domain-specific sentiment terms were manually compiled and added to the lexicon together with their associated scores. To obtain a richer lexicon articles covering diverse topics were chosen.

As a result SentiSAIL's sentiment lexicon in Spanish grew from the initial 286 to 2654 patterns. Note for comparison that SentiSAIL English lexicon comprises currently 2830 patterns. The development of Spanish resources was concluded by revising and expanding the lists of negations, boosters, phrases and idioms. The support of new languages in SentiSAIL can be achieved by taking steps equivalent to those taken for Spanish feature creation.

SentiSAIL is implemented in Perl. SentiSAIL performance speed is proportional to $log_2 N$, where N is the number of sentiment lexicon patterns in the language processed. Logarithmic performance speed is the result of running binary search on the sentiment lexicon. As SentiSAIL is typically deployed in a near real-time environment, high speed is a requirement.

IV. Evaluation and Results

Evaluating sentiment analysis systems is challenging, since there is no single ground truth. Each person classifies the observed text into one of the available sentiment classes depending on his/her cultural and educational background, age, political views, current mood and emotional state, etc. Thus the relation of the average inter-annotator agreement rate to

TABLE I. PERFORMANCE EVALUATION OF SENTISAIL IN SPANISH.

	Annotator 1	Annotator 2	Annotator 3	Average
Training set				
Annotator 1	-	76%	81%	**78%**
Annotator 2	-	-	77%	
SentiSAIL (Aggregation)	73%	65%	72%	70%
SentiSAIL (Averaging)	79%	71%	72%	74%
SentiSAIL (Maximization)	83%	73%	76%	**77.3%**
SentiSAIL (Maximization, SentiStrength features)	47%	41%	44%	44%
Testing set				
Annotator 1	-	77%	78%	**76%**
Annotator 2	-	-	73%	
SentiSAIL (Aggregation)	73%	68%	75%	72%
SentiSAIL (Averaging)	73%	66%	71%	70%
SentiSAIL (Maximization)	77%	74%	75%	**75.3%**
SentiSAIL (Maximization, SentiStrength features)	46%	43%	50%	46.3%

the average SentiSAIL-annotator agreement rate is chosen as an evaluation criterion for SentiSAIL. If the mentioned average rates are comparable, the performance of SentiSAIL system is considered as good as that of a human annotator.

The experimental setup comprises two stages. The first stage evaluates SentiSAIL's performance of the newly supported language - Spanish. The objective of the second stage is to compare SentiSAIL performance on the original German and Russian datasets, illustrated in [8], and on the Spanish dataset, introduced newly in this paper to the performance on the parallel corpora translated into English. The translations were performed automatically using the SDL Language Weaver (5.3.32 release), which is a statistical state-of-the-art MT tool [7]. The statistical translation models are generated automatically by applying machine learning technique on parallel collections of human translations.

The performance evaluation of SentiSAIL is reported in [8] on self-collected and labeled trilingual text corpus. The training dataset includes 32 news articles in English, 32 - in German and 48 - in Russian. The testing dataset comprises 50 news articles in each language. Since SentiSAIL is a lexicon-based method (as opposed to a machine learning based one), the training dataset was employed to extract additional domain-specific sentiment words manually, but not to train a classifier. We introduce an equivalent corpus in Spanish, comprising 100 traditional media articles, divided equally into training and testing datasets.

Table I details the experiments on the Spanish corpus. Identical experiments are conducted on training and testing datasets separately to show that the performance rates on the training dataset and unfamiliar data are comparable. Both training and testing datasets were labeled by 3 annotators by sentiment class labels (Positive, Negative, Neutral, Mixed). The average agreement rate among 3 annotators on training texts reached 78% (Table I). The following 3 lines in Table I present the agreement rates of SentiSAIL with the annotators, using the line scoring algorithms Aggregation, Averaging and Maximization in sequence. The best scoring algorithm is Maximization with 77.33% rate, which is competitive with the average human agreement rate of 78%. The next row in Table I shows that the improvement of the Spanish lexicon by SentiSAIL over the initial SentiStrength lexicon is considerable, having improved the performance rate from 44% to 77.33%. The main reason is that the initial SentiStrength lexicon is very short (286 words) and lacks stemming. The majority of sentiment terms are not detected and the classification is neutralized (42 out of 50 texts were classified as neutral). SentiSAIL achieves equivalent performance accuracy while running the same set of experiments on a previously unseen dataset (Testing set section in Table I).

The second stage of the experimental setup evaluates the impact of translation on the trilingual corpus. Since the Maximizaton algorithm scored the highest, it is chosen in the further experiments. Table II shows that the average inter-annotator agreement rate on the German training dataset scored 79.17% and SentiSAIL-annotators average agreement rate even outperforms it with 81.25% [8]. Running the equivalent experiment in English, i.e., performing sentiment analysis on the German into English translated corpus and using the English sentiment lexicon, yielded exactly the same average performance accuracy - 81.25% (Table II). Whereas the average performance rate on the original Russian corpus scored 82.99%, the equivalent rate on the English translated corpus decreased slightly to 80.9% (Table II). The third portion in Table II reports the empirical results on the newly supported language - Spanish. The average SentiSAIL-annotators agreement rate scored 77.33%, which is almost as high as the inter-annotator rate (78%). The average accuracy on the parallel English corpus recorded the highest decrease of 5% among 3 translated languages.

Table III presents the results of the identical experimental setup as Table II, but on testing datasets. Here the performance rate drop as an outcome of English translation of the trilingual corpora remains within negligible 1%. Table III also shows that SentiSAIL analysis accuracy on unfamiliar and training data are comparable.

V. CONCLUSION

Firstly, the work presented the development and evaluation of Spanish resources for the multilingual sentiment analysis tool SentiSAIL. Secondly, it explored empirically the impact of MT on sentiment analysis performance. The translation quality of the SDL Language Weaver allowed to achieve equivalent performance rates on original and translated parallel corpora while performing bipolar sentiment analysis by SentiSAIL. The original corpora were compiled in the traditional media domain in German, Russian and Spanish. The translation output language was English, supported by the majority of the state-of-the-art sentiment analysis systems. The performance decrease in the worst case remained within negligible 5%. The

TABLE II. PERFORMANCE EVALUATION ON THE ORIGINAL GERMAN, RUSSIAN, SPANISH TRAINING DATASETS AND THE EQUIVALENT ENGLISH TRANSLATIONS [8].

	Annotator 1	Annotator 2	Annotator 3	Average
		German training set		
Annotator 1	-	78.1%	79.7%	**79.2%**
Annotator 2	-	-	79.7%	
German original	92.2%	73.4%	78.2%	81.3%
English translation	92.2%	73.4%	78.2%	81.3%
		Russian training set		
Annotator 1	-	84.4%	79.2%	**82%**
Annotator 2	-	-	82.3%	
Russian original	86.5%	84.4%	78.1%	83%
English translation	85.4%	82.3%	75%	80.9%
		Spanish training set		
Annotator 1	-	76%	81%	**78%**
Annotator 2	-	-	77%	
Spanish original	83%	73%	76%	77.3%
English translation	78%	70%	69%	72.3%

TABLE III. PERFORMANCE EVALUATION ON THE ORIGINAL GERMAN, RUSSIAN, SPANISH TESTING DATASETS AND THE EQUIVALENT ENGLISH TRANSLATIONS [8].

	Annotator 1	Annotator 2	Annotator 3	Average
		German testing set		
Annotator 1	-	85%	76%	**76.7%**
Annotator 2	-	-	69%	
German original	81%	80%	77%	79.3%
English translation	80%	83%	72%	78.3%
		Russian testing set		
Annotator 1	-	93%	93%	**92.7%**
Annotator 2	-	-	92%	
Russian original	92%	88%	90%	90%
English translation	90%	89%	89%	89.3%
		Spanish testing set		
Annotator 1	-	77%	78%	**76%**
Annotator 2	-	-	73%	
Spanish original	77%	74%	75%	75.3%
English translation	76%	71%	80%	75.7%

conclusion drawn as an outcome of the extensive experimental setup is that substituting multilingual sentiment analysis by English sentiment analysis via MT may be an acceptable alternative, leading to inconsiderable performance drop. Such a setup may be advantageous when lacking the appropriate resources for a particular language and when fast deployment is crucial. In practical terms, the trade-off between the cost of the MT system and the effort for the development of language specific resources needs to be taken into consideration.

Future work will be in the direction of extending the list of languages further and evaluating the performance on data from multilingual social media platforms.

REFERENCES

[1] A. Montoyo, P. Martnez-Barco, and A. Balahur, "Subjectivity and sentiment analysis: An overview of the current state of the area and envisaged developments," Decision Support Systems, vol. 53, no. 4, 2012, pp. 675 – 679.

[2] E. Demirtas and M. Pechenizkiy, "Cross-lingual Polarity Detection with Machine Translation," in Proceedings of the Second International Workshop on Issues of Sentiment Discovery and Opinion Mining, ser. WISDOM '13. New York, NY, USA: ACM, 2013, pp. 9:1–9:8.

[3] X. Wan, "Co-training for cross-lingual sentiment classification," in Proceedings of the Joint Conference of the 47th Annual Meeting of the ACL and the 4th International Joint Conference on Natural Language Processing of the AFNLP (ACL-IJCNLP). Suntec, Singapore: ACL, 2009, pp. 235–243.

[4] I. Chetviorkin and N. Loukachevitch, "Evaluating Sentiment Analysis Systems in Russian," in Proceedings of the 4th Biennial International Workshop on Balto-Slavic Natural Language Processing, Sofia, Bulgaria, 2013, pp. 12–17.

[5] P. Gonçalves, M. Araújo, F. Benevenuto, and M. Cha, "Comparing and combining sentiment analysis methods," in Proceedings of the 1st ACM Conference on Online Social Networks (COSN 2013). Boston, USA: ACM, 2013, pp. 27–38.

[6] B. Pang, L. Lee, and S. Vaithyanathan, "Thumbs up?: sentiment classification using machine learning techniques." in Proceedings of the ACL conference on Empirical methods in natural language processing (EMNLP '02), Philadelphia, PA, USA, 2002, pp. 79–86.

[7] R. Soricu, N. Bach, and Z. Wang, "The SDL Language Weaver Systems in the WMT12 Quality Estimation Shared Task," in Proceedings of the 7th Workshop on Statistical Machine Translation. Montreal, Canada: 2012 Association for Computational Linguistics, 2012, pp. 145–151.

[8] G. Shalunts and G. Backfried, "SentiSAIL: Sentiment Analysis in English, German and Russian," in Proceedings of the 11th International Conference on Machine Learning and Data Mining, ser. MLDM '15, Hamburg, Germany, 2015, pp. 87–97.

[9] M. Thelwall, K. Buckley, G. Paltoglou, D. Cai, and A. Kappas, "Sentiment Strength Detection in Short Informal Text," J. American Society for Information Science and Technology, vol. 61, no. 12, Dec. 2010, pp. 2544–2558.

[10] G. Backfried et al., "Open source intelligence in disaster management," in Proceedings of the European Intelligence and Security Informatics Conference (EISIC). Odense, Denmark: IEEE Computer Society, 2012, pp. 254–258.

[11] A. Balahur and M. Turchi, "Multilingual Sentiment Analysis Using Machine Translation?" in Proceedings of the 3rd Workshop in Computational Approaches to Subjectivity and Sentiment Analysis, ser. WASSA '12. Stroudsburg, PA, USA: Association for Computational Linguistics,

2012, pp. 52–60.

[12] "Bing Translator," http://www.bing.com/translator, accessed: 2016-07-31.

[13] "Google Translate," https://translate.google.com, accessed: 2016-07-31.

[14] P. Koehn et al., Moses: Open Source Toolkit for Statistical Machine Translation. Association for Computational Linguistics, 6 2007, pp. 177–180.

[15] R. Mihalcea, C. Banea, and J. Wiebe, "Learning Multilingual Subjective Language via Cross-Lingual Projections," in Proceedings of the Association for Computational Linguistics (ACL), Prague, Czech Republic, 2007, pp. 976–983.

[16] T. Wilson, J. Wiebe, and P. Hoffmann, "Recognizing Contextual Polarity in Phrase-Level Sentiment Analysis," in Proceedings of HLT/EMNLP, Vancouver, Canada, 2005, pp. 347–354.

[17] J. Wiebe and R. Mihalcea, "Word sense and subjectivity," in Proceedings of the 21st International Conference on Computational Linguistics and the 44th Annual Meeting of the Association for Computational Linguistics. Sydney, Australia: ACL, 2006, pp. 1065–1072.

[18] C. Banea, R. Mihalcea, J. Wiebe, and S. Hassan, "Multilingual subjectivity analysis using machine translation," in Proceedings of the Conference on Empirical Methods in Natural Language Processing (EMNLP '08). Honolulu, Hawaii: ACL, 2008, pp. 127–135.

[19] C. Banea, J. M. Wiebe, and R. Mihalcea, "A bootstrapping method for building subjectivity lexicons for languages with scarce resources," 2008.

[20] C. Banea, R. Mihalcea, and J. Wiebe, "Multilingual subjectivity: Are more languages better?" in Proceedings of the 23rd International Conference on Computational Linguistics (COLING '10). Beijing, China: ACL, 2010, pp. 28–36.

[21] R. Remus, U. Quasthoff, and G. Heyer, "Sentiws - a german-language resource for sentiment analysis," in Proceedings of the 7th conference on International Language Resources and Evaluation (LREC), Valletta, Malta, 2010, pp. 1168–1171.

[22] P. J. Stone, D. C. Dunphy, M. S. Smith, and D. M. Ogilvie, The General Inquirer: A Computer Approach to Content Analysis. Cambridge, MA: MIT Press, 1966.

[23] S. Momtazi, "Fine-grained german sentiment analysis on social media," in Proceedings of the 8th International Conference on Language Resources and Evaluation (LREC). Istanbul, Turkey: European Language Resources Association (ELRA), 2012, pp. 1215–1220.

[24] I. Chetviorkin and N. Loukachevitch, "Extraction of Russian Sentiment Lexicon for Product Meta-Domain," in Proceedings of the 24th International Conference on Computational Linguistics (COLING), Bombay, India, 2012, pp. 593–610.

[25] A. Moreno-Ortiz, C. Perez-Hernandez, and M. A. Del-Olmo, "Managing multiword expressions in a lexicon-based sentiment analysis system for spanish," in Proceedings of the 9th Workshop on Multi-word Expressions, Atlanta, Georgia, USA, 2013, pp. 1–10.

[26] A. Moreno-Ortiz and C. P. Hernández, "Lexicon-based sentiment analysis of twitter messages in spanish," Procesamiento del Lenguaje Natural, vol. 50, 2013, pp. 93–100.

[27] E. Boldrini, A. Balahur, P. Martnez-Barco, and A. Montoyo, "Emotiblog: an annotation scheme for emotion detection and analysis in non-traditional textual genres," in Proceedings of the 5th International Conference on Data Mining (DMIN). Las-Vegas, USA: CSREA Press, 2009, pp. 491–497.

[28] J. Brooke, M. Tofiloski, and M. Taboada, "Cross-linguistic sentiment analysis: From English to Spanish," in Proceedings of Recent Advances in Natural Language Processing (RANLP). Borovets, Bulgaria: RANLP 2009 Organising Committee / ACL, 2009, pp. 50–54.

[29] M. Taboada, J. Brooke, M. Tofiloski, K. Voll, and M. Stede, "Lexicon-based methods for sentiment analysis," Computational Linguistics, vol. 37, no. 2, 2011, pp. 267–307.

[30] R. M. Veronica Perez Rosas, Carmen Banea, "Learning Sentiment Lexicons in Spanish," in Proceedings of the 8th International Conference on Language Resources and Evaluation (LREC). Istanbul, Turkey: European Language Resources Association (ELRA), 2012, pp. 3077–3081.

[31] M. M. S. Missen, M. Boughanem, and G. Cabanac, "Opinion mining: Reviewed from word to document level," Social Network Analysis and Mining, vol. 3, no. 1, 2013, pp. 107–125.

[32] T. Wilson, J. Wiebe, and P. Hoffmann, "Recognizing contextual polarity: An exploration of features for phrase-level sentiment analysis," Computational Linguistics, 2009, pp. 399–433.

[33] G. J. Norman et al., "Current emotion research in psychophysiology: The neurobiology of evaluative bivalence," Emotion Review, vol. 3, no. 3, 2011, pp. 349–359.

Car Sales Forecasting Using Artificial Neural Networks and Analytical Hierarchy Process

Case Study: Kia and Hyundai Corporations in the USA

Danial Shahrabi Farahani
Faculty of Management, Tehran University
Tehran, Iran
shahrabidanial@ut.ac.ir

Mansour Momeni
Faculty of Management, Tehran University
Tehran, Iran
mmomeni@ut.ac.ir

Nader Sayyed Amiri
Entrepreneurship Faculty, Tehran University
Tehran, Iran
nadersa@ut.ac.ir

Abstract - **In this study, we evaluate different effective factors related to marketing and sales and discuss the various prediction methods. The field of this study is the car industry and the tools used for classification, comparison and weight determination is the Analytical Hierarchy Process (AHP). Artificial Neural Networks are used for identifying the architecture and shaping the process of prediction. In order to do so, using a questionnaire presented to experts in the field, the factors affecting car sales in North America were identified and the processed weights obtained from these opinions were fed to the neural network as input, so that, ultimately, by teaching the network through different algorithms, the optimal solution can be obtained. The conceptual model of the research first identifies the factors affecting sales and then tries to determine the interconnection among the data. In order to compare the performance of this method, we needed a valid and established measure so that we can assess the methods based on it. Therefore, linear and exponential regression methods were selected to compare the degree of error and to obtain a more desirable final output which is closer to reality. The obtained result indicates the successful performance of the neural network compared to other selected methods and it was found that it has a lower Minimum Square Error (MSE) compared to others.**

Keywords- car sale prediction; analytical hierarchy process; artificial neural networks; feed forward network; multi-layer back propagation neural network; learning algorithm

I. INTRODUCTION

Management has always been significant for people, companies, and governments. Each one of these groups has dealt with this issue somehow and they try to maximize their wealth. Hence, they have to make the right decisions, one of which is the decision regarding (future) investments. This study evaluates the utilization of neural networks for predicting sales in the car industry and compares it with reality. It justifies the use of neural networks in this industry for the prediction process. Generally, car manufacturing industries include design, development, manufacturing, marketing and sale of different equipment for motor vehicles. The set of companies and factories involved in design, manufacturing, marketing, and sale of motor vehicles are a part of this industry. In 2008, more than 70 million motor vehicles including ordinary cars and commercial vehicles were manufactured around the world. In 2007, a total number of 71.9 million cars were sold in the world, with 22.9 million sold in Europe, 21.4 million sold in Asia and Pacific Region, 19.4 million sold in the US and Canada, 4.4 million sold in Latin America, 2.4 million sold in the Middle East, and 1.4 million sold in Africa. When the market was experiencing a recession in the US and Japan, Asia and South America significantly grew and got stronger. Moreover, it seems that large markets in Russia, Brazil, India and China have experienced a rapid growth. The car industry, as one of the largest industries in the world hosting a large amount of people, financial and time resources, is in dire need of accurate predictions of its future and its competitors in order to reach big and sensitive decisions. Perhaps one of the biggest concerns of the managers and manufacturers in the car industry and the investors in this field is the prediction of product sales and planning for the future manufacturing volume. If a manager can have a more accurate prediction regarding the future sales volume and car demand, they can absolutely optimize the investment volume, recruit workforce and optimally use time to reach optimal decisions and carry out macro strategies.

II. THE CONCEPTUAL MODEL OF THE STUDY

Five initial exogenous variables were used as the input for the neural network and the network was prepared for the entrance of the sixth variable; namely, the effect of season and month on buying behavior (see Figure 1). Then, the effect of the month was normalized and used as the main input for the network. Weights affecting the car sales were already extracted in previous studies; however, due to the specific geographical focus of this study, we needed to generate these effective weights. Therefore, the factors were extracted from electronic databases, particularly two prestigious studies in the car industry, and, after generating them and presenting questionnaires to experts in the same geographical region and integrating the sum of the weights, the viewpoints were ordered using analytical hierarchy process. In order to be used in other studies, the questionnaires were classified into sub-factors for each factor, too and the weights of the head factors were introduced into the system of the study. Regarding the introduction of seasonal and monthly effects, by identifying and analyzing high-sale and low-sale months and ranking these sites using the Excel software application, the months were ranked based on the sales volume from 2010 to 2015 and then they were normalized using Equation 1:

$$S_{iN} = \frac{S_i - S_{min}}{S_{max} - S_{min}} \quad (1)$$

Where

S_{max}: Equals the maximum value for each entry;

S_{min}: Equals the minimum value for each entry;

S_i: Is the value of the ith entry.

S_{iN}: Is the normalized value of the ith entry.

Due to the stability of criteria selection for humans, the data arising from individual judgment and their taste in time have stability and solidity. For instance, an individual who cares about safety, based on personality stability theory and selection stability, is very likely not to change his mind about his choice in the next five years. Therefore, after using fixed weights, due to the dynamic nature of neural networks, this study requires a dynamic measure for better training the network. In order to reach this, the seasonal and monthly data are used as the sixth variable for making the entries dynamic. The method for extracting monthly data for each country is different, since the coefficients of the months are different in each country. In the following, the monthly weights extraction process for the USA and the normalization method for these weights are discussed in detail [2].

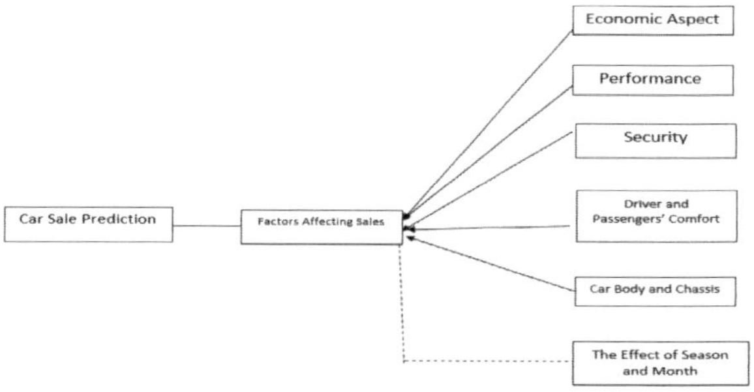

Figure 1: The Conceptual Model of the Study

The schematic conceptual model of the study is devised and presented for representation and simplification of the inputs and objectives framework. The conceptual model in this study is represented by expressing the factors affecting sales, categorization and the desired objective.

III. METHODOLOGY

Regarding objectives, this study searches for a scientific process for improving decision making about the future of the car industry, the time consumed, the energy, and the investment, as well as preventing the untimely manufacturing, which interferes with the economic cycle and leads to the loss of the industry. This can be used in governmental and non-governmental sectors, whether from the viewpoint of industrial policy making or the viewpoint of enterprise profitability. Regarding the type and nature, this study is a descriptive-analytical one since it evaluates and analyzes the current state of the market.

In this study, at first, the factors affecting car sales are identified based on previous studies and researches and then, these are presented to a panel of experts in order to be ranked.

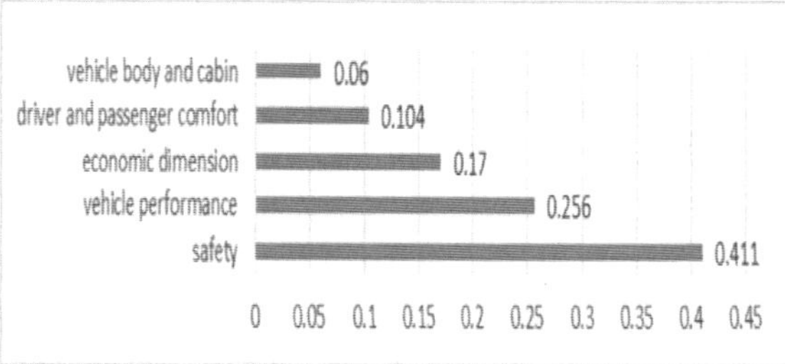

Figure 2: The Weights of the Factors Affecting Sales Obtained from the Software

Then, the semi-processed information is sent to the Expert Choice software application for final and ultimate processing and after obtaining the output as weights, they are presented along with the main input data to the neural network so that, while teaching the main data and using these weights, a better forecasting for the future can be obtained. Finally, the prediction data is compared to the real data so that the validity of the developed model can be measured. The statistical population of the study includes the market for the products of Kia and Hyundai corporations in the US and Canada from 2010 until 2015. This information is extracted from the formal electronic databases supervising the American industries as well as the databases of Kia and Hyundai corporations. In order to gather the required data for the theoretical sections (e.g. previous studies or introduction to artificial neural networks), the library method (using online databases, books, dissertations, and online articles) was used and for gathering the data related to the weights, the expert panel method was used and the opinions were integrated using the relevant software applications [8].

IV. DATA ANALYSIS

In this section, the multi-layer back propagation neural network is applied on the sales data for Kia and Hyundai corporations in the US and Canada from 2010 until 2015 in order to propose a model for predicting the car sales based on artificial intelligence. The 6 determining variables for car sales (economic, dimension, performance, safety, driver and passengers' comfort, dimensions, size, and the appearance of the car as well as the seasonal effects on sale) were used in two groups as the input for the network. In the first group, which includes the first five variables mentioned, the data was extracted using questionnaire from the expert panel and was fed into the group analytical hierarchy process. The cumulative results obtained from the Expert Choice software application were considered as the first group of inputs. The system was taught using these weights and was prepared for the second group of inputs, which include the seasonal effects on sale. The inputs of the artificial neural network have been normalized so that they can be between 0 and 1, and then they are fed into the neural network. In this study, a neural network with two hidden layers is used and the different network parameters (such as, the number of neurons, the type of network training algorithm, the fraction of the data tested by the network, and so on) were optimized using the neural network branch of MATLAB software application. Since the neural network toolboxes in MATLAB software application are intended to be used in ordinary and non-professional conditions and have a higher error compared to the manual configuration condition, this study uses the input codes obtained after performing a huge number of tests. In order to arrive at opinions relevant to the industry as well as the customers, this study uses the opinions of individuals who were unbiased and non-stakeholders while related to the car industry so that they can add both versions of an opinion to the questionnaire [3]. Table I represents the target data which include the sales volume of Kia and Hyundai cars in the USA from 2010 to 2015.

In order to extract the monthly effective data and the seasonal effect on buying behavior, we ranked the high-sale months using data classification in Excel software application and then the obtained rankings were normalized. This data, presented in Table II, is the input variables of the study for the artificial neural network to teach it and determine implicit relations between the network inputs and the network outputs. We use the term "implicit" because, in order to discover the relations among the data, the artificial neural network assesses the numbers in its black box. Hence, finding the exact relations and allocated weights by the network itself is highly complex, even impossible due to being highly time-consuming task.

TABLE I: SALES VOLUME DATA FOR KIA AND HYUNDAY CARS IN THE US

Month	2010	2011	2012	2013	2014
January	52626	65003	78211	80015	81016
February	58056	76339	96189	93816	90221
March	77524	106052	127233	117431	121782
April	74059	108828	109814	110871	119783
May	80476	107426	118790	120685	130994
June	83111	104253	115139	115543	118051
July	89525	105065	110095	115009	119320
August	86068	99693	111127	118126	124670
September	76627	87660	108130	93105	96638
October	73855	90092	92723	93309	94775
November	67324	86617	94542	101416	98608
December	75246	94155	98613	96636	110094

TABLE II: CLASSIFICATION AND RANKING OF HIGH-SALE TO LOW-SALE MONTHS

	Ranking in Each Year				
Month	2010	2011	2012	2013	2014
January	12	12	12	12	12
February	11	11	9	9	11
March	5	3	1	3	3
April	8	1	6	6	4
May	4	2	2	1	1
June	3	5	3	4	6
July	1	4	5	5	5
August	2	6	4	2	2
September	6	9	7	11	9
October	9	8	11	10	10
November	10	10	10	7	8
December	7	7	8	8	7

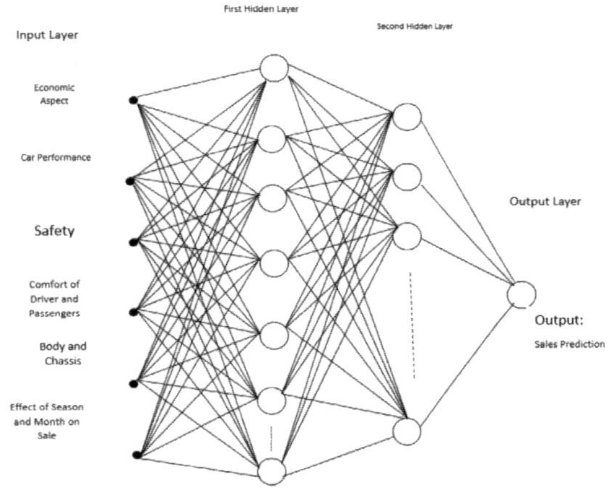

Figure 3: The Schematic Representation of the Neural Network Formed in the Study with Expected Inputs and Output

Due to the presence of an output at the end for predicting sales in each country (The US and Canada), a neuron is placed in the output layer of the neural network. The most important advantage of using this method is that even if the training accuracy for the network is not high, the network still keeps its generality [7]. Therefore, generally, the neural network involves six inputs and an output with two hidden layers. A schematic representation of the utilized neural network is presented in Fig.3.

The research data is categorized into three sections including training data, test data and evaluation data. The training data is simply used for adjusting the weights and biases of the neural network, while the test data is not involved in the training process of the network and it is just used for the generalization test of the network. The evaluation data is used for testing the generalization of the network in each stage of network training and then it is used for adjusting the network's weights and biases. MSE is used as a function of the neural network performance. In order to improve the performance of the network, the cross validation process is used for interrupting the training of the network. In this process, if the error of the network over the evaluation data after n times subsequent trainings is not improved, then the network training will be stopped in order to maintain the generalizability of the network. This study uses $n = 6$ as the criterion for stopping the network training. Another criterion used for maintaining the generalizability of the neural network is the gradient of the network in each repetition and, in this study, in order to reach the desired results, 1×10^{-5} is adopted [5].

V. Analyzing the Sensitivity of the Neural Network

In this section, the best algorithm for training the neural network and determining the number of neurons in the hidden layers is selected. Moreover, the sensitivity analysis is carried out on the fraction of data to be used as the test and evaluation data sets. Therefore, it has been tried to optimize the parameters of the neural network based on the network error.

VI. Selecting the Best Pattern for Network Training

The number of neurons in the first and second hidden layers are considered to be 10 and 1, respectively. By changing the network training algorithm, the training error over the test data is measured. The error obtained over the test data is used for selecting the network training algorithm based on a network with higher generalization capability [4]. Since the initial weights and biases of the network are selected randomly and these values affect the performance of the network, the neural network was carried out 30 times for each algorithm and the minimum error in these 30 runs was selected as a criterion for measuring the appropriate algorithm for training the network [6]. Accordingly, the results are presented in Fig.4.

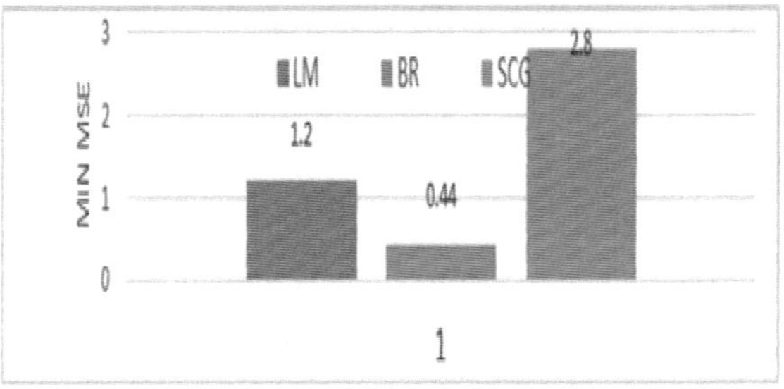

Figure 4: MSE Minimum Value over the Test Data for Different Neural Network Training Algorithms

Based on the results presented in Fig.4, training algorithms of *Trainlm* and *Trainbr* have the lowest error-based on the mean error MSE. Since the *Trainbr* algorithm has the lowest error, it is used for training the network.

VII. Determining the Optimal Value for the Number of Neurons in the First and Second Hidden Layers

Determining the number of neurons in hidden layers is of particular significance in the structure of neural networks. The presence of huge number of neurons in hidden layers will lead to the higher complexity of the neural network and increasing number of its adjustable parameters (weights and biases). Whereas, the presence of a fewer number of neurons in hidden layers can lead to a situation where the neural network is not able to efficiently describe the relations present between the inputs and output of the network. In order to determine the optimal number of neurons in the first and second hidden layers, by keeping all the other parameters constant, the first and second hidden layers vary between 5 and 12 and between 1 and 10, respectively, and the value of the minimum error (MSE) for each state over the test data is calculated. This computational tolerance is presented in Table III, along with extracting the optimal solution.

VIII. The Results Obtained from Training the Neural Network

Based on the sensitivity analysis carried out in the previous section and the adjustment of different parameters for the neural network, the following values are selected for the neural network and in order to reach the best results over the neural network, the network is run multiple times in order to obtain the lowest value of MSE.

TABLE III. COMPUTATIONAL TOLERANCE

Network Training Algorithm	*Trainbr*
The Fraction of Training, Test, and Evaluation Data	15%, 15%, and 70%
Neurons in the First Layer	10
Neurons in the Second Layer	1

After training the optimized neural network, Fig.5 is obtained for the error of the network. It is worth mentioning that after 8 repetitions from the beginning of network training, variations in the values of network parameters significantly reduced, indicating the convergence of the network in low repetitions. It should also

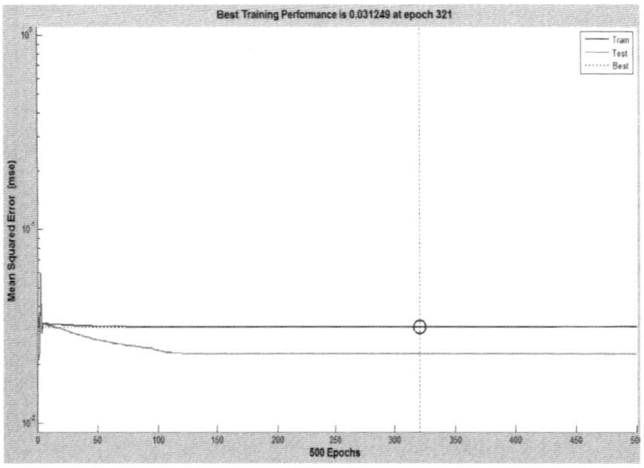

Figure 5: Error Curve for Optimized Neural Network over the Training and Test Data

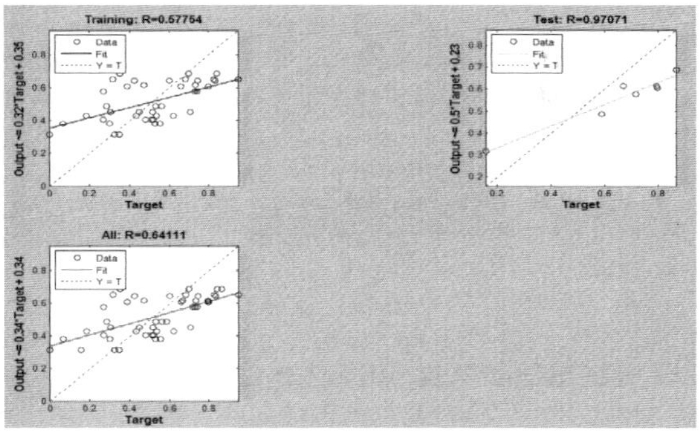

Figure 6: The Curve for Correlation among the Factors and Following the Regression Pattern

be said that the network training is carried out in Batch mode, which means that the selection of weights and biases of the network is done after applying all the training data. Another method is to update the weights and biases of the network after applying each individual input. In Fig.5, we trained and optimized the network using the Bayesian command. As mentioned before, the method with lowest error for optimizing the problem is to use the training algorithm. Perhaps, in most cases, the Levenberg-Marquardt (LM) algorithm provides a suitable solution. However, regarding the current study which differs from other studies, due to limited data at the input level and the lack of rich data for forming the network, the Bayesian algorithm provides a better optimization.

In the fields of management and economics, it is highly common to use the regression method for predicting a factor or some factors in the future. The regression method

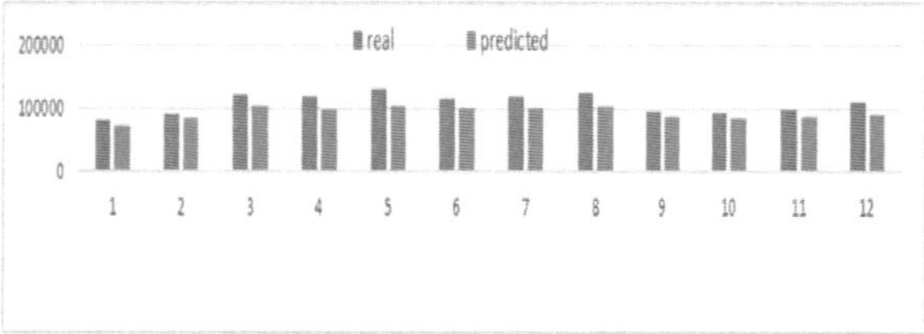

Figure 7: Comparing the Prediction of the Neural Networks with the Real Values of the Data

TABLE IV: COMPARING THE RESULTS FOR THE PERFORMANCEOF THE NEURAL NETWORK vs CONVENTIONAL PREDICTION METHODS

MSE		
Artificial Neural Network	Linear Regression	Exponential Regression
0.44 × 10 e8	1.64 × 10 e8	37 × 10 e8

uses data trends to predict the next step of the data. Generally, regression is classified as linear or non-linear or exponential. In this study, in order to evaluate the performance and efficiency of the neural network, the prediction data are compared to the real data as well as the data predicted by the regression method. The linear regression is closer to reality compared to the non-linear regression [10]. In order to facilitate the comparison, the data are simplified based on 10 to the power of 8 [1]. As can be inferred from Table IV, each model or method providing lower error compared to the real data, is more reliable and usable. In this study, the neural network is used as a pioneer network in minimizing the prediction error. Fig.7 shows how much the error of this claim is compared to the real data.

IX. CONCLUSIONS AND RECOMMENDATIONS

In this study, neural networks were used for predicting car sales. The important point and the differentiating aspect of this study compared to previous studies is using limited data which is considered one of the weaknesses of neural networks. However, at the end, with the proper architecture and training and using an optimal algorithm, this study was successful in optimizing this network even for limited data. The results obtained over training, test, and evaluation data indicate the capability of the neural network as one of the artificial intelligence methods for accurate prediction of car sales. Using the simulation carried out for the neural network and determining the method for changing car sales based on different parameters, it was concluded that the neural network is able to efficiently predict the normal trend of car sales based on the six factors of price, performance, safety, appearance, and comfort as well as the effects of months on the sale volume. Accordingly, it was concluded that based on the data utilized, the highest impact from car aspects on the sale are for safety and generally, the sales variations are influenced by the season and month. The trained neural network can be used in the future as a criterion for predicting car sales over limited data. Accordingly, before manufacturing the desired car, the trained neural network can be used to determine if this manufactured car attracts enough demand and sale capability or not or the investment will be influenced by demand risk loss. Based on the positive performance of neural network in this study, it is recommended to compare the artificial neural network and fitting curves for subjects with limited and poor data [9].

REFERENCES

[1] Abaspour, M., & Naseri, M. (2005). Proposing a Model for Predicting Share Prices of Iran Khodro Company Using Neural Networks. Paper presented at the The Fourth International Conference of Industrial Engineering

[2] Deepak Singhal, K. S., & Swarup. (2011). Electricity Price Forecasting Using Artificial Neural Networks. International Journal Of Electrical Power & Energy Systems, 33(3), 550-555.

[3] Firouzian, M., Mohammadian, M., & Ghafourian, H. (2006). Weight Allocation and Ranking of Factors Affecting Customer Satisfaction in Car Industry Using Analytical Hierarchy Process (AHP). Management Culture, 13, 37-64.

[4] Hanafizadeh, P. (2014). Artificial Intelligence and Fuzzy Logic. Tehran, Iran: Termeh Publications

[5] Hanafizadeh, P., Poursoltani, H., & Saketi, P. (2007). Comparative Study of Prediction Capability of Artificial Neural Networks Using Early Interruption Method and Autoregressive Time Series Process in Estimating Inflation Rate. Journal of Economic Research, 42(2), 25-36.

[6] Hudsun, Beale, M., Hagan, M., & Demuth, H. (2015). Neural Network Toolbox.

[7] Menhaj, M. (2008). Fundamentals of Neural Networks. Tehran, Iran: Publications of Amir Kabir Industrial University

[8] Sato, Y. (2005). Questionnaire Design for Survey Research; Employing Weighting Method. ISAHP. Honolulu Hawaii. Graduate School of Policy Science.

[9] Zarei, M., Khademi Zare, H., & Fakhrzad, M. B. (2013). Optimizing Energy Consumption Basket and Clustering Residential Buildings by Improving Fuzzy Neural Network through AHP Architecture and Weights. General Management Research, 6(19), 129-152

[10] Zou, H. F., Xia, G. P., Yang, F. T., & Wang, H. Y. (2007). An Investigation And Comparison Of Artificial Neural Network And Time Series Models For Chinese Food Grain Price Forecasting. Neurocomputing, 70 (16–18), 2913–2923.

Predicting Candidate Uptake For Online Vacancies

Corné de Ruijt[†‡], Sandjai Bhulai [†], Han Rusman[‡] and Leon Willemsens[‡]

[†]Faculty of Sciences
Vrije Universiteit
Amsterdam, the Netherlands
Email: s.bhulai@vu.nl
[‡]Endouble
The Netherlands
Email: {Corne, Han, Leon}@endouble.com

***Abstract*—The Internet has substantially changed how organizations market their vacancies and how job seekers look for a job. Although this has many benefits such as simplifying the communication, it can also cause problems. Some vacancies are obtaining more applications than can be handled by the recruitment department, while other vacancies may remain unfulfilled for a long time. Data analysis might reveal insights into what strategies are effective to solve these problems. To analyze these problems we therefore consider the predictability of the number of applications per vacancy per week, and to which extend this can be controlled using online marketing campaigns. After testing the predictive quality of several machine learning methods on a data set from a large Dutch organization we found that a Random Forest model gives the best predictions. Although these predictions provide insights into what recruiters and hiring managers can expect when publishing a vacancy, the error of these predictions can be quite large. Also, although the effect of online marketing campaigns on the number of applications is significant, predicting the effect from historic data causes problems due to collinearity and bias in the usage of these campaigns: a campaign is also a response to a small number of applicants who responded to the vacancy. Nevertheless, these predictions are insightful for both recruiters and hiring manager to manage their expectations when publishing a vacancy.**

***Keywords*–Recruitment analytics; HR analytics**

I. INTRODUCTION

The internet revolution has substantially changed how job seekers look for a job and how organizations attempt to attract job seekers [1]. Already in 2003, 94% of the global Fortune 500 companies were using a corporate recruitment website to attract job seekers [2], and online sources such as social media, online professional networks, and company websites are being used for effective employer branding [3]. Furthermore, the percentage of job seekers who are using the internet is growing steadily [4].

Advantages of using corporate recruitment websites have been discussed in previous studies, showing benefits including cost effectiveness, speeding up the hiring process, and ease of use both for recruiters and job seekers [5], [6], [7]. There is, however, yet another benefit of using corporate recruitment websites which has not been explored by previous research: it enables tracking the behavior of job seekers on the website using e-commerce software. By tracking this job seeker behavior, recruitment departments can obtain valuable insights on how to attract or repulse applications. This might lead to strategies for reducing recruitment lead time and cost.

To take a first step into exploring how vacancies attract job seekers and how this might be controlled, this study considers the predictability of the number of job seekers that will apply to an online vacancy per week. This metric is referred to as the application rate. In order to predict this metric, multiple machine learning techniques including Random Forest, Support Vector Regression, and Artificial Neural Networks were applied. The data used to predict the application rate included characteristics of the vacancy such as work location, required education level, and job title. Furthermore, also data describing whether the vacancy was used in online marketing campaigns such as Google Adwords, other vacancies on the website which might compete with the vacancy, and time related attributes such as the current recruitment lead time and application rates in weeks prior to the predicting period were used.

This paper has the following structure, Section II provides an overview of previous literature on the effectiveness of online recruitment websites will be given. Section III will discuss how data was obtained and prepared for analysis. In Section IV the findings from preliminary data analysis will be discussed which affects the choice of predictive models. Section V will give an overview of the methods that were used to predict the application rate. Finally, Section VI provides an overview of the predictive quality of these methods along with its implications.

II. RELATED WORK

The ability of corporate recruitment websites to attract job seekers has been investigated in multiple studies, often by sending questionnaires to either job seekers or employers. The results of these studies differ: some show the potential in terms of cost effectiveness, reducing recruitment leadtimes, and ease of use for both recruiters and job seekers [5], [6], [7]. Other studies however show a more modest perception: Brown [8] found that 75% of all job seekers find recruitment websites too complicated. This perception is shared by Maurer and Liu [9] who identified management of potential information excess on corporate recruitment websites as one of the key design issues for e-recruitment managers. Besides the excessive information organizations might send to potential job seekers, the opposite also holds. Vacancies might receive a large number of applications, including many unsuitable ones. Parry and Tyson [10] found that this is one of the reasons why a quarter of the organizations they examined who were using internet recruitment methods found it unsuccessful.

Data mining can play a role in managing the information spread by both the employer and job seeker. In particular, it can be used to investigate the relationship between recruitment efforts and recruitment outcomes. These relationships can be used to control the quality and quantity of applicants, and the quality of the employer's brand.

Previous research has not paid much attention to how data mining could be applied to manage the information spread by employers and job seekers apart from application selection [11], and resume parsing [12]. Although these methods automate part of the recruitment job, thereby enabling recruiters to handle a large number of applications, being able to control the quality and quantity of applicants would also decrease the workload of recruiters. Furthermore, fewer but better qualified applicants also means fewer rejections, which is beneficial for both job seekers and employers.

III. DATA GATHERING AND PREPARATION

A. *Data gathering*

To investigate whether the number of applicants who apply to a vacancy can accurately be predicted and controlled data was gathered from a large Dutch company which employs over 30,000 people and has on average 150 vacancies on its corporate recruitment website.

Data was gathered from three systems: first from an application tracking system (ATS) in which vacancy characteristics are stored such as work location, required education level, and working hours. Second, data was gathered from the corporate recruitment website's Google Analytics account. In particular, how many job seekers visited the corporate recruitment website per week, and how frequent job seekers followed different paths from the website's landing page to the application submit page (the webpage visited after having submitted an application). Also, Google Analytics is capable to keep track of whether job seekers visited the website via a paid hyperlink which was part of an online marketing campaign. This data was used to determine which vacancies had been used in online marketing campaigns. Third, the number of weekly tweets the recruitment department published via their recruitment Twitter account was gathered, along with whether certain vacancies were referred to in a tweet via a hyperlink.

Combining these three data sources gives per vacancy v, per time period t (in weeks) the vacancy characteristics of v, whether v was used in certain online marketing campaigns, and how many job seekers navigated from the landing page to the vacancy's submit page during time period t. This dataset was extended with time related data such as the recruitment lead time at time t, and application rates of a vacancy in weeks prior to week t.

The data set was split into a test- and training set. The training set contained all values between 2013-08-26 and 2015-09-31, whereas the test set contained all values between 2015-10-01 and 2015-12-31. This split was chosen for two reasons: first, at the time of splitting the data set there was no knowledge of possible time dependency in the data. If the application rate would include this time dependency then validating the predictive model on the last period of the total data set would produce the most realistic evaluation. Second, three months is the maximum period for which it is safe to assume that the vacancy portfolio over that period is known.

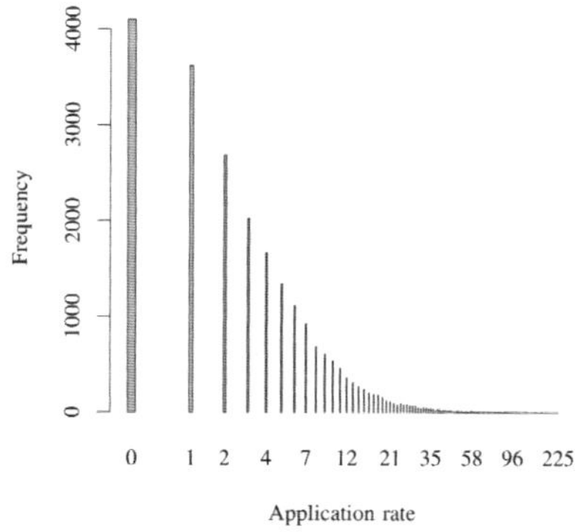

Figure 1. Histogram application rate

B. *Data preparation*

To improve the quality of the data set multiple operations were performed. Attributes related to work location and job title contained many possible categorical values, which was not practical for analysis. To reduce the number of categorical values the locations were clustered based on similarities in their application rate probability density. These probability densities were clustered using the K-means clustering algorithm by Hartigan and Wong [13]. To find an appropriate number of clusters the Akaike Information Criteria (AIC) was used, which was computed for $K = 1, \ldots, 10$ clusters. If a cluster had fewer than 100 observations the observations were assigned to the cluster closest to the overall mean application rate. Besides location attributes the job title had even more unique values, which made the usage of the probability density unpractical. As an alternative similar job titles were identified and clustered manually.

In order to identify attributes having a small variance, the frequency cut off from the *nearZeroVar* function of the caret package was used [14]. Since all predictors are either binary, categorical or discrete it was possible to apply this procedure on all predictors. Let $N_{i,j}$ be the frequency of a value i of category j. Furthermore, let $N_{(l),j}$ be the lth order statistic of $N_{1,j}, \ldots N_{n,j}$, then we have frequency ratio: $F_j = \frac{N_{(n),j}}{N_{(n-1),j}}$. Thus F_j gives the ratio of the most frequent and second most frequent value of attribute j. Attributes were removed from the data set if $F_j > 19$.

During the last data preparation step categorical attributes were dummified into binary vectors. The predictor values x_{ij} were normalized using $\tilde{x}_{ij} = \frac{x_{ij} - \bar{x}_j}{s(x_j)}$. Here $\bar{x}_j$ and $s(x_j)$ are the mean and standard deviation over the values of attribute j respectively.

IV. EXPLORATORY DATA ANALYSIS

A. *The application rate*

When considering possible probability distributions of the application rate a Poisson distribution would come first to mind. However, as Fig. 1 suggests, the Poisson distribution does not seem to fit the data well: the application rate's distribution is more zero inflated and overdispersed than a Poisson distribution. Dependent on the nature of the vacancy, a log-normal or negative binomial distribution is more appropriate. The distribution also confirms previous research stating that some vacancies can attract a large number of applications [10]. In fact, 10% of the rates accounts for 53% of all applications.

B. The total number of applications and sessions

Besides considering the distribution of the application rate also the predictability of the total number of applications per week was considered. To predict these metrics the structure of the vacancy portfolio and the used online marketing campaigns were used as predictors. This analysis might already give an indication of how online marketing campaigns can affect both the traffic to the website and the number of applications. Furthermore, if the residuals of this model would be highly correlated this could be an indication of time dependency, which would effect the selection of predictive models for the application rate.

To predict the number of applications and sessions per week, the status of the online vacancy portfolio and the number of vacancies subject to certain online marketing campaigns were used as predictors. The status of the vacancy portfolio was determined by counting the number of online vacancies having certain characteristics such as the same location, work area, job description, and required education level. A linear regression model was used to determine the effect of the online vacancy portfolio and online marketing campaigns on the total number of sessions and applications. This linear regression model did not include any interaction effects. Although also more sophisticated methods can be applied, the number of observations was relatively small compared to the number of predictors. Therefore, using more sophisticated methods was likely to cause overfitting. A backwards AIC algorithm was used to include only those predictors having the most predictive value.

Applying these methods gives an R^2 value of 0.68 and 0.56 when predicting the number of sessions and number of applications respectively. The models also indicate that it is difficult to determine the exact effect of online marketing campaigns on the total number of weekly sessions and applications. Although the marketing campaigns are significant, the campaigns are frequently used in combination with each other which makes it difficult to distinguish the effect of a single campaign.

This can easily be seen if we compute the condition indices and variance decomposition proportions as proposed by [15]. If we add up the variance decomposition proportions obtained from the number of vacancies subject to Facebook, Indeed and Google campaigns over the largest condition indices (85, 102 and 128 resp.), this sum becomes 0.692, 0.797 and 0.91 respectively, which are larger than the threshold value of 0.5. A possible remedy for this collinearity is to add more characteristics of the campaigns to the data set, such as the profiles used in a Facebook campaign. This was however not considered in this study.

Besides collinearity, an increase in online marketing campaigns can also be a response to a small number of applications, which makes the estimated effect of online marketing campaigns on the number of session and applicants biased.

When considering the residuals of the models predicting the number of weekly sessions and applications, a Box-Pierce test showed that these residuals were correlated. However, when examining the autocorrelation and partial autocorrelation functions this correlation turns out to be small: both the auto correlation and partial autocorrelation show a maximum absolute correlation of 0.21, at lag 2 and 1 respectively. Therefore, for simplicity, it was found acceptable to assume that the residuals were uncorrelated. As a result it was assumed that the total number of applications per week is independent of the date of the measurement.

C. Best sources

Also the relationship between the number of sessions originating from different websites via different devices and the number of weekly applications was considered. Again a linear regression model was used to avoid overfitting. Since visitors to the corporate recruitment website can originate from many different sources only the top four sources causing most traffic were considered, whereas smaller sources were combined in an 'other' category. Interestingly, the source device combinations causing most traffic to the website did not produce most applications. Where visitors originating from Google on a desktop produced most traffic to the website, changes in direct traffic on either desktop, mobile or tablet and traffic from the corporate website were the main drivers for changes in the number of weekly applications.

V. METHODS

A. Method selection

To determine which methods would be most suited to predict the application rate a number of considerations were taken. First, since the application rate is count data its prediction is considered as a regression problem. Second, exploratory data analysis found that the data is more zero inflated and overdispersed than a Poisson distribution. Therefore, predictive models which incorporate zero inflation and overdispersion are preferred. Third, during exploratory data analysis it was found that when predicting the total number of applications per week the residuals of this model are only slightly correlated. As a result it was assumed that the total number of applications per week is independent of the date of the measurement, though it still can be dependent on other time indicators such as the current recruitment lead time.

Fourth, the data set still contained a large number of attributes, some of which might not be useful for the predictive model. To reduce the number of attributes, methods which included variable selection were preferred. Fifth, since a grid search was applied to find good model parameters, methods which were able to produce good results within reasonable time were preferred (i.e., methods that took more than 1 hour to compute a single predictive model using a 1.6 GHz dual-core Intel Core i5 processor were disregarded). Sixth, methods which have been applied successfully in other regression application were preferred.

Using these criteria seven methods were identified: Linear elastic net, Poisson elastic net, Tweedie elastic net, Classification And Regression Trees (CART), Random Forest, Support Vector Regression (SVR), and Artificial Neural Networks (ANN).

B. Method overview

1) Linear elastic net: Linear elastic net is a method which attempts to minimize the sum of squared error plus a linear combination of the lasso and Ridge penalty. Let $PSSE(\lambda, \beta, \alpha)$ be the penalized sum of squared error with λ the weight of the penalty. α indicates to which extend either the Ridge or lasso penalty is taken into account, and β is the effect vector to be estimated. $PSSE(\lambda, \beta, \alpha)$ is given by:

$$\begin{aligned} PSSE(\lambda, \boldsymbol{\beta}, \alpha) = & \frac{1}{2N}\sum_{i=1}^{N}(y_i - \beta_0 - x_i^T\boldsymbol{\beta})^2 \\ & +\lambda\left[(1-\alpha)\frac{1}{2}||\boldsymbol{\beta}||^2 + \alpha||\boldsymbol{\beta}||_1\right] \end{aligned} \tag{1}$$

To minimize (1) the glmnet R package was utilized, which applies a coordinate descent algorithm to estimate β [16]. To determine good values for λ and α a grid search was applied. For λ, $K = 100$ uniformly spread values between $\lambda_{max} = \frac{max_l|\langle x_l, y\rangle|}{N\alpha}$ and $\lambda_{min} = \epsilon\lambda_{max}$ were used. To find a good value for α, values from 0 up to 1 with increasing steps of 0.2 were used.

2) Poisson elastic net: Poisson elastic net is a combination of a generalized linear regression model and elastic net using the link function $g(\mu_i) = log(\mu_i)$, where $\mu_i = \mathbb{E}(y_i|\mathbf{x}_i)$. Instead of the sum of squared error the log-likelihood is used to estimate $\boldsymbol{\beta}$. Let PLL be the penalized log-likelihood, then $\boldsymbol{\beta}$ is found by maximizing (2).

$$\begin{aligned} PLL(\lambda, \boldsymbol{\beta}, \alpha) = & \frac{1}{2N}\sum_{i=1}^{N}\left[y_i\mathbf{x}_i^T\boldsymbol{\beta} - \exp\left(\mathbf{x}_i^T\boldsymbol{\beta}\right)\right] \\ & -\lambda\left[(1-\alpha)\frac{1}{2}||\boldsymbol{\beta}||^2 + \alpha||\boldsymbol{\beta}||_1\right] \end{aligned} \tag{2}$$

To maximize (2), again the glmnet R package was used. In case of Poisson regression, glmnet iteratively creates a second order Taylor expansion of (2) without the penalty, using current estimates for $\boldsymbol{\beta}$. This Taylor expansion is then used in a coordinate descent algorithm to update β [16], [17]. To find appropriate values for λ and α the same grid search as in linear elastic net was applied.

3) Tweedie elastic net: To incorporate the fact that the application rate is more zero inflated and overdispersed than a Poisson distribution the Tweedie compound Poisson model was used. The Tweedie compound Poisson model can be represented by $Y = \sum_{i=1}^{n} X_i$, where Y is the responds vector, n a Poisson random variable, and X_i are i.i.d. Gamma distributed with parameters α and γ. The penalized negative log-likelihood is given by (3) [18].

$$\begin{aligned} PLL(\lambda, \boldsymbol{\beta}, \alpha) = & \sum_{i=1}^{n}\left[\frac{y_i\exp\left[-(\rho-1)(\mathbf{x}_i^T\beta)\right]}{\rho-1} + \frac{\exp\left[(2-\rho)(\mathbf{x}_i^T\beta)\right]}{2-\rho}\right] \\ & +\lambda\left[(1-\alpha)\frac{1}{2}||\boldsymbol{\beta}||^2 + \alpha||\boldsymbol{\beta}||_1\right] \end{aligned} \tag{3}$$

To minimize (3), the HDTweedie R package was used. This method applies an iterative reweighted least squares (IRLS) algorithm combined with a blockwise majorization descent (BMD) [18]. To find appropriate values for λ the standard procedure from HDTweedie was used, which first computes λ_{max} such that $\beta = 0$, and then sets $\lambda_{min} = 0.001\lambda_{max}$. The other $m - 2$ values for λ are found by projecting them uniformly on a log-scale on the range $[\lambda_{min}, \lambda_{max}]$. For α the values from 0.1 to 0.9 with an increase of 0.2 were used. For ρ we used $\rho = 1.5$.

4) Classification And Regression Trees (CART): To construct a regression tree the rpart implementation in R was used [19]. This implementation first constructs a binary tree by maximizing in each node $SS_T - (SS_R + SS_L)$, where SS_T is the sum of squared error of the entire tree, and SS_R and SS_L are the sum of squared errors of the left and right branch respectively. The tree constructions stops when further splits would violate a constraint on the minimum number of observations in each node.

Second, the constructed tree is split into m sub-trees. Let $R(T)$ be the risk of tree T, which is the sum of squared error in the terminal nodes of T. CART computes the risk of each sub-tree tree, which is defined by $R_\alpha(T) = R(T) + \alpha|T|$ using K-fold cross validation. The term $\alpha|T|$ is an additional penalty on the size of the tree. The final tree is the sub-tree which minimizes the average sum of squared error over the K-fold cross validation. The method described here is referred to as the "ANOVA" method.

Alternatively, rpart also has the option to maximize the deviance $D_T - (D_L + D_R)$, where D is the within node deviance assuming that the response originates from a Poisson distribution. To find an appropriate value for α a grid search was applied using $\alpha \in \{0.001, 0.01, 0.1, 0.3\}$, both for the ANOVA and Poisson models.

5) Random Forest: A Random Forest model was produced using the RandomForest package in R [20]. Random Forest constructs T unpruned regression trees T_i, where in each split only d randomly chosen predictors are considered. A prediction $\hat{y}_i$ is then created by $\hat{y}_i = \frac{1}{T}\sum_{i=1}^{T} T_i(x)$, thus the average over all trees. To find the appropriate number of trees a grid search was applied using 50, 100 and 500 trees. Furthermore, at each split 61 randomly sampled attributes were considered.

6) Support Vector Regression: Support Vector Regression is the regression alternative of Support Vector Machines. Given the linear regression problem: $y_i = \mathbf{w}^T\mathbf{x}_i + b + \epsilon$, SVR attempts to find the flattest hyperplane $\mathbf{w}^T\mathbf{x}_i + b$ such that for all data points $i = 1, \ldots, N$ we have $|y_i - (\mathbf{w}^T\mathbf{x}_i + b)| < \epsilon$. Also incorporating slack variables ζ_i and ζ_i^*, the problem can be described as (4).

$$\begin{aligned} \min \quad & \frac{1}{2}|\mathbf{w}||^2 + C\sum_{i=1}^{n}(\zeta_i + \zeta_i^*) \\ \text{s.t.} \quad & y_i - \mathbf{w}^T\mathbf{x}_i - b \leq \epsilon + \zeta_i, \quad i = 1, \ldots, N \\ & \mathbf{w}^T\mathbf{x}_i + b - y_i \leq \epsilon + \zeta_i^*, \quad i = 1, \ldots, N \\ & \zeta_i, \zeta_i^* \geq 0 \end{aligned} \tag{4}$$

Since the solution to (4) only depends on inner products between vectors $\mathbf{x}_i$, the problem can be transformed into a higher dimension without much extra computation using kernels [21]. For the computation of the SVR the R kernlab package was used [22]. Although in this study initially both a linear kernel (hence no kernel), and the RBF kernel: $\kappa(x_i, x_j) = \exp\left(-\frac{||x_i - x_j||^2}{2\sigma^2}\right)$ were considered, not using a kernel surprisingly had a large negative effect on the runtime and was therefore disregarded. To find appropriate values for ϵ and C a grid search was applied using: $\epsilon \in \{0.01, 0.1, 1\}$ and $C \in \{1, 10\}$

7) Artificial Neural Networks: In this study we considered a feed-forward Artificial Neural Network with a single hidden layer. To find the weights the nnet R package was used, which utilizes an L-BFGS algorithm to find the appropriate weights [23], [24]. A grid search was applied to find an appropriate number of units in the hidden layer. During the grid search 1, 5, 10, 30, and 50 hidden units were considered.

C. Method evaluation

To evaluate the quality of predictive models two scenarios were distinguished. The first scenario assumes that application rates in weeks prior to the predicting period are known, which is comparable with predicting one week ahead. The second scenario assumes these application rates to be absent, and is more comparable with predicting 2 to 12 weeks ahead. These two scenarios are indicated by including PAR, and excluding PAR.

To evaluate the quality of the predictions two error measures are used: the root mean squared error: $RMSE = \sqrt{\frac{1}{n}\sum_{i=1}^{n}(\hat{y_i} - y_i)^2}$, where $\hat{y_i}$ is the predicted value for actual y_i, and the determination coefficient: $R^2 = 1 - \frac{SS_{res}}{SS_{tot}}$, with $SS_{res} = \sum_{i=1}^{n}(\hat{y_i} - y_i)^2$, the residual sum of squares, and $SS_{tot} = \sum_{i=1}^{n}(y_i - \bar{y})^2$, the total sum of squares. A 10-fold cross validation was applied to obtain accurate estimates for the quality of the predictions over the training set in both scenarios. Furthermore, a final prediction over the test set was made using the model showing the best results over the training set to estimate out of sample performance.

VI. Results

A. Method comparison

Table I shows the best results per model when applying a 10-fold cross validation on the training set. The table indicates that Random Forest produced the best results both when predicting with and without PAR. Table I also indicates that multiple methods such as artificial neural networks without PAR, Poisson elastic net and Tweedie elastic net with PAR did not produce accurate results. Furthermore, Table I indicates that the added value of including previous application rates into the model is relatively small. Therefore, the predictive model would only produce slightly better results when predicting short term (1 week), in comparison with prediction long term (2 to 12 weeks).

When considering the quality of the models indicated in Table I it is important to note that the $RMSE$ is largely influenced by some large application rates which are difficult to predict. This can also be derived from the errors the Random Forest model makes on the test set (Fig. 2). In fact, 90% of the errors are smaller than 9.63, and the average absolute error over this 90% is 2.43.

TABLE I. Results 10-fold cross validation

Method	Best $RMSE$ including PAR	Best R^2 including PAR	Best $RMSE$ excluding PAR	Best R^2 excluding PAR
Linear elastic net	11.82	0.35	11.87	0.34
Poisson elastic net	15.53	0	NA	NA
CART ANOVA	10.72	0.46	11.12	0.42
CART Poisson	10.17	0.52	10.75	0.46
Random Forest	9.38	0.59	9.93	0.54
Tweedie elastic net	13.86	0.03	11.62	0.37
SVR	10.58	0.46	11.28	0.41
ANN	11.14	0.42	17.35	0

While predicting the application rate, also the predictive value of online marketing campaigns was considered. To determine the importance of these campaigns the following procedure was used. For each tree of the forest the reduction in the sum of squared error when splitting on one of the D randomly selected attributes was computed. These reductions are summed up over all trees for each variable to obtain an overall picture of the decrease in residual sum of squares per predictor.

By comparing the reduction in the sum of squared error for each variable a comparison can be made between the effect of online marketing campaigns and other attributes. From this comparison we found that the effect of online marketing campaigns on the the application rate is small. Most variance is explained by predictors related to the application rate in prior weeks, the job title, the current recruitment lead time, and the contractual hours required. However, in contrast to the model predicting the total number of applicants, the online marketing campaigns do show a positive effect on the application rate.

B. Test set evaluation

Since Random Forest produced the most promising results when applying 10-fold cross validation this model was evaluated on the test set. The results are shown is Table II, whereas the distribution of the error on the test set is given in Fig. 2. The quality of the prediction was slightly worse than the average error obtained from 10-fold cross validation. Furthermore, just as the training set also the test set contained some large application rates which had a large negative effect on the $RMSE$.

TABLE II. Results applying Random Forest on test set

Performance metric	Value including PAR	Value excluding PAR
MAE	5.25	6.35
MSE	100.44	123.99
RMSE	10.02	11.13
Residual mean	1.53	1.81
Residual sd	9.90	10.98
R^2	0.44	0.32

VII. Conclusion

This paper considered the predictability of the number of weekly applications per vacancy and to which extend this metric can be controlled. To investigate this question a dataset from a large Dutch organization employing more than 30,000 employees was considered. To predict the number of weekly

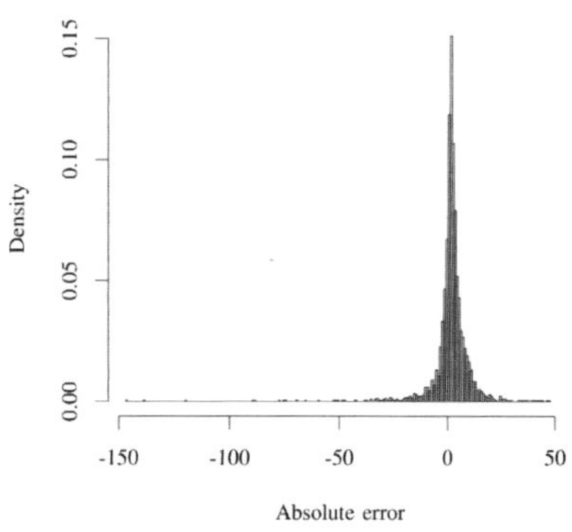

Figure 2. Test set error with PAR

applications per vacancy multiple machine learning methods were applied, of which Random Forest returned the best results with a root mean squared error of 9.38 and 9.93 when the predictors included and excluded application rates in weeks prior to the predicted week.

From closer examination of the errors two conclusions can be drawn. First, even though the predictions are quite accurate in most situations, i.e., have an error of less than 5 applicants, some vacancies can attract a large number of job seekers which the model finds hard to predict. As a result it will be more difficult to act on these predictions. On the other hand, both the predictions and insights into the variability of these predictions are helpful to manage the expectations recruiters and hiring managers might have when publishing a vacancy. In particular, recruiters should manage vacancies expecting a large number of applications carefully to avoid excess of applications. Also, recruiters could consider how attractive vacancies can be used to market less attractive vacancies, for example by generalizing the vacancy such that it may refer to both popular and less popular job positions.

Second, from analyzing the effect of online marketing campaigns on the number of applications per vacancy per week this effect is positive, though quite small. Also, it is likely that when estimating the effect of online marketing campaigns from historic data this effect will be biased: vacancies which do not attract many applications are more likely to be used in online marketing campaigns and there might be collinearity between the campaigns. Therefore, we were not able to draw a clear conclusion on the effect of online marketing campaigns and how this can be used to control the number of applications.

VIII. FURTHER WORK

Although the amount of data recruitment departments are storing is increasing, the usability of this data for research can be limited. This study did not take into account the quality of new employees, individual job seeker behavior, and other incentives than online marketing campaigns due to limitations in obtaining this data either due to legal constraints, time constraints, or incomplete data sources. Including these data sources could provide new insights into how the quantity and quality of applications can be controlled.

REFERENCES

[1] D. L. Van Rooy, A. Alonso, and Z. Fairchild, "In with the new, out with the old: Has the technological revolution eliminated the traditional job search process?" "International journal of selection and assessment", vol. 11, no. 2-3, 2003, pp. 170–174.

[2] R. Greenspan, Job seekers have choices, 2003, URL: https://www.clickz.com/job-seekers-have-choices/76679/ [accessed 2016-07-25].

[3] L. Abbot, R. Batty, and S. Bevegni, Global Recruiting Trends 2016, 2015, URL: https://business.linkedin.com/content/dam/business/talent-solutions/global/en_us/c/pdfs/GRT16_GlobalRecruiting_100815.pdf, [accessed 2016-07-27].

[4] F. Suvankulov, "Job search on the internet, e-recruitment, and labor market outcomes," DTIC Document, Tech. Rep., 2010.

[5] R. R. Zusman and R. S. Landis, "Applicant preferences for web-based versus traditional job postings," Computers in Human Behavior, vol. 18, no. 3, 2002, pp. 285–296.

[6] I. Lee, "The evolution of e-recruiting: A content analysis of fortune 100 career web sites," Journal of Electronic Commerce in Organizations (JECO), vol. 3, no. 3, 2005, pp. 57–68.

[7] P. Gibson and J. Swift, "e2c: Maximising electronic resources for cruise recruitment," Journal of Hospitality and Tourism Management, vol. 18, no. 01, 2011, pp. 61–69.

[8] D. Brown, "Unwanted online job seekers swamp HR staff," Canadian HR reporter, vol. 17, no. 7, 2004, pp. 1–2.

[9] S. D. Maurer and Y. Liu, "Developing effective e-recruiting websites: Insights for managers from marketers," Business horizons, vol. 50, no. 4, 2007, pp. 305–314.

[10] E. Parry and S. Tyson, "An analysis of the use and success of online recruitment methods in the uk," Human Resource Management Journal, vol. 18, no. 3, 2008, pp. 257–274.

[11] S. Strohmeier and F. Piazza, "Domain driven data mining in human resource management: A review of current research," Expert Systems with Applications, vol. 40, no. 7, 2013, pp. 2410–2420.

[12] D. Çelik and A. Elçi, "An ontology-based information extraction approach for résumés," in Joint International Conference on Pervasive Computing and the Networked World. Springer, 2012, pp. 165–179.

[13] J. A. Hartigan and M. A. Wong, "Algorithm as 136: A k-means clustering algorithm," Journal of the Royal Statistical Society. Series C (Applied Statistics), vol. 28, no. 1, 1979, pp. 100–108.

[14] M. Kuhn, "Building predictive models in R using the caret package," Journal of Statistical Software, vol. 28, no. 5, 2008, pp. 1–26.

[15] D. A. Belsley, "A guide to using the collinearity diagnostics," Computer Science in Economics and Management, vol. 4, no. 1, 1991, pp. 33–50.

[16] J. Friedman, T. Hastie, and R. Tibshirani, "Regularization paths for generalized linear models via coordinate descent," Journal of statistical software, vol. 33, no. 1, 2010, p. 1.

[17] T. Hastie and J. Qian, Glmnet Vignette, 2014, URL: http://www.web.stanford.edu/~hastie/Papers/Glmnet\textunderscoreVignette.pdf [accessed 2016-07-25].

[18] W. Qian, Y. Yang, and H. Zou, "Tweedies compound poisson model with grouped elastic net," Journal of Computational and Graphical Statistics, vol. 25, no. 2, 2016, pp. 606–625.

[19] E. J. Atkinson and T. M. Therneau, "An introduction to recursive partitioning using the rpart routines," Rochester: Mayo Foundation, 2000.

[20] A. Liaw and M. Wiener, "Classification and regression by randomforest," R news, vol. 2, no. 3, 2002, pp. 18–22.

[21] A. J. Smola and B. Schölkopf, "A tutorial on support vector regression," Statistics and computing, vol. 14, no. 3, 2004, pp. 199–222.

[22] A. Karatzoglou, A. Smola, and K. Hornik, The kernlab package, 2007, URL: https://cran.r-project.org/web/packages/kernlab/kernlab.pdf [accessed 2016-07-25].

[23] D. C. Liu and J. Nocedal, "On the limited memory bfgs method for large scale optimization," Mathematical programming, vol. 45, no. 1-3, 1989, pp. 503–528.

[24] B. Ripley and W. Venables, Package 'nnet', 2016, URL: https://cran.r-project.org/web/packages/nnet/nnet.pdf [accessed 2016-07-25].

Almost Squares in Almost Squares: Solving the Final Instance

Daan van den Berg
University of Amsterdam,
Faculty of Science,
Amsterdam, The Netherlands
Email: D.vandenBerg@uva.nl

Florian Braam, Mark Moes, Emiel Suilen, and Sandjai Bhulai
Vrije Universiteit Amsterdam,
Faculty of Sciences,
Amsterdam, The Netherlands
Email: florianbraam@gmail.com, mark_moes@hotmail.com,
emiel.suilen@gmail.com, s.bhulai@vu.nl

***Abstract*—The "almost-squares in almost-squares" (Asqas) problem is a rectangle packing problem in which a series of almost-squares (rectangles of dimensions $n \times (n+1)$) needs to be placed inside an almost-square frame without open areas or overlaps. Asqas-34, consisting of almost-squares $1 \times 2, 2 \times 3, \ldots, 34 \times 35$, remains unsolved. This paper shows Asqas-34 is the only remaining unsolved instance of Asqas, and describes several solutions to Asqas-34, and the methods used to find them.**

Keywords–Asqas; almost-squares in almost-squares; rectangle packing problem.

I. INTRODUCTION

Rectangle Packing Problems come in a broad variety and have quite a practical appeal besides their theoretical interest. Minimum-waste fabric cutting in clothes manufacture, maximum storage in warehouses, and optimal arrangement of text and advertisements in newspapers all involve finding the best arrangement of a set of rectangles [1]. While its industrial relevance has been recognized for some time (see, e.g., [2]–[4]), closely related bin packing problems also show a quite remarkable and very interesting extension to scheduling issues [5], where they provide a practical foothold for optimization problems in logistics and planning.

Almost-square packing problems are a special class of rectangle packing problems. A sequence of n almost-square tiles $(1 \times 2, 2 \times 3, \ldots, n \times (n+1))$ must be placed inside a small as possible rectangular frame, with no overlap and as little possible unused space. Most notable is the work of [6], who optimally solved these problems up to $n = 13$ by hand, and up to $n = 26$ by computer, meaning they found exact-fit configurations within frames of appropriate dimensions. Fig. 1 displays the Asqas-8 problem, which is the third of five instances of almost-squares-in-almost-squares, having 8 consecutive almost-square tiles of $1 \times 2, \ldots, 8 \times 9$ to be placed in an almost-square frame, in this case 15×16.

In this paper, we present a solution to the $n = 34$ problem instance, which is not only a relatively large instance of the almost-square packing problem, but also belongs to the slightly more exclusive class of almost-squares-in-almost-squares (Asqas) as well. This is a set of exactly five problem instances for which it is known that a frame of exact fit could have almost-square dimensions as well. The $n = 34$ instance of almost-squares has exactly 13 exact-fit frames, of which 35×408 is the most eccentric and 119×120, the almost-square one, is the most concentric. Erich's packing center, an extensive collection of open and solved packing problems maintained by prof. Erich Friedmann of Stetson University (see [7]) contains solutions to the first four instances of Asqas, but leaves the fifth open. It is this instance that we solve, but it is also the last open instance of Asqas, which we will firstly show.

The structure of the paper is as follows. We discuss the five instances of the Asqas problem in Section II. In Section III, we describe how border sets can help to reduce the complexity of the problem. This is used in Section IV to create borders of the tiles. Finally, in Section V we solve the interior of the border, which leads to the solution of the Asqas-34 problem.

II. THE FIVE INSTANCES OF ALMOST-SQUARES-IN-ALMOST-SQUARES

There are exactly five instances of Asqas and its proof relies on the observation that there is an intriguing bijective function from Asqas to geometry and triangular numbers in number theory closely reminiscent of homeomorphic topological conjugacies used in chaotic discrete dynamical systems [8]. Since a sequence of n almost-square tiles $(1\times2, 2\times3, \ldots, n\times(n+1))$ must be placed inside an almost-square frame, the first check should be whether such a frame actually exists for a given n, or equivalently, whether the summed area of all the separate tiles is equal to the area of an almost-square frame (of any size). More formally put: an Asqas-instance of size n exists only if there is a natural number p such that Equation (1) holds:

$$\sum_{i=1}^{n} i(i+1) = p(p+1). \tag{1}$$

As it turns out, there are exactly five values of n for which the equation holds, and the proof is underpinned by the existence of a near-trivial relation between the sequence of almost-square tiles $1, \ldots, n$ and the triangular numbers $1, \ldots, n$. Fig. 2 shows that summing the first n triangular numbers (bottom row) leads to the nth tetrahedral number. If this number happens to be a triangular number as well, then the existence of an Asqas-instance with the same n is guaranteed by a simple relation between summing triangular numbers (TR) and summing almost squares (AS) – the kth triangle is exactly half the area of the kth almost-square. Note that the relation critically depends on the existence of a triangular number for the nth tetrahedral number (in this case TR_4 for TH_3) and there are only five tetrahedral numbers (TH_1, TH_3,

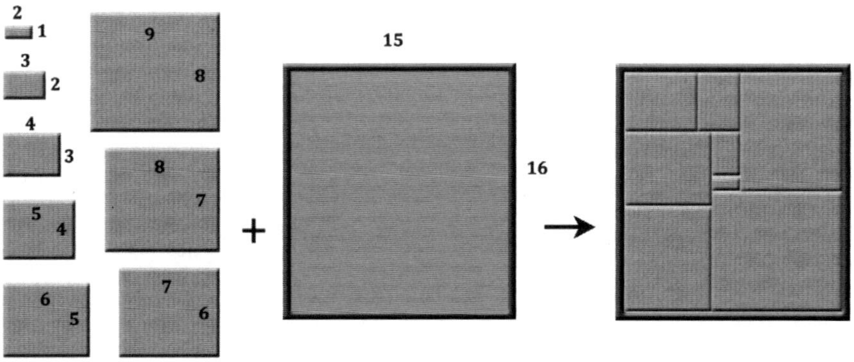

Figure 1. Illustration of the Asqas-8 problem.

TH_8, TH_{20} and TH_{34}) which have a corresponding triangular number. For this reason, there are exactly five Asqas-instances.

The area of any almost-square k is exactly twice the area of the corresponding triangular number k. Since the sum of the areas of the first n almost-squares should be expressible in $p(p+1)$ for the problem instance to exist, the question easily translates to whether the sum of the first n triangular numbers yields a new triangular number. However, the sum of the first n triangular numbers is most commonly known as a tetrahedral number, since 'stacking' subsequent triangles yields a tetrahedron, and as such the question becomes "which tetrahedral numbers are also triangular numbers?". The answer is given by [9]: only the 1st, 3rd, 8th, 20th, and 34th tetrahedral numbers have corresponding triangular numbers (the 1st, 4th, 15th, 55th, and 119th respectively). This ensures us that Asqas-34 is both the largest and the only remaining unsolved instance of Asqas.

A point worth noting is that a similar approach has been adopted for assessing instances of consecutive squares-in-squares; the sum of the series $(1 \times 1, 2 \times 2, \ldots, n \times n)$ gives a square pyramidal number P_n. Only two numbers are both square and pyramidal: $P_1 = S_1 = 1$ and $P_{24} = S_{70} = 4{,}900$ [10], the first being trivial and the second, consisting of the first 24 consecutive squares having no solution at all [11]. This instance is a special cases of 'perfectly squared squares' (see [12], [13]) and a nice visual overview can be found at [14].

III. Border Sets and Eligible Border Sets

When considering any tight configuration of tiles in a frame as a sequence, the number of possible arrangements is equal to $n!$. In the almost-square case, tiles can be put either horizontally or vertically, doubling the possibilities for each individual tile, and as such increasing the total number of configurations by a factor 2^n. For the case of Asqas-34, the number of possible arrangements is therefore equal to Expression (2):

$$34! \cdot 2^{34} = 507{,}206{,}086{,}632{,}656 \cdot 10^{34} \approx 5 \cdot 10^{48}. \quad (2)$$

Roughly speaking, any number of states exceeding 10^{20} becomes too cumbersome for calculation on a single computer within reasonable time.

Our heuristic approach is mainly fed by the observation that for Asqas-20, larger tiles are situated in the border of the frame. Asqas-20 has 54,992 solutions having a total of 9,812 different borders. Fig. 3 shows that the number of tiles in these borders follows a narrow distribution (left), with larger tiles more prevalent than smaller tiles (right), and some of the larger tiles (14×15, 17×18, 18×19 and 19×20) being present in the border of almost every solution. For this reason, it makes sense to start looking for solutions to Asqas-34 with larger tiles in the border.

For this purpose, without loss of generality, we split the set of tiles of the $n = 34$ instance into 'border sets' of b tiles, and the remaining 'interior sets' of $34 - b$ tiles. The number of any possible border sets of size b then equals $\binom{34}{b}$ and each of these has $b! \cdot 2^b$ of possible configurations, whereas the complementary interior set is left with $34 - b$ tiles, with $(34-b)! \cdot 2^{34-b}$ configurations. As such, the size of the state-space can better be viewed as in Expression (3):

$$\binom{34}{b} \cdot b! \cdot 2^b \cdot (34-b)! \cdot 2^{34-b}, \quad (3)$$

for any b in the range 1 to 34. The initial drawback is that for our approach to be complete, we have to repeat this procedure for every $b = 1, 2, \ldots, 34$ and as such multiply the gross calculations with 34. This however, turns out to be a small investment with a huge return. Firstly, it allows us to filter out 'eligible border sets' from which potentially valid borders can be constructed from non-eligible border sets with relative computational ease. The second advantage is rather practical: the compartmentation of the state space allows designated areas to be marked as 'covered', and even if no solution was to be found it would serve as progress for other teams working on the subject. But the third advantage, directly related to the second, is that by compartmenting the state space into borders of size b and interiors of size $34-b$, we can start an optimized complete search in the area of the smallest border sets – which have the largest tiles on average. This assumption however, was not thoroughly investigated and therefore starting here was a clear cut heuristic: an educated guess.

Sifting eligible border sets from discardable non-eligible border sets was done simply on the global constraint of perimeter: every set has a maximum perimeter ($p_{\max}$) and a

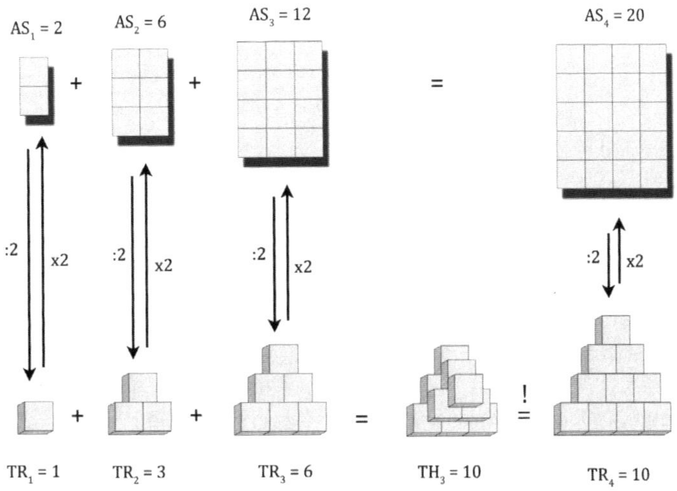

Figure 2. Relation between the sum of almost squares and triangular numbers.

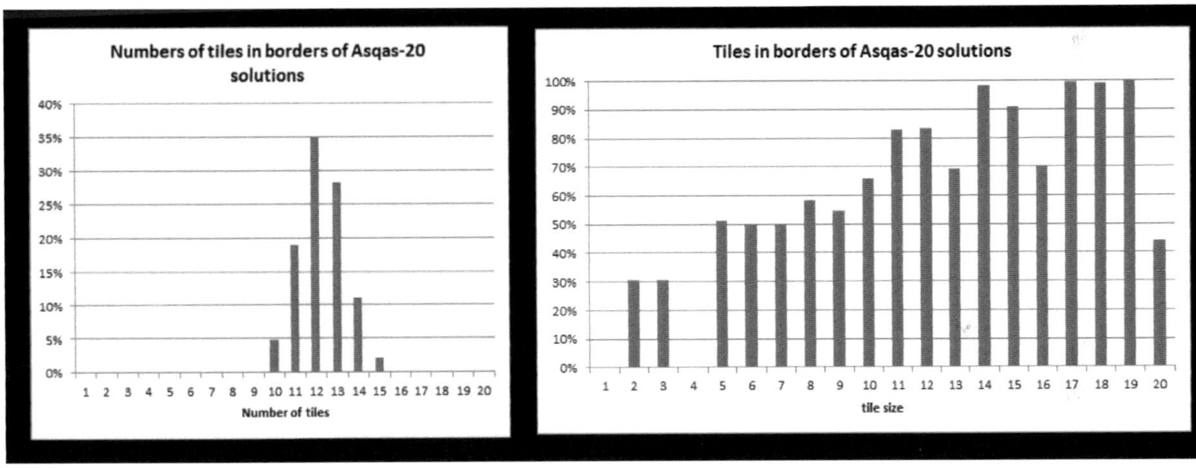

Figure 3. Distribution of the number of tiles in Asqas-20.

minimum perimeter ($p_{\min}$). The maximum perimeter is the greatest distance that any set of tiles can cover when placed along the inside of the frame in constructing a border from that set. It assumes the largest tiles to be put in the corners and all others with their long sides on the frame. As such, $p_{\max}$ is the sum of all the long sides of tiles in the set, plus the short sides of the four largest tiles in the set. The minimum perimeter assumes the opposite: placing the smallest tiles of the set in the corners of the frame and all others with their short sides on the frame, and as such is the sum of the short sides of all tiles in the set, plus the long sides of the four smallest tiles. The total length of the Asqas-34 frame is 119 + 119 + 120 + 120 = 478 and as such any set which has $p_{\min} \leq 478 \leq p_{\max}$ was to be marked *eligible*; all others were discarded. It is easy to see there are no eligible 3-border sets (too short) and no eligible 31-border sets (too long), but it should be noted that for various reasons, many of the eligible border sets have no validly constructable borders at all. The perimeter-approach has the great advantage of being computationally very effective, allowing the number of eligible border sets to be greatly reduced in a few days on a single stand-alone computer. On an abstract level, this procedure somewhat resembles the approach described by [15], using global constraints for packing rectangles as it "it leads to improvement in execution times", which of course, in terms can make an unsolvable problem solvable.

IV. Making borders of 12 tiles

The reduction from all border sets to eligible border sets only greatly varied with the number of tiles involved in a set, but was most drastic at its extremes. Table I shows that the number of border sets with b tiles is exactly $\binom{34}{b}$, but only a small fraction of these meet the eligibility-criterion of having enough but not too much length to potentially construct

TABLE I. NUMBER OF BORDER SETS IN THE REDUCTION.

set size	#sets	#eligible sets		(cont.)	(cont.)	(cont.)
≤ 11	var.	0		21	927,983,760	788,458,963
12	548,354,040	30		22	548,354,040	502,691,341
13	927,983,760	18,014		23	286,097,760	256,326,310
14	1,391,975,640	749,552		24	131,128,140	104,965,820
15	1,855,967,520	10,072,560		25	52,451,256	33,285,209
16	2,203,961,430	64,774,105		26	18,156,204	7,530,562
17	2,333,606,220	238,039,950		27	5,379,616	1,053,473
18	2,203,961,430	552,324,976		28	1,344,904	69,036
19	1,855,967,520	863,895,027		29	278,256	933
20	1,391,975,640	958,043,855		≥ 30	var.	0

a border of 478 units long. The percentage eligible sets is smallest at its extremes, for $b = 12$ and $b = 29$.

As our heuristic assumed that a solution of the Asqas-34, if existent, was likely to have larger tiles situated in the border, and the smaller sets necessarily consist of larger tiles, these two factors led us to explore all eligible border sets consisting of 12 tiles. There are only 30 of those sets, having a total of $30 \cdot 12! \cdot 2^{12}$ = 58,859,716,608,000 $\approx 5.9 \cdot 10^{13}$ possible borders, a number small enough to exhaustively compute on a stand-alone computer with a simple backtracking algorithm. Fig. 4 shows that the number of valid borders per eligible 12-set differs considerably, but roughly follows the fluctuations of $p_{\max}$. Sets have been numbered #1 – #30 following tile size (#1 having the largest tiles) but the number of valid borders shows no relation to this numbering (horizontal axis). Remarkably enough, the inset shows that when plotted in a log-normal scale the distribution of sets almost follows a straight line with a slope of -0.12 and intercept 6.13 (correlation coefficient: -0.994).

Of the $5.9 \cdot 10^{13}$ possible configurations, only 4,425,341 actually turned out to be valid borders (see Fig. 4). The border-construction algorithm was complete, and effectively ignored flip-isomorphic borders and partial-flip-isomorphic borders. Two borders are flip-isomorphic if a complete horizontal or vertical flip changes one into the other, and two borders are partial-flip-isomorphic if flipping two adjacent tiles in the border leaves the shape of the interior unchanged. It is worth noting that it is theoretically quite possible that other isomorphic borders were still present in our set, and the only way to ensure this is storing the exact polygon shape of the remaining interior and the accompanying set of interior tiles. We never bothered, for the storage capacity and checking algorithm needed for this mechanism to work appears to greatly exceeded its practical benefit, if any.

The total number of 4,425,341 borders constructable from any 12 tiles is fairly comprehensive, but each of them still needed its remaining 22 tiles to be arranged in at most $22! \cdot 2^{22}$ configurations, yielding a total of 4,425,341 $\cdot$ 471,440,074,852,053 $\cdot 10^{13}$ = 208,628,309,228,586 $\cdot 10^{20} \approx 2 \cdot 10^{34}$ possible configurations to explore, still far too many to analyze on a stand-alone computer. From here, we put our faith in all the optimizations we could think of for solving the interior, the computational power of third and fourth generation Distributed ASCI Supercomputers (DAS-3 and DAS-4), and the correctness of our heuristic intuition.

V. SOLVING THE INTERIOR

A pilot run showed that the calculation time for deciding whether any given valid border had a solvable interior, e.g., contained a complete Asqas-34 solution, was extremely unevenly distributed. Whereas the vast majority of borders was decided in a few minutes at most, approximately one in thousand took nearly a day to be completely puzzled out. In a worst-case scenario, this would stall even a supercomputer of 100 calculating nodes for over a month with all the quickly decidable borders waiting behind it. To effectively manage this risk, to maximize the number of analyzed borders or, ultimately, to find a solution to Asqas-34, we set up a small server with 4,439 text files, each containing at most $1,000$ border configurations, effectively covering all 4,425,341 borders of 12 tiles. The text files' content was arranged in accordance with the 30 different sets, but the files were randomly distributed over 80 nodes of DAS-3 grid computers and up to 90 nodes of DAS-4 grid computers located throughout The Netherlands and Belgium, each node running several instances of the interior solver (see Fig. 5 for the computational setup).

Each instance of the interior solver comprised an optimized complete backtracking algorithm that, on startup, retrieved one text file with 1,000 borders from our server, read the first border from the file, placed the 12 tiles inside the frame and commenced an exhaustive backtracking routine using the remaining 22 tiles to solve the interior. The tiles were placed starting on the first empty position bottom-left, and starting off with the largest tile standing up first. It optimized in three ways: firstly, whenever the first row was not completed, the search for the border was cut off and dismissed as unsolvable. Second, if a row was completed, it was checked for "impossible gaps", mostly high and narrow spaces which could not be filled by any combination of tiles. Third, rectangles were not reversed, meaning that any two consecutively placed tiles in the interior forming a rectangle were not checked in reverse order. This has an optimizing effect but the apparent drawback of missing solutions that only differed by a partial swap of two tiles. That effect however, was nearly insignificant as the number of solutions turned out to be so small they could be hand-checked.

The text file server tracked the progress per file, but also per border to minimize the "redo" time in case results came back incomplete.

The employed DAS3- and DAS4-nodes were located at VU and UvA universities in Amsterdam, Technical University Delft, Leiden University (LIACS), the astronomical ASTRON center in Drenthe, and at the Lab for Perceptual Dynamics of the Catholic University in Leuven, Belgium. Each DAS-3

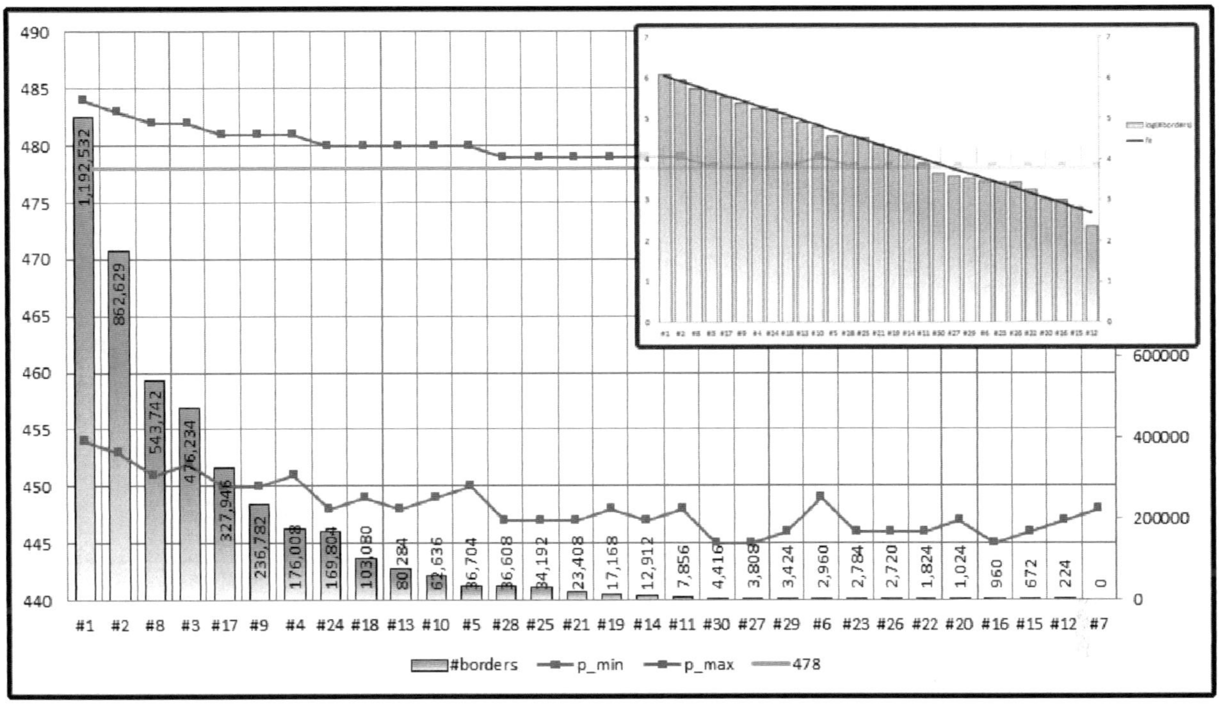

Figure 4. Number of valid borders per eligible 12-set.

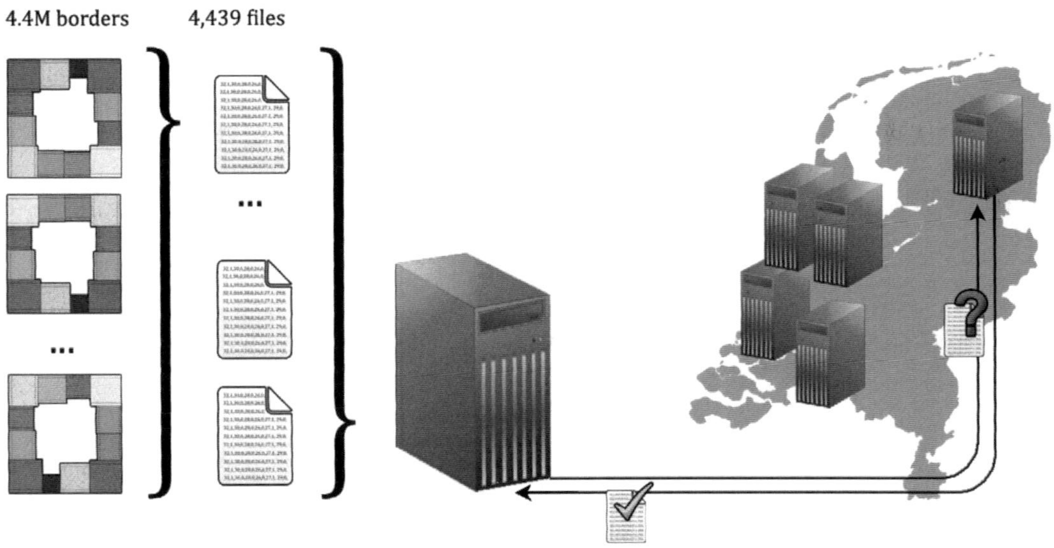

Figure 5. Setup for the solving the Asqas-34 problem.

node can simultaneously run up to four instances of an interior solver, each DAS-4 node up to eight. It is very hard to give an exact run-time estimate since each of these computers is used in a great variety of tasks, has highly volatile availability, occasionally malfunctions, was temporarily shut down for maintenance or were refused reservations for unknown reasons. So although we have completed the entire 12-set, it is quite hard to give an accurate run time estimate.

For a project of this scale, we can give a reasonable upper bound estimate: the entire set was exhaustively investigated in 80 days, running between 800 and 1,000 instances of the interior solver in parallel for between 96 and 116 hours a week. In this time, it found exactly 15 unique solutions to the Asqas-

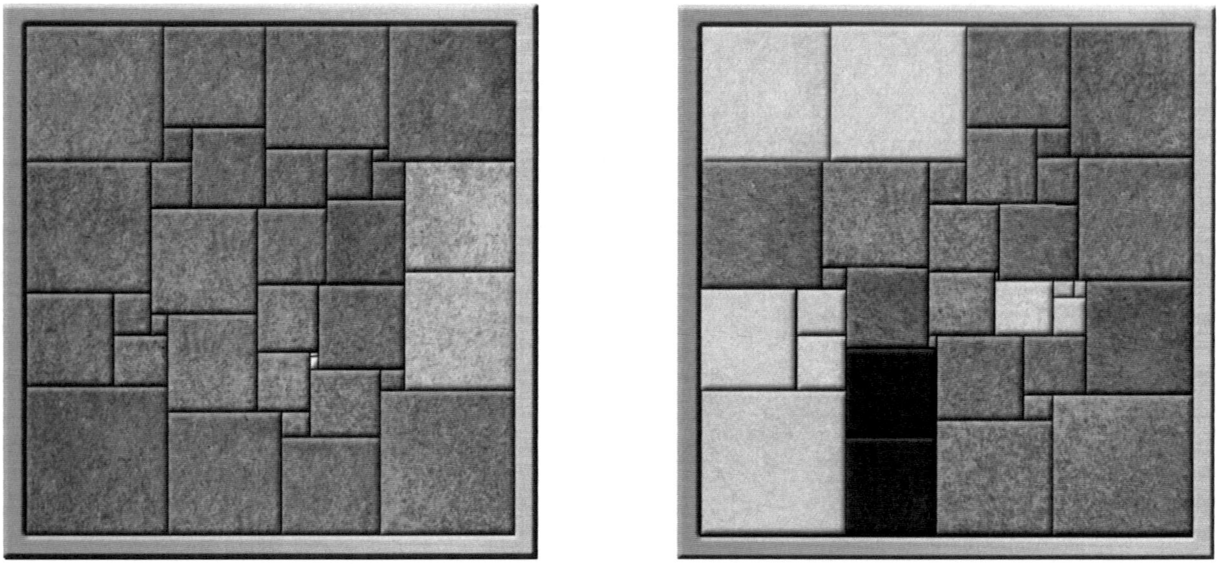

Figure 6. Two solutions to Asqas-34.

34 problem, which are its only solutions with 12 tiles in the border. Nonetheless, solutions with 13 or 14 border tiles are known to exist, because they can be constructed from one of the found solutions. Fig. 6 depicts two solutions to Asqas-34. Note that as both solutions have isomorphic solutions from a complete horizontal or vertical flip, the left hand solution holds potentially three others solutions from flipping either pair of highlighted tiles. The right hand solution can be transformed into at least 255 other solutions by flipping tiles or groups of tiles (highlighted and darkened), some of which have more than 12 tiles in the border.

ACKNOWLEDGEMENTS

Our thanks go to Cees van Leeuwen and Marco Maas for letting us use their server at the Laboratory for Perceptual Dynamics at Catholic University in Leuven, and their support in doing so. Further gratitude is to Rena Bakhshi (VU), Guillaume Pierre (VU), and especially Dion Gijswijt from TU Delft for proofreading this paper so thoroughly.

REFERENCES

[1] A. Lodi, S. Martello, and M. Monaci, "Two-dimensional packing problems: A survey," *European Journal of Operational Research*, vol. 141, pp. 241–252, 2002.

[2] K. A. Dowsland and W. B. Dowsland, "Packing problems," *European Journal of Operational Research*, vol. 56, pp. 2–14, 1992.

[3] L. Kantorovich, "Mathematical methods of organising and planning production," *Management Science*, vol. 6, pp. 366–422, 1960.

[4] M. Formann and F. Wagner, "A packing problem with applications to lettering of maps," in *Proceedings of the Seventh Annual Symposium on Computational Geometry, SCG '91*, 1991, pp. 281–288.

[5] J. E.G. Coffman, M. Garey, and D. Johnson, "An application of bin-packing to multiprocessor scheduling," *SIAM Journal of Computing*, vol. 7, no. 1, 1978.

[6] H. Simonis and B. O'Sullivan, "Almost square packing," in *Integration of AI and OR Techniques in Constraint Programming for Combinatorial Optimization Problems*. Springer-Verlag Berlin, 2011, pp. 196–209.

[7] E. Friedman, "Erich's packing center," URL: http://www2.stetson.edu/ efriedma/packing.html, 2005, retrieved: August 29, 2016.

[8] R. A. Holmgren, *A first course in discrete dynamical systems*, 2nd ed. Springer, New York, 1996, chapter 9.

[9] E. T. Avanesov, "Solution of a problem on figurate numbers (russian)," *ActaArith.*, vol. 12, pp. 409–420, 1966/1967, via http://mathworld.wolfram.com/TetrahedralNumber.html.

[10] G. Watson, "The problem of the square pyramid," *Messenger. Math.*, vol. 48, pp. 1–22, 1918.

[11] E. W. Weisstein, "Perfect square dissection," URL: http://mathworld.wolfram.com/PerfectSquareDissection.html, 2012, retrieved: August 29, 2016.

[12] R. L. Brooks, C. Smith, A. Stone, and W. Tutte, "The dissection of rectangles into squares," *Duke Math. J.*, vol. 7, no. 312–340, 1940.

[13] A. Duijvestijn, "Simple perfect squared square of lowest order," *J. Combin. Theory Ser. B*, vol. 25, no. 2, pp. 240–243, 1978.

[14] Retrieved: August 29, 2016. [Online]. Available: www.squaring.net

[15] H. Simonis and B. O'Sullivan, "Using global constraints for rectangle packing," in *Proceedings of the first Workshop on Bin Packing and Placement Constraints BPPC 2008, associated to CPAIOR 2008*, 2008.

Twitter Analytics for the Horticulture Industry

Marijn ten Thij, Sandjai Bhulai
Vrije Universiteit Amsterdam,
Faculty of Sciences,
Amsterdam, The Netherlands
Email: {m.c.ten.thij, s.bhulai}@vu.nl

Wilco van den Berg
GroentenFruitHuis,
Zoetermeer, The Netherlands
Email: vandenberg@groentenfruithuis.nl

Henk Zwinkels
Floricode,
Roelofarendsveen, The Netherlands
Email: h.zwinkels@floricode.com

Abstract—**In our current society, data has gone from scarce to superabundant: huge volumes of data are being generated every second. A big part of this flow is due to social media platforms, which provide a very volatile flow of information. However, leveraging this information, which is burried in this fast stream of messages, poses a serious challenge. A vast amount of work is devoted to tackle this challenge in different business areas. In our work, we address this challenge for the horticulture sector, which has not received a lot of attention in the literature. Our aim is to extract information from the social data flow that can empower the horticulture sector. In this paper, we present our first steps towards this goal and demonstrate key examples of this empowerment.**

Keywords–Twitter; horticulture; social media analytics.

I. Introduction

In recent years, there have been a lot of overwhelming changes in how people communicate and interact with each other, mostly due to social media. It has revolutionized the Internet into a more personal and participatory medium. Consequently, social networking is now the top online activity on the Internet. With this much subscriptions to social media, massive amounts of information, accumulating as a result of interactions, discussions, social signals, and other engagements, form a valuable source of information. Social media analytics is able to leverage this information.

Social media analytics is the process of tracking conversations around specific phrases, words or brands. Through tracking, one can leverage these conversations to discover opportunities or to create content for those audiences. It is more than only monitoring mentions and comments through social profiles, mobile apps or blogs. It requires advanced analytics that can detect patterns, track sentiment, and draw conclusions based on where and when conversations happen. Doing this is important for many business areas since actively listening to customers avoids missing out on the opportunity to collect valuable feedback to understand, react, and provide value to customers.

The retail sector is probably the business area that utilizes social media analytics the most. More than 60% of marketeers use social media tools for campaign tracking, brand analysis, and for competitive intelligence [1]. Moreover, they also use tools for customer care, product launches, and influencer ranking. Social media analytics is also heavily used in news and journalism for building and engaging a news audience, and measuring those efforts through data collection and analysis. A similar use is also adopted in sports to actively engage with fans. In many business areas one also uses analytics for event detection and user profiling. A vast amount of work is devoted to tackle the challenges in the mentioned business areas. In our work, we address this challenge for the horticulture sector, which has not received a lot of attention in the literature.

The horticulture industry is a traditional sector in which growers are focused on production, and in which many traders use their own transactions as the main source of information. This leads to reactive management with very little anticipation to events in the future. Growers and traders lack data about consumer trends and how the products are used and appreciated. This setting provides opportunities to enhance the market orientation of the horticulture industry, e.g., through the use of social media. Data on consumer's appreciation and applications of products are abundant on social media. Furthermore, grower's communication on social media might indicate future supply. This creates a need for analytic methods to analyze social media data and to interpret them.

In this paper, we present our first steps towards this goal and demonstrate key examples of this empowerment. We start with discussing related research in Section II. In Section III, we describe our dataset that we used in the analysis. Next, we present the results of our data analysis in Section IV. Finally, we conclude the paper in Section V with some discussion and future work.

II. Related Research

Many studies have focused on detecting trends and/or events using data obtained from Twitter, examples are building a prediction system for the number of hit-and-runs [2], or detecting locations of earthquakes [3], or detecting flu spreads and activity [4], [5]. Currently, researchers have extended their scope to a wide range of fields where these methods are being applied.

An example of such a field is journalism. In one of the first descriptive works analyzing the network and content of Twitter, Kwak et al. [6] found that it is mainly used for News (85% of the content). This lead to further analysis of the spread of news in Twitter. For instance, [7] studies the diffusion of news items in *Twitter* for several well-known news media and finds that these cascades follow a star-like structure. Furthermore, [8] studies the life cycle of news articles posted online and describes the interplay between website visit patterns and social media reactions to news content. Through this, the authors show that this hybrid observation method can be used to characterize distinct classes of articles and find that the overall traffic that the articles will receive can be modeled accurately. Also, [9] focuses on Twitter as a medium to help journalists and news editors rapidly detect follow-up stories to the articles they publish and they propose to do so by leveraging transient news crowds, which are loosely-coupled groups that appear in Twitter around a particular news item, and where transient here reflects the fleeting nature of news.

Another active field of study where Twitter is used is in the sports industry. For instance, [10] examines the effectiveness of using a filtered stream of tweets from Twitter to automatically identify events of interest within the video of live sports transmissions. They show that using just the volume of tweets generated at any moment of a game actually provides a very accurate means of event detection, as well as an automatic method for tagging events with representative words from the twitter stream. Also, [11] investigates to what extent we can accurately extract sports data from tweets talking about soccer matches and show that the aggregation of tweets is a promising resource for extracting game summaries. Building on the knowledge of these previous works, [12] describes an algorithm that generates a journalistic summary of an event using only status updates from Twitter as a source. Finally, [13] uses sentiment analysis on tweets of players and other data to model performance of NBA players.

A last example of a sector where Twitter data can be used is the retail industry. For instance, [14] analyzes the perceived benefits of social media monitoring (SMM) and finds that SMM enables industrial companies to improve their marketing communication measurement ability. Also, [15] develops a framework for leveraging social media information for businesses, which focuses on sentiment benchmarks. Furthermore, [16] analyzes the use of social media by destination marketing organizations and finds that they are exploring several ways to leverage social media. Finally, [17] discusses the setup and the key techniques in social media analytics and gives an overview of the possibilities for the industry.

In this work, we use Twitter to empower the horticulture industry by analyzing topic-relevant tweets.

III. Dataset

In this section, we describe how we obtained the tweets that we use in our analysis. These tweets are scraped using the filter stream of the Twitter Application Programming Interface (API) [18]. We use two streams (called "Netherlands (NL) general" and "NL specific"), which are set up with the goal to scrape as many Dutch tweets as possible.

In the "NL general" stream, we use filter stream with the option **track**, where a list of words must be defined. All tweets containing one of these words are caught. We define a list of general Dutch words (e.g., *'een, het, ik, niet, maar, heb, jij, nog, bij'*, which translates to *'a, the, I, not, but, have, you, still, with'*). In total, this list consists of 130 words. Then, "NL specific" uses the filter stream combining **track** and **follow**. For this option, we add a list of user IDs for which all tweets are caught. For this list, we include local news outlets and other news-heavy Twitter accounts, such as neighborhood police accounts. In total, we define a list of 1,303 users. Examples of accounts are *@NUnl, @TilburginBeeld*. The list of terms consists of 395 entries (e.g., *'brandweer, politie, gewond, ambulance'* which translates to *'fire brigade, police, injured, ambulance'*). Note that any caught tweet may be contained in multiple streams, we have not distinguished duplicates in our dataset.

Since we do not have access to the Twitter Firehose, we do not receive all tweets that we request due to rate limitations by Twitter [19]. To give an insight in the volume of tweets that we analyze, we display the total number of tweets that we received on a monthly scale in Table I, which shows that the number of tweets we receive per month is steady throughout the year. All months contain at least 30 million tweets that contains the keywords we used. Using such a large tweet dataset allows us to do studies into less popular topics, without a large loss of accuracy.

TABLE I. NUMBER OF RECEIVED TWEETS FROM AUGUST 1ST 2014 TO AUGUST 1ST 2015.

	Received
August 2014	36,364,128
September 2014	29,418,425
October 2014	32,298,112
November 2014	36,597,687
December 2014	37,065,838
January 2015	38,377,668
February 2015	34,454,250
March 2015	38,722,934
April 2015	33,931,939
May 2015	34,492,494
June 2015	33,274,631
July 2015	31,078,206
Total	416,076,312

For the real-time analysis of Twitter-information, we set up our own Twitter scraper using the Twitter API. Here, we used a list of product names, provided by our partners from GroentenFruitHuis and Floricode, to locate possibly interesting tweets. Again, we tailored these lists to acquire Dutch tweets and used to language filter provided by the Twitter API to ensure that all received tweets are indeed Dutch. The terms are split up into two lists, one containing fruits and vegetables, e.g., apple, orange, and mango, and the other containing flowers and plants, e.g., tulip, rose, and lily.

IV. Data studies

After retrieving the tweets, the first step towards empowering the sector is knowing what kind of information can be retrieved from the social feed. To investigate this, we performed several studies, for which we present the results below. These studies range from an analysis of what is discussed at the current time in Twitter, to a study into the frequency of postings with regards to particular products, to an analysis of the online footprint caused by real-life events.

A. GfK time series

For this analysis, we have used the year long data of Twitter messages from August 2014 to August 2015 and counted the number of occurrences of fruit products mentioned in the text of the tweets. From these mentions, we construct a weekly time series reflecting the number of mentions. Then, we compared these numbers to sales numbers of the most occurring product

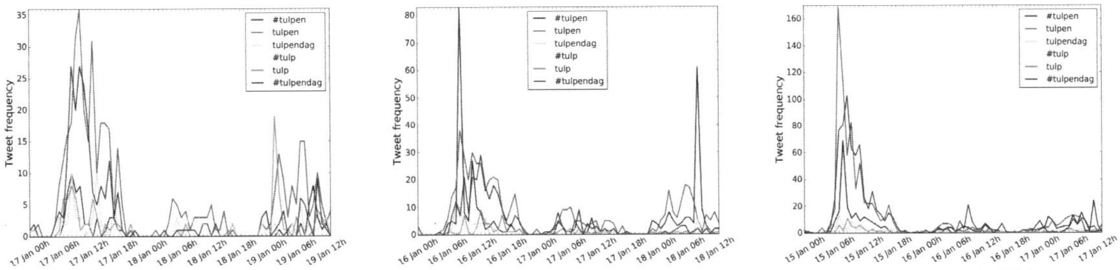

(a) Tulpendag in 2014 (b) Tulpendag in 2015 (c) Tulpendag in 2016

FIGURE 1. TULIP DAY TWEET FREQUENCIES DURING THE DAY ITSELF AND THE TWO DAYS AFTER THE EVENT.

type of these products. Thus, we compared the number of Dutch tweets mentioning 'pears' or 'pear' to the number of Conference pears that are sold in the same time-frame. Similarly, we compared the number of tweets mentioning 'apple' or 'apples' to the number of Elstar apples that are sold. In Figure 2, we present these time series, normalized on the maximum value in the series. In this figure, we see that in both cases the time series for the tweets and the sales are comparable. Using an eight-hour shift for the sales time series, we find a Pearson correlation coefficient of 0.44 for the apples series and a coefficient of 0.46 for the pears series.

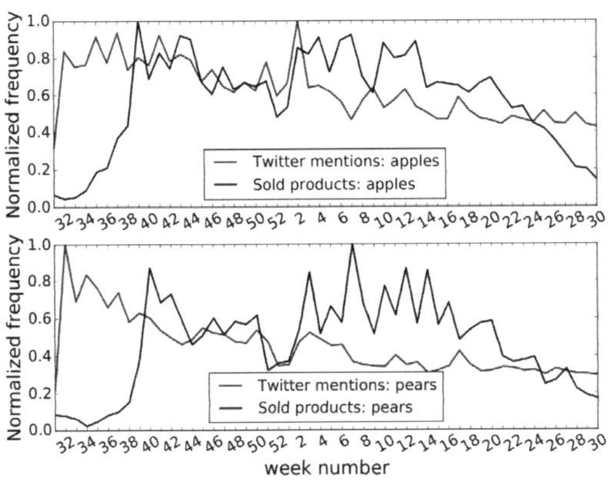

FIGURE 2. WEEKLY NORMALIZED TWITTER MENTIONS AND SALES.

These results indicate that it could be possible to predict the sales of a product type eight weeks in advance, however, this will need to be confirmed using other product types.

B. Tulip day

As a kick-off of the tulip season, which indicates the period in which a large variety of tulips is available at the vendors, the Dutch tulip growers organize the so-called Tulip day in Amsterdam. During this day, growers place a field of a large range of different tulips on the Dam in Amsterdam. During a few hours in the afternoon, visitors are allowed to pick the tulips in this field. For this event, we analyzed the presence on Twitter over a few years. For 2014, 2015, and 2016, we counted the occurrences of the tags 'tulip', 'tulips', and 'tulip day', both during the event and the two days after the event. The results of this study are presented in Figure 1. Here, we clearly see an increase in the number of mentions of the Tulip day on Twitter, this increase in mentions coincides with an intensified campaign by the growers and the governing body to broaden the attention to the Tulip day event. This analysis shows that the impact of the effort by marketing can be measured through Twitter analysis.

C. Top 10 rankings

The studies we discussed so far are based on a static collection of tweets. Another approach to extract value from Twitter is to see what a continuous feed of messages contains. To better understand how the products we are interested in are discussed on Twitter on a real-time basis, we set up two lexicons as described at the end of Section III. Using these lexicons, we scan Twitter in real-time for tweets that match these products. Using the tweets we receive this way, we can analyze what is currently discussed about these products. As a first step, we visualize this information in a top-10 application. The main page of this application shows the top 10 most discussed products on Twitter in the last day for both fruits/vegetables and plants/flowers, of which an example is shown in Figure 3. By clicking on one of the products in these top lists, we are redirected to a page, shown in Figure 4 for bananas, which shows us both the current messages mentioning the product and a detailed analysis of these messages, e.g., in terms of the most occurring tokens and a time series in which the terms are mentioned.

D. Story detection

The real-time data is also used for the detection of stories and discussions that suddenly pop-up. We do this by clustering incoming tweets by their tokens, using the Jaccard index. For sets A and B, this index equals

$$J(A,B) = \frac{|A \cap B|}{|A \cup B|}.$$

If two tweets are more similar than a predefined threshold, which we set at 0.4, then these two tweets will be represented by the same cluster. Therefore, if a topic is actively discussed on Twitter, it will be represented as a cluster in our story detection. Since these clusters are renewed every hour we add

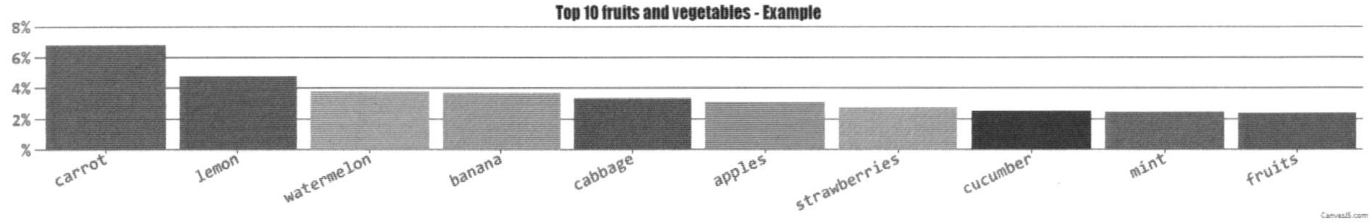

FIGURE 3. EXAMPLE OF THE TOP 10 DISCUSSED FRUITS AND VEGETABLES ON TWITTER.

the notion of stories, which clusters the clusters over time. By doing this, we can also track which clusters are prevalent for a longer period of time and therefore will be very likely to be of value for the industry. A current implementation of this method has been successfully implemented for the news reporting industry. This system can be found at [20].

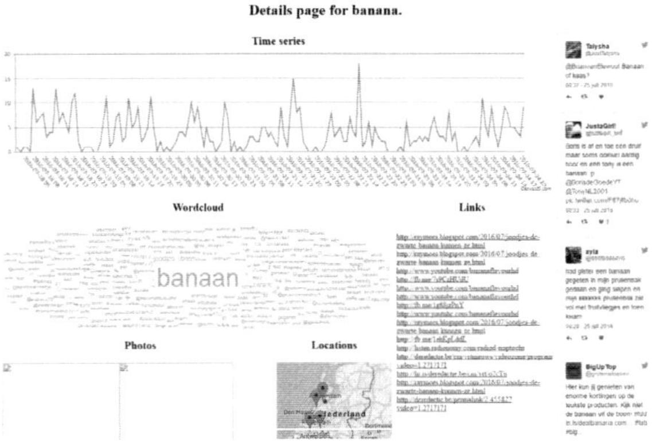

FIGURE 4. EXAMPLE OF DETAILS PAGE FOR TWEETS MENTIONING BANANAS.

V. DISCUSSION AND FUTURE WORK

In this paper, we describe our first steps towards empowering the horticulture industry by analyzing topic-relevant tweets in Twitter. During our first exploration of the Twitter data, we encountered some interesting results. For instance, we found that there could be predictive power in the number of times a specific product is mentioned on Twitter for the future sales numbers of that particular product. Furthermore, we developed methods to visualize the current industry specific content in real-time and filter out interesting information in the process.

These ideas can be fruitfully adopted in marketing analytics to directly measure the impact of marketing activities. Furhermore more, Section IV-A yields promising result in the production planning. These first results provide a good basis for further study.

ACKNOWLEDGMENTS

We thank RTreporter for supplying access to their tweet collections for our analyses.

REFERENCES

[1] D. Metric. Social media bechmark report. Retrieved: August 29, 2016. [Online]. Available: http://www.netbase.com/blog/why-use-social-analytics (2013)

[2] X. Wang, M. Gerber, and D. Brown, "Automatic Crime Prediction using Events Extracted from Twitter Posts," in Social Computing, Behavioral-Cultural Modeling and Prediction. Springer, 2012, vol. 7227, pp. 231–238.

[3] T. Sakaki, M. Okazaki, and Y. Matsuo, "Earthquake shakes Twitter users: real-time event detection by social sensors," in Proceedings of the 19th international conference on World wide web. ACM, 2010, pp. 851–860.

[4] E. Aramaki, S. Maskawa, and M. Morita, "Twitter catches the flu: detecting influenza epidemics using Twitter," in Proceedings of the Conference on Empirical Methods in Natural Language Processing. Association for Computational Linguistics, 2011, pp. 1568–1576.

[5] A. Signorini, A. M. Segre, and P. M. Polgreen, "The use of Twitter to track levels of disease activity and public concern in the us during the influenza a h1n1 pandemic," PLoS One, vol. 6, no. 5, 2011, p. e19467.

[6] H. Kwak, C. Lee, H. Park, and S. Moon, "What is Twitter, a social network or a news media?" in Proceedings of the 19th international conference on World wide web. ACM, 2010, pp. 591–600.

[7] D. Bhattacharya and S. Ram, "Sharing news articles using 140 characters: A diffusion analysis on Twitter," in Advances in Social Networks Analysis and Mining (ASONAM), 2012 IEEE/ACM International Conference on. IEEE, 2012, pp. 966–971.

[8] C. Castillo, M. El-Haddad, J. Pfeffer, and M. Stempeck, "Characterizing the life cycle of online news stories using social media reactions," in Proceedings of the 17th ACM Conference on Computer Supported Cooperative Work & Social Computing, ser. CSCW '14. New York, NY, USA: ACM, 2014, pp. 211–223. [Online]. Available: http://doi.acm.org/10.1145/2531602.2531623

[9] J. Lehmann, C. Castillo, M. Lalmas, and E. Zuckerman, "Transient news crowds in social media," in Proceedings of the Conference on Weblogs and Social Media, ser. ICWSM. AAAI, 2013, pp. 351–360.

[10] J. Lanagan and A. F. Smeaton, "Using Twitter to Detect and Tag Important Events in Live Sports," Artificial Intelligence, vol. 29, no. 2, 2011, pp. 542–545. [Online]. Available: http://www.aaai.org/ocs/index.php/ICWSM/ICWSM11/paper/download/2821/3236

[11] G. Van Oorschot, M. Van Erp, and C. Dijkshoorn, "Automatic extraction of soccer game events from Twitter," in CEUR Workshop Proceedings, vol. 902, 2012, pp. 21–30. [Online]. Available: http://ceur-ws.org/Vol-902/paper_3.pdf

[12] J. Nichols, J. Mahmud, and C. Drews, "Summarizing sporting events using twitter," in IUI '12: Proceedings of the 2012 ACM international conference on Intelligent User Interfaces. ACM, 2012, pp. 189–198. [Online]. Available: http://dl.acm.org/citation.cfm?doid=2166966.2166999$\backslash$npapers3://publication/doi/10.1145/2166966.2166999

[13] C. Xu, Y. Yu, and C.-K. Hoi, "Hidden in-game intelligence in nba players' tweets," Commun. ACM, vol. 58, no. 11, Oct. 2015, pp. 80–89. [Online]. Available: http://doi.acm.org/10.1145/2735625

[14] J. "Järvinen, A. Töllmen, and H. Karjaluoto, "Marketing Dynamism & Sustainability: Things Change, Things Stay the Same...". Springer International Publishing, 2015, ch. "Web Analytics and Social Media Monitoring in Industrial Marketing: Tools for Improving Marketing

Communication Measurement", pp. 477–486. [Online]. Available: http://dx.doi.org/10.1007/978-3-319-10912-1_157

[15] W. He, H. Wu, G. Yan, V. Akula, and J. Shen, "A novel social media competitive analytics framework with sentiment benchmarks," Information & Management, vol. 52, no. 7, 2015, pp. 801–812, novel applications of social media analytics. [Online]. Available: http://www.sciencedirect.com/science/article/pii/S0378720615000397

[16] S. Hays, S. J. Page, and D. Buhalis, "Social media as a destination marketing tool: its use by national tourism organisations," Current Issues in Tourism, vol. 16, no. 3, 2013, pp. 211–239. [Online]. Available: http://dx.doi.org/10.1080/13683500.2012.662215

[17] W. Fan and M. D. Gordon, "The power of social media analytics," Commun. ACM, vol. 57, no. 6, Jun. 2014, pp. 74–81. [Online]. Available: http://doi.acm.org/10.1145/2602574

[18] Retrieved: August 29, 2016. [Online]. Available: https://dev.twitter.com/streaming/reference/post/statuses/filter

[19] Retrieved: August 29, 2016. [Online]. Available: https://dev.twitter.com/rest/public/rate-limits

[20] Retrieved: August 29, 2016. [Online]. Available: http://www.rtreporter.com

Using Data Mining Techniques for Information System Research Purposes – An Examplary Application in the Field of Business Intelligence and Corporate Performance Management Research

Karin Hartl, Olaf Jacob
Department of Information Management
University of Applied Sciences Neu-Ulm
Neu-Ulm, Germany
karin.hartl@hs-neu-ulm.de, olaf.jacob@hs-neu-ulm.de

Abstract—**Corporate Performance Management (CPM) is a management concept based on performance measures. These measures are supplied by Business Intelligence (BI), which transformed information technology in companies from data storage solutions towards decision support systems. It is believed that BI enhances CPM and that BI needs CPM for a purposeful commitment. To gain a detailed insight in the relationship between these two constructs a Data Mining approach is used. Data Mining is a data driven statistical approach for knowledge discovery. In comparison to commonly used Information System research approaches, like Structural Equation Modelling, in Data Mining no hypothesis have to be developed beforehand. Therefore, otherwise undiscovered patterns, information and hypothesis embedded in a given dataset can be discovered. As an example, Association Rule Discovery has been applied to a questionnaire based dataset investigating the relationship between BI and CPM. The results of the Data Mining approach show indeed more detailed information about the connection of BI and CPM than the usually applied research methods Exploratory Factor Analysis and Structural Equation Modelling.**

Keywords-Data Mining; Association Rule Discovery; Business Intelligence; Corporate Performance Management.

I. INTRODUCTION

This research aims to explore the connection between Business Intelligence (BI) and Corporate Performance Management (CPM) to make the business value of BI tangible. The approach used is Data Mining. Data Mining are data-driven and hypothesis free methods, identifying patterns, information and hypothesis embedded in a given dataset [23][16]. In Information System (IS) research – especially regarding the connection between BI and CPM – Explanatory Factor Analysis (EFA) and Structural Equation Modelling (SEM) are the commonly used approaches. Before applying the statistical analysis, research assumptions and hypothesis have to be developed and later confirmed with data collected for this specific research purpose. This approach has one major limitation, its reliance on human imagination for generating research assumptions [20]. Instead, Data Mining techniques are working up from the data [23]. Hypothesis are not necessarily developed beforehand, making the detection of new and unexpected connections in the dataset possible. It is believed, that more detailed knowledge can be discovered by using exploratory Data Mining techniques.

Association Rule Discovery is a widely used and well-known Data Mining method and therefore has been identified as a suitable first approach in exploring the value Data Mining has for IS research. Association Rule Discovery searches for structural connections in a dataset, formulate If-Then-Statements and can take all available research criteria into account. In this research example, the results of the Association Rule Analysis could allow conclusions on the BI capabilities supporting successful CPM. As both CPM and BI consist of several characteristics, the Data Mining approach could help to focus on the important features in each area too.

In Section 2, a short introduction on the importance of the thematic research background is given, pointing out why an investigation of the connection between BI and CPM is necessary. Section 3 discusses the subject related research and the empirical approaches used in these studies. In Section 4, the motivators for using the non-traditional IS research approach Data Mining are evaluated. In Section 5, the research approach to the exemplary subject is described, and, in Section 6 the results for this example are presented. Section 7 discusses the sample results and the conclusion in Section 8 summarizes the benefits of using the Data Mining approach.

II. THEORY AND RESEARCH BACKGROUND

The challenge companies have to face nowadays for success and existence proves to be increasingly difficult. Globalization intensifies the competition and digitalization leaves enterprises with an immense amount of mainly unstructured data. These data and the contained information, however, are assumed to be the key to ensure the survival of an enterprise in the rapidly changing business environment. BI as a method of analysing data and the business environment promises companies to support their decision making process [1][23]. The support is achieved by acquiring, analysing and disseminating information from data significant to the business activities [7]. Accordingly, BI is seen as a source for quality data and actionable information. This implies that the appropriate use of BI systems supports the success of organizations [10].

As BI projects are not exempt from the increasing pressure in companies to justify the return on IT investment, the business value of BI needs to be measured [18]. Due to the abstract nature of BI, capturing its value is a strategic challenge [14][28]. Generally, BI systems do not pay for themselves strictly by cost reduction. Most BI benefits are intangible and hard to measure [18]. Williams and Williams [28] point out that the business value of BI lies in its use within the management processes. Therefore, the concept of CPM evolved, which is understood as the appropriate context to prove the value proposition and benefits of BI [14][15]. It is defined by Gartner as "an umbrella term that describes all processes, methodologies, metrics and systems needed to measure and manage the performance of an organization" [3]. CPM presents the strategic deployment of BI solutions and is born out of a company need to proactively manage business performance [4][13]. Inferentially, CPM needs BI to work effectively on accurate, timely and high quality data and BI needs CPM for a purposeful commitment [3]. As a consequence, it is expected that the effectiveness of CPM increases with the effectiveness of the BI solution and therefore company success improves as well [22].

III. Subject Related Research

In the last couple of years, various studies regarding the relationship between BI and performance management emerged.

Miranda [15] brought BI into context with CPM by summarizing CPM as a business management approach that supports companies in their way of operation by using business analysis. CPM is identified as a suitable framework for determining the business value of BI. Although no observable empirical background and foundation is provided, this article supplies the foundation for more detailed research in the field, including the following.

Empirical studies on the investigation of the connection between BI and CPM have mainly been realized just recently. Aho [1] evaluates the differences and similarities between BI and CPM by conducting a literature study and action oriented research. The results indicate that BI and CPM need to work together to be efficient and effective. However, the rather weak empirical background does not deliver any details on the relationship of BI and CPM.

Yogev et al. [29] address the question of the business value gained by implementing a BI system in an enterprise by using a process oriented approach. The research model identifies key BI resources and capabilities as possible explanatory factors of the value creation that can be accomplished with the implementation and application of a BI system. Hypothesis are formulated and tested using Explanatory Factor Analysis (EFA) and Structural Equation Modelling (SEM). The results illustrate that BI has a positive effect on both the operational and the strategic level of the company. Nevertheless, the empiricism does not provide any details about the BI related resources creating this positive effect.

Saed [24] investigates the relationship between BI and business success using regression and correlation analysis. While these statistical techniques provide room for detailed results, only aggregated explanations have been provided.

Richards et al. [22] are the first to directly investigate the impact and connection of BI on CPM using EFA and SEM. The research model supposes that BI directly influences and supports measurement, planning and analytics. The effectiveness of planning, measurement and analytics, again, influences the effectiveness of the company processes. Through a large-scale survey, sample data has been collected. Afterwards, with EFA the number of variables comprised in the questionnaire has been reduced followed by the Partial Least Square (PLS) analysis. Even though the research identifies a direction of how BI influences CPM, the specific BI mechanisms that do so are not defined.

This research project complements the subject related work, as the previous findings have been used as the initial point. But besides discovering and proving a positive connection between BI and CPM, these researches lack detail. Instead of grouping the characteristics and measurement items describing BI and CPM with EFA and SEM together, all items are considered separately. It is believed that this approach helps to get an in-depth insight into the relationship between BI and CPM.

IV. Motivation for the Data Mining Approach

The common approach in the research field of determining the value of BI is using EFA first and then CFA second. With the EFA correlating items are organized together in groups and summed up as a factor [2]. Data can be structured and reduced this way. This structured and reduced data are then analysed with the PLS method by seeking the optimal predictive linear relationship to assess the previously defined causal relationship [26][27]. The creation of factors for compacting information might be the right approach for many research subjects, but it must not be the only correct approach to explore connections in IS research. It is assumed that Data Mining can highly contribute to the subject. Data Mining is a data driven approach and supports the discovery of new and sometimes unexpected knowledge [20]. Instead of only testing assumed hypothesis, with Data Mining otherwise undiscovered data attributes, trends and patterns can be explored [6]. Especially with explanatory Data Mining techniques, a better understanding of connections in the dataset can be achieved [5]. Although Data Mining is often only seen as most suitable for large datasets, Natek and Zwilling [17] disclose that the use of small datasets in general are not limiting the use of the tool. Data Mining can be understood as an extension of statistical data analysis and statistical approaches [9]. Both approaches aim to discover structure in data, but Data Mining methods are generally robust to non-linear data, complex relationships and non-normal distributions [25]. These differences between Data Mining and the commonly used statistical approaches are assumed to supply more detailed and surprising results for the research field of BI and CPM. In particular, the research is working with Association Rule Discovery. Through Association Rule Discovery, the research aims to identify the strongest co-occurrence relationships between BI and CPM. It is believed that the results indicate the BI items most supporting to a successful and effective CPM. Furthermore, the outcomes will most likely provide more detailed insights in the relationship of BI and CPM.

V. Research Method and Results

A. Research Procedure

In the Data Mining literature, two main research procedures can be found, the Cross Industry Standard Process for Data Mining process model (CRISP-DM) or the overall procedure model Knowledge Discovery in Data bases (KDD) [5]. Both have the main process steps in common. The ones shown in Fig. 1 will be followed in this research. As the dataset is comparatively small, no selection of the appropriate dataset was seen as necessary. Therefore, the starting point for the data analysis was the pre-processing of the data. The data has been cleansed and missing, as well as conflicting values corrected. Cleve and Lämmel [5] suggest alternatives for dealing with missing values depending on the data structure. The important items of the questionnaire are formatted as Likert scale items and can be interpreted as metric data. Metric data can be pre-processed by replacing the missing values in the sample by the mean value of all item-based compiled answers. Alternatively, the mean values can be stated by contemplating the datasets closest to the dataset with the missing value. This idea follows the k-nearest neighbours (kNN) approach. Joenssen and Müllerleite [11] assess the kNN approach as practicable imputation method for missing Likert scale values if the dataset is small. Therefore, the missing values in the dataset were imputed using the kNN approach. After pre-processing, the data have been transformed in the required format for the applicable Data Mining technique. The applied Apriori Algorithm needs binary data [5]. Therefore, the Likert scale items have been transformed into binary variables. In the penultimate step, the data have been mined. Afterwards, in the discussion, the outcomes have been interpreted and evaluated. The interpretation and evaluation presupposes a subject knowledge background. As in every research, not all findings are valuable and of real-life meaning. Hence, only sensible research results should be discussed and applied. The decision about the sensibility of the research rests with the researcher and field experts.

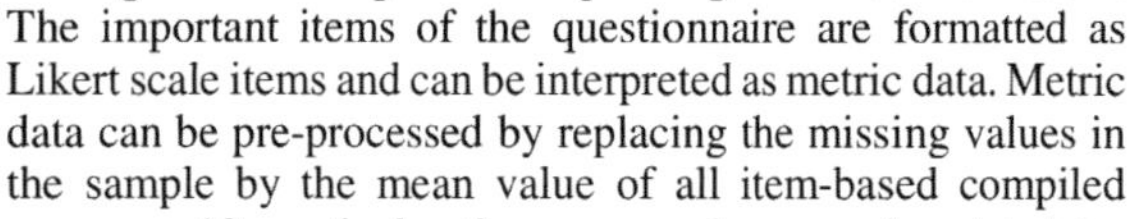

Figure 1. Research Procedure Model KDD

B. Data Collection

This research is based on the findings of [8], where a set of criteria that is seen as suitable to represent CPM on one hand, and BI on the other hand, has been identified. After an additional evaluation and definition of the pre-defined items, 20 CPM related items and 28 BI related items have been selected for further research (Table 1). A study has been conducted to bring the criteria of both fields together and to clarify the relationship between BI and CPM. Therefore, the identified criteria have been transformed into questionnaire items, which had to be answered on a five-point Likert scale. The anchor points at the ends of the scale have been "does not apply" and "fully applies" and an additional definition "applies half and half" for the mid stage has been defined. The data collection has taken place from December 2014 until March 2015 using telephone interviews and an online questionnaire. Subjects were German companies who use BI for supporting their performance management. Hence, decision makers from management, controlling and IT were addressed. In total 169 questionnaires were completed resulting in a response rate of 11.3%. The participating companies are mainly mid-sized to large German firms belonging to the manufacturing industry.

VI. Analysis and Results

Data Mining as a technique to discover new and unexpected patterns and relationships in data is the approach used to explore connections and associations between the BI and CPM criteria. In comparison to correlation or regression analysis, many Data Mining techniques do not imply connections in advance but discover them automatically. Association Rule Discovery is a popular pattern discovery method [20]. With association rules, co-occurrence relationships between data items can be discovered, taking into account as many research items as needed and available [5]. This indeed can lead on the upside to more detailed results and on the downside to an enormous amount of discovered association rules. Unmanageable amounts of association rules easily can be organized by instating measures to evaluate and select association rules based on their potential interestingness for the researcher [20]. These interestingness measures include *Lift*, *Support* and *Confidence* [5][16]. To generate association rules, many algorithms are available. The Apriori Algorithm is the classic procedure and works in two steps [21][30]. First, frequent itemsets exceeding the pre-defined *Support* threshold are identified. Therefore, the Apriori Algorithm initially finds itemsets containing of one item only. In the following steps, the algorithm includes one more item each round to the previously identified frequent itemsets until no more frequent itemsets are found [30]. Second, out of all frequent itemsets exceeding the pre-defined *Support* threshold confident association rules are generated. Hence, all identified frequent itemsets are separated into two subsets. The measure influencing which rules are understood as interesting is the *Confidence* measure [5].

In this research, Association Rule Discovery has been applied to find relation rules between BI and CPM. Before applying the Apriori Algorithm to the compiled dataset using the freeware Data Mining tool RapidMiner, the data had to be transformed into binary variables. This transformation can be done directly in RapidMiner. Questionnaire characteristics "does not apply" to "applies half and half" (1-3) have been transformed to *does not apply* and "does apply" and "fully applies" (4-5) to *does apply*. Furthermore, the minimum levels for the interestingness measures have been defined. Only association rules ($X \rightarrow Y$) with a minimum $Support \geq 0.6$ have been considered as interesting, meaning that in at least 60% of the cases in the dataset the association rule has to show [16]. The confidence level has been set at $Confidence \geq 0.7$. This determines that in at least 70% of the rules where the first part of the rule (X) is shown, the second part of the rule (Y) has to show as well [16]. The measure *Lift* needs to be $Lift > 1$ to show

TABLE I OVERVIEW BI AND CPM ITEMS

BI items	**CPM items**
BI1_1: Clear roles and responsibilities for operating the BI systems	CPM1_1: Business management processes are transparent and traceable for managers
BI1_2: Data consistency ("Single Version of the Truth")	CPM1_2: Business management process are documented throughout the company
BI1_3: 24/7 operation of the BI systems	CPM1_3: Business management processes are communicated throughout the company
BI1_4: Only compulsory BI tools are used	CPM2_1: Business management processes base on a common database
BI1_5: Data integrity during simultaneous use	CPM2_2: Management methods are fully automated and linked without manual support
BI1_6: Clear roles and responsibilities for the BI-development between the company's departments and the IT throughout the whole enterprise	CPM2_3: Data in business management processes are complete
BI1_7: BI-architecture is documented	CPM2_4: Decision makers manual expenditure to edit reports is marginal
BI1_8: Master data changes are traceable	CPM3_1: Data in business management processes are relevant
BI1_9: BI relevant master data can be saved in various versions	CPM3_2: Data in business management processes are current
BI2_1: Use of feature set for predictive forecasting	CPM3_3: Effective use of external data (market data)
BI2_2: Use of feature set for describing data analysis	CPM4_1: Alignment of business management processes across all business functions
BI2_3: Use of feature set for information visualization	CPM4_2: Alignment of business management processes across all business units
BI3_1: Use of applications for scenario modelling	CPM4_3: Alignment of strategic and operational planning
BI3_2: Use of applications for statistical analysis	CPM5_1: Use of measurable indicators in all business functions
BI4_1: Each BI project is carried out using a standardized procedure model	CPM5_2: Use of measurable indicators in all business units
BI4_2: Each BI project bases on a standardized design method	CPM5_3: Use of measurable indicators in all operational business processes
BI4_3: Documentation standards for BI projects are clearly defined	CPM5_4: Use of measurable indicators in all strategic business processes
BI4_4: BI projects use agility	CPM6_1: Existence of feedback loops in operational business processes (e.g., complaint management)
BI5_1: Use of applications for adding describing comments	CPM6_2: Existence of feedback loops in strategy development (adjustment of vision, mission and the company's strategy to environmental changes)
BI5_2: Use of applications for sharing comments throughout the enterprise	CPM6_3: Existence of feedback loops in strategic planning processes
BI5_3: Use of applications for automatic text processing and Text Mining	
BI6_1: Denotations and spellings are standardized in the BI databases	
BI6_2: BI tools for strategic business management are interoperable	
BI6_3: Manual expenditures for ensuring standardized spelling and denotations are marginal	
BI7_1: Applications for mobile usage of the BI Systems are available	
BI7_2: Applications for the mobile usage of the BI Systems are used	
BI8_1: Use of BI applications for implementing alerts linked to automated workflow data in operational business processes	
BI8_2: Use of BI applications for implementing alerts linked to automated workflow data in strategic business processes	

a positive dependency between the items of a rule for the occurrence of the items [5]. Regarding the minimum settings of the measures, 103 association rules have been discovered.

Association rules do not imply causality. They find items that imply the presence of other items [20]. As the research focus is on the benefits of BI for CPM, the attention lies on association rules beginning with BI items, leaving 52 association rules to evaluate. The association rules with the highest *Support* are shown in Table 2.

It is conspicuous that especially the CPM items *Data in business management processes are relevant* and *Data in business management processes are current* apply in a company, if specific BI items apply either. In more detail, these two CPM items most likely apply in a company, if in addition to the items in Table 2 the following BI items apply as well:

- *Data consistency ("Single Version of the Truth"),*
- *Only compulsory BI tools are used,*
- *Master data changes are traceable,*
- *Clear roles and responsibilities for the BI-development between the company's departments and the IT throughout the whole enterprise.*

Also, the BI item *Use of applications for automatic text processing and Text Mining* is found in combination rules with the item *Clear roles and responsibilities for operating with the BI system* and *Data integrity during simultaneous use*. Different from these two, *Use of applications for automatic text processing and Text Mining* has the characteristic does not apply. Still, the CPM items *Data in business management processes are relevant* and *Data in business management processes are current* apply, indicating that data currency and relevance is rather given if Text Mining and context processing tools are not used in a company.

Furthermore, the association rules illustrate that:

TABLE II. STRONGEST ASSOCIATION RULES, STARTING WITH BI ITEMS

BI items		CPM items	Interestingness
Data integrity during simultaneous use=applies	→	Data in business management processes are relevant=applies	Support=0.83 Confidence=0.92
Clear roles and responsibilities for operating the BI systems=applies	→	Data in business management processes are relevant=applies	Support=0.80 Confidence=0.93
Data integrity during simultaneous use=applies	→	Data in business management processes are current=applies	Support=0.78 Confidence=0.86
Data integrity during simultaneous use=applies and Clear roles and responsibilities for operating the BI systems=applies	→	Data in business management processes are relevant=applies	Support=0.76 Confidence=0.93
Data integrity during simultaneous use=applies	→	Data in business management processes are relevant=applies and Data in business management processes are current =applies	Support=0.74 Confidence=0.83
Clear roles and responsibilities for operating the BI systems=applies	→	Data in business management processes are current=applies	Support=0.74 Confidence=0.86
Clear roles and responsibilities for operating the BI systems=applies	→	Data in business management processes are relevant=applies and Data in business management processes are current =applies	Support=0.73 Confidence=0.84
24/7 operation of the BI systems=applies	→	Data in business management processes are relevant=applies	Support=0.70 Confidence=0.91

- *Use of BI applications for implementing alerts linked to automated workflow data in strategic business processes* does not apply,
- *Use of applications for sharing comments throughout the enterprise* does not apply,
- *Use of applications for adding describing comments* does not apply,
- *Use of applications for automatic text processing and Text Mining* does not apply

the CPM item *Management methods are fully automated and linked without manual support* does not apply as well.

VII. DISCUSSION

CPM is a management strategy for decision support [19]. This support is achieved by using measures and KPI's (Key Performance Indicator) from data. The information gained is used by decision makers and managers to monitor the companies target achievements. If necessary, strategy, processes and goals are adjusted to ensure the company's survival and success. Data is the quintessence in CPM but only useful if provided when needed and of high quality. The association rules show that if BI items related to the subject of data quality and data provision (e.g., *Data consistency, Data integrity during simultaneous use*) are high and apply in a company the *Data in the business management processes are relevant* and *current*. The rules illustrate the connection between data and business management processes and therefore the connection between BI and CPM. Supported with high quality data, decision makers can act and rely on actionable information to manage the enterprise. The rules underline the function of BI as a decision support tool needed for a successful CPM. The concentration on business management processes as the CPM part of the rule highlights the understanding of CPM as a multiplicity of business management processes connected and integrated into each other [12]. If the processes in a company are managed, based on needed high quality data, it is the initial point for an overall effective CPM. Nevertheless, a CPM strategy is not implemented in one run. The implementation is a slow process carried out in sub-steps [19]. The focus of the association rules on *Data in business management processes is relevant* and *current* supports this theory. It is indicated that first the attention has to lie on the management processes separately. Once a company is working on high quality data when needed, a good connection throughout the enterprise is given as well. The lack of association rules containing further CPM items might be an indicator that most companies are assumedly still working on implementing a thorough performance management.

The second set of association rules discovered that if no opportunity to use and share comments within an enterprise is given as well as the opportunity to use unstructured data a full automation and linkage of the company's management methods without manual support is not given as well. Management methods are ideally accepted process descriptions for dealing with certain issues (e.g., Balanced Scorecard) [19]. These methods can only be successful if goal oriented, understood and used continuously [19]. Consequently, management methods are focused on the definition and analysis of measures. For all measures to be useful, a reference magnitude is needed, which can be supplied by adding and sharing comments. Furthermore, the association rules imply that fully automated management and planning methods are dependent on the use of comments for ensuring transparency as well. Only if supported by describing comments, automated management processes and planning methods are understandable throughout a company and manual support is minimalized.

Text Mining enables knowledge discovery from semi-structured or unstructured data. This is a rather advanced analysis method of BI and the rules indicate that if there is no or not much *usage of automatic text processing and Text Mining, Data in business management processes* are still *relevant* and *current* but the *Management methods* are not fully *automated or linked without manual support*. Text Mining is an advanced research method used to gain new information from texts. The association rules suggest, that this feature of BI is rather not important for the data currency and relevance in the business management processes. Therefore, it might to be ignored in the establishment process of CPM. But it seems to be interesting once the automation of management methods without manual support wants to be achieved.

The association rules discovered only comprise 3 different CPM related items *Data in business management processes are current, Data in business management processes are relevant* and *Management methods are fully automated and linked without manual support*. This awakes the awareness that BI is not the only technological support in companies. Enterprise Resource Planning Systems (ERP), Customer Relationship Systems (CRM) and Supply-Chain-Management System (SCM) also play an important role for a successful performance management. Before focusing on implementing a BI solution, the predominant step might be to focus on existing software first and afterwards built an effective BI solution on top.

VIII. CONCLUSION

In comparison to the subject related research, the results of the Data Mining approach show more detailed information about the connection of BI and CPM. Instead considering BI and/or CPM as a whole, with Data Mining all BI and CPM features have been taken into account, allowing researchers and practitioners comprehensive insights into the relationship between these two interdependent disciplines. Besides simply proving a positive relationship, the research outcomes allow conclusions on a path of action for improving a company's CPM through the correct usage and implementation of BI. Although these inferences still need further investigation in practice, it has been possible to identify the BI and CPM items with the strongest connection through association analysis. Inferentially, the Data Mining approach presents itself as a suitable research procedure in IS research.

But this research still is only a first step in exploring the possibilities Data Mining holds for IS research. Future studies need to evaluate if and how Data Mining can be used to gain detailed research insights.

REFERENCES

[1] M. Aho, "The Distinction between Business Intelligence and Corporate Performance Management - A Literature Study Combined with Empirical Findings", Proceedings of the MCSP 2010 Conference, 2010.

[2] K. Backhaus, B. Erichson, W. Plinke, and R. Weiber, Multivariate analysis: An application-oriented introduction, 13th edn., Springer, Berlin, 2011.

[3] J. Becker, D. Maßing, and C. Janiesch, "An evolutionary process model for introducing Corporate Performance Management Systems", Data Warehousing, pp. 247–262, 2006.

[4] www.researchandmarkets.com/reports/1055897, retrieved: 2, 2015.

[5] J. Cleve and U. Lämmel, Data Mining, De Gruyter Oldenbourg, München, 2016, p. 187, 216 ff., 235.

[6] M. L. Gargano and B. G. Raggad, "Data Mining - a powerful information creating tool", OCLC Systems & Services: International digital library perspectives, 15(2), pp. 81–90, 1999.

[7] M. Hannula and V. Pirttimäki, "Business intelligence empirical study on the top 50 Finnish companies", Journal of American Academy of Business, 2(2), pp. 593–599, 2003.

[8] K. Hartl, O. Jacob, F. H. Lien Mbep, A. Budree, and L. Fourie, "The Impact of Business Intelligence on Corporate Performance Management", Proceedings of the 49th HICSS Conference, pp. 5041–5051, 2016.

[9] J. Jackson, "Data Mining; A Conceptual Overview", Communications of the Association for Information Systems, 8(1), pp. 267–296, 2002.

[10] O. Jacob and F. H. Lien Mbep, "Factors to Determine the Value of Business Intelligence to Corporate Performance Management", University of Applied Sciences Neu-Ulm, 2014.

[11] D. W. Joenssen and T. Müllerleite, "Missing Data in Data Mining", HMD Praxis der Wirtschaftsinformatik, 51(4), pp. 458–468, 2014.

[12] M. Lang, ed., Handbook of Business Intelligence: Potentials, Strategies, Best Practices, 1st edn., Symposion, Düsseldorf, 2015.

[13] F. H. Lien Mbep, O. Jacob, and L. Fourie, "Critical Success Factors of Corporate Performance Management (CPM) Literature Study and Empirical Findings", BUSTECH Conference Proceedings, pp. 6–14, 2015.

[14] http://legacy.wlu.ca/documents/22449/07_Measuring_the_Benefits_of_BI_Viva.pdf, retrieved: 02, 2016.

[15] S. Miranda, "Beyond BI: Benefiting from CPM Solutions", Financial Executive, 20(2), pp. 58–61, 2004.

[16] R. M. Müller and H.-J. Lenz, "Business Intelligence", Springer Berlin Heidelberg, Berlin, Heidelberg, 2013.

[17] S. Natek and M. Zwilling, "Data Mining for small student datasets - knowledge management system for higher education teachers", Management, Knowledge and Learning Conference, pp. 1379–1398, 2013.

[18] S. Negash, "Business Intelligence", The Communications of the Association for Information Systems, 13(1), pp. 177–195, 2004.

[19] K. Oehler, Corporate Performance Management with Business Intelligence tools, Hanser, München, 2006.

[20] K.-M. Osei-Bryson and O. Ngwenyama, "Advances in Research Methods for Information Systems Research: Data Mining, Data Envelopment Analysis, Value Focused Thinking", Springer, New York, 34, 2014.

[21] H. Petersohn, Data Mining: Methods, Processes and Application Architecture, Oldenbourg, München, 2005.

[22] G. Richards, W. Yeoh, A. Y.-L. Chong, and A. Popovic, "An empirical study of business intelligence impact on corporate

performance management", Proceedings of the Pacific Asia Conference on Information Systems 2014, pp. 1–16, 2014.
[23] S. Rouhani, A. Ashrafi, A. Zare Ravasan, and S. Afshari, "The impact model of business intelligence on decision support and organizational benefits", Journal of Enterprise Information Management, 29(1), pp. 19–50, 2016.
[24] R. A. Saed, "The Relationship between Business Intelligence and Business Success: An Investigation in Firms in Sharjah Emirate", American Journal of Business and Management, 2(4), pp. 332–339, 2013.
[25] A. J. Stolzer and C. Halford, "Data mining methods applied to flight operations quality assurance data: a comparison to standard statistical methods", Journal of Air Transportation, 12(1), pp. 6–24, 2007.
[26] N. Urbach and F. Ahlemann, "Structural equation modeling in information systems research using partial least squares", JITTA: Journal of Information Technology Theory and Application, 11(2), pp. 5–40, 2010.
[27] V. E. Vinzi, C. Wynne, J. Henseler, and H. Wang, Handbook of partial least squares: Concepts methods and applications, Springer, Berlin, 2010.
[28] S. Williams and N. Williams, "The Business Value of Business Intelligence", Business Intelligence Journal, 8, pp. 30–39, 2003.
[29] N. Yogev, L. Fink, and A. Even, "How Business Intelligence Creates Value", Proceedings of the ECIS Conference, 2012.
[30] R. Agrawal and R. Srikant, "Fast Algorithms for Mining Association Rules", Proceedings of the 20th VLDB Conference Santiago, Chile, pp. 487-499, 1994.

Travelled Distance Estimation for GPS-based Round Trips: Car-Sharing Use Case

Angel J. Lopez*†, Ivana Semanjski*, Dominique Gillis*, Daniel Ochoa† and Sidharta Gautama*
*Department of Telecomunications and Information Processing
Ghent University
St-Pietersnieuwstraat 41, B-9000 Ghent, Belgium
Emails: {angel.lopez, ivana.semanjski, dominique.gillis, sidharta.gautama} @ugent.be
†Facultad de Ingeniería en Electricidad y Computación
Escuela Superior Politécnica del Litoral, ESPOL
Campus Gustavo Galindo Km 30.5 Vía Perimetral, P.O. Box 09-01-5863, Guayaquil, Ecuador
Emails: {alopez,dochoa} @espol.edu.ec

***Abstract*—Traditional travel survey methods have been widely used for collecting information about urban mobility although, since middle of the 90's Global Position System (GPS) has become an automatic option for collecting more precise data of the households. But how good is the collected data? many studies on mobility patterns have focused on the GPS advantages and leaving aside its issues. However, when it comes to extract the frequency of the trips and travelled distance this technology faces some gaps due to related issues, such as signal reception and time-to-first-fix location that turns out in missing observations and respectively unrecognised or over-segmented trips. In this study, we focus on two aspects of GPS data for a car-mode, (i) measurement of the gaps in the travelled distance and (ii) estimation of the travelled distance and the factors that influence the GPS gaps. To asses that, GPS tracks are compared to a ground truth source. Additionally, the trips are analysed based on the land use (e.g., urban and rural areas) and length (e.g., short, middle and long trips). Results from 170 participants and more than a year of GPS-tracking show that around 9% of the travelled distance is not captured by the GPS and it affects more to short trips than long ones. Moreover, we validate the importance of the time spent on the user activity and the land use as factors that influence the gaps on GPS.**

Keywords*—*Data quality; travelled distance; CAN-BUS data; GPS data

I. INTRODUCTION AND RELATED WORK

Traditional travel survey methods have been widely used in transportation research as a tool for collecting information at an individual or household level (e.g., description of demographics, travel patterns, trip purpose and mode choice) [1]. Yet, respondents have the tendency to omit short stops, such as post office and ATM and when it comes to numerical answers, travel time is rounded to simple values like 10, 15, 30 minutes interval. Likewise it happens to the travelled distance [2].

Nonetheless, with the introduction of the Global Position System (GPS) and its first adoption on transportation studies in the middle of the 90's, where Wagner [2] reports one of the first studies that uses GPS for collecting information of 100 households through logger devices installed in their vehicles, since that it has been extensively used in combination with others datasets. Studies [3], [4], and [5] have already demonstrated the possibility to use GPS data in Transportation research by capturing the characteristics of different types of trips. Later studies, such as [6] and [7] evaluated the use of processed GPS data for both trip tracking and transportation-mode detection without the support of questionnaires. Their results showed that trip identification deviates slightly from the census data whereas for mode detection it was not possible to distinguish between transportation modes with similar speed, for instances bus and car trips. Trip reporting and therefore travelled distance are challenging issues that can be achieved by detecting the transition between transportation-modes although, if many transitions are detected for a single-mode trip, it turns out in over-reporting of trips and under-reporting of distance. In studies [8] and [9], the GPS trajectories are split using features, such as speed and distance, it applies a good common-sense knowledge of the world, describing that the start and end points of walk segment may be changes of transportation mode and Liao et al. [10] uses an probabilistic approach to estimate those changes. Zheng et al. [11] shows that extracting trip frequencies is a challenging task, despite his method classifies transportation-mode with an accuracy of 76%, the precision for trip counting is below 30% due to the over-segmentation, which actually shows that many studies report the classification error as a proportion of miss-classification regardless the over-segmentation. A way to overcome that is by merging the consecutive trips with similar transportation-mode using heuristics on the distance and time between trips or by smoothing the classification outcomes [12].

However, signal reception and time-to-first-fix (TTFF) are well known issues of GPS, both of them affecting the reported distance [13]. Signal reception is mainly influent for external factors that can block or reflect the signal, it can lead with either *signal loss* due to poor satellite reception (e.g., underground travel, bridges and tunnels) or multi-path errors aka *urban canyoning errors* because they appear in urban canyons where the signal is reflected by buildings [14]. TTFF aka *cold/warm start* is the delay in getting the first observation when the GPS device has been off for a period of time, which turns out in missing observations at the beginning of the trip [15].

In this study, we use tracking data from a fleet of shared cars to (i) assess the gaps present in the GPS-based distance and their possible effect in mobility studies, and (ii) to estimate the travelled distance and the relevant factors that influence the GPS gaps. To accomplish the previous points, we need a ground truth source that reports the driven kilometres when the car is used, therefore the odometer-sensor is chosen and its data is accessible through the Controller Area Network bus (CAN-bus) [16]. CAN-bus is known as a protocol for high performance and high reliable serial communication links between electronic control units (e.g., sensors), and it is mainly used in the field of automotive and industrial control applications [17]. CAN-bus has been used together with GPS data to estimate mobility parameters in off-road vehicles, such as resistance force and wheel slip under different terrain conditions [18], where a GPS logger was used to gather the ground speed and trajectory; and the gross power and rotational speed were extracted from the CAN-bus. Furthermore, given that GPS trajectories are spread across different type of land use, we use a Geographic Information System (GIS) to make a distinction between trips in urban and rural areas.

The remainder of this paper is organised as follows. Section II describes the datasets and methods for assessing GPS gaps on the car mode. Section III presents the case study and the outcomes of this research and Section IV summarise the findings by drawing conclusions on it.

II. Methodology

The data from the present research is drawn from two sources (a) a car-sharing company named *Cambio* [19] that opened its operation in Belgium in 2002, and at this time (June 2016), it is available in 35 cities with 369 stations, 862 cars and more than 24.000 users. *Cambio* provided us a dataset with the reservation details (e.g., distance, duration, start and ending times) based on CAN-bus data. (b) GPS data that are collected through loggers installed on selected cars from the car-sharing company.

A. Dataset description

As one of the interests in this study is to identify the differences in GPS-based distance and the actually driven kilometres, we use the car odometer-sensor data as a ground truth. The access to that such a data is possible through the CAN-bus. A CAN-bus is known as a protocol for high performance and high reliable serial communication links between electronic control units in the field of automotive and industrial control applications [17], for example it is typically used to control and automatically calibrate the engine performance in a vehicle. It was developed as a multi-master message broadcast system [20] where each element on the network can send a message (e.g., temperature, state of charge) independently to the entire network, being the bus priority defined by the message identifier [21]. The dataset contains information about the car reservation, including the total distance, reservation period (e.g., duration), identifiers (cars/client/reservation), start and ending times.

A limitation of this dataset concerns to its granularity, which is at the reservation level, therefore the reservation period represents the total duration of the reservation rather than the travel time, as an illustration, a reservation starts when the car is picked up from the car charging station and it ends when the car returns back to the charging station. Consequently, the reservation period contains not only the travel time but also the time spent on the participant activities for instances time doing shopping, time visiting someone, etc. Nonetheless, the travelled distance and the starting time (first trip segment) are not affected for the aforementioned limitation.

GPS has been used in several studies (Section I) and it allows tracking targets through their geographical location, where a GPS logger is a device for collecting locations and other measurements, such as speed, altitude, heading, accuracy and timestamp. It can have either a built-in or external antenna and the data can be stored in the internal memory for being downloaded later on, or sent it to a centralised repository through the network. For collecting the data, a GPS logger *GenLoc 53e* [22] is installed in the cars, the device can send the tracking data through the cellular network to a centralised system in which it is processed. A frequency of 1 Hz is used for collecting the GPS data and the logger only collects observations when the car is turned on (i.e., the GPS logger automatically starts when the car is turned on and stops when the car is turned off), therefore it can occur that a single reservation includes more than one trip, which is expressed as follow:

$$R_i = \{S_1^{(i)}, ..., S_m^{(i)}\} \qquad (1)$$

where, R_i represents the ith reservation, $S_j^{(i)}$ is the jth trip segment within a reservation R_i, such as $S_j^{(i)} \in \{S_1^{(i)}, ..., S_m^{(i)}\}$ and m is the number of trip segments per reservation.

B. Data quality

To assess the quality of the GPS-based distance, we calculate missing distance and the TTFF using the following formulations:

$$\text{Missing distance}_{\text{prop}} = 1 - \frac{\sum_{S_j^{(i)} \in R_i} d(S_j^{(i)})}{\sum_{i=1}^{N} d(R_i)} \qquad (2)$$

$$\text{Missing distance}_{\text{avg}} = \frac{1}{N}\sum_{i=1}^{N}\Big(d(R_i) - \sum_{S_j^{(i)} \in R_i} d(S_j^{(i)})\Big) \qquad (3)$$

$$\text{TTFF}_{\text{avg}} = \frac{1}{N}\sum_{i=1}^{N}\Big(t(S_1^{(i)}) - t(R_i)\Big) \qquad (4)$$

where $d()$ and $t()$ are functions to extract the distance and start time respectively, $S_1^{(i)}$ represents the first trip segment of a reservation R_i, and N is the number of observations.

Equation (2) is the proportion of missing distance and it calculates the overall missing distance for all reservations. Nevertheless, it can also be applied to a set of trips based on some conditions, such as land use and trip groups. However, this formulation faces two possible outcomes, when the outcome is positive it represents an under-reported distance, whereas it is negative when the distance is over-reporting. This last scenario can be explained by the GPS accuracy because under certain conditions (e.g., tunnel, bridge, parking lots) turns out in jumps around the same location. Those points can add an extra distance to the trip.

Equation (3) is the average missing distance and it is expressed in kilometres and (4) is the average of time-to-first-fix, it calculates an average of time difference between the reservation start time and the timestamp of the first GPS location.

C. Land use

A key research focus of this study is to assess the GPS gaps, where the land use provides an extra perspective to analyse those gaps in rural and urban areas, given that the GPS signal reception could be affected for the high density of large structures (e.g., buildings, bridges). A GIS tool allows to identify the land use of a trip [23] (i.e., whether a trip was performed on either rural or urban area) in such a way that trips are matched within an administrative area (boundary area classified as rural or urban) through the origin and destination points. Consequently, a precise land use identification relies on the completeness of the geographical information for the administrative areas.

The administrative areas (in which the trips were performed) are extracted from ©OpenStreetMap contributors (OSM) [24]. OSM is an open access platform for geospatial vector data and it is often considered complete and appropriate for planning studies in comparison to other commercial counterparts [25].

D. Regression method

To explain the gaps in GPS data, the factors that influence the data collection are identified through a linear regression. Linear Regression methods are techniques for modelling the relationships between a scalar dependent variable and its explanatory or independent variables aka covariates, that relationship is modelled through a error term ε, a random variable that adds noise to the linear relationship between the dependent and independent variables [26], therefore the model is expressed as follows:

$$\mathbf{y} = \mathbf{X}\beta + \varepsilon \tag{5}$$

where $\mathbf{y}$ is the dependent variable or response variable, $\mathbf{X}$ represents the explanatory variables, β the regression coefficients or effects and ε is the error term.

III. Case Study

The data on this study are part of the Olympus project, a Flemish initiative to promote the introduction of electric vehicles in Belgium. It was a common project between suppliers, integrators and users of shared mobility, aiming at developing tools and systems to enhance multimodal travel behaviour. Therefore, the multimodal travel behaviour was monitored, both from the vehicle perspective as from the personal perspective. From the vehicle perspective, GPS loggers were installed on shared electric cars, showing how these were used in terms of frequency, trip length, origins and destinations.

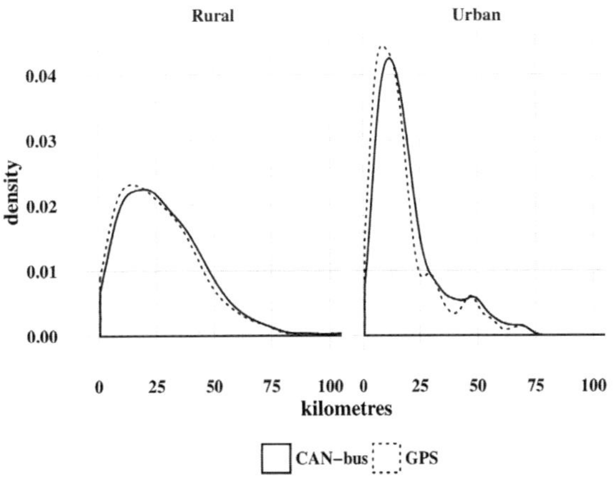

Figure 1. Travelled distance density based on land use for GPS logger and CAN-bus data

Data collection was performed between 2012 and 2013 in the Belgian cities Ghent, Antwerp and Leuven, involving 170 participants.

A. Descriptive analysis

A summary of the travelled distance reported by the CAN-bus data and GPS logger is depicted in Table I, where we can notice clear differences on the reported average distances.

TABLE I. A SUMMARY OF THE TRAVELLED DISTANCE (KM)

Data	min	median	mean	max
CAN-bus	2.0	19.0	23.9	106.0
GPS Logger	0.6	17.2	21.8	104.6

In order to get an analysis at different levels, we group the trips based on the travelled distance into three categories, such as short, middle and long trips. Table II shows the conditions for those groups.

TABLE II. GROUP OF TRIPS BASED ON THE TRAVELLED DISTANCE

Group	Description
Short trip	less than 10 km.
Middle trip	between 10 and 25 km.
Long trip	more than 25 km.

Those groups and the land use allow to identify which type of trips are mainly affected when it comes to GPS tracking.

The missing distance for the GPS logging can be noticed in Fig. 1, where the GPS density curve is shifted to the left side with respect to CAN-bus curve in both rural and urban areas, this is another indication of missing distance based on the land use.

B. Distance measurement gaps

For the travelled distance by car, we consider the missing distance as the difference between the odometer distance (e.g., distance obtained from the CAN-bus data) and the logging distance (e.g., distance reported by the GPS logger) as it shows in (2), it turns out that on average 9% of the travelled distance is not captured by the GPS logger (Fig. 2). It means that for an average trip with distance 23.9 km the GPS will report on average 2.1 km less (Table I).

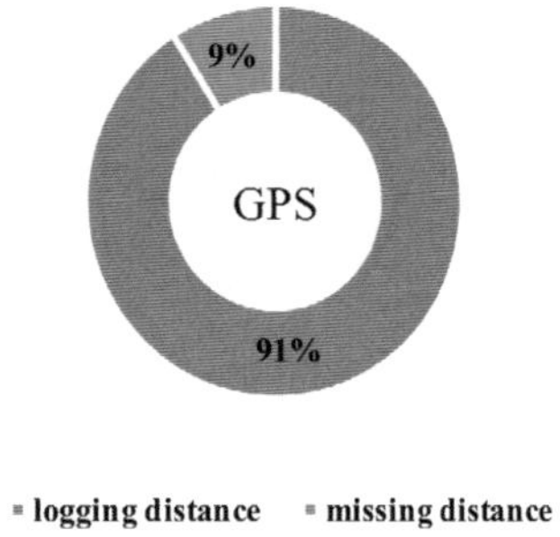

Figure 2. Global missing distance for a car mode using GPS

From the groups, we calculate the travelled distance for both GPS and CAN-bus data. Fig. 3 shows the missing data for short, middle and long trips within groups of different land used, in which, urban areas affect more to the short and middle distance trips (around 81% and 83% respectively) than the long trips (Table III). Besides, the GPS logging performs better for long trips in both urban and rural areas, logging 92% and 95% respectively.

TABLE III. A SUMMARY OF THE GPS GAPS BASED ON THE LAND USE

			TTFF (min)		Missing distance (km)	
	Group	Trips	Median	Mean	Mean	Percentage
Rural	Short	82	4.6	7.8	0.9	11.9%
	Middle	190	6.1	7.0	1.9	10.1%
	Long	292	5.6	8.3	2.0	4.6%
Urban	Short	161	5.5	16.5	1.4	19.3%
	Middle	326	5.9	10.8	2.9	16.9%
	Long	189	6.2	7.8	3.6	8.5%

To our understanding, part of the missing data could be related to the cold/warm start issue that is present on the GPS technology, where it is required a period of time before fixing the first location. Therefore we assess the TTFF using (4), which makes use of the starting time as an argument.

C. Explanatory factors

To explain the travelled distance a regression model is fitted to the GPS data, where the dependent variable is provided by the CAN-bus data as a travelled distance and from the GPS data we extract the covariates, such as distance, duration, average speed and number of trips per reservation.

Others covariates, such as land use is obtained using GIS, where the origin and destination points are used for classifying the trips within a rural or urban area. Finally, the time spent on the user activity (purpose of mobility) is calculated from the reservation time and the trip duration. Table IV shows a full description of the covariates.

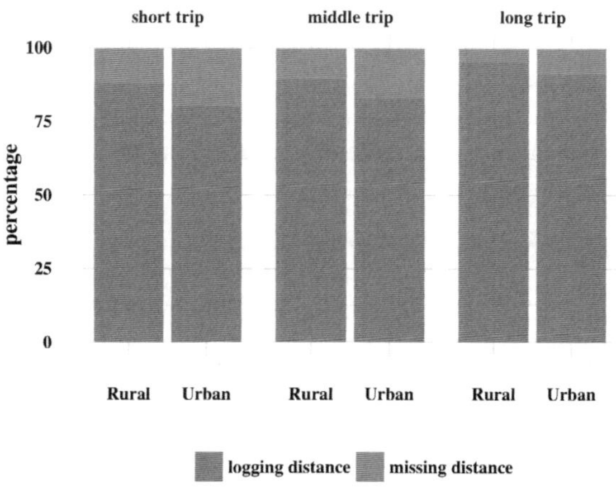

Figure 3. Percentage of missing data for different group of trips

TABLE IV. MODEL COVARIATES

Covariate	Description
Distance	Logging distance from the GPS data (km)
Duration	Travelled time for the logging distance (min)
Trip segments	Number of trip segments per reservation
Average speed	Average speed for the trip (km/h)
Time spent	Time spent on the user activity (e.g., shopping)
Time spent per trip	Average time spent per trip
Land use	Land use for the trip (e.g., urban, rural)

A summary of the fitted models is depicted in Table V, where the covariate coefficient is estimated using a regression model and its significant level is based on the p-value. Based on *model 3*, the number of *trip segments* seem to be not significant, on the other hand from *model 4* we can notice that the average speed is a good predictor and makes the *duration* less significant.

Time spent shows significant results on *model 5*, it means that the waiting time within trips (e.g., time when the car is parking) is important factor for modelling the travelled distance because it adds more periods of cold/warm start to the GPS logger (i.e., a higher waiting time increases the chances of missing data). And it is even more significant when it is combined with the *trip segments* as an average of *time spent* on a particular activity per *trip segments* (e.g., time spent over trip segments). Land use is another influential variable its coefficient indicates that for each trip in the urban area it will add around a kilometre to the total distance. Based on the R^2, *model 7* explains better the travelled distance as a function of the covariates: distance, average speed, time spent per trip and land use.

IV. CONCLUSION

In this paper, we measure the gaps in the GPS-based distance using CAN-bus data as a ground truth, likewise the factors that influence those gaps were identified through regression models. It was found that on averages 9% of the travelled distance is not captured for the GPS logger, this is important, considering that many mobility studies are

TABLE V. MODELS RESULT

	Dependent variable: Travelled distance (km)						
	(1)	(2)	(3)	(4)	(5)	(6)	(7)
Distance	0.976*** (0.013)	1.032*** (0.020)	1.044*** (0.021)	0.888*** (0.049)	0.905*** (0.017)	0.920*** (0.017)	0.930*** (0.016)
Duration		−0.047*** (0.013)	−0.061*** (0.016)	0.019 (0.024)			
Trip segments			0.250 (0.155)				
Average speed				7.180*** (2.232)	5.854*** (1.177)	4.701*** (1.247)	5.196*** (1.225)
Time spent					0.008*** (0.002)	0.003 (0.003)	
Time spent per trip						0.015*** (0.006)	0.019*** (0.004)
Urban area							1.062*** (0.388)
Constant	2.837*** (0.324)	3.698*** (0.402)	3.247*** (0.488)	0.535 (1.060)	0.457 (0.477)	0.709 (0.482)	−0.076 (0.565)
AIC	1967	1957	1956	1949	1928	1923	1916
BIC	1979	1972	1976	1968	1947	1946	1940
R^2	0.944	0.946	0.946	0.948	0.950	0.951	0.952
Adjusted R^2	0.944	0.946	0.946	0.947	0.950	0.951	0.952

Note: *p<0.1; **p<0.05; ***p<0.01

Covariates: coefficient and coefficient error in brackets.
AIC: Akaike information criterion, *BIC:* Bayesian information criterion.

being conducted using GPS data, and their outcomes might underestimate the actual travelled distance. Although, it will depend on the type of land use where the trips are carried out. In our findings, the rural area reports 6% of missing distance whereas the urban area about 13%, which is a clear indication that urban areas are more susceptible to issues related to the signal reception, affecting in around one kilometre to the reported distance (based on the *model 7*).

Moreover, the model also includes the cold/warm start as a function of the time spent on the user activity per trip, which provides an average waiting time between trips. This last factor should be considered when it comes to the trip reporting because in real situations round trips have more than a single trip and long periods of waiting time, consequently, it adds a delay for getting the first valid location.

Part of the missing distance could be corrected by interpolating the missing GPS points within a trip. Using a road network is feasible to route (provide alternative trajectories between two points by a given transportation mode) and align the points to a valid location. However, it becomes complicated when the missing part is at the beginning of the trip because there is not any reference point to interpolate that part. This is the case of the cold/warm start.

Our findings also contrast with other study [27] that reports 4% of missing data (comparison among theoretic GPS points rather than travelled distance) for a driving mode using smartphones as tool for GPS data collection. However, a smartphone does not have long periods of being off, hence we could assume that TTFF is not having a big influence on the data collection.

Future directions are focused on the GPS data quality for other transportation modes (e.g., walking, biking and public transportation) and also the differences across the collection methods, for example, passive and active logging.

ACKNOWLEDGMENT

The authors thank their respective institutions, Ghent University, Escuela Superior Politécnica del Litoral (ESPOL), and The National Secretary of Higher Education, Science, Technology and Innovation of Ecuador (SENESCYT) for its support through the scholarship program Open Call 2012-I.

REFERENCES

[1] S. Handy, "Methodologies for exploring the link between urban form and travel behavior," *Transportation Research Part D: Transport and Environment*, vol. 1, no. 2, pp. 151–165, 1996.

[2] D. P. Wagner, "Lexington area travel data collection test: GPS for personal travel surveys," *Final Report, Office of Highway Policy Information and Office of Technology Applications, Federal Highway Administration, Battelle Transport Division, Columbus*, pp. 1–92, 1997.

[3] L. Yalamanchili, R. Pendyala, N. Prabaharan, and P. Chakravarthy, "Analysis of Global Positioning System-Based Data Collection Methods for Capturing Multistop Trip-Chaining Behavior," *Transportation Research Record: Journal of the Transportation Research Board*, vol. 1660, pp. 58–65, jan 1999. [Online]. Available: http://trrjournalonline.trb.org/doi/10.3141/1660-08

[4] G. Draijer, N. Kalfs, and J. Perdok, "Global Positioning System as Data Collection Method for Travel Research," *Transportation Research Record: Journal of the Transportation Research Board*, vol. 1719, pp. 147–153, jan 2000. [Online]. Available: http://trrjournalonline.trb.org/doi/10.3141/1719-19

[5] J. Wolf, D. Dr, and R. Guensler, "Using GPS data loggers to replace travel diaries in the collection of travel data," Ph.D. dissertation, 2000.

[6] A. Bolbol, T. Cheng, I. Tsapakis, and J. Haworth, "Inferring hybrid transportation modes from sparse GPS data using a moving window SVM classification," *Computers, Environment and Urban Systems*, vol. 36, no. 6, pp. 526–537, nov 2012. [Online]. Available: http://linkinghub.elsevier.com/retrieve/pii/S0198971512000543

[7] N. Schuessler, K. Axhausen, and N. Schüssler, "Processing Raw Data from Global Positioning Systems Without Additional Information," *Transportation Research Record: Journal of the Transportation Research Board*, vol. 2105, pp. 28–36, dec 2009. [Online]. Available: http://trrjournalonline.trb.org/doi/10.3141/2105-04

[8] L. Zhang, M. Qiang, and G. Yang, "Mobility Transportation Mode Detection Based on Trajectory Segment," *Journal of Computational Information Systems*, vol. 8, pp. 3279–3286, 2013.

[9] Y. Zheng, Y. Chen, Q. Li, X. Xie, and W.-Y. Ma, "Understanding transportation modes based on GPS data for web applications," *ACM Transactions on the Web*, vol. 4, no. 1, pp. 1–36, 2010.

[10] L. Liao, D. J. Patterson, D. Fox, and H. Kautz, "Learning and inferring transportation routines," *Artificial Intelligence*, vol. 171, no. 5-6, pp. 311–331, apr 2007. [Online]. Available: http://linkinghub.elsevier.com/retrieve/pii/S0004370207000380

[11] Y. Zheng, L. Liu, L. Wang, and X. Xie, "Learning transportation mode from raw gps data for geographic applications on the web," in *Proceeding of the 17th international conference on World Wide Web - WWW '08*, no. 49. New York, New York, USA: ACM Press, 2008, p. 247. [Online]. Available: http://portal.acm.org/citation.cfm?doid=1367497.1367532

[12] A. J. Lopez, D. Ochoa, and S. Gautama, "Detecting Changes of Transportation-Mode by Using Classification Data," in *18th International Conference on Information Fusion (Fusion 2015)*. Washington, DC: Information Fusion (Fusion), 2015, pp. 2078–2083. [Online]. Available: http://ieeexplore.ieee.org/stamp/stamp.jsp?tp={&}arnumber=7266810{&}isnumber=7266535

[13] M. Flamm, C. Jemelin, and V. Kaufmann, "Combining person based GPS tracking and prompted recall interviews for a comprehensive investigation of travel behaviour adaptation processes during life course transitions," in *11th World Conference on Transportation Research*, Berkeley, 2007.

[14] N. Schuessler and K. Axhausen, "Identifying trips and activities and their characteristics from GPS raw data without further information," Tech. Rep., 2008. [Online]. Available: http://e-collection.library.ethz.ch/view/eth:30471

[15] P. Stopher, Q. Jiang, and C. FitzGerald, "Processing GPS Data from Travel Surveys," in *2nd international colloqium on the behavioural foundations of integrated land-use and transportation models: frameworks, models and applications*, Toronto, 2005, pp. 1–21.

[16] I. S. O. Standard, "Iso 11898, 1993," *Road vehicles–interchange of digital information–Controller Area Network (CAN) for high-speed communication*, 1993.

[17] K. Turski, "A global time system for CAN networks," in *Proceedings of the 1st International CAN Conference*, vol. 13, no. 3, Mainz, 1994, pp. 31–36.

[18] A. Suvinen and M. Saarilahti, "Measuring the mobility parameters of forwarders using GPS and CAN bus techniques," *Journal of Terramechanics*, vol. 43, no. 2, pp. 237–252, 2006.

[19] "Cambio Belgium a car-sharing company," http://www.cambio.be, retrieved: July, 2016.

[20] M. Farsi, K. Ratcliff, M. Barbosa, K. Ratcliff, and M. Farsi, "An overview of Controller Area Network," *Computing & Control Engineering*, vol. 10, no. June, pp. 113–120, 1999. [Online]. Available: http://digital-library.theiet.org/content/journals/10.1049/cce{_}19990304

[21] R. Bosch, "CAN Specification Version 2.0," *Rober Bousch GmbH, Postfach*, vol. 300240, p. 72, 1991.

[22] "Erco and Gener genlog53e," http://www.ercogener.com, retrieved: July, 2016.

[23] P. Stopher, E. Clifford, J. Zhang, and C. FitzGerald, "Deducing mode and purpose from GPS data," *Institute of Transport and Logistics Studies*, 2008.

[24] "OpenStreetMap contributors," http://www.openstreetmap.org/copyright, retrieved: July, 2016.

[25] H. H. Hochmair, D. Zielstra, P. Neis, and P. N. Hartwig H. Hochmair, Dennis Zielstra, "Assessing the Completeness of Bicycle Trail and Designated Lane Features in OpenStreetMap for the United States and Europe," *Proceedings of the Transportation Research Board 92nd Annual Meeting*, vol. 19, no. 1, pp. 1–21, 2013.

[26] J. Neter, M. H. Kutner, C. J. Nachtsheim, and W. Wasserman, *Applied linear statistical models*. Irwin Chicago, 1996, vol. 4.

[27] S. Vlassenroot, D. Gillis, R. Bellens, and S. Gautama, "The Use of Smartphone Applications in the Collection of Travel Behaviour Data," *International Journal of Intelligent Transportation Systems Research*, pp. 17–27, 2014. [Online]. Available: http://link.springer.com/10.1007/s13177-013-0076-6

Forecasting Travel Behaviour from Crowdsourced Data with Machine Learning Based Model

Angel J. Lopez[1,2]; Ivana Semanjski[1]; Sidharta Gautama[1]
[1] Ghent University, Department of Telecomunications and Information Processing,
Ghent, Belgium
Emails: {angel.lopez, ivana.semanjski, dominique.gilles, sidharta.gautama} @ugent.be
[2]Facultad de Ingenierıa en Electricidad y Computacion
Escuela Superior Polit´ecnica del Litoral, ESPOL
Guayaquil, Ecuador
Emails: alopez @espol.edu.ec

Abstract—**Information and communication technologies have become integral part of our everyday lives. It seems as logical consequence that smart city concept is trying to explore the role of integrated information and communication approach in managing city's assets and in providing better quality of life to its citizens. Provision of better quality of life relies on improved management of city's systems (e.g., transport system) but also on provision of timely and relevant information to its citizens in order to support them in making more informed decisions. To ensure this, use of forecasting models is needed. In this paper, we develop support vector machine based model with aim to predict future mobility behavior from crowdsourced data. The crowdsourced data are collected based on dedicated smartphone app that tracks mobility behavior. Use of such forecasting model can facilitate management of smart city's mobility system but also ensures timely provision of relevant pre-travel information to its citizens.**

Keywords-travel behavior; smart city; crowdsourceing; transport planning.

I. INTRODUCTION

Influence of information and communication technologies (ICT) on transport planning is not new. On one hand, transport planning involves multiple complex models that try to generalize dynamic features of human and cargo movements, needs for mobility and forecasts future states of the system. On the other end, ICT constantly develops, which includes higher processing powers and calculation capabilities, innovative protocols and growing number of available sensors. Thus, integration of ICT tools into transport planning process is twofold challenging and requires constant synchronization between available technology and transport planning needs. A lot has been done in this field over last decades, particularly in recent years when role of ICT is getting integrated at the higher level enabling development of smart cities [1]-[8]. In this context, location acquisition technologies play an important basis for smart city applications [9][10]. Smart cities as urban development concept aim to integrate ICT solutions in a secure fashion to manage a city's assets (e.g., local departments' information systems, transport systems, hospitals, power plants, water supply networks, waste management, etc.). The goal of building a smart city is to improve quality of life for its residents by using technology to improve the efficiency of services and to enable more informed decision making process on both policy makers' and citizens' ends. When it comes to the transport aspect of smart cities, location information acquisition is often supported by Global Navigation Satellite Systems (GNSS) data. GNSS comprehends a constellation of satellites providing signals from space that transmit positioning and timing data to GNSS receivers. The receivers then use this data to determine location. Probably the best know GNSS system is Global Positioning System (GPS) developed by USA's NAVSTAR, but other systems like Russia's Global'naya Navigatsionnaya Sputnikovaya Sistema (GLONASS) and China's BeiDou Navigation Satellite System are operational while some others are on its way to ensure global coverage like European Union's Galileo system. In the literature, there are some interesting examples of GNSS use for extraction of origin-destination (OD) matrices [11]-[14], validation of travel behaviour models [15][16] or rush hour analysis [17][18]. Furthermore, when analysing the use of GNSS data for mobility studies we can distinguish between implementation of (a) dedicated GNSS sensor and (b) integrated GNSS sensors. The first one usually includes dedicated sensor placed into a vehicle or portable GNSS device that individual carries in order to log his mobility behaviour. In these studies samples are usually limited in size (e.g., due to discipline that is required from responded in order to carry the device with him) or bias in transport modes coverage (e.g., device tracks only motorised transport modes). The second one involves integration of GNSS chipsets into devices that are not primary dedicated to location purposes. Probably the most common device of such kind today is a mobile phone [19]. As mobile phones have more sensors integrated (e.g., cameras, accelerometers, etc.) and individuals usually carry them without considering it to be a burden, they exhibit potential to overcome above mentioned limitations and deliver a rich datasets for mobility studies. Most often these datasets are referred as crowdsourced data. Nevertheless, little is known about the potential of crowdsourced data for smart city mobility management. And even less about the context of personalized mobility services and the interactions between a city and its transport system users. While only scarce literature tackles this idea [20][21], in this article we contribute to this line of research by using crowdsourced data from smartphones and a support vector machine algorithm to forecast transport mode one will use for the upcoming travel. Forecasting is based on a set of given conditions (location, trip's purpose, time of day, etc.). We see this as a potential application that can be used to enable timely relevant indication of intended mobility behaviour. This way relevant transport information and incentives can be provided in order to support making of more informed mobility related decisions. Furthermore smart city mobility management can be supported with this information to ensure timely management of transport related activities and services.

This paper is structured as follows: after the Introduction, Section 2 provides detailed description of the data collection procedure and adopted support vector machines approach. Section 3 summarizes the result of the transport mode forecasting procedure and is followed with discussion section. Finally, Section 5 highlights major conclusions drawn from the observed insights.

II. METHOD AND DATA

A. Data collection

Data on mobility behavior is collected via an Android smartphone application Routecoach [22], which is developed at Ghent University in Belgium. The Routecoach application was a part of sustainable mobility campaign in province of Flemish-Brabant. The main aim of the campaign was to develop an evaluation and planning toolkit for mobility projects, which is transferable and can be adopted by planners [23]. The data collection process lasted from January to April 2015. Over this period, in total, 8303 users actively participated by downloading the freely available application and collecting the data on more than 30,000 trips.

For our analysis, we used a part of overall dataset that included only 'interactively' (also called 'actively') [19] logged trips that were collected in area of city of Leuven. The city of Leuven (Fig.1) is the capital of the province of Flemish-Brabant and located about 25 kilometers east of Brussels (capital of Belgium). The two cities are well connected with road, rail and bike highway. Leuven itself is a very dynamic city that is a home to one of the largest universities in the region. The city's daily dynamics results in a lot of traffic and also related traffic congestion. This is particularly noticeable across the ring road that surrounds the city center and main road axes that bring regional traffic to the city. Potentially for this reason, the use of public transportation (only bus is available) in the city has seen a fivefold increase in last 20 years. Also, the use of active transport modes is quite common as just cycling contributes to the city's modal share with 17-20% [24].

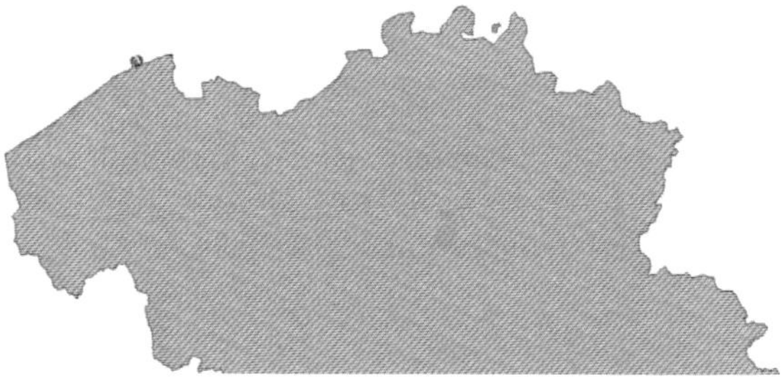

Figure 1. Location of city of Leuven in Flanders region.

As already mentioned, for our research we used only 'actively' logged trips. 'Active' logging comprehends that the logged data are validated by users. This way, through the application itself, users can confirm transport mode that they are using or indicate a reason for the trip (trip purpose) while data are being logged. In addition, for the completed trips users can perform data quality control. Data quality control is made possible over dedicated web portal (Fig. 2). Through the web portal, participants can access to their personal trip logs and use friendly, geographic information system (GIS), interface. This interface visualizes exiting trips but can also be used to report on additional trip data, correct wrongly introduced information or report on personal points of interest (like home or work locations).

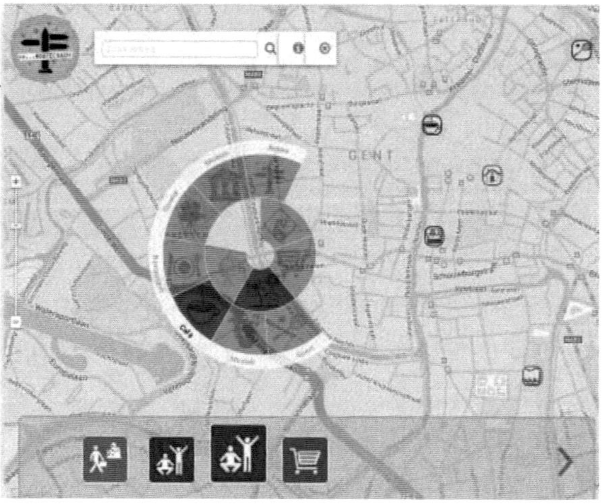

Figure 2. Geo interface for data validation and quality control.

Our sub dataset consist of 17,040 validated trips created by 292 individuals, meaning that each individual in average made around 60 trips. Most of the trips were made by car and least by public transport (Fig.3). The distribution of validated trips over 24 hours clearly indicates morning and afternoon peaks (Fig. 4).

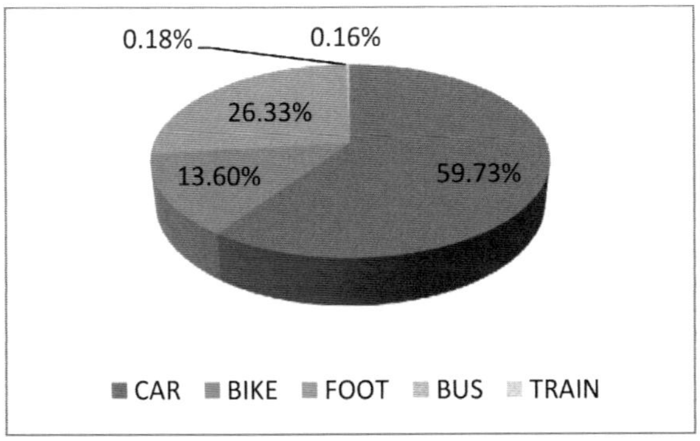

Figure 3. Modal split (validated trips).

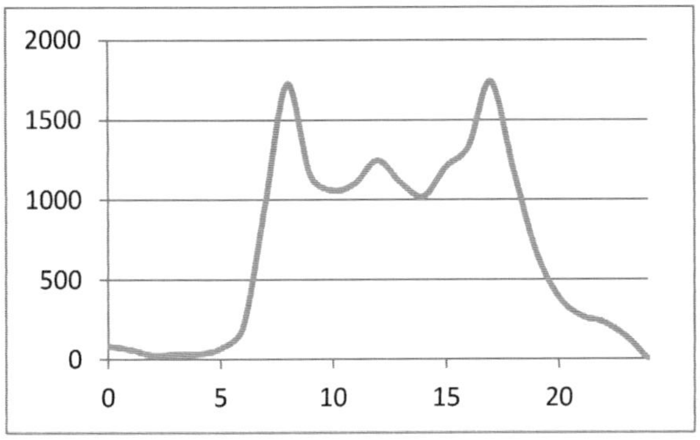

Figure 4. The distribution of validated trips over 24 hours.

A detail description of attributes collected for each trip is given in Table 1.

B. *Support vector machines classification*

Support vector machines (SVM) are supervised machine learning algorithm that is based on the concept of decision hyperplanes. These decision hyperplanes separate between observations that have different class membership in multidimensional feature space. Quite often, it is not so easy to separate between observations, and different mathematical functions (kernels) are used to map them in order to separate among different classes. For this reason, firstly, a training dataset is introduced. The training dataset is a dataset where class membership is know in advance for each observation. This dataset serves to train the model so that, as good as possible, decision hyperplanes are selected. Later, to test the success rate of the first step, and the selected decision hyperplanes, a new dataset is introduced. This second dataset, called test dataset, also has known class membership for each observation. This knowledge of the class membership is used to objectively test the outcome of the trained model. The objectivity is based on the fact that newly introduced dataset contains observations on which the initial model was not trained, thus it allows more fair evaluation of the model results. After the selection of decision hyperplanes is confirmed on the test dataset it is considered that the model will give fair results when data with unknown class membership are introduced to it. More detailed overview of SVM algorithm can be found in literature [25]-[27].

TABLE I. DESCRIPTION OF VARIABLES

Variable	Acronym	Description
User's ID	userid	Unique identifier of the user/device
Trip's ID	tripid	Unique identifier of the trip
Trip's start time	starttime	Year, month, day, hour, minute and second when trip started
Trip's stop time	stoptime	Year, month, day, hour, minute and second when trip ended
Trip's start location	startpoint	Geographic location of the trip's origin point
Trip's end location	endpoint	Geographic location of the trip's destination point
Distance	distance	Distance between trip's origin and destination points measured in kilometres
Transportation mode	transportmode	Transportation mode used for the trip
Trip's purpose	purpose	The purpose of the trip made (go to work, shopping, recreation, school…)
Working day identification	week day	Boolean value that indicates if the day when trip started is a working day
Holiday identification	weekend	Boolean value that indicates if the day when trip started is a holiday or weekend

In our study, we divided complete data set in two parts; 75% has been used as training and 25% as test dataset. Sampling was random and insight into distribution of trip lengths between training and test dataset reveals quite balanced representation of different trip lengths in both samples (Fig.5). The input dataset consists of trip observations for every individual, where each trip is considered to be a path between two locations made by one transport mode. Each trip is described with variables listed in Table 1.

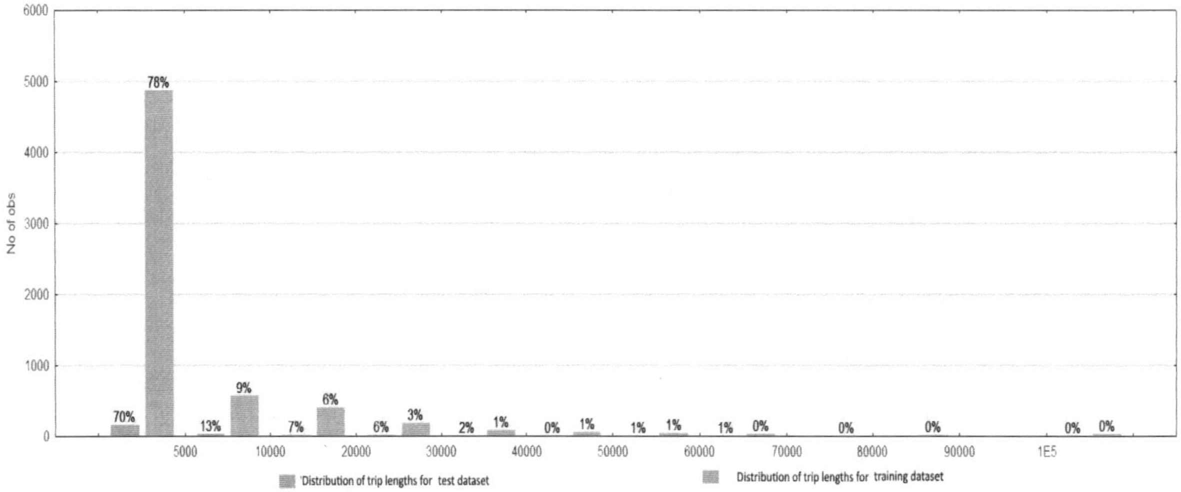

Figure 5. Success rate in relation to the trip lengths.

For the SVM classification, we applied C-SVM type. The forecasting minimization error function for the applied C-SVM is defined as:

$$\frac{1}{2}w^T w + C \sum_{i=1}^{N} \xi_i \quad (1)$$

subject to constraints:

$$y_i(w^T \phi(x_i) + b) \geq 1 - \xi_i \quad (2)$$

$$\xi_i \geq 0 \quad (3)$$

Where $i=1, \ldots, N$, C is the capacity constant, w represents the vector of coefficients, b is a constant, and ξi are parameters for handling non-separable inputs and ϕ stands for kernel function. Kernel function used in our example is radial basis function that transforms input to the feature space as defined by (4):

$$K(X_i, X_j) = \phi(X_i) \cdot \phi(X_j) = X_i, X_j. \quad (4)$$

The value of parameters C and γ is defined in training phase based on the result of 10- fold cross validation. The obtained values were 3 for C and 0.2 for γ. The output variable of the model was a transport mode one will use for a next trip and forecasting time frame was one hour.

III. RESULTS

Overall success rate of the forecasting model was 82% (Table 2). The most challenging part was to create decision hyperplanes that separate between trips made with private car, bike and public transportation (bus) as this resulted in more than 1000 support vectors for bike and car transport modes.

TABLE II. MODEL RESULTS

Kernel type	Radial Basis Function
Classification accuracy	81.87%
Number of SVs	2921 (1 bounded)
Number of SVs (BIKE)	1187
Number of SVs (BUS)	687
Number of SVs (CAR)	1033
Number of SVs (FOOT)	5
Number of SVs (TRAIN)	9

Considering each transport mode individually (Fig. 6), it was easiest to predict when one will use personal vehicle for the next trip. A detailed look into confusion matrix reveals occurrence of miss-classifications between transport modes bike, car and foot (Fig. 7). In most of the cases trips that were predicted to be made by car were forecasted to be made by bike or foot. Potentially, insight into weather conditions could give more details on context of miss-classifications and in future phase model can be extended to integrate these insights. Furthermore, Fig. 8 and 9 show more details on trip purposes for the forecasted trips. Quite different distributions indicate how important the availability of information on the purpose of travel is when predicting transport mode to be used for travel.

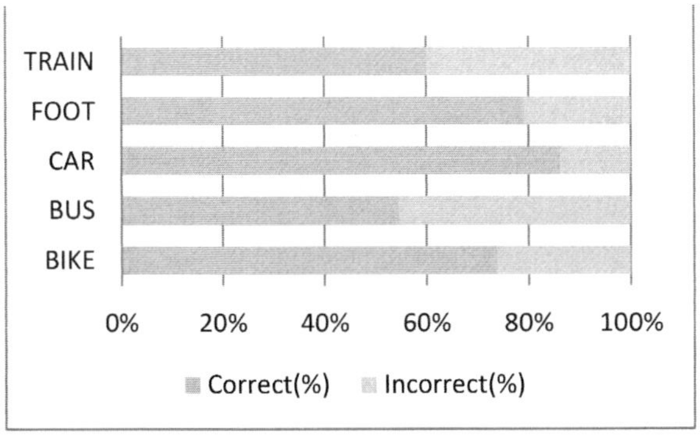

Figure 6. Model's success rate at transport mode levels

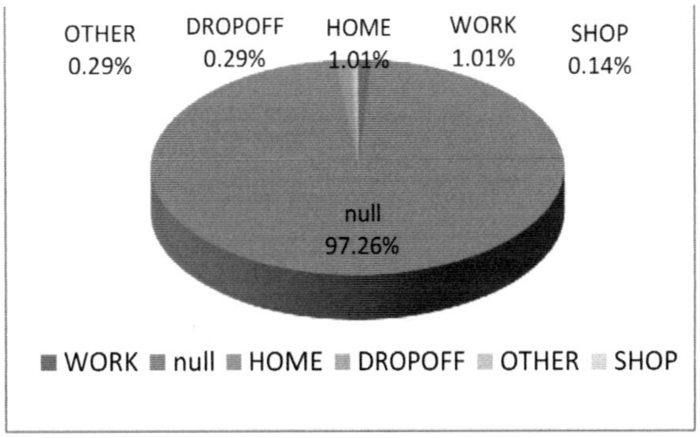

Figure 7. Purpose of trips for which transport mode was incorrectly forecasted.

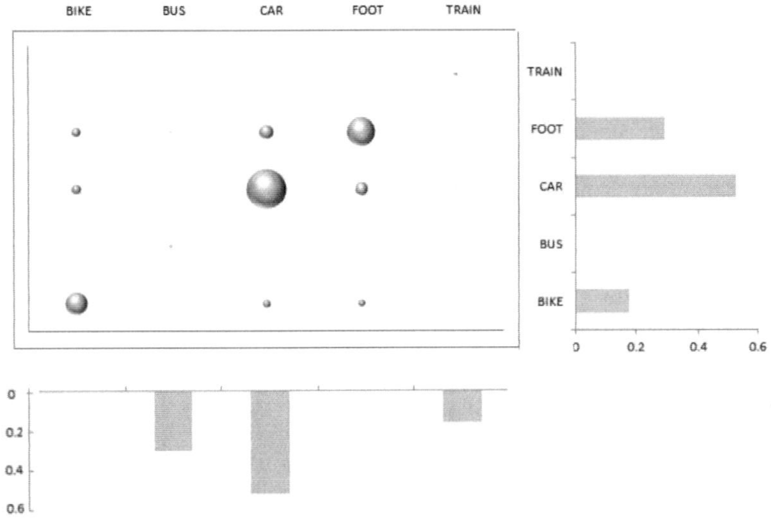

Figure 8. Confusion matrix.

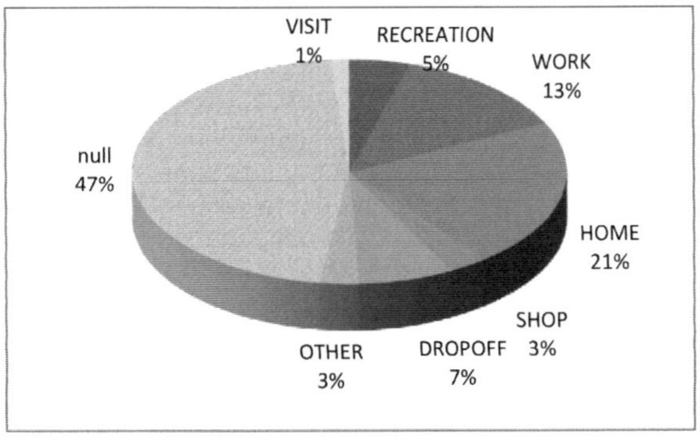

Figure 9. Purpose of trips for which transport mode was correctlly forecasted.

IV. DISCUSSION

Although the implemented SVM model has a quite high success rate (82%), still there is a place to improve forecasting results by additional extensions and considerations based on the gained insights. Firstly, since the model would give a good forecast in a bit more than eight out of ten trips, when implemented to provide pre-travel information, it could be useful to provide information on two transport modes that are most likely to be used. This way the model outcomes could be of higher relevance to the user and have outweighing role when user is considering more than one option. Furthermore, this way provision of such information could be also integrated into the city's transport management system and provided information can be coordinated with city's preferences. For example, if city wishes to promote new public transport line, or bike route, it can add additional weight to these options in the model so that this information is provided to the user whenever feasible route using promoted options exists. In addition, there is a highest confusion between use of private car and active transport modes like bike and foot, which are the two ends of the sustainable mobility spectrum. It is worth to examining in future research in more details a context of trips for which confusion happened. Potential reasons include bad weather conditions when users are more prone to use private cars but also different trip purposes (e.g., one is more likely to use private car to drop-off multiple family members than for recreation). First reason can successfully be examined by fusing weather data and crowdsourced dataset. This insight car provide more descriptive context of the confusion occurrence. Second challenge is the familiarity of trip purpose. As forecasting time frame was an hour, this means that trip purpose should be known in advance. However, unless user indicates this information, a need to make a trip for certain reason should also be forecasted. This adds additional complexity to the model and can impact the success rate of the forecast. Therefore, it could be beneficial to investigate in more details complementarity of trip purpose forecasting models with transport mode forecasting and evaluate added value they give to each other.

Compared with results from literature [20], where gradient boosting trees were used to forecast transport mode one will use for the next trip, our results achieved with the support vector machines based model have around 10% higher success rate. This shows potential of support vector machines based model to be extended to incorporate other data sources and to be successfully implemented in order to support smart city mobility planning and managing process.

V. Conclusion

Support vector machines based model achieved success rate of 82% in forecasting transport mode one will use for the next trip. This shows high potential to implement such a model into smart city mobility system management and planning processes as it can result in development of more advanced pre-travel information service. Furthermore, gained insights already indicate potential future extensions of the model in order to ensure higher usability of the output results and improved relevance to the end users.

Acknowledgment

This research is funded by INTERREG North-West Europe project New Integrated Smart Transport Options (NISTO), the Flemish government agency for Innovation by Science and Technology and the Flemish Institute for Mobility.

References

[1] E. Tranos and D. Gertner, "Smart networked cities?" Innovation: The European Journal of Social Science Research. 25, pp. 175–190, 2012.

[2] P. Neirotti, A. de Marco, A. C. Cag, G. Mangano, and F. Scorrano. Current trends in Smart City initiatives: Some stylised facts. Cities, 38, pp. 25–36, 2014.

[3] I. Marsa-Maestre, M. A. Lopez-Carmona, J. R. Velasco, and I. A. Navarro, "Mobile Agents for Service Personalization in Smart Environments". Journal of Network and Computer Applications, 3, pp. 30–41, 2008.

[4] S. Beswick, Smart Cities in Europe: Enabling Innovation; Osborne Clarke: London, UK, 2014.

[5] G. J. A. Alonso and A. Rossi, New Trends for Smart Cities; ATOS: Bezons, France, 2011.

[6] L. Atzori, A. Iera, and G. Morabito, "The Internet of Things: A survey". Computer Networks, 54, pp. 2787–2805, 2010.

[7] T. Nam and A. Pardo, "Conceptualizing Smart City with Dimensions of Technology, People, and Institutions". In Proceedings of the 12th Annual International Conference on Digital Government Research, College Park, MD, USA, 12–15 June 2011.

[8] The Climate Group, ARUP, Accenture & The University of Nottingham. Information Marketplaces, The New Economics of Cities; The Climate Group, London, UK, 2011.

[9] G. C. Lazaroiu and M. Roscia, "Definition methodology for the smart cities model". Energy, 47, pp. 326–332, 2012.

[10] Y. Lu and Y. Liu, "Pervasive location acquisition technologies: Opportunities and challenges for geospatial studies". Computers, Environment and Urban Systems, 36, pp. 105–108, 2012.

[11] R. M. Pulselli, C. Ratti, and E. Tiezzi, "City out of Chaos: Social Patterns and Organization in Urban Systems". International Journal of Design & Nature and Ecodynamics, 1, pp. 125–134, 2006.

[12] J, Novak, R. Ahas, A. Aasa, and S. Silm, "Application of mobile phone location data in mapping of commuting patterns and functional regionalization: A pilot study of Estonia". Journal of Maps, 9, pp. 10–15, 2013.

[13] O. Järv, R. Ahas, and F. Witlox, "Understanding monthly variability in human activity spaces: A twelve-month study using mobile phone call detail records". Transportation Research Part C: Emerging Technologies. 38, pp. 122–135, 2014.

[14] S. Iqbal, C. F. Choudhury, P. Wang, and M. C. González, "Development of origin-destination matrices using mobile phone call data". Transportation Research Part C: Emerging Technologies, 40, pp. 63–74, 2014.

[15] F. Liu, D. Janssens, J. Cui, Y. Wang, G. Wets, and M. Cools, "Building a validation measure for activity-based transportation models based on mobile phone data". Expert Systems with Applications, 41, pp. 6174–6189, 2014.

[16] Y. Yuan, M. Raubal, and Y. Liu, "Correlating mobile phone usage and travel behavior—A case study of Harbin, China". Computers, Environment and Urban Systems, 36, pp. 118–130, 2012.

[17] H. Bar-Gera, "Evaluation of a cellular phone-based system for measurements of traffic speeds and travel times: A case study from Israel". Transportation Research Part C: Emerging Technologies 15(6), pp. 380-391, 2007.

[18] O. Järv, R. Ahas, E., Saluveer, B. Derudder, and F. Witlox,

"Mobile Phones in a Traffic Flow: A Geographical Perspective to Evening Rush Hour Traffic Analysis Using Call Detail Records". PLoS ONE, 7(11), pp. e49171, 2012

[19] I. Semanjski and S. Gautama, Sensing Human Activity for Smart Cities' Mobility Management, InTech, 2016 (In Press)

[20] I. Semanjski and S. Gautama, "Smart City Mobility Application—Gradient Boosting Trees for Mobility Prediction and Analysis Based on Crowdsourced Data", Sensors, vol. 15, no. 7, pp. 15974-15987, 2015.

[21] I. Semanjski, A. Lopez Aguirre, J. De Mol and S. Gautama, "Policy 2.0 Platform for Mobile Sensing and Incentivized Targeted Shifts in Mobility Behavior", Sensors, vol. 16, no.7, pp. 1035-1053, 2016

[22] Ghent University, "Routecoach," Google Play, [Online]. Available: https://play.google.com/store/apps/details?id=com.move.routecoach. [Accessed 27 May 2016].

[23] New Integrated Smart Transport Options, "NISTO," [Online]. Available: http://www.nisto-project.eu. [Accessed 03 MarcN 2016].

[24] Official mobility statistics for Flanders, OVG, [Online] Available: http://www.mobielvlaanderen.be/ovg/. [Accessed 27 May 2016].

Datamining and Big Freight Transport Database

Analysis and forecasting capabilities

Massimiliano Petri, Antonio Pratelli
Dept. Civil and Industrial Engineering
University of Pisa
Pisa, Italy
email: m.petri@ing.unipi.it, antonio.pratelli@ing.unipi.it

Giovanni Fusco
Centre National de la Recherche Scientifique
Université de Nice Sophia Antipolis
Nice, France
email: giovanni.fusco@unice.fr

Abstract—**Transport modeling, in general, and freight transport modeling, in particular, are becoming important tools for investigating the effects of investments and policies. Freight demand forecasting models are still in an experimentation and evolution stage. Nevertheless, some recent European projects, like Transtools or ETIS/ETIS Plus, have developed a unique modeling and data framework for freight forecast at large scale to avoid data availability and modeling problems. Despite this, important projects using these modeling frameworks have provided very different results for the same forecasting areas and years, giving rise to serious doubts about the results quality, especially in relation to their cost and development time. Moreover, many of these models are purely deterministic. The project described in this article tries to overcome the above-mentioned problems with a new easy-to-implement freight demand forecasting method based on Bayesian Networks using European official and available data. The method is applied to the Transport Market study of the Sixth European Rail Freight Corridor**

Keywords - Freight Demand Model; Bayesian Networks; European Freight Corridor; Demand Forecasting

I. INTRODUCTION AND GOALS

Nowadays, there is a large interest in developing a mathematical tool in the field of freight transport modeling for investigating the effects of investments and policies, involving large number of resources. However, freight demand forecasting models are still in the evolution stage [21] for the following reasons:

- lower seniority (about 10 years) than the respective passenger models;
- high number of decision-makers to consider (companies, shippers, carriers, logistics operators, port operators, deposits, etc.);
- variety of products transported (in terms of categories, dimensions, weight, value, etc.);
- high variability in decision-making processes;
- limited availability of information (data often aggregated, dated, partial, heterogeneous, etc.).

To take into account the complexity of freight transport system, researchers have proposed a wide array of models belonging to the aggregate or disaggregate model types [1] and to three different fields: the modelling of the relationship between transportation and economic activity, logistic decision making and processes and the link between traffic flows and networks [2].

Recently, European projects like Transtools [3] ETIS/ETIS Plus [4][22] have developed a unique modeling and data framework to forecast freight flows at large scale to avoid data availability and modeling problems [20]. Despite this, very important projects, using these modeling frameworks, have provided very different results for the same forecasting areas and years, giving rise to serious doubts about the results quality, especially in relation to their cost and development time. For example, there is a very high divergence between the results of the two projects Prog-Trans and TransTools for truck flows (Germany in TransTools has an increase in freight transport tonnage in 2005-2020 of about 10% while in Prog-Trans this value is about 50%) [5].

This is a general problem for freight modeling and forecasting, with a high complexity analysis level applied to a very large scale, bringing uncontrollable errors.

Moreover, many of these models are purely deterministic in results, giving no information about their estimation errors or the probability of the occurrence of forecast values. Other problems include forecasting different scenarios with very long-term simulations. We think that projects of national/European importance would benefit from the contribution of probabilistic data-driven models that take into account the uncertainties and variability of attributes and scenarios, especially for long-term estimates, in order to have more truthful decision-support.

There are a lot of freight demand models [15], with some methods similar to the one adopted here, like the use of Trend Analysis/Time series or Neural Networks [16], but Bayesian Networks have the advantage to allow the introduction in the model of expert knowledge and the possibility to verify the results [23] that are in the form of an easy-to-understand oriented causal graph among variables and not complex or black-box relations, like with Neural Networks [6].

The objective is mainly to understand quantitative and qualitative aspects of future traffic demand and evaluate possible future scenarios according to most relevant and influencing variables of the freight market [7]. We also want to overcome the above-mentioned problems with a new freight demand forecasting framework based on Bayesian Networks and using European official and available data. The model has to be easy to implement, not onerous and give probabilistic results in less time, with an estimation error similar to the more complex methods. It should be capable of giving the order of magnitude of forecasted freight flows for strategic decision making at a very early phase of policy development, and be complementary to more traditional, more precise, but much more expensive freight models for later stages of analysis.

Section II, of this paper deals with a new methodology for freight demand forecast, which is divided into four main explanatory parts. The structure of the study is referred in part A; part B is related to preliminary data analysis; part C concerns decision tree models used in multivariate classification; lastly, the Bayesian network forecasting model is described in part D. Finally, Section III is for comments, conclusions and insights on future developments.

II. A New Methodology for Freight Demand Forecast

Within our study, we applied the general demand forecast methodology to freight flows within the Transport Market study of the Sixth European Rail Freight Corridor. The European parliament and the Council adopted on 22 September 2010 the EU Regulation 913/2010 concerning a European rail network for competitive freight. Within this framework, the EU identifies nine rail corridors; in particular, Rail Freight Corridor.6 (RFC6) allows railway connections among Spain, France, Italy, Slovenia and Hungary, also providing links with rail freight corridors 1, 2, 3, 4, 5 and 7 (see violet line in Fig.1).

Regulation 913/2010 sets two main goals:

- To develop the rail freight corridors in terms of infrastructure capacity and performance, to meet market demand on both quantitative and qualitative layers;
- To lay the groundwork for the provision of good quality freight services, to meet customer expectation.

Regulation 913/2010 requires a Transport Market Study (TMS) for each freight corridor, developed according a clear "corridor perspective", with a coherent structure for the entire corridor, and not as a collection of studies focused on individual Member States. The Transport Market Study is intended as the basis for the assessment of the customer needs.

The main goal of the TMS for RFC6 is to provide a clear understanding of the current conditions of the multimodal freight market along the corridor as well as to develop short and long term traffic forecasts (volumes and modal split/modal shift), also including the effect of actions and measures related to the implementation of the Corridor itself.

Consequently, the Transport Market Study is aimed at:

- Analyze the current situation in terms of transport demand and supply and economic context;
- Analyze the transport market in terms of customer needs and deliver information on modal choice process;
- Provide transport demand projections after the implementation of the corridor itself.

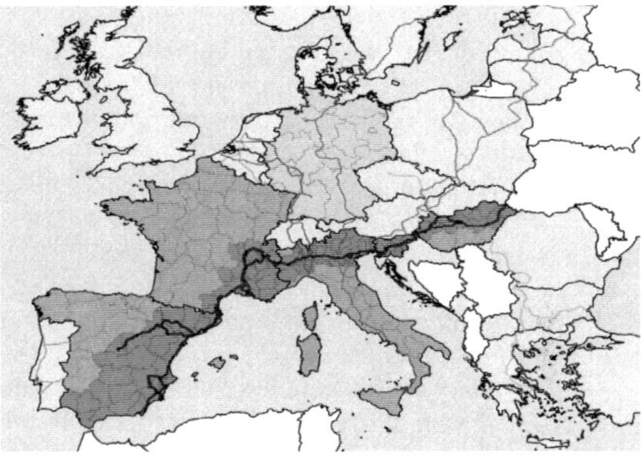

Figure 1. Rail Freight Corridor 6 (RFC6).

A. *Structure of the study*

To this, the study is organized in three Phases:

- Phase 1: Analysis of the present situation;
- Phase 2: Survey (Releaved Preferences-RP and Stated Prefereces-SP surveys);
- Phase 3: short and long term transport demand forecasts.

Phase 1 provides direct final results and creates the background to structure, design and implement Phase 2 and Phase 3. In particular, Phase 1 is aimed at providing a sound analysis of the present socio-economic situation and of the future scenario in the Countries crossed by Corridor 6 within the wider EU framework, making clear the full picture and deriving first qualitative policy indications and guidelines.

Consequently, Phase 1 provides information in terms of:

- Present and future economic magnitude of Countries and/or regions along Corridor 6;
- Present transport demand across the Corridor (macro-flows among Countries and/or regions, including flows to areas not directly served by the Corridor itself);
- Future transport demand (at the macro-level) in terms of likelihood of increase (macro potential demand and macro role of the railway transport in terms of modal split, volumes and values of carried goods based on the evolution of the future competitive positioning of countries crossed by Corridor 6).

Phase 2 aims to engineer and implement surveys on the decision path in the choice of transport mode. In particular, the surveys and their analysis provides a complete picture of the main factors affecting the choice of transportation, like:

- transport cost;
- travel time;
- risk of delay in delivery;
- risk of damage or theft.

The surveys are aimed at several transport market actors:

- manufacturing firms which directly organize the shipping / receiving of goods;
- intermediaries which organize the transport of goods on behalf of producers and/or final users;
- operators of rail transport networks and intermodal centers.

Based on results of Phases 1 and 2, Phase 3 provides estimates of freight transport that could be carried out on Corridor 6 at the different time horizons (2015 and 2030).

Phase 3 is divided into two distinct steps:

- estimate of the total (road and rail) freight transport demand in 2015 and 2030;
- estimate of the modal split road / iron as a function of hypothetical scenarios characterized by the variation of the main features of the transport (cost, time, delay, damage / theft).

The present paper is then aimed at explaining key quantitative and qualitative analysis of the Rail Freight Corridor.6 Transport Market Study,the methodology and its detailed results regarding the datamining methods used for actual state analysis (Phase 1) and for the freight transport model implementation (Phase 3-first step).

The key steps of the different activities based on the datamining techniques performed and described here are:

- the input data analysis;
- the Decision Tree Induction model analysis [8] (Witten and Frank, 2000);
- the final freight demand forecasting by Bayesian Network models ([9] and more particularly [10], [18] for their use as spatial strategic forecasting tools).

These steps are logically connected. The input data analysis allows to know how each input variable influences the actual freight flow dynamics in terms of relative growth (i.e. percentage variation between reference years 2005 and 2010) to understand which variables are directly (with the uni-variate analysis) or indirectly (bi-variate and tri-variate analysis) related to it. The Decision Tree classification refines this preliminary analysis with a complex multi-variate elaboration having as target variable always the freight flow dynamics (the evolution of the freight flows between 2005 and 2010). Finally, the Bayesian Network models use as input data only the most influencing variables in order to avoid irrelevant data in the model, resulting in errors and reduction in the forecasting capacity.

The Bayesian Network models were finally used to forecast freight flows in different scenarios. More precisely, the final traffic forecasts were carried out according to three different estimates of GDP growth for the study area: basic, optimistic, conservative. The demand forecasting models were developed with reference to two different geographic areas: at first, the analysis were conducted with reference to the mobility data of whole European O/D Matrix, later it was decided to focus only on the area interested by Corridor 6 and to calibrate the model accordingly in order to obtain more reliable estimates.

B. The Preliminary Data Analysis

A first socio-economical analysis was made to evaluate and estimate the scenario for important input variables. For example, population and its evolution can be considered as a proxy of future trends for goods production and demand. The total population is about 184 million, against a European population of about 521 million. Corridor countries population has been growing faster (CAGR +0,8%) than Europe as a whole (CAGR +0,4%), despite a negative trend in Hungary (Table 1).

TABLE I. GROSS DOMESTIC PRODUCT (BN €) AND POPULATION (M) (SOURCE: ELABORATIONS ON EUROSTAT DATA)

	GDP			Population		
Zone	2008	2011	CAGR % (2003-11)	2008	2011	CAGR % (2003-11)
Spain	1.087,70	1.063,40	3,9	45,3	46,2	1,3
France	1.933,20	1.996,60	2,9	64	65	0,6
Italy	1.575,10	1.579,70	2,1	59,6	60,6	0,7
Slovenia	37,3	36,2	4,3	2	2,1	0,3
Hungary	105,5	99,8	3,8	10	10	-0,2
Europe	13.152,80	13.499,50	3,1	515,9	521	0,4
Corridor	4.738,90	4.775,60	2,9	181	183,9	0,8

Despite the negative impact of the economic downturn on the relevance of historical trends, medium term forecasts (in particular at year 2030) can provide a higher level of consistency, neutralizing short term fluctuations. At year 2030, in real prices GDP grows (base case) of about 28% both for countries crossed by Corridor 6 and for Europe, but with significant internal differences (France and Spain grows more; Italy, Slovenia and Hungary grows less). GDP growth rate is assumed according specific annual forecasts (made available in winter 2013) for year 2012, 2013 and 2014 and on average trends since 2015 on (average official long term trends to 2060, to neutralize short terms fluctuations) (Table 2 and 3).

To cope with uncertainty in long term forecasts, low and high sensitivity scenarios (GDP growth higher or lower than in base case) are introduced.

The statistical initial data analysis was carried out on the whole road and rail ETIS Origin-Destination Freight Flows Matrix in Europe for 2005 and 2010 years. Origins and

Destinations in this database are known at the NUTS 2 level.

TABLE II. GROSS DOMESTIC PRODUCT GROWTH RATES (AVERAGE % CHANGE OVER THE PREVIOUS YEAR) (SOURCE: ELABORATIONS ON DG EC.FIN. DATA)

Zone	2012	2013	2014	2015	2020	2025	2030
Spain (F)	-1,40%	-1,40%	0,80%	1,60%	1,60%	1,60%	1,60%
France (G)	0,00%	0,10%	1,20%	1,70%	1,70%	1,70%	1,70%
Italy (H)	-2,20%	-1,00%	0,80%	1,30%	1,30%	1,30%	1,30%
Slovenia (I)	-2,00%	-2,00%	0,70%	1,30%	1,30%	1,30%	1,30%
Hungary (J)	-1,70%	-0,10%	1,30%	1,20%	1,20%	1,20%	1,20%
Europe (K)	-0,20%	0,20%	1,60%	1,40%	1,40%	1,40%	1,50%
Corridor (L)	-1,10%	-0,60%	1,00%	1,50%	1,50%	1,50%	1,50%

TABLE III. GDP GROWTH RATES BY SCENARIO (AVERAGE % CHANGE; 2011-X) (SOURCE: ELABORATIONS ON DG EC.FIN. DATA)

	2015			2030		
Zone	Low	Basic	High	Low	Basic	High
Spain (F)	-0,50%	-0,10%	0,30%	0,80%	1,20%	1,70%
France (G)	0,50%	0,70%	1,00%	1,00%	1,50%	1,90%
Italy (H)	-0,70%	-0,30%	0,10%	0,60%	1,00%	1,40%
Slovenia (I)	-1,00%	-0,50%	-0,10%	0,50%	0,90%	1,30%
Hungary (J)	-0,20%	0,20%	0,50%	0,60%	1,00%	1,30%
Europe (K)	0,40%	0,70%	1,10%	0,90%	1,30%	1,70%
Corridor (L)	-0,10%	0,20%	0,50%	0,80%	1,30%	1,70%

The original road 2005 O/D matrix has thus about 134.000 O/D pairs while the corresponding 2010 matrix has only 102.000 O/D pairs. 88.000 O/D couples are common to the two matrices. Taking into account only these common data (88.000 O/D pairs), we lose around 4% of total flows (containing also flows not interesting directly the Corridor 6). For each O/D couple an evolution rate between 2005 and 2010 could thus be calculated. Together with freight flows, the starting data include twenty variables belonging to different fields like economy, geography and transportation and are summarized in Table 4.

TABLE IV. LIST OF THE INITIAL VARIABLES (IN ROSE COLOR ARE INDICATED THE VARIABLES CHANGING FOR THE THREE SCENARIOS (BEST, REGULAR AND WORST).

ID	Indicator	Starting year	Forecast year1	Forecast year2	Scale start year	Scale forecast year
1	GDP (Gross domestic product) of NUTS2i	DELTA 2005 10	DELTA 2010 15	DELTA 2010 30	NUTS2	NUTS0
2	GDP (Gross domestic product) of NUTS2j	DELTA 2005-10	DELTA 2010-15	DELTA 2010-30	NUTS2	NUTS0
3	Total population of NUTS2i	2010	2010	2010	NUTS2	NUTS0
4	Total employment of NUTS2j	2010	2010	2010	NUTS2	NUTS0
5	GCF (Gross capital formation) of NUTS2j	DELTA 2005-10	DELTA 2010-15	DELTA 2010-30	NUTS0	NUTS0
6	PMGS (Production of Manifactured Goods Sold) of NUTS2j	DELTA 2005-10	DELTA 2010-15	DELTA 2010-30	NUTS0	NUTS0
7	PV (Production value by industry) of NUTS2j	DELTA 2005-10	DELTA 2010-15	DELTA 2010-30	NUTS0	NUTS0
8	IG (Import of goods) of NUTS2j	DELTA 2005-10	DELTA 2010-15	DELTA 2010-30	NUTS0	NUTS0
9	EG (Export of goods) of NUTS2i	DELTA 2005-10	DELTA 2010-15	DELTA 2010-30	NUTS0	NUTS0
10	Total Freigth flows betwwen NUTS2i and NUTS2j	DELTA 2005-10	DELTA 2010-15	DELTA 2010-30	NUTS2	NUTS2
11	Minimum distance betwwen NUTS2i and NUTS2j	2010	2010	2010	NUTS2	NUTS2
12	Macroregion Name of NUTS2i	2010	2015	2030	NUTS1	NUTS1
13	Macroregion Name of NUTS2j	2010	2015	2030	NUTS1	NUTS1
14	NMF - Net migration flows of NUTS2j	DELTA 2005-10	DELTA 2010-15	DELTA 2010-30	NUTS0	NUTS0
15	NMF - Net migration flows of NUTS2i	DELTA 2005-10	DELTA 2010-15	DELTA 2010-30	NUTS0	NUTS0
16	Unemployment rate of NUTSi	2010	2010	2010	NUTS0	NUTS0
17	Transport taxation revenues of NUTS2i (million of €)	DELTA 2005-10	DELTA 2010-15	DELTA 2010-30	NUTS0	NUTS0
18	Transport taxation revenues of NUTS2j (million of €)	DELTA 2005-10	DELTA 2010-15	DELTA 2010-30	NUTS0	NUTS0
19	Diesel price of NUTS2i (€/litre)	DELTA 2005-10	DELTA 2010-15	DELTA 2010-30	NUTS0	NUTS0
20	Diesel price of NUTS2j (€/litre)	DELTA 2005-10	DELTA 2010-15	DELTA 2010-30	NUTS0	NUTS0

This general data analysis phase explores the freight flow dynamics. Its correlation with the main variables, some of which are normally used in Transport Distribution Models (like distance, population and GDP) while others are not included in these models but can be used in data-driven Bayesian Network learning (for example unemployment rate, the variation of origin export and destination import or binary variables like the belonging to the EU) [17].

The starting data analysis is divided in three parts of increasing complexity: orthogram, bi-variate and tri-variate analysis. The following analyses concern only road and rail freight flows because they are the most interesting for Corridor 6 study area (Fig.1).

The first part of preliminary data analysis uses some correlation tools at different complexity levels; for the simplest part, we elaborated some bi-variate correlation analysis, for example:

- Distance – Delta flow 2010/2005
- Population 2010 – Delta flow 2010/2005
- Unemployment 2010 – Delta flow 2010/2005
- Delta Export 2010/2005 – Delta flow 2010/2005

Increasing the complexity, we elaborated a tri-variate analysis like for the correlation between Origin Delta GDP, Destination Delta GDP and Delta flow 2010/2005.

Before using Datamining methods, we have also implemented some Orthogram analysis, like for the two following variables: UE Belonging - Delta flow 2010/2005.

The bi-variate analysis shows that correlation of freight flow dynamics is practically absent both with the distance between Origin and Destination (measured in kilometers on the transportation networks), with Origin Population, with unemployment rate at the Origin or with the Origin Export Variation and with the Destination Import Variation (Import and Export variations are known at the country level).

The tri-variate analysis correlates simultaneously the freight flow variations with Origin and Destination GDP variations. The 3D scatterplot, with a smoothing interpolation effect (Fig. 2) indicates an overall positive correlation between these three variables with more specific local trends.

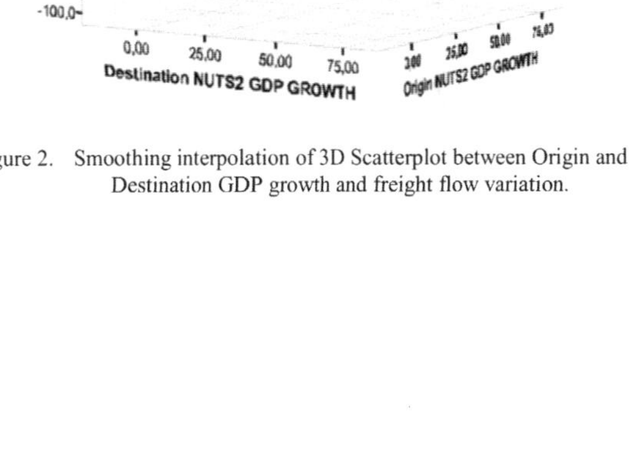

Figure 2. Smoothing interpolation of 3D Scatterplot between Origin and Destination GDP growth and freight flow variation.

For better understanding this last point, two 2D scatterplots are extracted from the 3D diagram (Fig. 3). The correlation is similar for the destination and origin GDP variations. Curiously, a positive flow growth characterizes even negative GDP variations, showing, for some countries, an inverse correlation, which could indicate a profound restructuring of the economy following the integration in the European market. More than linear flow growths are to be observed beyond 75% of GDP increase rate (more evident for Origin than Destination).

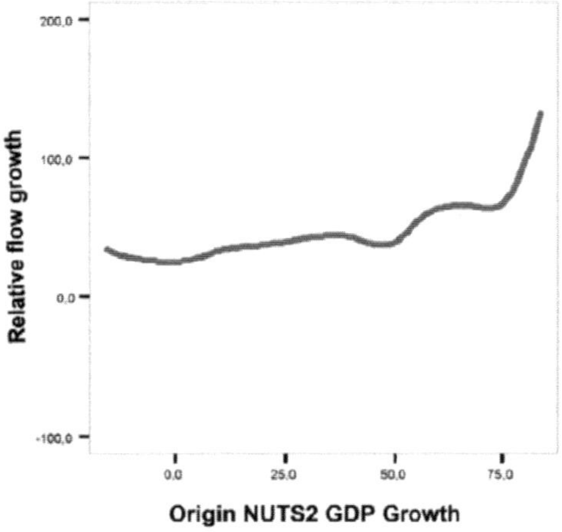

Figure 3. The results of two bi-variate analysis corresponding the previous tri-variate one

The orthogram analysis (Fig. 4) allows studying the correlation between different kinds of variables (categorical and numeric for example).

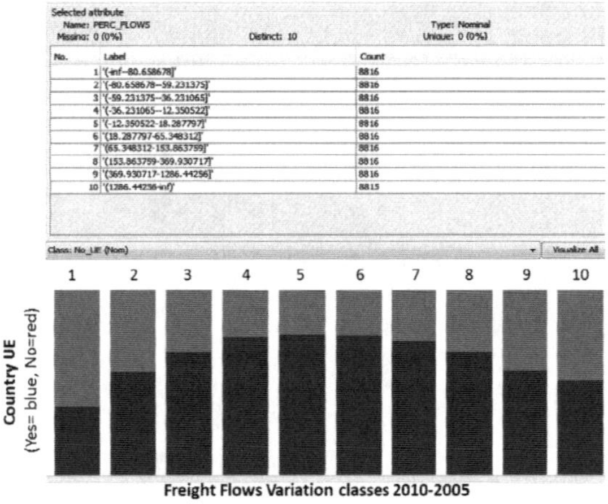

Figure 4. The Orthogram analysis (freight flow variation are indicated in percentage).

The analysis shows that 2005-2010 freight flow variation is correlated with the belonging or not of each area to the EU: there is a clear distinction between areas belonging to the EU and the other areas. EU Countries have more stable freight flows while non-EU Countries have opposite behaviors with some showing a big increase of freight flows and others a considerable decrease. These bi-modal behaviors are difficult to model with classical Transport Distribution Models. This first analysis already shows the interest of using different, more exploratory methods, like Decision Tree Induction and Bayesian Network modeling.

C. The Decision Tree Induction Classification

Decision Tree models are useful multivariate classification instruments allowing analysis of data correlation on the base of a target variable, O/D freight flow relative growth. Moreover, instead of regression models where we need to hypothesize a shape of the correlation (linear, cubic, exponential, etc.), Decision Tree models don't require any assumption and give more than one type of correlation. Finally, the IF THEN framework is very useful and understandable for users and Decision Tree models can be used as a preliminary phase for the Bayesian Network modeling in order to understand the most influential variables to simulate the target one. Decision Trees Induction is an inductive classificatory technique belonging to the Data-Mining and to the Knowledge Discovery in Databases fields. It will be applied to the complete list of variables (Table 4), keeping the O/D freight flow relative growth as target variable.

The extracted classifier has a percentage of Correctly Classified Instances of about 38%, which appears relatively inaccurate. However, the analysis shows two main points:

- the classification ability is higher for the first and last flows variation classes and for the class nearest to zero;
- once again, distance (DIST_2010) between the individual Origins and Destinations does not have a relevant influence.

The analysis suggests introducing new variables so to add detail in the information (GDP at NUTS 2 Level, Internal, Belonging to EU and others) and to add interaction between territorial dimensions at NUTS2 and NUTS0. The new variables are:

- Internal (indicates if an O/D couples belong to the same country);
- No_EU (indicates if an O/D couples belong to EU countries or not);
- Delta GDP 2010-2005 at NUTS2 level;
- Flow 2005 (to indicate flow level before the 2008 economic crisis);

- EU15_CH_NO (indicate whether a flow belongs to the 15 EU member states before 2004 plus Switzerland and Norway);
- Weight of the exit flow for a given origin = Fij/Fi.;
- Weight of the entry flow for a given destination = Fij/F.j;
- Weight of exports to Country J from i = FiJ /Fi.;
- Weight of imports from Country I to j = FIj/F.j

where FiJ means total flows from NUTS2 i to all Country J while F.j means total exit flows to NUTS2 j.

Introducing these new variables, the extracted Decision Tree identifies the variable "weight of the exit flow" as the most important one and shows the relatively chaotic evolution of flows for non-EU countries. Decision Trees results for the whole ETIS O/D Matrix describe a non-unique freight traffic evolution, with different variables explaining flow growth for each country and mainly different from countries belonging or not to the early EU member states. The only shared important variable is the weight of the exit flow (Fij/Fi) showing the relative importance of the economic relation between the origin and destination areas with respect to all the exit flows.

The Decision Tree extracted from the same variables but including only O/D flows belonging to the area of interest for Corridor 6 shows clearly two different dominant behaviors:

- the first one is related to the countries with more stable economy and freight market where the only element that explains the freight dynamic is the actual weight of outgoing flows (this concerns more than 50% of total flows);
- the second one is the already noted bi-modal behavior.

D. *The Bayesian Network Forecasting Model*

The Decision Tree technique produces knowledge only for the pre-processing phase. The limit of this technique is mainly due to the difficulty of the application of the rules extracted from the sample to the whole population:

- first, it is possible that a combination of conditional attributes never occurred in the extracted rules (IF part), whereas it can be present in the prevision dataset; the problem would then be to compute the relative conditional probability distribution;
- second, it could also be possible not to find a rule exactly identical (in the IF part) with the record to be classified: this problem can be solved only with the search of an attribute set close enough to the one to be classified.

Due to these possible situations, the extracted influent variables were used as input variables to implement a Bayesian Network. Bayesian Networks are more suitable to predict phenomena due to their robustness (they can couple statistical robustness from data-mining to expert knowledge directly implemented in the model, whereas Decision Trees are only based on data frequencies) and the possibility to make probabilistic inference so to have a probability values attached to predictions. Even in the absence of expert knowledge (as in our application), prior probabilities in the network initialization produce non-null probabilities for combination of attributes that are not present in the learning data-base. Through Bayesian learning algorithms from data [11], the model links the variables in acyclic and directional graphs, showing their reciprocal influence in a cause-effect relationship between "parent" and "child" nodes. Finally, a conditional probability table is calculated for each dependent variable (with incoming link in the node), detailing the probabilistic relationship between the values of the "parent" and "child" variables. Unconditional probability tables are calculated for independent variables (without incoming links in the node). Learning algorithms search for the best possible combination of structure (links among nodes) and parameters (probability values in the tables) within a subspace of possible solutions. The best solution is found through likelihood maximization, knowing the empirical data.

Different Bayesian Network models were calculated from data covering the whole ETIS O/D Matrix, or just the area of interest for Corridor 6. Continuous variables were discretized in eight classes of equal frequencies (other discretizations were also attempted). Each model allows probabilistic inference of O/D freight flow relative growth between 2005 and 2010 from 2005 and 2010 data. Under the assumption of model stationarity, the probabilistic relationships embedded in the model can be used to infer O/D freight flow relative growth between 2010 and 2015 (end hence 2015 freight flows) from 2010 data and scenarios on 2015 data. A more problematic stationarity assumption was also used in order to forecast 2030 freight flows.

1) The forecast for the whole ETIS O/D matrix

The final model set up for the whole ETIS O/D Matrix (Fig. 5) shows that the most important variables are essentially two. One is the GDP national growth in the country of origin (NUTS2 GDP growth had too many missing data to produce statistically significant links in the model); the other one is the relative importance of the outflow for the origin (weight of the exit flow Fij/Fi.). The mutual information analysis (resumed by the position of each node within the model) shows a clear clustering of economic (with internal circle in dark grey) and geographic (without internal circle) variables.

A first validation of the extracted Bayesian Network concerns its predictive power in inferring the value of the target variable of flow relative growth knowing the other variables. The resulting confusion matrix shows that the model can predict values of the target variable with a total precision of 25%, when considering the prediction of the exact variation class, but of more than 50% when considering prediction of the right class or of the two (eventually one) nearest ones (flow growth rates are discretized in eight classes). The second validation tests the model generalizability (or presence of over-fitting problem) through a ten-fold cross validation (that is to say the iterative use of 9/10 of the total O/D data to build the network and 1/10 of the total O/D data to validate it). Results of the cross validation are very similar to the initial model, which leads us to the conclusion that the model does not have particular over-fitting problems. During the cross validation, another validation of the model regards the stability of its network structure (called confidence analysis) and relative variable dependencies (represented from the arc connections) in the ten simulated networks. The arcs directly connected with the target variable (flow_growth) remain always the same and are present in all the networks produced within the cross validation (100%).

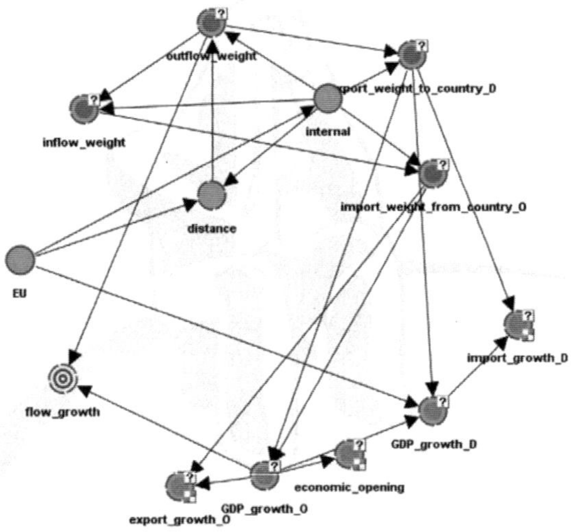

Figure 5. The Bayesian Network model (whole ETIS O/D Matrix)

A first problem of this methodology arises when we need to use the probabilistic results of the Bayesian Network inside the Discrete Choice model [12] that is based on deterministic values of total demand and, based on Revealed Preferences/Stated Preferences interviews (RP/SP, [19]), elaborates probabilistic results on the modal split. In our application, modal split predictions are carried out using the weighted average of the median value of each flow variation class. An example is shown in Fig. 6, with a probability distribution for the target variable freight flow growth. For each of the eight classes, the central value is reported in the right column and is used to calculate the expected mean value (-26.17% in the example) as the weighted average (on the predicted probabilities) of the mean class values.

TABLE V. DEMAND FORECAST (WHOLE ETIS O/D MATRIX) FOR 2015 AND 2030 SCENARIOS

YEAR	Freight flows (road and rail) of the whole ETIS O/D Matrix	
2005	17.752 million of tons	
2010	16.229 millions of tons	
2015	16.367 - 17.037 millions of tons	Delta 2010-15: 0%:+5%
2030	19.530 - 26.167 millions of tons	Delta 2010-30: +20%:+61%

Once the Bayesian Network model is calibrated for 2010 (base year), scenario values can be defined for 2015 and 2030 for the main economic variables. Subsequently, the most probable values of freight flow growth can be inferred through the Bayesian Networks for very O/D couple in 2015 and 2030.

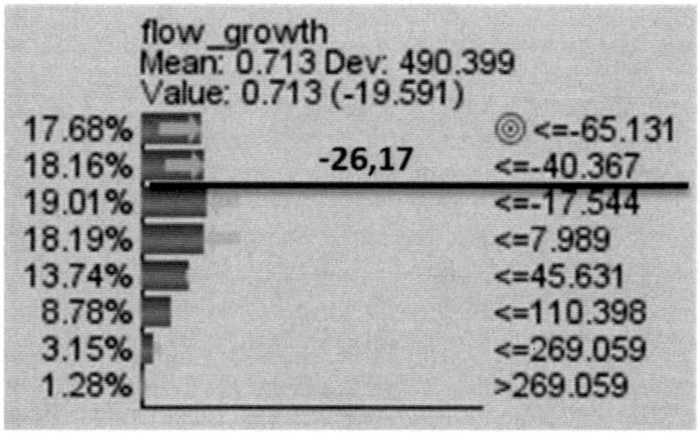

Figure 6. Bayesian Network (whole ETIS O/D Matrix): evaluation of the mean flow prediction

The scenarios for the economic variables are as follows:

- Base scenario: 2015 and 2030 forecast baseline (natural development of the market from the current situation);
- Optimistic scenario: GDP growth forecast increased by 30%;
- Conservative scenario: GDP growth forecast decreased by 30%.

2) The forecast for the Corridor 6 study area

A second Bayesian Network model was developed more specifically for the area concerned by Corridor 6. Flows are grouped as follows:

- Internal, with Origin AND Destination in Corridor zones;
- Exchanges, with Origin OR destination in Corridor zones;
- Transits, with Origin AND Destination outside of Corridor zones.

Once again, under 5-year and 20-year stationarity assumptions, freight flows were inferred for 2015 and 2030, using the most probable values of flow relative growth. The forecasts for Corridor 6 flows (see Table 6 and Fig. 7) shows that the flows variation in 2015, relative to 2010 base year and considering the three scenarios, lies between -1% (conservative scenario) and +10% (optimistic scenario), with very low probability of having total flow decrease and high probability of having total flow increase, although small in quantity. The results of the demand forecast for 2030 show a general long-term increase of traffic flows with high percentage variation from the conservative scenario, with a 27% of increase to a 96% of increase for the optimistic one.

It is very difficult to verify these results. We thus tried to compare our results with those produced by a recent work by the French Ministry of the Environment [14]. This is one of the few comparable works to ours, in terms of geographical extension of the study area.

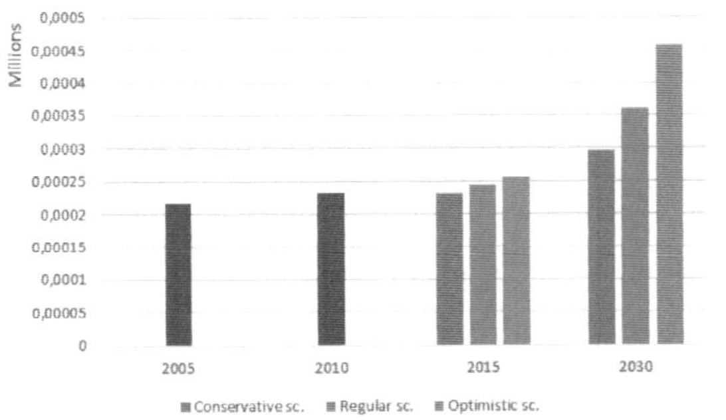

Figure 7. Road and Rail flows in the Corridor 6 catchment Area (including transit)

The study on freight flows through the Pyrenees predicts the following annual average freight flow growth rates between the Iberian Peninsula and the rest of Europe between two scenarios: 2.9% (low scenario) and 4.5% (high scenario).

TABLE VI. EVOLUTION OF FREIGHT FLOWS CONCERNING CORRIDOR 6 CATCHMENT AREA (INCLUDING TRANSIT)

YEAR	Freight flows (road and rail) of Interesting O/D couples	
2005	217 million of tons	
2010	233 millions of tons	Delta 2005-2010: +7,3%
2015	230 - 256 millions of tons	Delta 2010-15: -1%:+10%
2030	297 - 457 millions of tons	Delta 2010-30: +27%:+96%

By applying these growth rates to the observed 2005 freight flows within the area of interest for Corridor 6 (data derived from the 2005 ETIS O/D matrix), the estimated 2010 road and rail freight flows from the Iberian Peninsula to the rest of the catchment area of Corridor 6 would be much higher than the ones actually recorded within the ETIS 2010 O/D Matrix (Table 7).

TABLE VII. COMPARISON OF EVOLUTION OF FREIGHT FLOWS THROUGH PYRENEES BETWEEN THE FRENCH STUDY AND THE ETIS REAL VALUES (VALUES IN MILL. OF TONS)

ETIS 2005	Study on freight flows through Pyrenees - 2010 estimates		ETIS 2010
	Low scenario	High scenario	
10,86	12,5	13,5	11,68

TABLE VIII. COMPARISON OF PREVISION OF FREIGHT FLOWS THROUGH PYRENEES BETWEEN THE FRENCH STUDY AND OUR RESULTS (VALUES IN MILL. OF TONS)

YEAR	Freight Transport of Pyreneer' study - Estimates 2010		Our study on RFC 6		
	Low scenario	High scenario	Conservative	Regular	Optimistic
2015	14,8	16,9	11,5	11,9	13,6
2030	22,7	32,6	16,3	17,3	24,4

Table 8 provides a comparison between 2015 and 2030 forecasted freight flows in the two studies (the study of freight flows through the Pyrenees provides estimates in 2025, but due to the hypothesized linearity of the evolution, it was possible to determine the "most likely forecast" in 2030).

III. CONCLUSIONS AND FUTURE DEVELOPMENTS

The data-driven methodology applied within this work seems to be very promising from many points of view. First of all the data it needs are easy to find from official European level sources (even if more complete economic data-bases at the NUTS 2 level could have improved the performance of our models). Secondly, the methodology, because of its simplicity, is applicable in the short term, through model updating by incremental learning or new model development; it will thus be possible to update forecasts, as new data are available and to follow multi-temporal economic dynamics. Moreover, the Bayesian Network framework adopted allows the recognition of different flow evolutions (which is similar to having multiple transport distribution system equations based on different calibrated parameters) and their application in the forecasted scenarios. In addition, a comparison of the results with some official studies shows that our results are acceptable estimates.

The starting database for this first application covers two base years, namely 2005 and 2010, which are a very particular period for the European economy (arrival of new member states in 2004 and deep economic crisis after 2008), with some peculiar correlations and dynamics among economic, transportation and social variables. Availability of the 2015 version of the ETIS database will allow data-driven model development over the 2005-2015 period, which should produce more reliable results. Of course, the development of new infrastructures or geo-economic dynamics (entrance of new member states in the EU) will always be exogenous to the model, and the use of timeor cost-distances could be used instead of km-distance to better model the impact of transportation networks on the study area. Finally, the stationarity hypotheses on the links between economic, geographic and transportation variables are much more appropriate for short-term forecast (5 years) than for long-term ones (20-30 years).

A further point to be developed is the link between the total demand forecast and the following modal split scenarios. The use of average prediction values necessary for this further methodological step involves the loss of the richness of the Bayesian Network results that is the probability distribution of the estimated flows demand. We are presently trying to use Monte Carlo simulation approaches [13] in order to extract a large number of possible deterministic demand values from the demand probability distribution. Subsequently, a modal choice probabilistic distribution will be derived from each of these values. It will then be possible to estimate an overall probability distribution for flows by mode and the results will be expressed in terms of values accompanied by statistical parameters such as mean, variance, and quartiles.

The methodology is similar to that used in Mixed Discrete Choice Models.

Another option would be to develop the entire demand forecast that is the generation and the modal distribution of freight flows, within the Bayesian Network framework. It will then be possible to preserve a consistent probabilistic approach for flows estimation by transport mode.

REFERENCES

[1] L. Tavasszy, "Freight Transport: from neighbring countries and from thos far away (in Dutch)", Nijemegen: Radboud Universiteit, 2006.

[2] M. Ben-Akiva, H. Meersman, E. Van de Voorde, "Freight Transport Modelling", Emerald Group Publishin Limited, 2013, ISBN 978-1-78190-285-1

[3] Burgess A. et al., "Final Report TRANS-TOOLS (TOOLS for TRansport Forecasting ANd Scenario testing) Deliverable 6". Funded by 6th Framework RTD Programme. TNO Inro, Deft, Netherlands, 2008.

[4] NEA Transport research and training BV, "Core Database Development for the European Transport policy Information System (ETIS), Final Technical Report v1", 2005.

[5] M. Petri, G. Fusco, A. Pratelli, "A new data-driven approach to forecast freight transport demand", Computational Science and ITS Applications, 14th International Conference (ICCSA 2014) Proceedings part IV, Springer-Verlag Berlin Heidelberg, 2014, pp. 401-416, ISSN: 0302-9743.

[6] D. Floreano, C. Mattiussi, "Neural Network Handbook (in Italian)", Mulino Editrice, Bologna, 1996.

[7] H. Meersman and E. Van de Voorde, "The Relationship between Economic Activity and Freight Transport", in Freight Transport Modelling, edited by Ben-Akiva et. Al., Emerald Group Publishing, 2013.

[8] I. H. Witten and E. Frank, "WEKA – Machine Learning Algorithms in Java", University of Waikato, Morgan Kaufmann Publishers, 2000.

[9] J. Pearl, "Causality – Models, Reasoning and Inference", Cambridge University Press, Cambridge, 2000.

[10] G. Fusco, "Handling Uncertainty in Interaction Modelling in GIS: How will an Urban Network Evolve?", in H. Prade et al. (Eds.) "Methods for Handling Imperfect Spatial Information", Berlin, Springer, 2010, pp. 357-378

[11] F. V. Jensen, "Bayesian Networks and Decision Graphs", Springer, New York, 2001.

[12] M. Ben-Akiva and S. R. Lerman, "Discrete choice analysis", MIT Press, Boston, 1985.

[13] K. E. Train, "Discrete Choice Methods with Simulation – Second Edition", Cambridge University Press, USA, 2009, ISBN: 9780521766555

[14] Ministère de l'Écologie, du Développement durable et de l'Énergie, Direction des Transports Terrestres-Bureau d'Informations et de Previsione Economiques, "Analysis and Development of freight flows crossing the Pyrenees (in French)", Issy Edition BIPE, 2005.

[15] K. M. Chase, P. Anater and T. Pelan, "Freight Demand Modelling and Data Improvement - The Second Strategic Highway Research Program", Transport Research Board, Washington D.C., 2013.

[16] NCHRP - National Cooperative Freight Research Program "Freight-Demand Modeling to Support Public-Sector Decision Making", Transport Research Board, Washington D.C., 2010.

[17] C. Caplice and S. Phadnis, "Driving Forces Influencing Future Freight Flows - NCHRP", web-only document 195, Transport Research Board, Washington D.C., 2010.

[18] G. Fusco, "Geo-prospective approach and random probabilistic modelling (in French)", Cybergeo: European Journal of Geography [Online], Systems, Modelling, Geostatistics, document 613, 2012, http: //cybergeo.revues.org/25423; doi:10.4000/ cybergeo.25423.

[19] R. Danielis and L. Rotaris, "An analysis of freight transport demand using stated preference data: a survey and a research project for the Friuli-Venezia-Giulia region", Trasporti Europei (13), 1999.

[20] A.Albert and A. Schafer, "Demand for Freight Transportation in the U.S.; A High- Level View", Journal of Transportation Statistics, 2013.

[21] D.Inaudi, G. De Jong and M. Arnone, "A mathematical model for evaluating some of freight transport scenarios in the North-West of Italy (in Italian)", in XXXII Italian Conference about Regional Science, 2013.

[22] M. Chen, "ETIS and TRANS-TOOLS v1 Freight demand" in CTS-seminar – European and National Freight demand models, 1 March 2011, Stockolm, 2011.

[23] S. Onsel, F. Ulengin, O. Kabak and O. Ozaydin, "Transport Demand Projections: A Bayesian Network Approach", 13th World Conferenze on Transport Research, July 15-18, 2013 – Rio de Janeiro, Brazil, 2013, ISBN: 978-85-285-0232-9H.

Seaplane Traffic in the Republic of Croatia

Pero Vidan, Merica Slišković, Nikola Očašić
Faculty of Maritime Studies
University of Split, Split, Croatia
pvidan@pfst.hr

Abstract— **Seaplane traffic in the European Union has been growing constantly over the last decade. The International Air Transport Association (IATA) predicts an even higher annual growth rate of the seaplane traffic in the near future. The development of seaplane services results from the capacity overload of the existing airports and the demand for point-to-point connections with minor destinations. Due to the length of its coastline and other natural features, the Republic of Croatia is one of the EU member states experiencing a rapid increase in seaplane traffic. The state has been forced to amend a number of acts and regulations. In 2016 seaplane service network in Croatia consists of 16 destinations. Seaplane service was not recognized in Croatia law. Therefore, implementation such service needed previous revision of Croatia legislation. This includes researching of influence to environment, especially to pollution of air, water and influence of noise. Because of need of positioning of seaplanes port in maritime ports which are crowded during the season, maritime study of safety of traffic due to positioning of seaports and public perception regarding the safety of maritime traffic.**

Keywords-Seaplane; Traffic, Safety; Seaplane Service in the Republic of Croatia.

I. INTRODUCTION

The seaplane traffic in the European Union has been growing by 5% per year [8]. The International Air Transport Association (IATA) predicts an even higher annual growth rate of the seaplane traffic in the near future. The development of seaplane services results from the capacity overload of the existing airports and the demand for point-to-point connections with minor destinations [8]. The European Union experiences a considerable increase in sites intended for building seaplane ports, especially on lakes and islands. 24% of EU's smaller aircraft are intended for passenger transport.

The development of the seaplane traffic started some 80 years ago, but the basic seaplane design has not changed much over the years. One of the reasons may be the relatively small share of seaplanes in the overall Commercial Air Transport. Most of them have been operated by private persons for non-commercial purpose. The ones engaged in liner service, they have been mostly used for connecting minor destinations and transporting a small number of passengers. However, the advantage of a seaplane service over a standard air service lies in the simplicity and low cost of the seaplane port infrastructure. In addition, seaplane ports do not charge high dues that otherwise affect the airfare considerably. Manoeuvring features of these crafts, while on the sea surface, are similar to those in seagoing vessels.

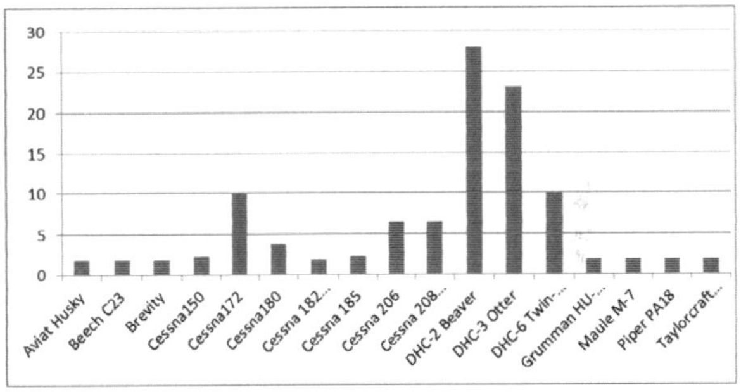

Graph 1. Share of small aircraft manufacturers in the EU fleet (%) [8]

Across the world, there are a number of places with extensive seaplane traffic. The examples include:

- Maldives – where seaplane services connect more than 40 dispersed tourist destinations with land-based airports. 24 Twin Otter craft perform over 150 flights daily, including scenic flights.
- Vancouver – where Vancouver Harbour Air Company operates 50 seaplanes connecting Vancouver Harbour with smaller 20-minute range destinations.
- Sea Air company has tried to establish a similar airline service in Greece, using 22 Twin Otter craft.
- Harbour Air Malta operates a liner service between Valleta and Gozo Island for weekenders and businessmen, in addition to performing scenic flights.

II. LEGISLATION OF THE REPUBLIC OF CROATIA

The transport of goods and passengers by maritime law in Republic Croatia, between Croatia's seaports represents the maritime cabotage that includes the coastal cabotage. The latter includes:

1. Seaborne transport of passengers and/or goods between mainland-based seaports without calling at the islands;
2. Supply provided to the offshore facilities: seaborne transport of passengers and/or goods between any

ports, plants or structures within the epicontinental shelf of the Republic of Croatia;

3. Insular cabotage, i.e., seaborne transport of passengers and/or goods between:

- Mainland-based seaports and ports at one or more islands;
- Ports at islands.

The establishment of seaplane traffic has led to the necessity of adapting the national *Maritime Code* and other relevant acts and regulations as this type of commercial maritime traffic has not been experienced before.

Croatia's legislation has been examining foreign acts, regulations and conventions referring to seaplanes, including the regulations that are internationally adopted and incorporated into the *International Convention on Safety of Life at Sea* (SOLAS 74), *International Convention for the Prevention of Pollution from Ships* (MARPOL 73/78), *International Load Line Convention* (LOADLINE 1966), *International Convention on Tonnage Measurement of Ships* (TONNAGE 1969), and Ordinance regulating specific security, safety and other measures when handling dangerous substances in port areas. In addition to general national regulations, the Regulations on navigation and order in ports specifically comply with the Ordinance on terms and methods of maintaining order in ports and conditions for using ports, the Ordinance on determining the class and limit of hazardous substances that can be handled in ports, the Ordinance on terms and methods of performing activities in free zones, and the Plan of ship waste management in the area under jurisdiction of the Port Authority. Other ordinances are the Ordinance on handling hazardous substances, conditions and forms of seaborne transport, loading and discharging of hazardous substances, bulk and other cargoes in ports, and on prevention of spreading oil spills in ports, the Ordinance on terms and methods of maintaining order in ports and other parts of internal waters and territorial seas of the Republic of Croatia, the Ordinance on amendments to the Ordinance on the safety of maritime navigation in internal waters and territorial sea of the Republic of Croatia and on the conditions and methods of performing the surveillance and regulation of the sea traffics, as well as the relevant regulations and technical requirements stipulated by *Croatian Register of Shipping* and by competent authorities of the flag-states where the above Conventions do not refer to some of their vessels.

Because, seaplanes are crafts which are considered being boats during manovring to the water and planes during flying to air, new regulations must be in short relation with international air regulation.

These restrictions and regulations can be found in: *National regulations are harmonized with European regulatory framework, given in this particular 'air traffic' part by Basic and implementing Regulations (Regulation (EC) No 216/2008, and Commission Regulation (EU) No 965/2012, Act on airports, Maritime Demesne and Seaports Act, Ordinance on water airports.*

Until 2012, the national legislation did not regulate the sites and conditions of seaplane landing and taking off operations, and the latter were treated as the emergency operations.

For establishing the commercial seaplane traffic it is of great importance to regulate the "seaports" as a dedicated water area (including all facilities, installations and equipment), entirely or partially intended for movement, take-off, water landing (alighting) and accommodation of seaplanes.

III. IMPACT OF SEAPLANES AND WATER AERODROMES ON THE ENVIRONMENT

Water airdromes have only a minor effect on the features and the overall shape of the existing scenery, due to the fact that these facilities use parts of seaports that are already engaged in accommodation of vessels and handling maritime traffic.

According to the analyses carried out by the project FUSETRA – Future Seaplane Traffic [9], aircraft should be more affordable, safer, cleaner and quieter in order to meet the criteria of the environmental sustainability of the air traffic. Sustainability may be defined in various ways, but it is generally agreed that the concept of sustainability implies responsible exploitation of natural resources worldwide. In terms of sustainable use of resources, one of the EU goals is to halve the emission of carbon dioxide (CO2) by 2020 and to reduce noise pollution and nitrogen oxide emission (NOx) by 80% in comparison to the values recorded in 2000 [9].

Figure 1. ECA Water aerodrome in Split [30].

During the flight, i.e., the period between taking off and landing on the water, the environmental impact of a seaplane is equal to the impact of any other aircraft. Various studies on the effects of seaplanes on the environment have been carried out primarily by seaplane owners [24]. The most comprehensive study was conducted by American military engineers (USACE) [25], concluding that seaplanes do not harmfully affect:

- Air quality,

- Water quality,
- Soil quality,
- Wildlife,
- Fisheries,
- Hydrology.

Water aerodromes affect local surface water circulation to some extent due to the small draft of the pontoon infrastructure whose designed draft usually amounts to 0.35 m, but they do not affect deep water circulation at all. As this infrastructure creates shadow and reduces the light below, some effects on the marine life should be taken into consideration.

The noise created under water cannot be calculated from the noise above water because the sources are different. Air noise primarily results from the seaplane's engine operation and movement of the craft through the water when landing or taking off. It should also be noted that, unlike vessels, seaplanes do not discharge sewage or oily waters, and that their hulls are not treated with toxic antifouling paints. There are no toilettes in seaplanes so that there is no risk of discharging faecal waste into the sea [12]. Furthermore, the exhaust emissions produced by seaplanes are released into the atmosphere high above the sea level, thus minimising the direct harmful impact on the marine environment [30].

TABLE 1. ESSENTIAL CHARACTERISTICS OF JET A1 FUEL WITH REGARD TO HEALTH, SAFETY AND ENVIRONMENT SOURCE: [19]:

Characteristic	Unit	Value
pH value (concentration and temp.):		Not applicable
Ebullition point / area:	°C	145.0 – 300.0
Flash point:	°C	38.00 (min)
Volatility:	(solid/gaseous):	Not applicable
Explosion limits:	vol. %	No data
Oxidation properties:		No data
Vapour pressure:	Pa	No data
Density at 15°C:	kg/m	775.0 – 840.0
Solubility (type of solvent indicated):	g/L	Not applicable
Solubility in water:	g/L	Not applicable
Octanol/water partition coefficient:	logPow	Not applicable
Viscosity (kinematic) at 100°C:	mm2/s	< 8.000
Vapour density (at 15°C):	kg/m3	No data
Evaporation rate:		No data
Auto-ignition temperature:	°C	260 – 410
Conductivity:	pS/m	50 – 600

Seaplane engines are not cooled by means of heat exchangers (water coolers) as is the case in marine engines so that there is no seawater circulating around the engines. After the engine shutdown, the excess fuel is collected in specially designed accumulators that are regularly emptied to prevent marine pollution.

TABLE 2. COMPARISON OF TEMPERATURE PROPERTIES FOR SOME FUELS [27]

Fuel	Flash point	Auto-ignition temperature	Freezing point
Ethanol (70%)	16.6°C	363°C	
Petrol (Gasoline)	– 43°C	246°C	
Diesel	> 62°C	210°C	
Jet fuel	> 38°C	210°C	
Jet A	> 38°C	210°C	< – 40°C
Jet A-1	> 38°C	210°C	< – 47°C
JP5	> 60°C		< – 46°C
JP7	> 60°C		
Jet B	– 18°C		
Kerosene	> 38°C – 72°C	220°C	
Biodiesel	> 130°C		

Seaplane engines are not cooled by means of heat exchangers (water coolers) as is the case in marine engines so that there is no seawater circulating around the engines. After the engine shutdown, the excess fuel is collected in specially designed accumulators that are regularly emptied to prevent marine pollution.

During the manoeuvring of the seaplane on the sea surface, there is little or no turbulence of water at the seabed. Therefore, the sediments on the sea bottom that some forms of benthic life depend upon are not disturbed [24].

The impact of a seaplane on the mechanical properties of the sea mass is negligible due to the fact that the craft's entire propulsion system is above the water level.

The most common jet fuel used by seaplanes is JET A1. According to its chemical composition, JET A1 is the kerosene grade fuel (refined paraffin). This fuel is stable when properly stored and used, i.e. when not exposed to heat sources, flames, sparks and excessive temperatures. Incomplete combustion may result in CO (carbon monoxide), SOx (sulphur oxides) or H2SO4 (sulphuric acid) [19].

Jet A1 fuel is produced in compliance with international standards with a flashpoint above 38°C and the lowest pure point temperature of - 47°C [27].

In the Republic of Croatia, fuel bunkering is defined and regulated by *Ordinance on handling hazardous substances, conditions and forms of seaborne transport, loading and discharging of hazardous substances, bulk and other cargoes in ports, and on prevention of spreading oil spills in ports* (Official Gazette: 51/05, 127/10, 34/13, 88/13), *Ordinance on terms and methods of maintaining order in ports and other parts of internal waters and territorial seas of the Republic of Croatia* (Official Gazette 90/05), and by *Ordinance on water airports* (Official Gazette 36/14).

Standards for emissions from aircraft are internationally defined and incorporated into the legislation of each member state of the International Civil Aviation Organization (ICAO) [28]. Article 123 of *Croatia's Air Transport Act* (Official Gazette: 69/09, 84/11, 127/13) states that "noise and exhaust gases produced by a taking-off and landing aircraft must be below maximum allowed limits for the noise level and exhaust gases, as defined by ordinances referring to this Act and complying to the relevant EU regulations". Presently, Croatia's legislation does not contain regulations defining maximum levels of exhaust gases produced by aircraft, but the *Air Protection Act* (Official Gazette: 130/11, 47/14) and related sub-law regulations have been harmonised with the effective *EU's Directive 2008/50/EC of the European Parliament and of the Council of 21 May 2008 on ambient air quality and cleaner air for Europe* [28].

TABLE 3.COMPARISON OF AIR TRAFFIC TO OTHER EMISSION SOURCES SOURCE: [6]

FUEL CONSUMPTION			
Air traffic (million tons/year)		Total (million tons/year)	
176		3140	
EMISSIONS			
Pollutant	Air traffic (million tons/year)	Other sources (million tons/year)	Source
CO_2	554	20,900	Combustion of fossil fuels
H_2O	222	45 525,000	Oxidation of methane into the stratosphere; Evaporation from the Earth's surface
NO_x	3.2	$2{,}9 \pm 1{,}4$ 90 ± 35	Transfer stratosphere – troposphere; Anthropogenic sources
CO	0.26	600 ± 300 1490	Oxidation of methane Anthropogenic sources
CH	0.1	90	Anthropogenic sources
Soot	0.0025	-	-
SO_2	0.176	0.0625 134	Stratospheric aerosol; Combustion of fossil fuels

The International Civil Aviation Organization (ICAO), through the Committee on Aviation Environmental Protection (CAEP) responsible for defining regulations and new standards related to noise and emissions from aircraft, has made efficient efforts in further reduction and restriction of emissions produced by aircraft engines which harmfully affect the environment [28].

As a member of ICAO, Croatia is obliged to comply with the standards described in the Book II of the Annex 16 to the ICAO Convention on International Civil Aviation [16].

These standards define the limits that the aircraft engines have to meet regarding the emissions of nitrogen oxides (NOx), carbon monoxide (CO), volatile organic compounds (VOC) and smoke point. The standards do not define the limits for particulate matter (PM) that also results from fossil fuel combustion, but there are a number of states whose national legislation define the boundary limits for PM as well.

Fuel consumption of seaplanes per minute of flight is larger than fuel consumption in seaborne vessels, and the emission of CO2 is larger correspondingly [9]. However, the distance covered by seaplanes per minute is much greater. The distance of 100 nautical miles is covered by a seaplane operating in Europe in 60 minutes, whereas an average fast surface vessel would take 180 minutes [16].

The introduction of a new seaplane service increases the overall seaport traffic and exhaust emissions, and yet this harmful influence on the environment is not enough strong to compromise the air quality. Furthermore, seaplanes use JET A-1 fuel (kerosene) that does not contain some of the volatile organic compounds (VOC) that are present in marine heavy fuel oils. Jet fuel also contains less sulphur so that, correspondingly, smaller SOx emissions are recorded.

One of the major obstacles to the growth of seaplane services is insufficient familiarization with the environmental impacts of this form of transport. The ICAO, through the already mentioned Committee on Aviation Environmental Protection (CAEP), has been efficient in further reduction and restriction of noise produced by aircraft engines, which harmfully affects the environment [28].

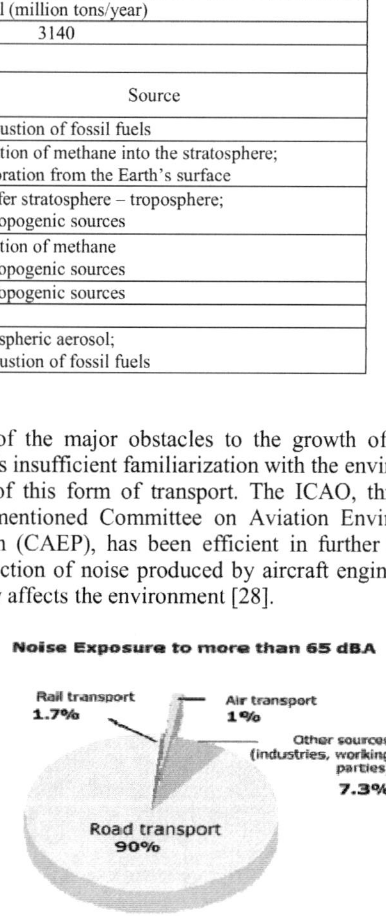

Graph 2. Exposure to noise over 65 dB in the European Union [29]

According to the data presented by the European Commission, only 1% of noise over 65 dB is created by air traffic, while the share of road traffic amounts to 90% [29]. The major problem is the noise produced by seaplanes during taking off and landing operations. The noise is estimated at 75 dB (A), i.e. well over ambient noise. Taking into consideration that during these relatively short periods a seaplane creates more noise than a vessel under way, the take-off/landing zone should be designed in such a way that flying over inhabited areas at low height is avoided. Evans [7] measured the noise produced by a 650 ccm Kawasaki scooter; the noise amounted to 83 dB (A) at low speeds and up to 90 dB (A) at high speeds [7]. Examples of various noise levels are shown in Table 4.

TABLE 4 EXAMPLES OF NOISE LEVELS FOR VARIOUS OPERATIONS [9]

Noise	Noise level (in dB)
Military aircraft	120+ dB(A)
Scooter (Jet ski)	110 dB(A) on lake
All-terrain vehicles	85 dB(A) during general operations
Planing boat	65-95 dB(A) on lake
Seaplane	75 dB(A) only on take-off over an area of 300 m (20 sec)
Car interior	68-73 dB(A) at 30 mph (50 km/h)
Normal conversation	65 dB(A)

TABLE 5 CROATIA'S MAXIMUM PERMISSIBLE NOISE LEVELS IN OPEN ENVIRONMENT [15]

Noise zone	Purpose of the environment	Maximum permissible noise emission level LRAeq in dB(A)	
		Day (Lday)	Night (Lnight)
1	Zone intended for rest, recovery and therapy	50	40
2	Zone intended exclusively for habitation and residence	55	40
3	Zone of mixed purpose, mostly for housing	55	45
4	Zone of mixed purpose, mostly business area with housing	65	50
5	Business zone (production, industry, warehouses, services)	▪ At the building plot boundary within the zone, the noise must not exceed 80 dB(A) ▪ At this zone's boundary, the noise must not exceed permissible noise levels in the neighbouring zone(s)	

The noise level produced by seaplanes is higher than the noise levels for other surface vessels but is not within the range that is considered harmful [9]. Regulation on the maximum permissible noise levels in the environment in which people work and live (Official Gazette 145/04) defines 5 noise zones, depending on their purpose and time during the day. These levels are shown in Table 5.

Maximum noise load in Croatia is expected during tourist season. Presently the seaplane operations are scheduled only during daytime so that the annoying noise levels are avoided at night. Increased seaplane noise is produced only during taking off and landing. As these operations are performed at the regulatory distance of 300 meters off the coast, it can be concluded that the noise does not considerably affect the observed area.

IV. IMPACT OF SEAPLANES ON SAFETY

In Europe, there are various regulations governing the seaplane traffic. Many of them are rather strict, particularly with regard to the safety and environment preservation. In many countries these regulations have become obsolete and are neither in line with demands for seaplane services nor in line with the latest seaplane aviation technologies [4].

- Major obstacles to the development of seaplane traffic arise from:
- Prejudice and public perception regarding the safety of maritime traffic,
- Strict regulations, and
- Inability to build infrastructure for seaplane accommodation.

Seaplane traffic is governed by regulations on seaborne and airborne transport. According to the COLREGS [1][2][7] definition, a seaplane is a craft designed for manoeuvring in air and on water surface. There has been a significant growth in the development of seaplane services over the last five years, particularly in the USA, Canada and Australia [20]. Pontoons and jetties for seaplane accommodation have been increasingly built in China as well. The great demand for seaplane services has resulted in a number of projects and studies related to seaplane traffic, in particular regarding the effects of seaplane traffic on the maritime traffic in ports.

FUSETRA identified the requirements for seaplanes, passengers, operators and manufacturers in Europe. With reference to the FP5 project, concluded that the seaplane traffic in Europe has a great potential due to the development of Europe's transport network and the abundance of rivers, lakes and islands. He established the standards for 11 major Polish ports capable of accommodating seaplane [9].

In 1994, the US Federal Aviation Administration (FAA) released the Advisory Circular for seaplane bases and associated facilities, replaced by the amended Advisory Circular in 2013 [16]. When discussing the safety of navigation of seaplanes and vessels in ports, the collision risks can be analysed by using DEMETEL method [15], [23]. So far, only partial studies on seaplane traffic and its effects on maritime traffic have been published. They use the simulation of traffic flow in ports by applying queueing theory [4], [6] multiple factor method and the simulation of dominance by applying Arena software for simulating heterogeneous traffic of vessels and seaplanes. The principle of analysing individual system components [7], [8], [9] and other theories and methods were also used. So far, the only licensed seaplane operator in the Republic of Croatia is European Coastal Airlines (ECA). The company has more than 200 employees. Its fleet consists of eight De Havilland Twin Otters and one Grumman G 21 Goose. Twin Otter seaplanes connect over 16 destinations in Croatia and Italy (Figure 23) and the corporate plans include expanding of operations to Montenegro and Albania. In 2015, ECA performed 24,000 flights transferring 221,000 passengers [30].

Canadian De Havilland DHC-6 Twin Otter is a STOL (Short Take-off and Landing) (Figures 3 and 4) seaplane manufactured by Viking Air Company. It has been designed to carry passengers and/or cargo, and is able to perform landing and take-off operations using floats, wheels or skis. It has been the best-selling passenger seaplane model ever, able to accommodate 19 passengers.

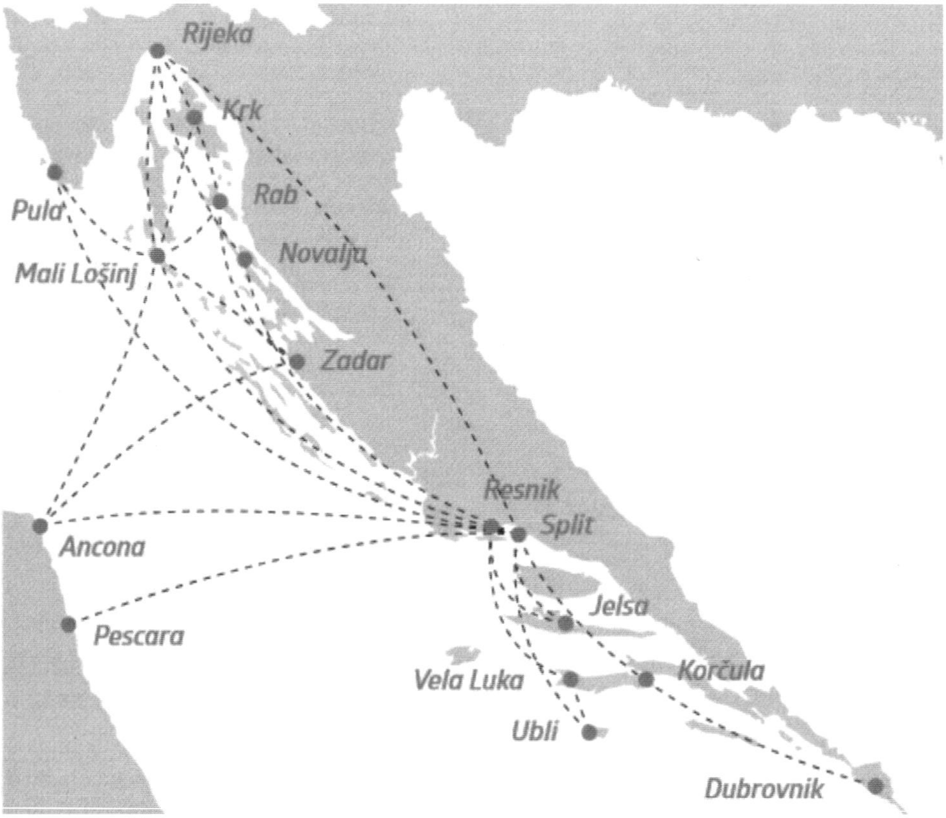

Figure 2. ECA's seaplane destinations in Croatia and Italy [30]

Figure 3. DHC-6 Twin Otter.

Seaplane navigation performance is observed through:

- Manoeuvrability, and
- Traffic features.

Manoeuvring performance of seaplanes during taxiing is similar to the performance of surface vessels, but it differs considerably during take-off and landing operations.

Cruise speed during take-offs and landings ranges from 40 to 108 knots). Compared to the speed of vessels when approaching or leaving port (5-10 knots), it is obvious that the seaplane speed during take-off and landing operations is about 10 times higher than in boats and ships. Given the seaplanes' high speeds in a relatively confined area, it is important to give way to seaplanes when performing these operations. Taking off operations take place at the distance of 350 m from the area allocated for manoeuvring [2][3].

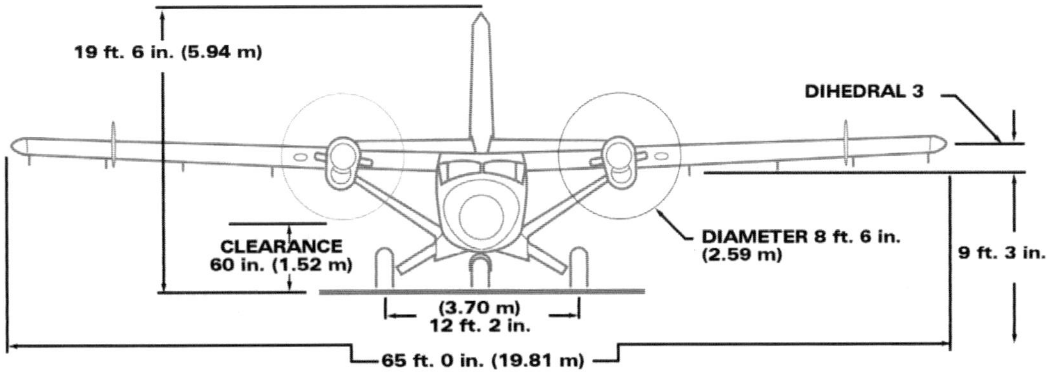

Figure 4. Dimensions of the DHC-6 Twin Otter's wing span and propellers. [13]

When performing take-off and landing over the areas intended for such operations in Croatia, seaplanes do not comply with the regulations on general restrictions of speed, otherwise imposed on surface vessels. If the seaplanes perform commercial air service they can take off or land only in the area allocated for these operations, i.e., at least 300 meters off the coats, except in case of emergency or force majeure.

Landing and take-off operations are usually allowed only during daylight, in suitable meteorological conditions that ensure good visibility. All participants in maritime traffic within the seaplane landing and take-off areas have to manoeuvre with caution. All vessels, yachts and boats with or without mechanical propulsion have to leave the area dedicated to take-off and landing of seaplanes not later than 30 minutes before these operations take place, and act according to the instructions given by the seadrome operator who is authorised to ensure and take adequate security and safety measures in line with relevant statutory regulations.

TABLE 6. MANOEUVRING FEATURES OF THE DHC-6 TWIN OTTER SEAPLANE. [12]

FEATURES	
Engines PT6A-34	
Taking off (runway)	406 m / 1,333 ft.
Flying over 50 ft. obstacles before starting to land	562 m / 1,843 ft.
Taking off (water)	374 m / 1,227 ft.
Flying over 50 ft. obstacles before starting to land	599 m / 1,965 ft.
Climb rate (per minute)	427 m / 1,400 ft.

The seaplane pilots have to perform the landing and take-off manoeuvers after making sure that the landing/take-off area is clear of any other maritime traffic participants. The area is usually properly marked with lights, buoys, daybeacons and daymarks in compliance with specific regulations and is marked in navigation charts issued in official maritime publications.

The wind strength and direction affect the seaplane's movement during take-off and landing operations. Windward take-off (towards the wind) considerably reduces the take-off distance. A DHC-6 Twin Otter typically requires 374 meters for taking off (Table 6), 300 meters for landing operation and 40-80 meters for stopping after touching the water. The seaplane may extend the stopping distance on the water to reduce hull stress and improve passengers' comfort. However, in emergency the craft is able to come to a halt 40 meters after touching the water surface. Strong winds and waves higher than 1.5 m may impede landing and take-off operations [5]. Turning the seaplane on the water is performed by means of the rudder and engines. As the DHC-6 Twin Otter is a double-engine craft, the rudder is fitted to the seaplane's tail but the two controllable pitch propellers ensure excellent manoeuvrability.

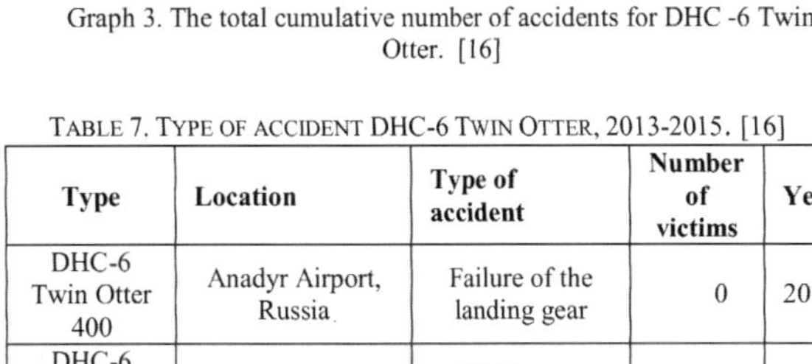

Graph 3. The total cumulative number of accidents for DHC -6 Twin Otter. [16]

TABLE 7. TYPE OF ACCIDENT DHC-6 TWIN OTTER, 2013-2015. [16]

Type	Location	Type of accident	Number of victims	Year
DHC-6 Twin Otter 400	Anadyr Airport, Russia	Failure of the landing gear	0	2014
DHC-6 Twin Otter 300	Maldives	Sinking on landing	0	2015
DHC-6 Twin Otter 300	Maldives	This meeting of the plane during the removal of the dock one of them	0	2015
DHC-6 Twin Otter	Enarotali Airport, Indonesia	Fly out to the runway	0	2015

300				
DHC-6 Twin Otter 300	Tequesquitengo Airport, Mexico	Fly out to the runway	0	2014
DHC-6 Twin Otter 300	La Tabatière Airport, Canada	Fly out to the runway	0	2014
DHC-6 Twin Otter 300	Woitape Airport, Papua New Guinea	Fall on approachin airport	4	2014
DHC-6 Twin Otter 300	USA, Boulder City Municipal Airport	Collision with helicopter	0	2014
DHC-6 Twin Otter 300	Nepal	Drop	18	2014
DHC-6 Twin Otter 310	Kudat Airport, Malaysia	Fly out to the runway	2	2013
DHC-6 Twin Otter 300	Jomsom Airport	Fly out to the runway	0	2013
DHC-6 Twin Otter 300	Greenland	Impact against a reef on landing	0	2013
DHC-6 Twin Otter 300	Sam Neua-Nathong Airport, Laos	The coup in the trees on takeoff	0	2013
DHC-6 Twin Otter 300	St. Anthony Airport, Canada	Fly out to the runway while landing in difficulty	0	2013
DHC-6 Twin Otter 300	Mount Elizabeth, Antarctica	Drop	3	2013
DHC-6 Twin Otter 300	Alifu Dhaalu Atoll, Maldives	The coup in while	0	2012
DHC-6 Twin Otter 300	Laguna Caballococha, Peru	Landing on rough weather, sinking	0	2012

TABLE 8. NUMBER OF ACCIDENT DHC TWIN OTTER 6-300/400. [16]

Year	DHC Twin Otter 6-svi	6-300	6-400	Accident with deats	Number of victims
2006	6	5		2	13
2007	7	6		4	42
2008	10	8		3	22
2009	7	5		3	31
2010	5	5		1	22
2011	6	5		2	8
2012	3	2		/	/
2013	6	6		2	5
2014	6	5	1	2(6-300)	22
2015	5	3		/	/

DHC-6 Twin Otter has been developed throw navigation equipment in period since it has been in operation. According to graph 3, the number of accident rapidly grow up, but this trend is followed by increasingly number of seaplanes in operation and increasing number of traffic in water aerodromes and airports.

According to Table 7, it might be concluded that most of accident are happening on airports. This type of airplane is easy and under influence of wind, especially during landing. Statistics show that victims were only in cases of dropping of seaplanes.

From the Table 8 it can be concluded that the annual average occur around 2 accidents with fatal consequences for the entire world fleet of Twin Otter DHC 6-300 / 400 , for different purposes and design. Given the number of aircraft it gives the approximate probability of an accident with fatal consequences about 3x10-3 per year per aircraft. Most of the accidents is a result of failures, strikes, adverse weather conditions, and mostly occur during landing and take-off. Collisions with ships not registered in the records of accidents [11].

V. CONCLUSION

Croatia is one of the first EU member states which launched the commercial seaplane service as a faster alternative way to reach destinations inland and abroad. However, this service is not public and it is used mostly during summer season. Other EU states with similar experience include Poland, Denmark and Greece. The limiting factors for the development seaplane traffic in the Republic of Croatia included insufficient information and familiarization with this type of transport that was, consequently, not recognized by the national legislation. However, over the last years, Croatian legislation has introduced a number of regulations and ordinances in order to create legal framework for seaplane traffic operations, in particular related to the entrance of seaplanes into ports, their landing, taxiing and taking off within port areas and the construction of seaports.

After years of legislation and investment issues, European Coastal Airlines became the first licensed seaplane operator in Croatia. In addition to the national and local governments, the venture was supported by the AdriSeaplanes project co-funded by the European Union and the IPA – Adriatic Cross-Border Cooperation Program. European Coastal Airlines presently maintains regular flights connecting 16 destinations in Croatia and Italy, and plans to expand operations over the rest of the Adriatic Sea by establishing seaports in Montenegro and Albania.

Various studies and research conducted across the world indicate that the seaplane traffic is safe and not presenting a serious threat to the air and marine environment. The development of this type of transport and the increasing demand indicate that the seaplane traffic is likely to grow considerably in the coming years, for the benefit of holiday-makers and the residents of 66 inhabited islands of Croatia.

REFERENCES

[1] Admiralty List of Lights and Fog Signals, NP 78-2014/15, UKHO.

[2] Canamar Alen, Seaplane Conceptual Design and Sizing, University of Glasgow, 2012.

[3] Department for Transport, Maritime and Coastguard Agency, 2010. http://www.mcga.gov.uk/c4mca/msn_1781-2.pdf (access: 2016-04-20

[4] DeRember D., Bay C., Seaplane Operations, 2004.

[5] DHC & Noise Statement

[6] Enquete-Kommission "Schutz der Erdatmosphäre" des Deutschen Bundestages, Mobilität und Klima, Economica Verlag, Bonn, 1994

[7] Evans, P. G. H., Canwell, P. J. & Lewis, E. 1992. Annex perimental study of the effects of pleasure craft noise upon bottle-nosed dolphins in Cardigan Bay, West Wales. European Research on Cetaceans 6: 43-4

[8] First results of the "FUture SEaplane TRAffic" study, FUSETRA, Aerodays Madrid 2011 (available at http://www.cdti.es/recursos/doc/eventoscdti/aerodays2011/6g4.pdf)

[9] Fusetra, Report on current strength and weaknesses of existing seaplane / amphibian transport system as well as future opportunities including workshop Analysis

[10] Richardson, W. J., Greene, C. R., Malme, C. I., & Thomson, D. H. 1995. Marine mammals and noise. Academic Press. San Diego.

[11] Maritimna studija "Hidroavionsko pristanište na dijelu lučkog područja Split, predio jugozapadni dio Sportske luke Mornar" (Maritime study "Seaplane dock in Split Port area, south-western part of the Sports harbour Mornar")

[12] Twin Otter Series 400 Viking

[13] Viking; Wave statement

[14] Uredba o ekološkoj mreži, NN 80/13) (Regulation on proclamation of the ecological network, Official Gazette of the Republic of Croatia 80/13)

[15] Uredba o određivanju područja i naseljenih područja prema kategorijama kakvoće zraka, NN 68/08 (Regulation on designation of zones and inhabited agglomerations according to categories of air quality, Official Gazette of the Republic of Croatia 68/08)

[16] http://aviation-safety.net/database/record.php?id=20130516-1 (access: 2016-06-13)

[17] http://portsplit.com/bazen-gradska-luka/ (access: 2016-06-24)

[18] http://www.boeing.com/resources/boeingdotcom/company/about_bca/pdf/statsum.pdf (access: 2016-06-24)

[19] http://www.ina.hr/UserDocsImages/stl/HRV/Gorivo_za_mlazne_motore_JET_A-1.pdf (access: 2016-06-24)

[20] http://www.legislation.gov.uk/ukpga/1949/67/section/52/enacted (access: 2016-06-24)

[21] http://www.members.tripod.com (access: 2016-06-24)

[22] http://www.mppi.hr/default.aspx?id=13830 (Ministry of Maritime Affairs, Transport and Infrastructure of the Republic of Croatia, June 2015) (access: 2016-04-02)

[23] http://www.planecrashinfo.com/cause.htm (access: 2016-06-24)

[24] http://www.seaplanes.org.au/PDF/Seaplanes_and_the_Environment.pdf

[25] http://www.seaplanes.org.au/PDF/Seaplanes-The_Facts.pdf (access: 2016-06-20)

[26] http://www.seaplanes.org/advocacy/booklet.pdf (access: 2016-06-24)

[27] http://www.mzoip.hr/doc/studija_o_utjecaju_na_okolis_.pdf

[28] https://bib.irb.hr/datoteka/140311.Steiner_SarajevoConference.doc - EC Green Paper on Future Noise Policy, European Commission, COM 96/540

[29] https://www.ec-air.eu/en/about

[30] http://www.fusetra.eu/documents/FUSETRA_D41_SWOT_v01strtot2.pdf (access: 2016-06-20)

WACIC Method – A Web Analytics Process to Perform Continuous Improvement in Digital Environments

Adriana T. Figueiredo
Faculdade de Tecnologia
UNICAMP
Campinas, Brazil
adrinit@gmail.com

Marcos Augusto F. Borges
Faculdade de Tecnologia
UNICAMP
Campinas, Brazil
marcosborges@ft.unicamp.br

Regina Lucia de O. Moraes
Faculdade de Tecnologia
UNICAMP
Campinas, Brazil
regina@ft.unicamp.br

Abstract - **The Web universe expands every day, providing access to multiple sources of information using different platforms and devices. Due to the increasing number of online users in the world, there are several reasons why corporations became interested in analyzing the traffic on their websites. From small to medium sized businesses, this analysis means dealing with large volumes of data, which can become a real struggle to perform without the support of Web Data Tools. In order to deal with this challenge, this paper proposes the WACIC- a Web Analytics Process to perform continuous improvement in digital environments. Beside the process definition, the paper proposes a set of artifacts to help the discussion and to register decisions.**

Keywords - Web Analytics; Metrics; Method; Google Analytics.

I. INTRODUCTION

Nowadays, understanding the habits of consumers who use the Web for daily activities is a point that draws attention and concern for companies. Transformations and innovations take place constantly on the Web, which leads companies to try to understand and meet the needs of online users. Websites focused on providing services need to operate dynamically, be agile and show continuous improvement [1].

Considering the constantly increasing number of online users in the world, there are various reasons for a company to be interested in analyzing the traffic on their Website, such as knowing if the Website is attracting visitors; what are the pages gaining more interest; to measure the budget invested; the conversion rate; among others [2][3].

Digital marketing, a relatively recent field of study from 1990, has recorded an expressive growth throughout the last decades. Companies started to meet the need for digital marketing strategies, aiming at a better position in the online environment. Besides, the concepts of visitation and navigation on the Web have gone through transformation throughout the last decade [4].

Today, users create their own content, communicate through social networks, give opinions and are constantly interacting in the virtual environment [4][5].

Consequently, the data analysis coming from the Web has gained increasingly greater space in organizations due to some key aspects, such as helping in evaluating the performance of a business and allowing the entrepreneurs to better know the market they are working in.

This analysis aims to make strategic decision making more effective and less risky [5]. This way, the importance of tools that aim to collect and analyse Web data has emerged. This concept earned the name Web Analytics, and it has redefined the way in which companies are monitoring online user's behavior, and even their decision making process [1][4][5][6].

Today, enterprises are exploring Web Analytics to discover facts they did not know before. This is an important task because the recent economic recession forced deep changes into most businesses, especially those that depend on mass consumers [2][3].

The goal of this article is to describe an approach of the use of Web Analytics tools in order to help organizations to reach a competitive differential founded on the analysis of data coming from their Websites.

The lack of a structured process, the difficulties and the divergences faced by companies during the adoption of Web Analytics motivated the proposed approach. It covers the common steps that are presented by different authors, along with new steps that are suggested and are relevant in the context of Web Analytics.

The contributions of this paper are:

- A reviewed and optimized method based on continuous improvement for digital environments, combined with steps commonly used by companies during the adoption of Web Analytics process;
- Monitoring artifacts that helps to store the information tracking between all the involved roles during the process
- A method that can be used by different companies that work on the Web in different contexts.

The remaining of the paper is divided as follows: Section II describes the related work; the fundamental steps of Web Analytics are found in Section III; Section IV presents the WACIC method; finally, the conclusion is found in Section V.

II. RELATED WORK

During the development of this work, traditional and/or standardized processes to guide the use of Web Analytics were not identified. Onwubiko [7] performed a research focused on the applicability of Web Analytics tools in data gathering and analysis to enhanced cyber situational awareness for monitoring critical online Web services.

Many different intelligence sources such as Web logs, browser fingerprints and mobile fingerprints were analysed, in terms of information protection. The author brings useful information regarding technical aspects, technical challenges in the applicability of specific tools and devices that support Web Analytics, but does not present a method to structure a Web Analytics process, like the one presented in this work.

Bengel et al. [8] describe the technical aspects of a research on adopting Web Analytics by directly implementing a tracking code (tag) on the website. This tag aids in automating the tracking and identification of marketing tags for websites overall, which would be a significant effort if done manually. It is an innovative implementation, and it surely provides a competitive advantage. But the paper does not go deeply in a procedural perspective, by emphasizing a process or a method to use Web Analytics tools for different contexts. Instead of that, authors focus on the technical aspects of the tag implementation, and provide a how-to for this implementation.

Although the authors provide an extensive technical explanation of the experiment, it could be difficult for beginners in Web Analytics context to embrace the technique described in the paper without a process methodology that supports the adoption. A Web Analytics approach is presented by Li and Baciu [9]. According to the authors, visual analytics of large data sets has become a challenge for traditional in-memory and off-line algorithms as well as in the cognitive process of understanding features at various scales of resolution. In the paper, they attempt a new Web-based framework for the dynamic visualization of large data.

Along with the technical aspects and challenges described during the data modeling, it is interesting that the authors demonstrate the effectiveness of their Web-based framework on different types of large datasets. This type of Web Analytics research is absolutely useful and provides a step forward in Web Analytics techniques, but this research does not provide the necessary support for those who are still in need of understanding the basics of the Web Analytics adoption.

In terms of standardized Web Analytics methods, Cassidy [10] and Phillips [11] provide an explanation that goes through the common steps and helps most organizations start the adoption of Web Analytics tools. The authors provide important information regarding how organizations can integrate their own processes with adoption of Web Analytics, and how to mitigate the risks of this integration.

This information helping to integrate processes, technology, and people into all facets of analysis to generate business value is useful, but it is important to highlight that the Web Analytics steps are described without considering a specific method or framework.

Some missing steps were identified, such as the tool definition (and criteria to choose the tool that best suits the needs) and a specific step for action plans after the analysis. These complementary steps are provided by the proposed process in this work.

In the next section, we describe in more detail the Web Analytics concept and what are the fundamental steps commonly used by companies that adopt Web Analytics.

III. FUNDAMENTAL STEPS - WEB ANALYTICS

As underlined by the authors Dehkordi et al. [4], Kaushik [5], Siegel and Davenport [6], Kotler, Kartajaya and Setiawan [13], there are three methods that are most used to evaluate the performance of strategies in digital environments.

Kaushik [5], Siegel and Davenport [6] mentioned the approach based on Web metrics (or Web Analytics); another approach is supported by financial indicators, according to Dehkordi et al. [4]; and the third approach is a hybrid of Web Analytics and financial indicators, according to Kotler, Kartajaya and Setiawan [13]. For this work, the Web Analytics is the chosen one to be studied.

There are some divergences regarding the exact definition of the concept of Web Analytics. Kaushik [5] synthesized it in an objective manner: "The objective of Web Analytics is to first and foremost improve the experience of online customers. It is not a technology to produce reports; it is a virtuous cycle for Website optimization."

The mentioned cycle is commonly supported by Web Analytics tools that extract data from Websites. Regardless of whether it is applied, the cycle is understood as a process of measurement, collection, analysis and production of navigation and interaction data reports, whose purpose is to understand the behavior and needs of the users for better optimization of Internet sites and pages.

The work of Kaushik [5] is more closely related to this work, since its steps, presented in Figure 1, were used and extended. However, these steps were described and have been carried out in an ad hoc manner by the organizations.

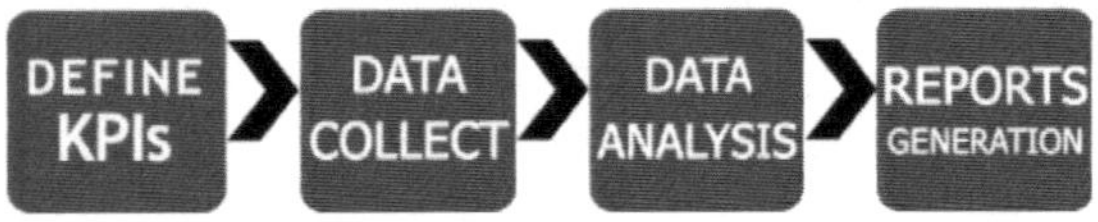

Figure 1. Fundamental steps of the Web Analytics Cycle.

The first fundamental step in the Web Analytics process is to define the MEASUREMENT to be used. Called by some authors KPI (Key Performance Indicators) DEFINITION, it consists of defining what should be measured and what one wants to analyze in order to guide the KPIs choice [1][5][14]. It is necessary to establish a frequency to observe each KPI, identifying successes and failures in the outlined goals and allowing for comparing the results.

Therefore, from time to time, some KPIs adjustments and modifications are necessary, and they should be quickly done so that opportunities to collect information are not lost [14]. In addition, some authors recommend an amount of 3 up to 5 KPIs in order to observe each Web Analytics cycle [1][5][6].

The second step consists of data COLLECTION which is usually done by a Web Analytics tool. According to Kaushik [5] and Jerath, Ma and Park [14], it can be said that all of the Web Analytics tools available have a common point: once enabled, the data collection is done in real time, continuously.

The third step consists of the ANALYSIS of the collected data. The administrators and/or analysts responsible for manipulating the tools and metrics can use specific tools and metrics or to segment the captured data (the forms and options vary according to the tool) for carrying out the analysis[1][5][6]. For Rosenzweig [15] this step is considered crucial, emphasizing the importance of the understanding of user behavior on the Web environment.

At last, the fourth step consists of the REPORTS GENERATION. In this step, it is common to organize the information provided based on the data analysis. There are countless forms and standards of documents for generating reports of the results and they vary according to the Web Analytics tool being used [1][5][16].

This section proposes an empowered and optimized adaptation of the fundamental steps.

In order to empower the Web Analytics adoption, a Web Analytics Process to perform continuous improvement in digital environments is proposed.

IV. THE PROPOSED METHOD

The method proposed for using Web Analytics is based on the fundamental steps described in the previous section. However, some steps were added in order to bring an adherent proposal to all types of organizations interested in practices based on Web Analytics tools. Also, the proposed method aims to solve the lack of standardized methods of Web Analytics application.

A. The Method Definition - WACIC

The method proposed is named WACIC – Web Analytics Continuous Improvement Cycle. It includes the fundamental steps and added two new steps. The first one is a specific step that helps to define the Web Analytics tool that best suits and supports the chosen KPIs. Normally, this step is not performed by most of companies; they usually choose the tool before the KPIs definition [1][6]. Plus, the choice itself is commonly based only on price and popularity, instead of considering the importance of the KPIs adherence to the tool.

The second new step consists of executing action plans based on the analysis. The actions should be executed in order to reach the goals outlined in the KPIs step. Besides the inclusion of these two new steps, the DATA ANALYSIS and REPORTS GENERATION were combined into one single step. This change is due to the fact that the analysis needs to be documented or organized to be provided to all involved roles, and the reports generated by the Web Analytics tools can be used as artifacts for this step.

Two cycles compose the WACIC: the FULL CYCLE and the CONTINUOUS CYCLE. The Full Cycle presents the Method flow as a whole, since the Action Plans implemented and executed will reflect in reaching the goals defined in the KPI step. The Continuous Cycle presents a cyclical flow where the action plans executed should be analyzed and re-executed until the expected result is reached. Once the goal is reached, the full cycle should start again, in order to define new KPIs so as to reach further improvements due to the continuous process.

The adaptation of the method is based on the concept of continuous improvement, through the PDCA (Plan, Do, Check and Act) framework. In the PDCA, the main activities are planning, executing, checking and verifying [17]. As such, an uninterrupted optimization method for product and service improvement is obtained, since as the PDCA cycle repeats itself, it is possible to come closer to outlined goals and reach the expected result.

In addition, the WACIC method integrates specific artifacts that help to consolidate and track all the information obtained during each of the steps and document the decisions during the process.

Moreover, the artifacts are a suggestion, and not mandatory. In case of an organization that does not have its own artifact to support the information tracking, the WACIC can help by suggesting the artifacts that is integrated by the proposed method.

Figure 2 presents the WACIC method and Figure 3 presents the artifacts integrated to the process.

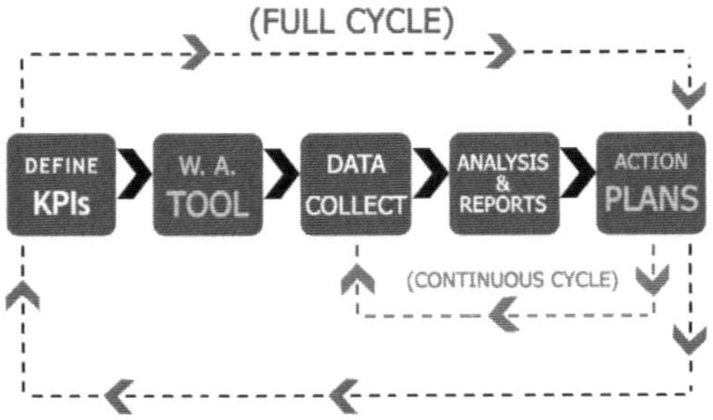

Figure 2. The WACIC method.

B. *KPIS Definition*

Besides the definition of measurements to be used provided by the fundamental step, three activities should be concluded during this step, aiming at addressing all the mandatory steps for KPIs definition. The activities can be carried out during one (or more, if necessary) alignment meetings. The participation of interested roles through means of communication with the data analysis team is essential and can be done either in person or through video conferences.

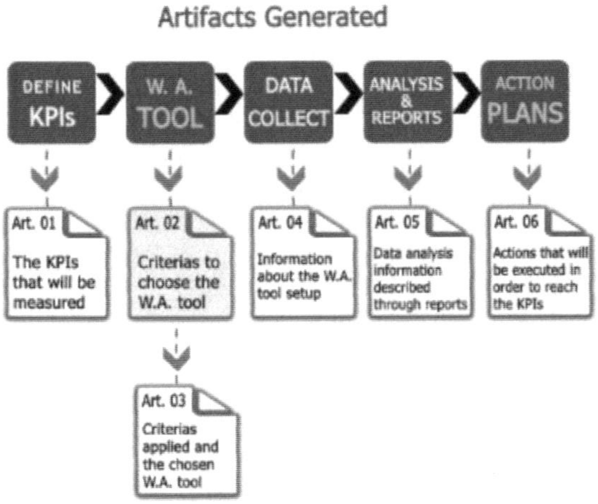

Figure 3. WACIC Artifacts.

During the first step, the activities should be carried out jointly, involving all of the relevant roles and awareness of the business goals.

Professionals tasked to conduct the Web Analytics process participate in this step, that is, Business Analysts, Project Managers, Directors and additionally, other professionals who carry out roles relevant to defining the performance indicators for the organization.

The activities in this step were defined as follows:

- *Organization Goals Definition and Understanding* - understanding of the organization's objectives provides greater assertiveness in the definition of the KPIs.
- *Motivation/Purpose for choosing the KPIs* - after understanding the organization's business objectives, it is necessary to justify the choice of the KPIs that will be defined. Which are the factors, on a technical or business level, that motivate the choice of the KPIs.
- *Definition of the KPIs* - this definition guides all of the following steps of the proposed method. Through the KPIs, it should be possible to understand if the Web environment under analysis is progressing or regressing.

TABLE I. KPIS DEFINITION

Art. 01 - KPIs definition	
[Company's name]	
[Website]	
[Focal Points of the Company (Name, e-mail and telephone)]	
[Duration of this step]	
Date / Meeting Place	
[Focal Points involved in this step (Name, e-mail and telephone)]	
Company's goals	[to be defined]
What motivates to choose each of the KPIs	[to be defined]
KPI 01	Description/ How it will be measured/ data collect period
KPI 02	Description/ How it will be measured/ data collect period

The following questions are examples of KPIs: "how many visitors or buyers access the organization's site daily"; "where the Website accesses come from and what is the peak number of accesses"; "what is being commented in the social networks regarding the organization"; "what are the consumer experiences of the Internet users (positive or negative reactions about the brand or product)". A proposal of an artifact resulting from this step is presented in TABLE I, which aims to document the information relevant to the KPIs definition.

Each organization that is the focus of the analysis generates an artifact containing the information. The artifact's fields indicate the participants for each activity, date and time of the meeting(s), what the business objectives discussed were, what the purpose and justifications for the defined KPIs were, and finally, the definition of the KPIs.

C. *Choosing the Web Analytics Tool*

The second step in the method consists of choosing the Web Analytics tool to capture the collection of data to be analyzed. The choice of the tool needs to be based on information defined in the first step. Bearing in mind the various tools for capturing Web data available, the method proposed here presents four criteria that help in more assertively choice of the most adequate tool to be used.

The criteria are described in TABLE II. The application of the first criterion considers the most current commonly used tools, which was considered bearing in mind the tools cited in the bibliographic sources.

TABLE II. CRITERIAS TO CHOOSE THE WEB ANALYTICS TOOL

Art. 02 - Criterias to choose the Web Analytics tool	
First	Most commonly used Web Analytics tools, nowadays.
Second	Logs based tools *versus* tags based tools
Third	Web Analytics tools that offers the features necessary to measure the KPIs defined in the first KPIs phase
Fourth	Costs and benefits of the tools

The second criterion is supported by the discussion of particularities that the Web Analytics tools present. That is, based on logs or measurement by tags. These two methods are, today, often used for analyzing Internet traffic. This criterion allows for the analysis of the KPIs considered to be adherent to the operation of the chosen Web Analytics tool. It identifies, basically, if the focus of the analysis is of a technical nature and/or focused on performance (the log method favors the collection and analysis of data through the server-side), or if the focus is the behavior/actions of the visitor (the method that uses tags favors the collection and analysis of data through the client-side).

The third criterion to be considered in the choice of the Web Analytics tool consists of choosing a tool that has the functions that allow for the proposed measurement. The types of metrics and KPIs stipulated vary according to the search objective. Then, the choice of the tool should consider if the functions necessary to meet and support the requested measurement are provided by it.

The fourth criterion consists of the evaluation of the cost/benefit of the tools researched. There are tools available for free and tools that require a specific cost. Depending on the result of the criteria previously applied, the options for tools mapped out are countless. However, it is necessary to evaluate if the cost of a paid tool will in fact be necessary for an organization.

TABLE III. CRITERIA APPLIED TO CHOOSE THE WEB ANALYTICS TOOL

Art. 03 - Criterias applied to choose the Web Analytics tool	
[Company's name]	
[Website]	
[Focal Points of the Company (Name, e-mail and telephone)]	
[Duration of this step]	
Date / Meeting Place	
[Focal Points involved in this step (Name, e-mail and telephone)]	
First Criteria	[results after the first criteria]
Second Criteria	[results after the second criteria]
Third Criteria	[results after the third criteria]
Fourth Criteria	[results after the fourth criteria]
Chosen Web Analytics tool	[to be defined]

The application of the criterion consists of the fundamental activity in the step proposed here. This activity should be carried out with the involvement of roles relevant to the choice.

At the end of this step, an artifact will be generated, referent to the choice of the Web Analytics tool. The artifact consists of a table for filling in information referent to the choice of the tool, as presented in TABLE III.

It is important to highlight that the Web Analytics tool do not need to be changed or replaced every time the WACIC flow restarts. Companies usually deal with costs, implementation and training of the Web Analytics tools, and those aspects should not be disregarded.

D. *Data Collect*

The third step of the continuous cycle consists of collecting the data. This step has some activities that need to be completed so that enabling the data capture is carried out.

The activities were divided as follows:

- *Installation of the tool* - for this activity, the manual and/or instruction steps provided by the chosen Web Analytics tools should be followed;
- *Configuration of the Website data capture* - to enable the tool, capture the data from the Website and store them for analysis;
- *Validation of the monitoring of the Website* pages - aiming to guarantee full coverage of the pages to be analyzed.

TABLE IV. DATA COLLECT

Art. 04 - Data Collect	
[Company's name]	
[Website]	
[Focal Points of the Company (Name, e-mail and telephone)]	
[Duration of this step]	
[Focal Points involved in this step (Name, e-mail and telephone)]	
Chosen tool	[to be defined]
Tool installation (OK / NOK)	[to be defined]
Tool configuration to capture data correctly (OK / NOK)	[to be defined]
Validation of pages – to make sure all of them are being tracked correctly (OK / NOK)	[to be defined]

People involved in the data capturing activities are basically people from the technical team and/or Web Analytics professionals who carry out the activities directly through the tool, and who monitor the Website.

It is necessary a focal point, a technical role, to verify if the tool is in fact collecting the data correctly, and if all of the pages are being analyzed so that the information relevant to the future analysis of the data is not lost. For this step, an artifact that describes the activities referent to the data collection was defined. The artifact can be seen in TABLE IV.

E. *Data Analysis Reports*

After the data collection, the analysis step on the collected data and the interpretation of these data by the tool begins. Using the defined KPIs as a base for analysis, the interpretation of the data is performed, with the aim of evaluating and understanding the involvement of the Website visitors.

This step can be described as a study of the collected data. The formalization of the study takes place through the generation of reports containing conclusions from the analysis. The data analysis and generation of the reports should be carried out by the roles relevant to his step, that is, professionals tasked with conducting the Web Analytics process, or Business Analysts, Project Managers, Directors and, additionally, other who can help to understand user behavior and refine the objective of the research.

TABLE V. DATA AND ANALYSIS REPORTS

Art. 05 - Data and analysis reports	
[Company's name]	
[Website]	
[Focal Points of the Company (Name, e-mail and telephone)]	
[Duration of this step]	
[Focal Points involved in this step (Name, e-mail and telephone)]	
Date and Meeting place	
KPIs/ Period of data collect	**Report Information**
[to be defined]	[to be defined]

The activities in this step can be carried out, preferably, during one (or more, if necessary) meeting in person, since the analyzed KPIs should be discussed. At the end of the data analysis phase, the reports generated by the tool will be used as artifacts from this step.

In addition to the generated reports, the TABLE V will present a summary of the content from the reports, facilitating its identification and interpretation.

F. *Action Plans (definition and execution)*

The fifth step consists of applying action plans that help to reach the objectives described in the first step of this cycle. Within an organization, an action plan may involve various departments and areas.

For each plan, three items should be defined, i.e., defining who will be responsible for carrying it out, the duration, and how the plan will be executed.

The action plan is derived from the analysis performed in the Analysis and Report Generation step, and consists of a practical way to reach the strategic objectives previously established in the first step of the method.

Professionals conducting the Web Analytics process and those designated to carry out the action plan must participate in this step, preferably in an in-person meeting.

The activities in this step consist of the execution of the action plans and vary according to the defined KPI and should be described and monitored through the artifact presented in TABLE VI. Each action plan details must be registered.

TABLE VI. ACTION PLANS

Art. 06 – Action Plans				
[Company's name]				
[Website]				
[Focal Points of the Company (Name, e-mail and telephone)]				
[Duration of this step]				
[Focal Points involved in this step (Name, e-mail and telephone)]				
Date and Meeting place				
[KPI DESCRIPTION]	[REPORT OF THE KPI]	[ACTION PLAN DEFINED]	DURATION OF ACTION PLAN - and its deadline	RESPONSIBLE TO EXECUTE ACTION PLAN (Name, telephone and e-mail)

It is important to highlight that in this step the cyclic flow of the method started. If one of the action plans executed does not present the expected result during a new data analysis, the continuous cycle is repeated with the aim of continuous improvement, until the KPI is achieved.

After the KPIs have been observed and reached, the complete cycle repeats itself. For this, it has a method where it will be possible to constantly collect, measure, analyze and implement improvements that are reflected in a better quality of the information made available to Website users.

V. CONCLUSION AND FUTURE WORK

This paper presented WACIC Method that has as a goal to standardize the use of Web Analytics and to integrated artifacts that guide and document decisions.

The validation of WACIC is being applied (still in progress) using two case studies from distinct Web environments, i.e., a corporate and an academic ones. The validation takes a long time because it needs to collect data for a significant period, analyze and understand the problems to define the action plan. Then, it is necessary to implement the plan and collect data again and compare the improvement towards the KPIs that were defined.

Based on previous works, there are companies that still have difficulties to create or follow a process that helps them to deal with Web data. Many of companies are still starting to use Web Analytics tools, and during this transition it is common to emerge doubts regarding how to use Web Analytics tool, what exactly should be measured or how should the process be executed in order to extract the maximum strength from Web Analytics tools.

One of the alleged reasons for the failure and/or lack of continuity of the investment in Web Analytics is related to the difficulty in structuring an adequate process or method. What is often seen are organizations that end up mixing concepts and guidance from various sources when applying Web Analytics, facing even more doubts and difficulties when they try to extract useful information.

This paper can help these companies to adopt the WACIC process and its artifacts, documenting decisions and achieving their goals more assertively through the Web Analytics.

Future work will present the challenges faced and the complete results of the method applicability and conclusions about its efficacy. Also will the action plans implemented and its impact to the products/services offered by the Websites analyzed will be described. It is expected to provide a map between the identified problems and solutions that efficiently improved the focused Web sites.

REFERENCES

[1] G. Blokdijk "Web Analytics - simple steps to win, insights and opportunities for maxing out success.", Complete Publishing, pp.186, 2015.

[2] Internet World Stats. Available at: http://www.internetworldstats.com/top20.htm . Last access in August, 2016.

[3] P. Russom "Big Data Analytics". TDWI best practices Report. TWI Research, 2011.

[4] G.J. Dehkordi, S. Rezvani, M. Salehi, S. Eghtebasi and A. Hasanabadi, "A conceptual analysis of the key success of business in terms of internet marketing". Interdisciplinary Journal of Contemporary Research in Business, 4 (1), pp. 811-816, 2012.

[5] A. Kaushik, "Web Analytics 2.0: the art of online accountability and science of customer centricity.", John Wiley & Sons, New York, 2009.

[6] E. Siegel and T. H. Davenport, "Predictive analytics: the power to predict who will click, buy, lie, or die." Willey, 2013.

[7] C. Onwubiko, "Exploring Web analytics to enhance cyber situational awareness for the protection of online Web services," 2016 International Conference On Cyber Security And Protection Of Digital Services (Cyber Security), London, 2016, pp. 1-8.

[8] A. Bengel, A. Shawki and D. Aggarwal, "Simplifying Web analytics for digital marketing," Big Data (Big Data), 2015 IEEE International Conference, Santa Clara CA, 2015.

[9] C. Li and G. Baciu, "VALID: A Web Framework for Visual Analytics of Large Streaming Data," 2014 IEEE 13th International Conference on Trust, Security and Privacy in Computing and Communications, Beijing, 2014.

[10] J. M. Cassidy, "What Is Web Analytics And How To Get Started: An Introduction To The Web Analytics Process." Paperback. CreateSpace Independent Publishing Platform, 2012.

[11] J. Philips, "Building a Digital Analytics Organization: Create Value by Integrating Analytical Processes, Technology, and People into Business Operations". FT Press Analytics Series, 1st edition, August 2013.

[12] C. Ryan and C. Jones "Understanding digital marketing: marketing strategies for engaging the digital generation", Kogan Page Limited, 2nd Edition, 2012.

[13] P. Kotler, H. Kartajaya and I. Setiawan "Marketing 3.0: from products to customers to the human spirit.", Wiley, 1st Edition, 2010.

[14] K. Jerath, L. Ma and Y. Park "Consumer click behavior at a search engine: the role of keyword popularity." Journal of Marketing Research,, 51 (4), pp. 480-486, 2012.

[15] E. Rosenzweig "Successful user experience: strategies and roadmaps", Chapter 11, Morgan Kaufmann, pp. 221-244, 2015.

[16] J. Järvinen and H. Karjaluoto "The use of Web Analytics for digital marketing performance measurement", Industrial Marketing Management, Vol. 50, pp. 117-127, 2015.

[17] J. Ning, Z. Chen and G. Liu, "PDCA process application in the continuous improvement of software quality," Proc. International Conference on Computer, Mechatronics, Control and Electronic Engineering, Changchun, 2010, pp. 61-65, doi: 10.1109/CMCE.2010.5609635.

[18] K. Shibata, H. Nakayama, T. Hayashi and S. Ata, "Establishing PDCA cycles for agile network management in SDN/NFV infrastructure, Ottawa, ON, 2015, pp. 619-625, doi: 10.1109/INM.2015.7140346.

Learning Analytics: Supporting Teaching and Learning through Learner's Data Analytics and Visualization

Ali Shiri
School of Library and Information Studies,
University of Alberta, Edmonton, Alberta, Canada
e-mail: ashiri@ualberta.ca

Abstract— **This paper reports on the design and development of a new learning analytics application for the Moodle learning management system. The uniqueness of this application lies in its ability to provide transparent access to learner's data interaction for both instructors and students. This application allows instructors to monitor their students' online learning activities, interaction and performance and facilitates the provision of personalized and enhanced advice to students. It also provides students with new visual and analytical tools and opportunities to regularly manage their learning activities and interactions in order to be able to compare their performance with their peers in an ongoing and real time manner. This paper addresses the target analytics conference theme.**

Keywords-Learning analytics; learner's big data; visualization; data analytics; learning management systems.

I. INTRODUCTION

The widespread development of online teaching and learning and the introduction of numerous online courses and programs have presented new challenges and opportunities for the institutes of higher learning to develop and apply new ways and tools for monitoring and evaluating online teaching and learning. Terms such as educational data mining, academic analytics and more commonly adopted term 'learning analytics' have been used in the literature to refer to the methods, tools and techniques for gathering very large online data about learners and their activities and contexts. The first International Conference on Learning Analytics and Knowledge (LAK 2011) [1] defines learning analytics as "the measurement, collection, analysis and reporting of data about learners and their contexts, for purposes of understanding and optimizing learning and the environments in which it occurs". Clow [2] provides a learning analytics life cycle to conceptualize successful learning analytics work, including four key components, namely learners, data, metrics, interventions. Learner means a student who may take an online course or courses that make use of a learning management system. The second step in the cycle is the generation and capture of data about or by the learners, including login and clickstream data. The metrics stage refers to the processing of data using various metrics, examples of which may include visualization, dashboards, list of at-risk students, comparison with previous cohorts, etc. The final stage of the cycle refers to, for instance, dashboards for learners in order for them to be able to compare their activities with their peers or previous cohorts, etc.

The advantages of learning analytics have been enumerated by Siemens et al. [3] and Siemens and Long [4], some of the important ones include:

- Early detection of at-risk students and generating alerts for learners and educators
- Personalize and adapt learning process and content
- Extend and enhance learner achievement, motivation, and confidence by providing learners with timely information about their performance and that of their peers
- Higher quality learning design and improved curriculum development
- Interactive visualizations of complex information will give learners and educators the ability to "zoom in" or "zoom out" on data sets,
- More rapid achievement of learning goals by giving learners access to tools that help them to evaluate their progress

A recent report on the state of learning analytics concludes that there is widespread interest, both within the academic community and beyond, in learning analytics and the possibilities they offer for tailoring educational opportunities to each learner's level of need and ability [5].

II. CONETXT AND PRIOR RESEARCH

There have been a number of learning analytics tools developed for various learning management systems, such as Moodle, Desire2Learn, Canvas and Blackboard. There are two general categories of learning analytics tools. The first category is exclusively designed to be used by instructors and course designers with features and functionalities for analyzing and visualizing data related to student activities. The second category provides additional features and functionalities for students, as well as instructors with access to learners' interaction and activity data. A significant number of these learning analytics tools are open source applications, some of which are still being developed and others have not been kept up to date. In the following, a review of ongoing and useful projects is presented.

SNAPP (Social Networks Adapting Pedagogical Practice) is a browser plugin that has limited functionality and creates social network diagrams that can be used to identify isolated students, network patterns and interaction occurring between student participants. This tool allows instructors to evaluate student behavioral patterns against learning activity, design objectives and intervene as required a timely manner [6]. It can be used within Moodle, Blackboard, and Desire2Learn.

The Moodle Analytics and Recommendations block is a small scale project that uses colour coded charts and tables to allow students to quickly view their participation. Teachers are able to view single, comparative analytics and global analytics. This block is not currently maintained up to date or supported [7].

LOCO-Analyst is an open source educational tool that provides teachers with feedback regarding student activities and usage. The application does not provide any features and functionalities for students to compare their learning data with their peers. This application is still being developed [8].

GISMO (Graphical Interactive Student Monitoring Tool for Moodle) is a graphical interactive monitoring tool that provides useful visualization of students' activities in online courses to instructors. Using GISMO instructors can examine students' attendance, reading of materials, and submission of assignments. While GISMO is designed to work with Moodle, the version available is not compatible with University of Alberta eClass platform. Another major limitation of the application is that GISMO focuses mainly on instructors and there is very limited functionality for students to be able to use the system and interact with their own data [9].

The Academic Analytic Tool (AAT) is an open source ongoing project at the Athabasca University, which allows instructors to access and analyze student behaviour data in learning systems. It enables them to extract detailed information about how students interact with and learn from online courses, to analyze the extracted data, and to store the results in a database and/or CSV/HTML files. While AAT is compatible with Moodle, it has primarily been developed for learning designers [10].

In addition to the above applications, there are other learning analytic tools developed for Blackboard, Desire2Learn and Canvas. The main point is that learning analytics are becoming an integral and expected component of learning management systems. In this paper we report on the design and development of a learning analytics application for eClass, a learning management system that is based on Moodle and is currently used by the University of Alberta in Canada and many universities around the world. This new application provides learning analytics functionalities for both students and instructors and given that it is created for an open source learning management system, it can be adopted by other universities and colleges that use Moodle as their learning management system.

Course and learning management systems such as Moodle hold very large data sets related to student interactions and activities. However, student tracking capabilities in these systems are usually limited and as a result the depth of extraction and aggregation, reporting and visualization functionality of these built-in analytics has often been basic or non-existent [11]. While Moodle has reporting functions for students and instructors, these functionalities are not easy to use. For instance, Moodle data can be downloaded as an Excel file, but it still requires analysis in order to be useful for students and instructors. The University of Alberta eClass environment does not currently have learning analytics tools to provide support for analyzing, visualizing and making sense of very large student and instructor activities datasets. The eClass reporting features and logs provide only limited and basic level data, such as time, IP address, course view, forum view, resource view, and actions such as 'add', 'delete', 'view' for forum or blog posts. These data points are presented separately from one another, with no analytical, comparative or visual functionality to allow for a real time understanding of the individual and class performance. Therefore, instructors are not able to use these data points in a multidimensional way to make detailed and comparative inferences about student activities and interactions within one particular course activity or across the entire course content. For instance, it is not possible for an instructor to a) comparatively and visually identify the most frequently used resources within a course, b) detect the kinds of resources used by high performing students in class, or c) identify the nature of course materials not used by low and average performing students. The overarching goal of the analytical tool reported here is to facilitate access to and making sense of learning data for students and instructors.

III. METHODOLOGY

This project will draw upon [2] learning analytics life cycle to design an application that will support the four stages of the learning analytics life cycle, namely learner, data, metrics and interventions. The learning analytics tool that will be designed in this project will support both instructors and students and will be compatible with the eClass environment. Moodle databases collect large multidimensional data files from student activities, clickthrough data, access to various digital objects, history of pages viewed, number of hits for each day of the course. However, this data is available in a tabular format and it is very difficult to understand the structure and organization of data or to be able to make sense of various types of data collected. The learning analytics tool that is developed in this project will provide the following key components:

- Data repository: Data collection and amalgamation
- Data transformation mechanism to organize and cluster raw data
- Data processing to support large data analysis

- Data and information visualization functionalities to visualize and demonstrate individual and comparative views of the following data points:
    - Logins
    - Submissions
    - Interaction with learning objects (resources accessed and frequency)
        - Frequently used content and media
    - Interaction with discussion forums, lessons, quizzes etc.
    - Student interaction and social networks
    - Blog and discussion forum analysis and visualization
    - Time spent (on individual pages, on average, across the course, etc.)
    - Detection of low, average and high performing students

The application makes use of a broad range of technologies, including PHP (Hypertext Preprocessor) and MySQL (Structured Query Language), information visualization technologies, and text and data analysis tools.

IV. LEARNING ANALYTICS TOOL FUNCTIONALITIES

The following graphs will depict a number of screenshots of our newly developed learning analytics application. The screenshots provide visual representation of learner's data analyzed using our application.

A. *Visual dashboard for engagement data*

Our application provides a number of features to analyze and visualize content engagement, forum engagement, forum usage over time and events by user over time. Fig. 1 shows an example of a graph that depicts students' engagement data across a number of activities, such as visiting various course webpages, interacting with forums, files or blocks.

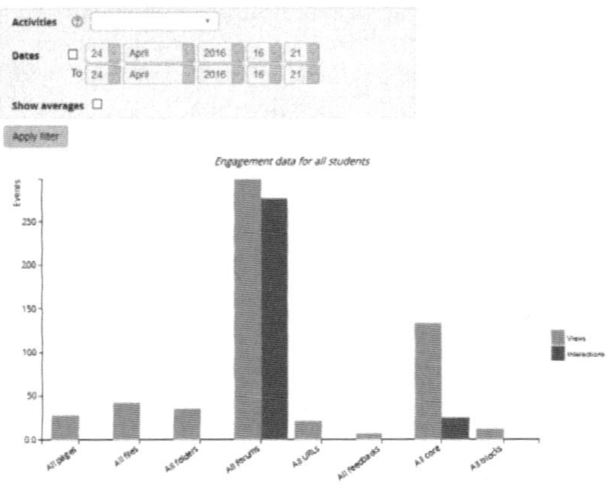

Figure 1. Visual dashboard for engagement data

Through this graph students are able to visually identify how students within a class have viewed and interacted with different parts and components of a course. It also allows individual students to choose a particular time range to view their own enganement and activities for the time period.

Fig. 2 provides a longitudinal view of engagment data for students. This functionality allows for a holistic view of all activities over a certain period of time. They can also choose a particular activity, such as contributing to a forum or blog and view how they have been using or interacting with the forum over time. This feature allows them to keep track of their own use of various learning objects over the period of a semester.

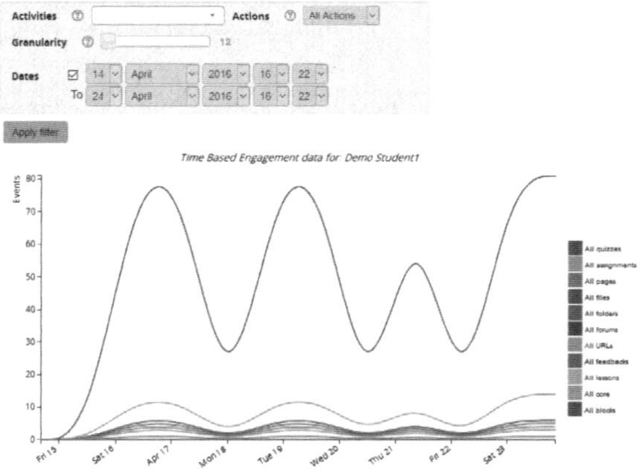

Figure 2. Time-based engagment data

The granularity function shown in Fig. 3 allows students to narrow down the timeline to days and hours. This function will be useful for identifying how active students are before or after a particular quiz.

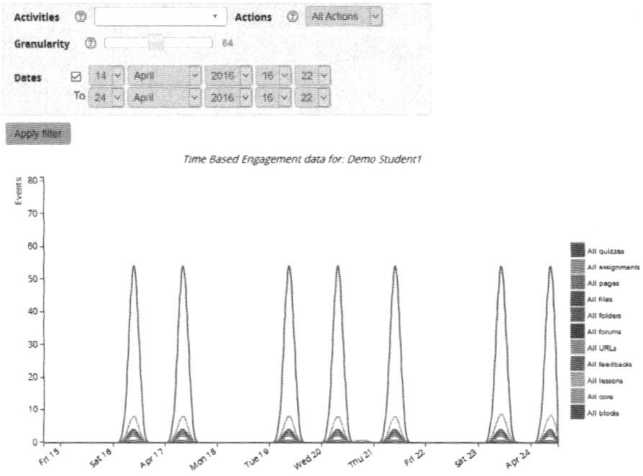

Figure 3. Time-based granularity for learning objects

B. Visual dashboard for weekly discussion and selected students

In order to allow students to gain a collective perspective of performance within a class, engagement data for all students are shown in Fig. 4. This graph is useful for instructors and students to quickly and visually see how students contribute to a discussion forum across several weeks.

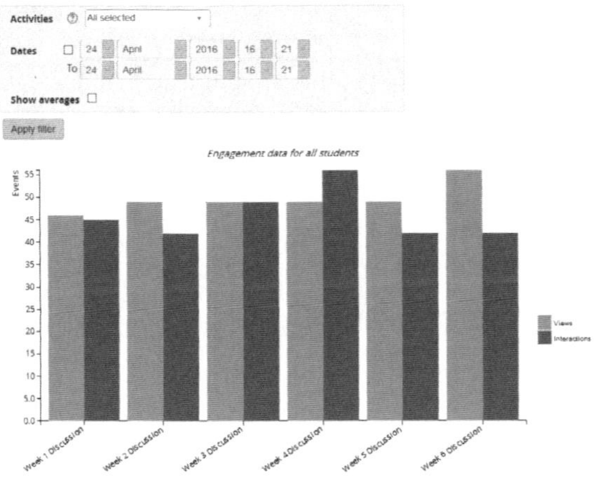

Figure 4. Weekly discussion engagement data for all students

Fig. 5 allows a student to gain a comparative perspective of how other students on average interacted with course content and where she stands.

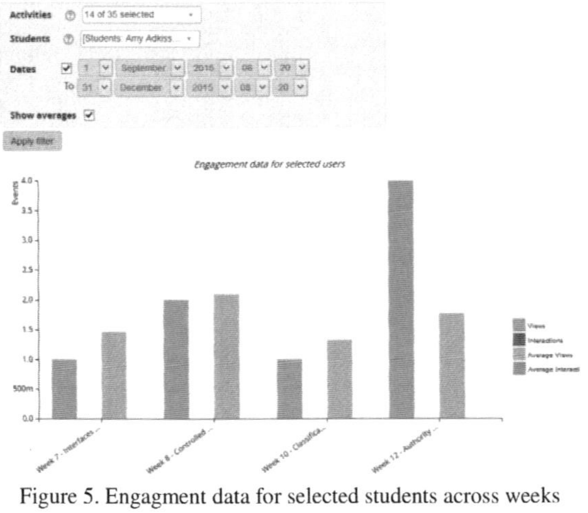

Figure 5. Engagment data for selected students across weeks

This will allow a student to see the level of engagement on the part of her fellow students.

V. Conclusion

The learning analytics tool that was reported in this paper provides a useful tool for universities and colleges that make use of the Moodle learning management system. This application supports instructors and students in monitoring learning and teaching activities and provides ways in which instructors can offer personalized and enhanced advice to students. The tool has the potential to be expanded to include department-level and campus-wide evaluation of learning and teaching to facilitate prediction, adaptation, personalization and intervention in the learning process.

For instance, at the department level, first year undergraduate courses with large enrollment can benefit from student engagement data analysis and visualization to allow the department to assess the usefulness of various learning objects and resources for a particular course. Further development of this application will focus on text analysis and visualization tools that will support instructors to create quick visual representations of large discussion forum data. We are currently conducting usability evaluation with students and instructors from a wide variety of disciplines to assess the ease of use, learnability and usability of our learning analytics tool. An initial analysis of the usability study data indicates a number of areas for further refinement of the tool, including the terminology used on the interface (e.g. views vs. interactions), analytical tools for the textual data on discussion forums, and ways to triangulate data with grades. Once the tool is finalized it will be shared openly with those using the Moodle system.

Acknowledgment

I would like to acknowledge the Teaching and Learning Enhancement Fund (TLEF) that was provided by the University of Alberta Centre for Teaching and Learning.

References

[1] 1st International Conference on Learning Analytics and Knowledge (LAK 11). https://tekri.athabascau.ca/analytics/about (retrieved June 2016)

[2] D. Clow, "The learning analytics cycle: closing the loop effectively." In *Proceedings of the 2nd International Conference on Learning Analytics and Knowledge* (pp. 134-138). ACM, April 2012.

[3] G. Siemens, D. Gasevic, C. Haythornthwaite, S. Dawson, S. B. Shum, R. Ferguson, K. E. Duval, and R. S. J. D. Baker, (2011). "Open Learning Analytics: an integrated & modularized platform." *Proposal to design, implement and evaluate an open platform to integrate heterogeneous learning analytics techniques.* http://www.elearnspace.org/blog/wp-content/uploads/2016/02/ProposalLearningAnalyticsModel_SoLAR.pdf (retrieved June 2016)

[4] G. Siemens and P. Long, "Penetrating the fog: Analytics in learning and education." *Educause Review*, *46*(5), pp. 30-32, 2011.

[5] R. Ferguson, "Learning analytics: drivers, developments and challenges." *International Journal of Technology Enhanced Learning*, 4(5/6) pp. 304–317, 2012.

[6] S. Dawson, A. Bakharia, and E. Heathcote, "SNAPP: Realising the affordances of real-time SNA within networked learning environments." In *Proceedings of the 7th International Conference on Networked Learning*, pp. 125-133, 2010.

[7] Moodle Blocks: Analytics and Recommendations: https://moodle.org/plugins/view.php?plugin=block_analytics_recommendations (retrieved June 2016)

[8] J. Jovanovic, D. Gaševic, C. Brooks, V. Devedžic, M. Hatala, T. Eap, and G. Richards, "LOCO-Analyst: semantic web technologies in learning content usage analysis". International Journal of Continuing Engineering Education and Life Long Learning 18, 1, pp. 54-76, 2008.

[9] GISMO: http://gismo.sourceforge.net/index.html (retrieved June 2016)

[10] S. Graf, C. Ives, N. Rahman, and A. Ferri, "AAT: a tool for accessing and analysing students' behaviour data in learning systems." In *Proceedings of the 1st International Conference on Learning Analytics and Knowledge* (pp. 174-179). ACM, February 2011.

[11] S. Dawson, " 'Seeing' the learning community: An exploration of the development of a resource for monitoring online student networking." *British Journal of Educational Technology*, *41*(5), 736-752, 2011.

Tourism Websites Network: Crawling the Italian Webspace

Alessandro Longheu, Giuseppe Mangioni, Marialaura Previti
Dipartimento di Ingegneria Elettrica, Elettronica ed Informatica (DIEEI)
University of Catania
Catania, Italy
e-mail: alessandro.longheu@dieei.unict.it, giuseppe.mangioni@dieei.unict.it, ml.previti@gmail.com

Abstract— **The relevance of tourism is increasing more and more in the globalized economy. To improve management of tourism activities, the analysis of tourism related data deserves a major attention. In this work, we investigate on the Italian tourism website network, exploiting crawling and classifying techniques in order to extract and analyze such network, with the final goal of providing useful information for tourism management stakeholders.**

Keywords— ***web pages categorization; text classification; Support Vector Machine (SVM); complex networks; tourism management.***

I. Introduction

Tourism is one of the main entries in globalized economy, and is becoming more and more a challenging issue in many research areas even apparently unrelated, as sustainable (tourism) development [1], health-care and well-being [2], as well as many others [3].

Even if the pervasive adoption of mobile devices and related apps for tourism resource discovery and management represent a cutting-edge topic [4], the huge amount of web sites currently available still represents the main data source for tourism information [5].

In this paper, we aim at focusing on the Italian website tourism network in order to analyze such network and its properties. Our final goal is to exploit this information to improve the comprehension about tourism phenomenon, for which a number of models have been proposed in the past with limited success in providing satisfactory insights [6].

Actually, each term of "Italian website tourism network" should be further specified according to topics we want to highlight:

- by "Italian" we mean any website containing information written in Italian language, since we believe that information in other languages may either represent a simple duplicate of the former, or they are not intended for the Italian webspace;

- by "website" we mean the site seen as the atomic unit of information, i.e., we gather (text) information from all pages belonging to the same site, of course, we limit the data amount stopping the of collecting web pages from the same site according a given depth;

- by "tourism" we mean that each site contains tourism related information, we perform the classification using a SVM based text classifier that has been develop using the KNIME software.

- finally, by "network" we mean that we aim at gathering hyperlinked Italian tourism websites. In particular, the crawling process used to build such a network starts from an initial seed made by official, institutional regional tourism websites, further considering all hyperlink contained within each visited page. The process is properly managed to avoid downloading huge amount of data, as explained below.

After the (large) crawling operation cited so far, we started to analyze such data. In this work, we consider in particular one of the first crawled Italian region ("Abruzzo") and we illustrate the related network and its analysis. These preliminary results are promising in terms of their relevance in providing significant information about how many Italian tourism websites are present, how they are connected and finally how such information can be exploited to improve tourism management.

The rest of paper is organized as follows: in Section II, an overview of related work about website classification is introduced, then in Section III we describe our work in more detail. In Section IV first results are presented, finally providing in Section V our conclusions and further works.

II. Web Content Classification

Web page classification is the process of assigning a web page to one or more categories. In recent years, several methodologies for the automatic classification of web pages have been introduced. The most common approach is based on web pages information content categorization: images analysis, text classification, metadata extraction, document structure analysis, etc.

To achieve this goal, F. Sebastiani [7] mainly focused on traditional textual classification based on supervised machine learning techniques, C. Lindermann [8] identified and analyzed structural properties, which reflect the functionality of a Web site to divide them into five most relevant functional classes, Z. Xu [9] proposed a statistical web page classification approach, which incorporates heterogeneous data sources extracted from web pages like title, metadata, anchor texts, URLs, links and formulates them into a common format of kernel matrix, P. Calado [10] used link information in combination with content information to improve classification results for web collections, A. Sun [11] proposed the use of Support Vector

Machine classifiers to classify web pages using both their text and context feature sets.

Although no new techniques are presented in this paper, we used a combination of the aforementioned to analyze the Italian tourist webspace.

Although there are various classifiers that allow to review the English-language texts, until today, no one has modified a classifier for the purpose of classifying large-scale texts in Italian language, so we have had to face this challenge to perform this work.

III. CRAFTING ITALIAN TOURISM WEBSITE NETWORK

A. *Overview*

As introduced in Section I, the work here proposed begins from considering a set of Italian official tourism websites (actually not shown here) that were manually classified.

We used these sites as a seed to start crawling, in particular we considered for each site its home page together with related first level pages (i.e., those directly linked by the home page), extracting all hyperlinks to proceed with crawling process, and retaining the whole text of such pages to further classify the site.

Each website will be a node in the network, and the crawling continues until a specified number of hops is reached, hence the overall network is built. This network may include site with non-italian language text, and/or unrelated to the tourism topic, therefore this is simply the network of (hyper)linked sites reachable from the seed.

In order to extract the subnetwork of Italian tourism websites, we first discard all sites whose language is not Italian, then we perform a classification to establish whether a site is about tourism or not, using the seed as a training set. All nodes that "survive" these filtering phases will compose the Italian tourism (sub)network.

Finally, to cope with crawling time and with the huge amount of data to analyze, we split the whole process over the 20 italian geographical regions. In the following, each step of our proposal is described in more detail.

B. *Filtering Crawled data*

After having crawled data, the next step was the filtering of web pages to get only the Italian ones, in fact an initial data analysis showed that most of tourist web pages are part of multilingual sites and are linked to foreign countries pages.

Foreign words can adversely affect the text classification because they can't be prefiltered with preprocessing instruments that use the Italian vocabulary (e.g., stemmers, word filter stop), therefore they are placed in the bag-of-word as they are.

Therefore we developed a whitelist filter used to discard web pages with a top-level domain different from .it, .com, .org, .net, .tv, .info, .eu, .ch, .at and .fr, then we filtered the selected pages using the java library language-detection [12] to further discard the pages with Italian domain, but written in a foreign language. Note that in the whitelist we included top level domain of countries bordering Italy since this geographic proximity sometimes implies that sites are bi-lingual, e.g. a .fr website is likely to include Italian text.

Today many websites are created using scripts, therefore extracting text useful for the classification is difficult and, in some cases, is also insufficient, then we need to preliminarily extract additional textual useful information to be added to the text from the body of the page. In order to do this, our filter not only performs the removal of tags and scripts, but preliminarily examines tags containing the metadata (HTML and OG [13]) of title, description and keyword and, after text cleaning, adds this information on top of the extracted text.

C. *Classification tool*

After a practical comparison of six most used free software tools for general data mining today available and thanks the Jovic [14] description of algorithms and procedures supported by these tools, we decide to use KNIME [15], an open-source general-purpose data mining tool based on dataflow architecture. This tool offers several configurable building blocks in the core installations and various extensions, including "text processing" and "mining" plugins that we have used to achieve our purpose.

D. *Training set*

Among the classification techniques analyzed [16][17], we decided to use Support Vector Machine (SVM) with Sequential Minimal Optimization (SMO) [18], a simple algorithm that quickly solves the SVM quadratic programming problem without any extra matrix storage and without invoking an iterative numerical routine for each sub-problem, significantly reducing training time.

The first step to use SVM is the creation of a data set, so, starting from a list of tourist web page URLs manually created searching on internet for hotels, travel agencies, tourist destinations, etc., with our filter we automatically extract text and save it in textual.

After this we have assessed the results and have discarded texts with insufficient size or content. The remaining texts became part of the tourist texts folder.

Similar work has been done to create non-tourist texts folder.

To evaluate the quality of the work performed, we created a KNIME program to do cross-validation (Fig. 1), i.e., to partition data into two segments: one used to train the model and the other used to validate it. In typical cross-validation, the training and validation sets must cross-over in successive rounds such that each data point has a chance of being validated against. We therefore repeated ten times the classification and produced an error rate table shown in Fig. 2, where during each cycle 9 folds are used as training set and the remaining one is the test set.

The results show that the average of classification accuracy is 89,75%.

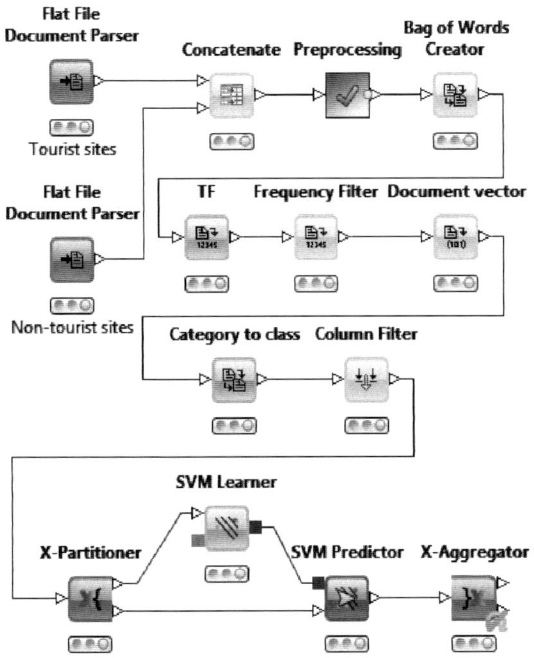

Figure 1. KNIME program used to validate training set.

Row ID	D Error in %
fold 0	5
fold 1	15
fold 2	10
fold 3	2.5
fold 4	10
fold 5	7.5
fold 6	10
fold 7	15
fold 8	15
fold 9	12.5

Figure 2. Error rate table.

E. Preprocessing

Any text written in any language contains a large number of elements common to all documents written in the same language, so these elements do not add any information content neither facilitate the document classification, rather they only increase computation time.

In the preprocessing phase, terms are manipulated in order to cut out elements that don't contain content, such as stop words, numbers, punctuation marks or to remove endings based on declination or conjugation by applying stemming.

While Puntuaction Erasure and Number Filter are the same for all languages, the other preprocessing block depend on the language to analyze, so we provided to Stop Word Filter a list of common terms in Italian language and used Snowball Stemmer, which allows the stemming of text in various languages (Fig. 3).

All terms survived to preprocessing are collected in a bag-of-word, which keeps the reference to the document belongs to, through this, the frequency with which a term appears in a document can be calculated and the terms less frequent can be removed. We set frequency filter threshold to 0,3%.

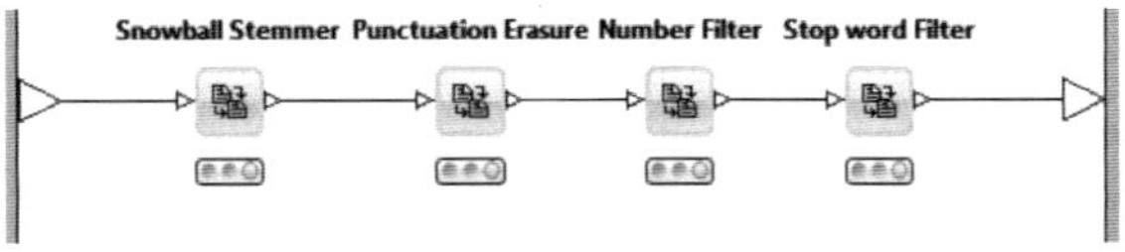

Figure 3. Content of preprocessing metanode.

F. Classification

The classification consists of two phases: learning and prediction (Fig. 4).

The first phase is carried out by the SVM learner, i.e., a block that trains the SVM on the input data using a polynomial kernel:

$$K(x, y) = (gamma * x^T y + bias)^{power}$$

where:

- x and y are vectors in the input space;
- *power* is the degree of the polynomial;
- *bias* and *gamma* are hyperplane coefficients.

Power was the only parameter we set to 1 in order to have a linear SVM.

We have provided to SVM learner the dataset previously validated to get the best hyperplane for the separation of the two sets of classification: tourist text and non-tourist text.

In the second phase, the SVM predictor takes as input the model proposed by SVM learner and an unclassified dataset equal to 1/3 of the total number of text.

To prevent unclassified data were more than classified ones, each folder containing text supplied from sites of a given region has been divided into sub-folders in order to keep the aforementioned proportion and the classification procedure has been iterated several times till all the data has been classified.

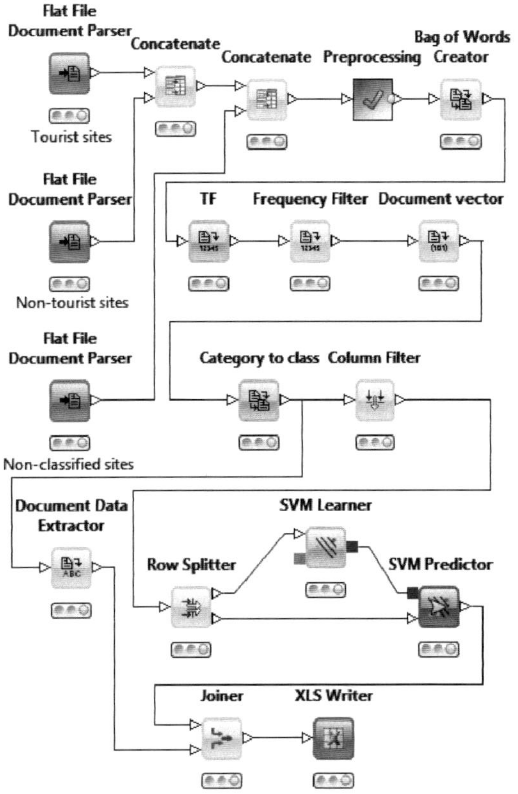

Figure 4. KNIME program used to classificate tourist and not tourist text.

IV. Preliminary Results

Abruzzo has been the first analyzed region. The crawler, starting to seeds of certainly tourist sites, crawled 14.482 sites on a total of 2.377.378 pages. Using aforementioned classificator, we discover that only 4.200 sites were in Italian language and among these, only 2169 were classified as touristic.

Each of these sites was considered as a network node. In Fig. 5, we show the Abruzzo network after deleting non-Italian nodes. In Fig. 6, we show the Abruzzo (sub)network with tourism websites only.

To better characterize the subnetwork, we assess its in-degree (Fig. 7) and out-degree (Fig. 8) distributions in two graphs with logarithmic scale. Both graphs exhibit a trend that can be approximated to a power laws distribution, although further studies are needed to determine the exact degree and parameters.

Analyzing the network with standard bow-tie model (Fig. 9), the strongly connected core consists of 7 nodes only, whereas input nodes are only 3 and 85 are output nodes. Tendrils, i.e., pages that link to and from the In and Out group but are not part of either, are 1194. The disconnected component includes 880 nodes. Bow-tie graph shows that the network core, i.e., the strongly connected part, is really small and there are many disconnected nodes. Furthermore, the large number of tendrils highlights that most of the nodes prefer to be pointed, but rarely link other tourist sites.

The reason is probably that a low level of cooperation among tourism operators is present, and this negatively affects the development of Italian tourism.

TABLE I. ABRUZZO CRAWLING RESULTS

Italian regional tourism authorities	#of sites crawled	# of pages crawled	#nodes	#of website in Italian language (#of nodes)	#of website classified as touristic (#of nodes)	#of connected components	#of nodes of the largest connected component
Abruzzo	14482	2377378	14482	4200	2169	873	1289

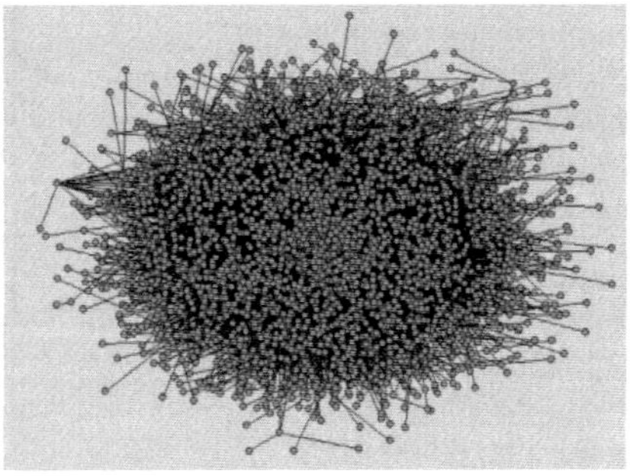

Figure 5. Italian nodes of Abruzzo network

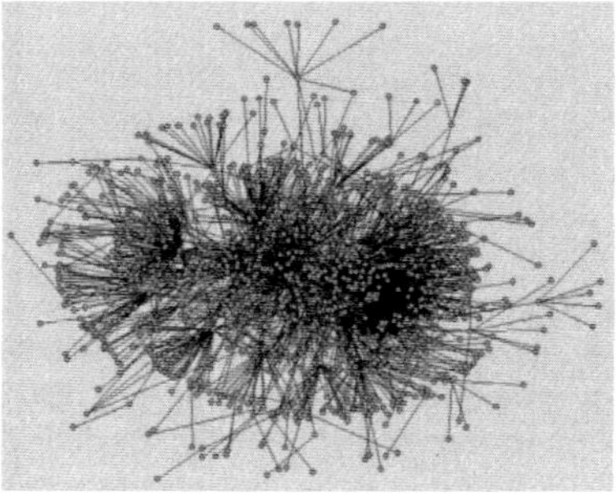

Figure 6. Tourism Italian nodes of Abruzzo network

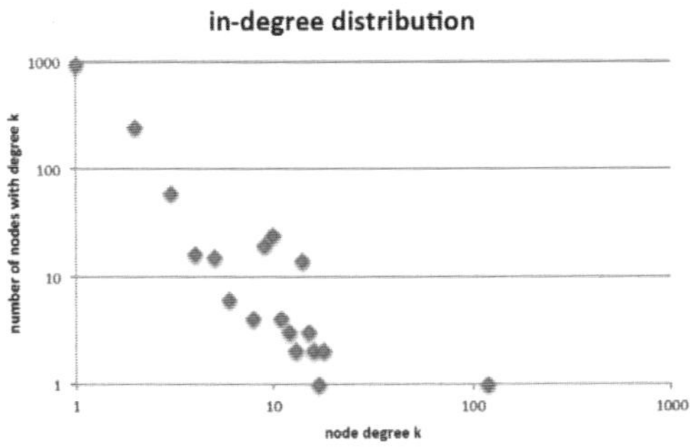

Figure 7. In-degree distribution of tourism nodes.

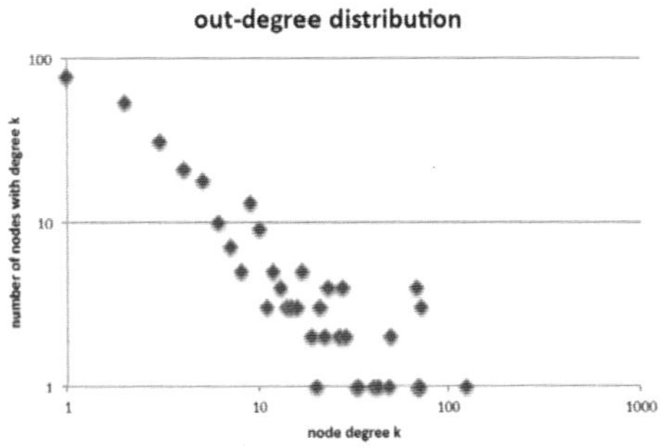

Figure 8. Out-degree distribution of tourism nodes.

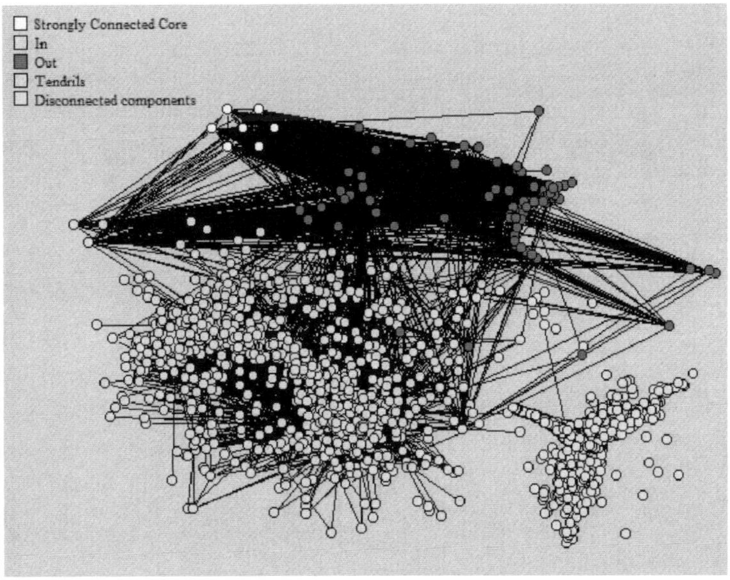

Figure 9. Bow-tie model of Abruzzo network.

V. CONCLUSIONS AND FUTURE WORKS

In this paper, the Italian tourism websites network has been extracted from a large set of crawled sites. Using a proper seed of tourism websites and an SVM-based classifier, we crafted the tourism network, then we focused on one of the 20 italian regional networks, analyzing and briefly discussing its feature. In particular, a really low level of cooperation seems to characterize the network, and this is probably due to an extreme competition among tourist operators that negatively affects the management of tourism itself.

Although at a first stage, this work seems promising in terms of its dimension (a large website data set has been considered), becoming a significant base for further analysis. In particular we are going to craft all other regional Italian networks, in order to get a global view of the overall Italian tourism website network (actually, part of this work has been already carried out [19]). Finally, we are also planning to compare our approach with other classification models.

We believe that the further analysis of such global network will provide tourism stakeholders with significant and detailed data to improve tourism management, also by leveraging results coming from other research areas, for instance trust and ranking [20][21], to score and exploit "relevant" tourism sites, or recommendation systems [22], to discover and endorse "useful" tourism sites.

REFERENCES

[1] J. Zhang, "Weighing and realizing the environmental, economic and social goals of tourism development using an analytic network process-goal programming approach." *Journal of Cleaner Production* 127: pp. 262-273, 2016.

[2] S. Pyke, H. Hartwell, A. Blake, A.Hemingway, "Exploring well-being as a tourism product resource."*Tourism Management* 55: pp. 94-105, 2016.

[3] L. Y. Y. Lu and J S. Liu, "A novel approach to identify research fronts of tourism literature." *Management of Engineering and Technology (PICMET), Portland International Conference on*. IEEE, pp. 2211-2217, 2015.

[4] A. Groth and D. Haslwanter, "Efficiency, effectiveness, and satisfaction of responsive mobile tourism websites: a mobile usability study."*Information Technology & Tourism*: pp. 1-28, 2016.

[5] I. Christensen, S. Schiaffino, and M. Armentano, "Social group recommendation in the tourism domain." *Journal of Intelligent Information Systems*: pp. 1-23, 2016.

[6] B. H. Farrell and L. Twining-Ward, "Reconceptualizing tourism."*Annals of tourism research* 31.2: pp. 274-295, 2004.

[7] F. Sebastiani, "Machine learning in automated text categorization." *ACM computing surveys (CSUR)* 34.1: pp. 1-47, 2002

[8] C. Lindemann and L. Lars, "Coarse-grained classification of web sites by their structural properties." *Proceedings of the 8th annual ACM international workshop on Web information and data management.* ACM, pp. 35-42, 2006.

[9] Z. Xu, I. King, and M. R. Lyu, "Web page classification with heterogeneous data fusion." *Proceedings of the 16th international conference on World Wide Web.* ACM, pp. 1171-1172, 2007.

[10] P. Calado, M. Cristo, E. Moura, N. Ziviani, B. Riberto-Neto, and M. A. Goncalves, "Combining link-based and content-based methods for web document classification." *Proceedings of the twelfth international conference on Information and knowledge management.* ACM, pp. 394-401, 2003.

[11] A. Sun, E. Lim, and W. Ng, "Web classification using support vector machine." *Proceedings of the 4th international workshop on Web information and data management.* ACM, pp. 96-99, 2002.

[12] http://developer.cybozu.co.jp/archives/oss/2010/10/language-detect.html [retrieved: July, 2016]

[13] A. Haugen, "The open graph protocol design decisions." *The Semantic Web–ISWC 2010.* Springer Berlin Heidelberg. pp. 338-338, 2010.

[14] A. Jovic, K. Brkic, and N. Bogunovic, "An overview of free software tools for general data mining." *Information and Communication Technology, Electronics and Microelectronics (MIPRO), 37th International Convention on.* IEEE, pp. 1112-1117, 2014.

[15] M. R. Berthold et al., "KNIME: The Konstanz information miner:version 2-0 and beyond" . *AcM SIGKDD explorations Newsletter* 11.1: pp. 26-31, 2009.

[16] T. N. Phyu, "Survey of classification techniques in data mining."*Proceedings of the International MultiConference of Engineers and Computer Scientists.* Vol. 1., pp. 18-20, 2009.

[17] S. B. Kotsiantis, "Supervised machine learning: A review of classification techniques.": pp. 3-24, 2007.

[18] J. C. Platt, "12 fast training of support vector machines using sequential minimal optimization." Advances in kernel methods : pp. 185-208, 1999.

[19] G. Mangioni, A. Longheu, and R. Baggio, "The Italian Tourism Webspace: a Complex Network Analysis". Poster presented at the 5th Workshop on Complex Networks, Bologna, pp. 727-734, 2014.

[20] V. Carchiolo, A. Longheu, M. Malgeri, and G. Mangioni, "Trust assessment: a personalized, distributed, and secure approach" Journal Concurrency and Computation: Practice and Experience (CCPE) Special Issue: Special Issue on intelligent distributed computing, Volume 24, Issue 6, pp. 605–617, 2012

[21] V. Carchiolo, A. Longheu, M. Malgeri, and G. Mangioni, "Network size and topology impact on trust-based ranking", in press on Intl Journal of Bio-inspired Computation (IJBIC), http://www.inderscience.com/info/ingeneral/forthcoming.php?jcode=ijbic [retrieved: July, 2016]

[22] V. Carchiolo, A. Longheu, M. Malgeri, and G. Mangioni, "Context-based global expertise in recommendation systems" International Journal of Computing and informatics – Informatica - ISSN: 1854-3871 - Volume 34, no. 4, pp. 409-418, Slovenia, 2010.

A Study of the OAuth 2.0 Protocol Extended Using SMS for Safe User Access

Chae Cheol-Joo
Dept. of R&D Information Convergence
Korea Institute of Science and Technology Information
Daejeon, Korea
cjchae@kisti.re.kr

Kwang-Nam Choi
Dept. of R&D Information Convergence
Korea Institute of Science and Technology Information
Daejeon, Korea
knchoi@kisti.re.kr

Abstract—**Recently, diverse Web services and applications have been provided to users. Since these services are provided to the authenticated users only, users need to go through the authentication process whenever they use the services. To take care of this kind of inconvenience, the Open Authorization (OAuth) protocol which allows a 3rd party application to have restricted access authority against Web services has emerged. This OAuth protocol provides convenient and flexible services to users, but it has security weaknesses in acquiring authority. Therefore, this study proposes a method to analyze and improve security loopholes, which can occur in the OAuth 2.0 protocol.**

Keywords - OAuth 2.0; User Access; Authentication; Authorization

I. INTRODUCTION

The OAuth is a protocol which authorizes the authority to use the services provided by diverse service providers after going through user authentication just once between the user and 3rd party application. Even though the OAuth provides convenience and scalability, it has several security loopholes in the authentication between the user and 3rd application. Unlike the weakness of the conventional Web application authentication, such problems can cause a serious security problem because once a user successfully passes user authentication once, he/she can get access to multiple services without additional authentication procedures [1][2].

Therefore, this study proposes a 3rd application and user authentication method which can analyze and overcome the security weaknesses of the OAuth protocol. This paper is structured as follows: In Section 2, the OAuth protocol is described. In Section 3, the security weaknesses which can occur in the OAuth protocol are stated. In Section 4, an authentication method which can overcome the security loopholes mentioned in Section 3 is proposed. In Section 5, conclusion is given.

II. USER AUTHENTICATION IN THE OAUTH 2.0

As a general procedure to operate the OAuth 2.0 protocol, the client requests an access token which represents authority to get access to resources to the resource owner. The authorization server issues the authority to get access to the resources after authenticating the client and user information. Then, the client is able to approach user resources. Figure 1 reveals the general operating procedures of the OAuth 2.0 protocol [3][4].

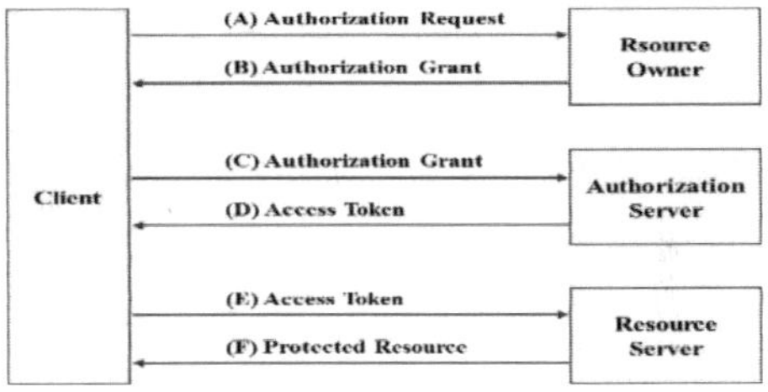

Figure 1. General Operating Procedures of the OAuth 2.0 Protocol.

III. SECURITY VULNERABILITY OF USER AUTHENTICATION IN THE OAUTH 2.0

In the OAuth protocol, if the access token having the authority to get access to resources is stolen, security vulnerability that users are able to approach resources using diverse applications occurs. In terms of a way to steal such access token, there are replay attack, phishing and spoofing which are the common network security problems. In this section the security vulnerability in which authority can be stolen through the said attacks in the OAuth 2.0 protocol [5] is described.

A. Acquisition of authorization code using replay attack

For replay attack, an attacker captures authorization code between the client and resource owner. Then, it can resend a request to the client to login to the resource owner's account associated with authorization code, using the captured authorization code redirection request. Through this kind of replay attack, an attacker is able to acquire the authority to get access to the resource server after getting the information on the resource owner.

B. Acquisition of ID and password using phishing

In order for the client to get the resource owner's information, it should pass the authorization server's authentication. In this process, an attacker is able to steal the resource owner's ID and passwords which are needed for authentication by creating a malicious client. Using the resource owner's ID and password stolen through phishing, an attacker is able to get the authority to login and use the resource server.

C. Acquisition of authorization code using spoofing

To attempt spoofing, the attacker first wiretaps and intercepts the authorization code. Then, it actually blocks the authorization code request to maintain the intercepted authorization code. Then, the attacker starts an initial session with the client. Once the session is begun, it can acquire the authority to get access to the resource service, using the intercepted authorization code.

IV. SAFE USER ACCESS AUTHORIZATION IN THE OAUTH 2.0 PROTOCOL USING THE SMS

In this section, a method to issue an access token which is the authority to get access to the resource server safely after authenticating the resource owner, using SMS (Short Message Service) before the issuance as a way to solve the security problems that can occur in the OAuth 2.0 protocol analyzed in Section 3. Figure 2 reveals the OAuth 2.0 protocol extended through SMS authentication to grant safe user authority.

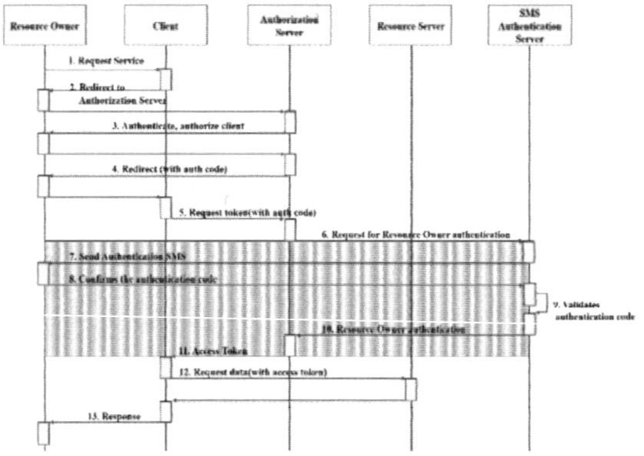

Figure 2. Proposed Method for more Safe User Asscess Grant.

To allow the SMS authentication server to send an email which includes authentication code to the resource owner safely in Step 6, Elgamal algorithm was adopted. The SMS authentication server creates a very large decimal (p) and creates and issues a public key ($y = g^a \bmod p$) which can be compared to a private key ($a \in p^*$) needed for the resource owner in the SMS authentication server.

In Step 7, the resource owner decrypts and authenticates $\{MAS_{SMS\ address}, User_{SMS\ address}, c_1, c_2, MAC_{MAS}, T_{MAS}\}$ received from the SMS authentication server.

Using the proposed method, the user authentication security vulnerability in the OAuth 2.0 analyzed in section 3 can be overcome as follows:

- In the replay attack vulnerability, a malicious attacker can resend a request to the client to login to the resource owner's account associated with authorization code after capturing and using the captured authorization code redirection request between the client and resource owner. Then, the attacker attempts to get the authority to approach the resource server by getting user information. In the proposed method, however, the issuance of an access token to the resource owner is authorized by using the SMS. Therefore, the attacker isn't able to get access to the resource server through the authorization code-based replay attack. In addition, even though the attacker retries replay attack using the SMS during authentication, the validity of TMAS received after going through the verification of $(T_{user} - T_{MAS}) \leq \Delta t$ is verified in the SMS authentication. Therefore, it is able to block replay attack.
- In phishing vulnerability, an attacker can attempt proxy authentication using the values entered by the resource owner after constructing a malicious client. However, the resource owner and SMS authentication server verify the MAC authentication code during the SMS authentication of the proposed method. Therefore, it is able to block the attacker's phishing.
- In spoofing vulnerability, an attacker wiretaps and intercepts authorization code and blocks the user's request. Then, it starts normal protocol, using the intercepted authorization code. In the proposed technique, however, SMS authentication on the user is only performed. Therefore, it is able to avoid spoofing vulnerability.

V. CONCLUSION

The OAuth protocol is developed for the purpose of standardizing different authentication methods. With this, therefore, users are able to use many other applications without going through additional authentication procedures. Even though the OAuth protocol provides convenience and scalability, it has several security loopholes in the authentication between the user and 3rd application. To overcome such security problems which can occur in the OAuth protocol, this study proposed a method which can authenticate user authority safely by verifying the authentication code, using the external authentication server.

The proposed method overcomes the security vulnerability of the OAuth protocol so that it is able to provide active services, compared to the conventional protocol. The proposed method-based OAuth protocol can prevent a security accident. In addition, it could be applied to the emerging OpenID and facilitate the protocol.

REFERENCES

[1] Meng-Yu Wu, Tsern-Huei Lee, "Design and Implementation of Cloud API Access Control Based on OAuth", In Proc. Of TENCON Spring Conference, 2013.

[2] http://en.wikipedia.org/wiki/OAuth

[3] D. Hardt, " The OAuth 2.0 authorization framework, " Internet Engineering Task Force(IETF) RFC 6749, 2012.

[4] E. Hammer-Lahav, Ed, "The OAuth 1.0 Protocol" , Internet Engineering Task Force(IETF) RFC5849, 2010.

[5] M. Jones and D. Hardt, " OAuth 2.0 Authorization Framework: Bearer token usage" , Internet Engineering Task Force (IETF) RFC6750, 2012.

AUTHOR INDEX